Captives of Liberty

EARLY AMERICAN STUDIES

Series editors:
Daniel K. Richter, Kathleen M. Brown,
Max Cavitch, and David Waldstreicher

Exploring neglected aspects of our colonial,
revolutionary, and early national history and culture,
Early American Studies reinterprets familiar themes and
events in fresh ways. Interdisciplinary in character, and
with a special emphasis on the period from about 1600
to 1850, the series is published in partnership with the
McNeil Center for Early American Studies.

A complete list of books in the series
is available from the publisher.

Captives of Liberty

Prisoners of War
and the Politics of Vengeance
in the American Revolution

T. Cole Jones

PENN

UNIVERSITY OF PENNSYLVANIA PRESS

PHILADELPHIA

Published by
University of Pennsylvania Press
Philadelphia, Pennsylvania 19104-4112
www.upenn.edu/pennpress

Printed in the United States of America on acid-free paper
1 3 5 7 9 10 8 6 4 2

A Cataloging-in-Publication record is available
from the Library of Congress
ISBN 978-0-8122-5169-2

To my loving parents, Randy and Connie Jones

Contents

Note on Style   *ix*

Introduction. Words About War   *1*

Chapter 1. The Vision of War   *12*

Chapter 2. The Novelty of War   *45*

Chapter 3. The Realities of War   *91*

Chapter 4. The Fortune of War   *139*

Chapter 5. The Vengeance of War   *187*

Conclusion. The Memory of War   *240*

List of Abbreviations   *251*

Notes   *253*

Index   *305*

Acknowledgments   *317*

Note on Style

I have made a concerted effort to accurately reproduce the often inconsistent eighteenth-century spelling, capitalization, and punctuation used in the sources I have consulted. When necessary for comprehension, I have added punctuation or clarifying words, which are clearly denoted in brackets. Throughout the book I have referred to those inhabitants of Great Britain's North American colonies who embraced the struggle against the Crown as "revolutionaries" or simply "Americans" and those who supported reconciliation with Britain as "loyalists." I have eschewed the laudatory or derogatory terms "patriot," "rebel," and "tory." Additionally, I have referred to those subjects of the Holy Roman Empire who served as British military auxiliaries as Germans or "Britain's Germanic allies." Only when I am sure the soldiers in question came from Hesse-Kassel or Hesse-Hanau have I called them Hessians, despite the widespread American practice of referring to all German auxiliaries as "Hessians." Similarly, I have referred to the indigenous inhabitants of North America as Native Americans or Indians except in instances where the sources allowed me to name the specific group or nation to which an individual belonged.

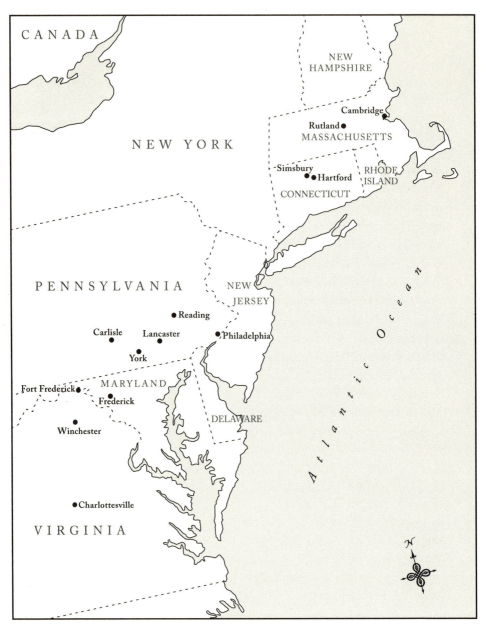

Map 1. Principal internment sites for British and German prisoners of war, 1775–83.

Introduction

Words About War

This is a story about the violence of war, the rules societies make to control it, and what happens when they abandon those restrictions. It is a story of an infant nation that enshrined the rules of war in its founding document—the Declaration of Independence—only to repudiate them in thought, word, and deed. It is a story of a cycle of violence, retaliation, and revenge so gruesome that it begged to be forgotten. At its center, this is a story about how a colonial war for independence became the American *Revolutionary* War.

* * *

In early December 1775, the elected representatives of the thirteen British colonies in America resolved to remind the government in London that even armed conflict has rules. Already aware of Thomas Jefferson's persuasive pen, the Continental Congress looked to the thirty-two-year-old Virginia delegate to draft a "declaration" protesting the British abuse of American prisoners of war and enunciating the stance that violence should be restricted to the field of battle. As Jefferson phrased it, Congress was determined that this conflict would "not be decided by reeking vengeance on a few helpless captives, but by atchieving success in the fields of war." Jefferson was the ideal choice for the declaration's draftsman. Few in Congress could boast either his depth of knowledge or his breadth of reading on the prevailing European conceptions of how war should be conducted. Like most of his fellow delegates, Jefferson believed that, though clearly misled by a tyrannical ministry, the British people remained "brave and civilized."[1]

To Jefferson's horror and indignation, however, in late 1775 it appeared as if the British had abandoned the contemporary European rules of war—in other words, the cultural norms of war—which emphasized restraining violence and treating enemy prisoners humanely, according to their military rank and social station. While these norms reflected the hierarchical social structure of monarchical Europe, enemy prisoners of all ranks benefited. Once captured, they were to be objects not of violence but of compassion. In his stern reproof, Jefferson reminded his British readers that "it is the happiness of modern times that the evils of necessary war are softened by refinement of manners and sentiment, and that an enemy is an object of vengeance, in arms and in the feild [sic] only." By contrast, royal forces seemed determined "to revive antient barbarism, and again disgrace our nature with the practice of human sacrifice." Time and again, British generals had made it clear that in their eyes the American conflict was not a war but a rebellion that had to be suppressed, violently if necessary. As Jefferson crafted his declaration, American prisoners starved in pestilent prisons under the constant threat of execution for treason, while British prisoners in American custody enjoyed "every comfort for which captivity and misfortune called." In deference to General George Washington's negotiations with his British counterpart, Jefferson's declaration was never sent, but Congress echoed his sentiments when it resolved on January 2, 1776, to indict the British for "the execrable barbarity, with which this unhappy war has been conducted." Despite deep provocation, Congress could take pride that the American cause had not been stained by such inhumanity.[2]

Three years later, as governor of Virginia, Jefferson penned a very different declaration on the conduct of war. In the intervening period, British and Native American raiding parties had plagued Virginia's frontiers; bands of armed loyalists had plundered its countryside; thousands of its enslaved Africans had fled to British lines, many taking up arms against their former masters; hundreds of Virginia's soldiers and sailors had perished in British jails and prison ships; and the Royal Navy had terrorized its coastline. To compound the governor's concerns, Congress had saddled Virginia with the responsibility of housing and feeding thousands of enemy prisoners anxious for an opportunity to rejoin their comrades. With a British army ensconced in Georgia and poised to march northward, it looked as if they might soon get their chance. In late 1779 Jefferson's Virginia was surrounded by enemies from both within and without, enemies who evinced no intention of observing "the usage of polished Nations; gentle and humane." Instead, as he apprised John Jay, they were guilty of committing "ravages and enormities, unjustifiable by the usage of civilized nations." This was the context in which Jefferson expressed a fundamentally different vision of the conduct of war from that which he had espoused in the waning days of 1775. As he noted to a Virginian officer in enemy custody, the

British had transformed the conflict into "a contest of cruelty and destruction," and henceforth Americans would "contend with them in that line, and measure out misery to those in our power." This was not an idle threat of proportional retaliation for British misdeeds as sanctioned by the European laws of war. This was the deliberate articulation of a radical alteration in the revolutionaries' conduct of the war, now to be carried out with "a severity as terrible as universal."[3]

Captives of Liberty explores this widespread, and largely unrecognized, transformation in the revolutionaries' conduct of war by analyzing how these Americans treated their enemy prisoners. During the eight-year conflict, American forces captured over seventeen thousand British and allied Germanic soldiers as well as thousands more armed loyalists and British mariners. The fledgling nation soon found the care and management of so many prisoners of war to be a daunting challenge. What was to become of these men? How should they be treated? Who would pay to house and feed them? Should they be released or held indefinitely? By answering these questions, this study reveals the factors that coalesced to revolutionize the American war effort, escalating its violence exponentially.[4]

* * *

A brutal war of vengeance was the furthest thing from the minds of colonial Americans in 1775. They were no strangers to unbridled violence, of course, having engaged in chronic conflict with the Native peoples of the continent since the early days of colonization, but with the possible exception of New England, warfare had been peripheral and distant for most Americans. Even during the Seven Years' War (1756–63), when thousands of Americans had served in the royal provincial forces, the brunt of combat had fallen on Britain's regular army and navy. Instead of the seasoned veterans of popular lore, most rebellious colonists entered the revolution armed only with an idealized conception of contemporary European warfare. They soon discovered that the realities of this new war looked nothing like their romanticized vision of restrained and humane strife. The experience of the conflict shocked and outraged revolutionary Americans. They demanded retribution.[5]

The Continental leadership had not intended to abandon the norms of European warfare, but by throwing off the hierarchical strictures of monarchical culture and embarking on an experiment in republican government, they unwittingly removed control over the direction of war from the hands of elite officers and diplomats, fundamentally altering how it would be prosecuted and who would have a say in ordering its conduct. Americans from across the social spectrum, including men and women who would have had no influence on the conduct of war in royal America, were no longer pawns in or spectators to conflict: they began to adjudicate its practice. Faced with increasing popular pressure for retaliatory violence, revolutionary leaders such as Jefferson, slowly and in fits and starts, began to reconsider their humane position on the conduct of war. The result was a torrent of violence that scholars have only recently begun to appreciate.[6]

Three principal factors account for this transformation. From the conflict's outset, the revolutionary leadership encountered a resolute enemy required by Parliament to deny American soldiers and sailors the status of legitimate combatants, instead labeling them as rebels and traitors. They faced the divided loyalties of their own population, inaugurating civil war. And most important, they failed to establish a monopoly on violence, the bedrock of early modern European state formation. Combined, these three imperatives shaped the very nature of the war they fought, transforming a limited struggle for colonial self-determination into a revolutionary conflict unlike any Anglo-Americans had seen for a century.

Although revolutionary Americans believed that their grievances justified taking up arms, British political and military officials considered them criminals in need of chastisement. How could they have done otherwise after the colonists had defied Parliament and killed the king's soldiers at Lexington and Concord? When suppressing rebellions, the British Army had a long history of denying the conventional European protections of war to insurgents in locales as diverse as Scotland, Ireland, Jamaica, and Acadia. While the cultural resemblance between the British and their American colonists was so strong that the violence of Britain's response never matched that of the preceding insurrections, the Crown's stance that the American conflict was an unlawful rebellion strongly influenced its military practice. American prisoners were the principal victims of Britain's effort to end the rebellion by force. Historians estimate that somewhere between 8,500 and 18,000 American soldiers, sailors, and privateers perished while in Crown custody, most aboard the infamous prison hulk *Jersey* in Wallabout Bay, Brooklyn. Despite the discrepancy in total numbers, scholars agree that roughly one-half of all Americans who fell into British hands during the war succumbed in captivity—a statistic unprecedented in eighteenth-century European warfare. The prisoners did not suffer in silence.

The revolutionary leadership wasted no time in capitalizing on their ordeals for propaganda purposes. As accounts of these abuses proliferated in the revolutionary press—usually exaggerated but rarely without some truth—ordinary Americans, thirsting for vengeance, began to demand retaliation. To infuriated revolutionaries, British prisoners looked like the ideal objects of revenge.[7]

Responding to the siren call of vengeance, revolutionary authorities retaliated first and most violently upon those Americans who took up arms in opposition to the "common cause." The conflict had been a civil war within the empire from the start, but the British ministry's decision to arm white loyalists, Native Americans, and former slaves to assist in the suppression of the rebellion launched an internecine conflict in which abuse would beget abuse for the remainder of the struggle. The revolutionary leadership's initial effort to shield suspected loyalists from the types of popular violence perpetrated during the imperial crisis collapsed after independence. Loyalism became treason and armed opposition rebellion against the nascent United States. Traditionally seen as beyond the pale of white Anglo-American civilization, the king's Indian and African American auxiliaries were more likely to face death or enslavement than moderation and generosity in American hands. The identification, demonization, and persecution of internal enemies were central to the revolutionaries' campaign to build support for the war effort. Once mobilized, ordinary Americans had few qualms about meeting counter-revolutionary fury with revolutionary ferocity. Contrary to popular narratives, this American-on-American violence was not limited to the backcountry of the Carolinas or to the no-man's-land of Westchester County, New York, but occurred wherever British forces could project enough power to encourage resistance. Fear of a phantom "fifth column" in their midst drove revolutionaries, elite and ordinary alike, to acts of shocking cruelty. When captured, loyalist "rebels" and "insurgents" no longer deserved the humane treatment due to prisoners of war, which the revolutionaries had so sedulously maintained at the conflict's outset. They could be imprisoned at whim, held with little prospect of release, beaten, tortured, and even summarily executed. This alteration in how the revolutionaries conceived of their enemies had dire consequences for their treatment of loyalist prisoners.[8]

Despite the popular outcry against British abuses and the exigencies of civil war, the revolutionary leaders' humane vision of warfare might have endured had they had the means of enforcing it. But Jefferson and his elite peers, as the ringleaders of a popular insurgency in the name of a new republic, did not possess a legitimate monopoly on organized violence. They were out-laws. Notwithstanding the fine clothes and florid prose of its leadership, the budding American state's sole claim to legitimacy derived from popular sup-port. Unlike European monarchs, whose positions rested on their ability to forcibly coerce their subjects, elite revolutionaries in Congress depended upon the backing of their constituents both to justify their existence and to wage the war. They could ill afford to ignore the will of the people. Moreover, the ideology and structure of republicanism, and its attendant suspicion of standing armies, severely curtailed their ability to direct the war effort and restrain its violence. In addition to its well-documented failure to supply the Continental Army with adequate provisions and munitions, Congress never granted its military branch the power or the purse necessary to adequately provide for enemy prisoners. Politically constrained from levying taxes, it had little choice but to outsource prisoner management to individual states. In this decentral-ized system, local authorities often interpreted congressional orders as mere suggestions. Provincial concerns trumped national ones throughout the contest. State governments, accountable to their citizens first, then Congress, jealously guarded the enemy prisoners under their control to exchange for their own citizens in British custody, contrary to Washington's desire for exchanges to be based on length of captivity alone. More seriously, once the prisoners were out of the general's hands, he could do little to guarantee their safety or humane treatment. Local officials, deeply mired in their own civil wars and constantly pressed by constituents to exact retribution for British atrocities, often escalated retaliation beyond proportionality. Prevented by Congress from ever entering into a general cartel for the exchange of prisoners with the British, Washington could do nothing but lament the prisoners' plight and the escalation of the war's violence.[9]

* * *

By analyzing how these factors influenced the revolutionaries' practice of war, *Captives of Liberty* questions the standard narrative of the conflict and its place in the broader history of the American Revolution. Americans have long viewed their revolution with the hindsight of revolutionary France's Reign of Terror, unsurprisingly underestimating the extent and importance of violence in founding the United States—after all, there was no guillotine in Philadelphia, and King George III survived the war with his head in place. The historian Gordon Wood, in summarizing this popular conception, notes that America's experience "does not appear to resemble the revolutions of other nations in which people were killed, property was destroyed, and everything was turned upside down." The revolutionaries were "too much the gentlemen" who "made speeches, not bombs." The apparent absence of widespread violence has prompted some historians to question whether the American Revolution was really revolutionary at all. Echoing the "consensus" school of American Revolution historiography, Timothy Tackett, a prominent scholar of the French Revolution, has recently argued that the American experience was "much closer to a war of independence than to a social revolution." For Tackett, "a comparison between it and the French Revolution has only limited value." Wood's seminal work, *The Radicalism of the American Revolution*, expressly challenges this assertion by tracing the social and political transformations wrought by the struggle for independence. America's revolution, he argues, "was as radical and social as any revolution in history." Yet the war's violence has no place in his narrative.[10]

Historians who have critiqued Wood for his apparent emphasis on ideas over actions, patricians over plebs, seeking instead to recover the agency of those disenfranchised by the Revolution, have done more to reveal the contested character of America's transformation from monarchy to republic, but their emphasis has been on the causes and consequences rather than the course of the conflict. Scholars often identified as "Neo-Progressives"—including Ray Raphael, Jesse Lemisch, T. H. Breen, Gary Nash, Alfred Young, and others—have documented a very different revolution that took place "out of doors," away from the halls of Congress or the genteel drawing rooms of the elites. They have noted the pivotal role ordinary Americans played in shaping the resistance movement, unleashing a wave of democratization the gentleman-founders never envisioned or desired. This revolution was far from unanimously supported, significantly more contested, and ultimately less complete than Wood's, but the battlefield and its aftermath are peripheral to their story. Its violence remains offstage.[11]

Although military historians have long taken the experience of the war seriously, they have traditionally separated the fighting into two categories: first as a limited conflict in the eighteenth-century European tradition between the regular forces of Great Britain and the nascent United States, and second as a "total" conflict between these two powers and their various Native American adversaries and civilian militias. Within this bifurcated conception, the Revolutionary War looks much like the colonial contests of the eighteenth century. The violence of the regular war has been downplayed, while that of the militia war has been emphasized. Unsurprisingly, historian John Shy's claim that the conflict was "militarily conservative" has endured, largely unchallenged.[12]

More recently, scholars have begun to address the process of revolution and its corresponding violence. They have taken up Allan Kulikoff's clarion call to understand "the Revolution as a war—a violent and protracted conflict." In so doing, they have done much to recover how revolutionary Americans experienced the brutality and terror of "America's first civil war." But highlighting this violence is not enough. We must seek to understand its social, cultural, and political causes and implications; if not, we will continue to accept a narrative of the American Revolution divided "into two halves." On the one side, a war for independence, destructive and repressive, and on the other, a political revolution, idealistic though unfinished. Breaking down this barrier requires making the connection between revolutionary political change and revolutionary violence.[13]

Enemy prisoners of war provide an ideal vantage point from which to view this relationship. Captured throughout the war and confined far from the battlefields where the Continentals and their British counterparts waged what one historian has called "the last great war of the *ancien régime*," prisoners were at the mercy of their captors, rarely capable of mounting significant resistance. Ready objects of vengeance and victims of violence, prisoners and their experiences in American captivity testify to the war's revolutionary transformation, yet their story has received little attention. Unlike American prisoners in British hands, the suffering of British and allied prisoners has been silenced—first by their captors, who were keen to put the war's violence behind them, and subsequently by scholars, who have accepted a carefully crafted myth of American moderation, humanity, and generosity.[14]

* * *

The revolutionary generation's moral victory is a comforting story in an age when memories of Guantanamo Bay and Abu Ghraib are still uncomfortably fresh. When I came to this project, one could not pick up a newspaper or turn on CNN without being confronted by a barrage of accounts of prisoner-of-war abuse. Political analysts and pundits, infatuated by what *Newsweek* termed "Founders Chic," delighted in contrasting contemporary American misdeeds with the founders' "virtuous" and "humanitarian" conduct of war. Intrigued by the juxtaposition, I scoured the existing literature on the subject for evidence supporting their claims. Abundant quotes from prominent revolutionary leaders emphasized the importance of the humane treatment of enemy prisoners to the American cause. Elias Boudinot, the first American commissary general of prisoners and future president of the Continental Congress, was not alone when he boasted in 1777 that "humanity to Prisoners of War has ever been the peculiar Characteristic of the american [sic] Army." It appeared as if the revolutionaries had been steadfast in their defense of the "laws of humanity" in the face of continual British atrocities—maybe there was something to American "exceptionalism" after all. Pursuing the topic further, I wanted to know why the revolutionaries embraced what historian David Hackett Fischer calls an "American Way of Fighting" that privileged "a policy of humanity." The answer in the archives bore little resemblance to Fischer's laudatory assertion that the revolutionaries conducted the war "in a manner that was true to the expanding humanitarian ideals of the American Revolution." These findings challenged my preconceptions both about how the war was fought and about the centrality of the war itself to the broader phenomenon of the Revolution.[15]

This story of America's descent into revolutionary violence proceeds in five parts. The first two chapters establish the context for understanding the dramatic transformations in the revolutionaries' conduct and analyze their treatment of British and allied prisoners during the first year of the struggle. Chapter 1 begins by examining the place of war within the intellectual and cultural world of Anglo-Americans on the eve of conflict with Great Britain. I explore the development of eighteenth-century Europe's culture of limited war, as well as its migration across the Atlantic, and argue that these norms shaped revolutionary Americans' *vision* of war—how it should, and would, be conducted. Chapter 2 chronicles the revolutionary leadership's struggle to maintain the norms of European warfare in the face of popular demands for retribution for alleged British misconduct during the campaign to capture Canada. In the aftermath of the Declaration of Independence, Congress, no longer hopeful for reconciliation, was motivated by the desire to appear as a legitimate nation-state in the eyes of potential European allies. The cries and lamentations of mistreated British prisoners would serve only to undermine that cause. Enemy captives were no longer simply the inconvenient by-products of revolt; they began to take on a symbolic meaning as tangible evidence of American martial prowess and national legitimacy.

As the war progressed and word of British abuse of American prisoners spread, the revolutionaries' vision of humane and moderate war began to fade. In Chapter 3, I turn to the treatment of prisoners during the British campaign to capture and pacify New York in 1776 and 1777. During this period, the threat of loyalist uprisings and the truly staggering mortality rate of prisoners in British hands persuaded ordinary Americans to reimagine their overseas foes as barbarians and loyalists as traitors. Reconceived in this way, the enemies of the Revolution were no longer entitled to the protections of "civilized" warfare. The ramifications of this shift become manifest in Chapter 4, which examines the fate of the British army that surrendered under the protection of the Convention of Saratoga in 1777. By nullifying the convention, Congress openly flouted the norms of the European culture of war that the revolutionary leadership had held sacrosanct at the commencement of hostilities. This radical departure from previous prisoner-of-war policy reflected a drastic shift in popular opinion. In the spring of 1778, retaliation had come to dominate the public discourse on prisoner treatment, and Congress resolved to ignore the demands for retribution no longer.

Chapter 5 looks at the brutal backcountry civil war that developed in the South after the fall of Charleston in 1780. During this phase of the conflict, exaggerated accounts of British brutality and loyalist opposition galvanized southern revolutionaries to wage a war of vengeance against Britons and loyalists alike. Embracing retaliation for enemy atrocities, the destruction of the property of enemy civilians, the revocation of surrender agreements, the wholesale arrest and imprisonment of enemy noncombatants, and the execution of prisoners of war, the revolutionaries engaged in a cycle of revengeful violence in the last years of the conflict that would have been unthinkable at its outset. The war in the South was not a contest over abstract political principles but an existential struggle for national, local, and individual survival. This was not the war the revolutionary elite had envisioned in 1775.

In the years following the Treaty of Paris (1783), revolutionary leaders, now claiming the mantle of the nation's founders, sought to leave the bloody business of war in the past as they imagined and constructed a new nation. To staunch nationalists like Henry Knox and Alexander Hamilton, the violence required to win independence was not only distasteful but also dangerous. Armed and angry American citizens might resort to violence against their new rulers just as they had against the king's representatives. These elite nationalists, without popular consent, conspired to tame what they saw as an "excess of democracy" let loose during the war. They got their way. The Constitution of 1787 firmly asserted the national government's monopoly on war's violence. Only Congress could declare war, raise troops, and make rules for their wartime conduct. Additionally, these men committed their new nation, through a series of international treaties, to waging the next war by the European rulebook.[16]

But it was not enough to restrain the violence of future conflicts; to claim national unanimity and respectability, the Revolution's violence had to be reimagined as virtuous, limited, and restrained. Postwar Americans celebrated the service and sacrifice of national martyrs, like fallen generals Joseph Warren and Richard Montgomery, while forgiving their enemies and forgetting their own part in the devastation. By sanitizing their narratives, early historians and history painters ironically reversed the war's own transformation by recasting a revolutionary conflict as a mere war for independence. With the outbreak of revolution in France and its subsequent violent escalation, the sanitizers redoubled their efforts to paint America's experience as different, even exceptional. Their efforts proved enduring. Americans came to embrace a largely bloodless narrative of their revolution in which the war and its violence were extraneous to the real story: the victory of democracy over despotism.[17]

Captives of Liberty centers the war, and its consequent horrors, in the scholarly debate about the character and consequences of the American Revolution. It argues that the political revolution, rejecting monarchy in favor of a republic founded upon popular sovereignty, had the unintended consequence of transforming the conduct of the war waged to achieve it. While the path to a war of vengeance was contingent and haphazard, once begun, it was not easily contained. Despite the efforts of many in the Continental leadership to restrain the escalating violence, the American republic, forged in the crucible of civil war, was not a European state. The Old World's hierarchical military culture, premised on the restraint of violence between "civilized" peoples, was unsustainable in the American conflict. Declarations of American "humanity" in the face of British "barbarity" were but a decorous facade that crumbled under the weight of popular pressure. By recovering the treatment of enemy prisoners in American hands, this book seeks to illuminate a side of the Revolution the founders preferred forgotten: the violence of the democratization of war.

Chapter 1

The Vision of War

George Washington had been in command of the infant Continental Army for just over a month when he penned a letter of stern reproach to a former comrade, British lieutenant general Thomas Gage, on "the Obligations arising from the Rights of Humanity, & Claims of Rank." Washington rebuked his opponent for the treatment of American prisoners confined in Boston. In his scathing reprimand, the American general asserted that these men, most of whom had been captured during the fighting at Bunker Hill in June 1775, were "thrown indiscriminately, into a common Gaol" overflowing with disloyal Bostonians, suspected spies, unruly redcoats, and common criminals. The wounded and sick sweltered alongside the healthy in the summer heat, with only a single bucket of water a day for both hydration and sanitation. The prisoners were deprived of nourishment and "the Comforts of Life" at the whim of the British provost officer. In the opinion of one prisoner, "The place seems to be an Emblem of Hell."[1]

For Gage, an officer who had served with distinction in the 1745 Jacobite Rebellion, the War of Austrian Succession (1740–48), and the Seven Years' War, chastisement from a man whose most impressive military accomplishment had simply been to survive the defeat of Major General Edward Braddock in 1755 must have smacked of the impudence of a rank amateur. The British general would not tolerate a lecture on the proper conduct of war from a novice and a traitor to his king and country. Gage reminded Washington that, "under the Laws of the Land," the Continental commander and his entire army deserved to hang for treason; simply foregoing summary execution was thus a sign of British mercy. He refused to countenance any claim of rank that was not derived from a king's commission; thus the officers would remain in the same jail with common criminals. Nevertheless, Gage strongly asserted that captured Americans had "hitherto been treated with care and kindness." He defended this assertion by invoking European customs for the treatment of prisoners of war: "To the Glory of Civilized Nations, humanity and War have been compatible; and Compassion to the subdued, is become almost a general system." This was language that Washington understood. Well-read in contemporary military literature and theory and a veteran of the most recent imperial conflict against the French, he shared a set of values about the conduct of war with his British antagonist. As Gage's comment indicates, European elites possessed a common culture of warfare, what Wayne Lee has defined as "a broadly understood set of cultural expectations about the uses and forms of war." By the late eighteenth century, Europe's culture of war emphasized controlling violence and protecting enemy prisoners.[2]

* * *

Examining the factors that limited war's destructiveness and improved the plight of prisoners in eighteenth-century Europe, as well as the migration of those factors across the Atlantic, illuminates revolutionary Americans' cultural expectations about the treatment of prisoners in 1775. It was these European norms that shaped the colonial elite's *vision* of how war should be conducted. While Americans had experienced over a century and a half of nearly endemic warfare with the indigenous peoples of the continent, they were largely unprepared to wage a European-style war. Nonetheless, revolutionary leaders thought they knew how such a conflict would unfold. They imagined that both sides would conform to the prevailing European standards of acceptable violence in warfare. This vision of restrained and limited war as conducted among "civilized" peoples conditioned the revolutionary leadership's response to captured British soldiers when fighting engulfed the colonies in the spring and summer of 1775. By treating their prisoners according to these European customs, influential revolutionaries (such as Washington) intended to demonstrate the legitimacy of their cause to their British enemies. Given the inherent illegitimacy of rebellion, they could hardly have done otherwise.

There was another vision of war available to colonial Americans, one that Washington, as a veteran of the Seven Years' War, knew well: retaliatory warfare. In the colonial wars of the eighteenth century, Anglo-American forces had encountered in Native Americans an enemy with a very different understanding of the norms of acceptable violence in warfare. While the British and their American auxiliaries had hoped to conduct military operations during that earlier conflict according to the practices of "civilized" nations, on the frontier, where war parties and rangers roamed, alleged atrocities committed by one side had been answered with revengeful reprisals by the other. Away from the judgmental gaze of their European superiors, Franco-Canadian and Anglo-American forces, in conjunction with their Native allies, escalated the violence well beyond Old World norms. Twenty years later Washington and many of his fellow American veterans of that war were determined that their dispute with Britain would never devolve into a similar cycle of retaliatory violence. In this new confrontation, enemy prisoners would be treated with humanity according to an idealized vision of European practice—or so they thought.

Prisoners of War in Early Modern Europe

In 1753, when twenty-one-year-old George Washington began his military career, the rules by which European powers conducted war were becoming increasingly rigid. Horrified by decades of sanguinary religious conflict, eighteenth-century princes, philosophers, jurists, clerics, and soldiers all sought to control the violence of European warfare. With monarchs rather than mercenaries directing its progress, war would be waged by standing armies of long-serving volunteers or conscripts, controlled by discipline, rules, regulations, and aristocratic officers, gentlemen who shared a code of honor. Battles would be bloody, but in their aftermath captured soldiers could expect adequate food, clothing, and quarters. Most important, they would be quickly released through an equitable exchange. Officers, as members of a pan-European aristocratic culture, could offer their parole (from the French meaning "speech" or "spoken word") of honor not to engage in hostile actions while considered a prisoner, thus enjoying considerable freedom until the cessation of hostilities or exchange for an officer of equal rank. This was European warfare as Washington envisioned it; but it had not always been this way.[3]

   During the previous century, Protestants and Catholics—believing salvation itself at stake—made little effort to temper the fury of war and proceeded to kill and maim one another on a scale not seen in Europe since antiquity. Bands of marauding mercenaries, owing allegiance to none but the highest bidder, pillaged, plundered, and purged their way across the continent. When prisoners of war were taken, their fate depended largely on the caprice of the captors. If he was a wealthy aristocrat or senior officer, a prisoner might be ransomed or exchanged for an equally wellborn captive held by the other side. For common soldiers and civilians, having little monetary value, the outcome was bleak. Housing and feeding large numbers of enemy prisoners were beyond the capacity of the ad hoc armies and nascent states that waged the religious wars. While occasional exchanges of prisoners did occur, those fortunate enough to be taken alive were sometimes impressed into the enemy's army, though most were simply put to death. The horrors of war were compounded by the prevalence of siege warfare. The populations of fortified cities and towns that resisted an enemy's conquest could expect the worst when the city's defenses failed—pillage, rape, and murder on a massive scale. Atrocities were legion, and the death tolls staggering. Prisoners of war and civilian men, women, and children paid the price for the religious and political affiliations of their social superiors.[4]

The 1648 Treaty of Westphalia, which ended the religious wars, did not signal the end of conflict in Europe, though it did usher in a series of changes in the practice of war that had the surprising effect of constraining its horrors. Significant alterations in the organization of armies, and even the states that raised them; the evolving culture of honor and restraint among the aristocracy; and the juridical tradition of the laws of war all coalesced in late seventeenth-century Europe to ensure that warfare in the eighteenth century would look remarkably different from that of centuries prior.[5]

Known to scholars as the "military revolution," the early modern period witnessed a series of developments in technology, tactics, and organization that had a profound influence on the conduct of war and the fate of its prisoners. Beginning with the introduction of gunpowder and culminating in the creation of the tax-supported, centralized, and bureaucratic states necessary to pay and provide for the large armies required to employ the new weaponry, these changes consolidated the control of warfare in the hands of European monarchs. On the eve of the eighteenth century, the crowned heads of Europe had achieved a near-complete monopoly on military violence. Fractious nobles, whose confessional squabbles had brought about decades of unfettered violence, now found an outlet for their destructive impulses in the officer corps of state-sponsored standing armies. Serving at the pleasure of the Crown, these armies could wage wars with limited aims, such as the expansion of territory or control of dynastic succession. Throughout the century, monarchs agreed to resolve their disputes on the field of battle. With war the sole domain of kings (and queens), the battlefield, rather than the farmer's cottage, parish church, or village square, became the primary locus of human destruction, thus mitigating the most violent excesses of wars past.[6]

The military revolution also improved the treatment of prisoners of war by increasing the value of an individual soldier's life. While the common foot soldier of medieval Europe was expendable in the eyes of his knightly superiors, the rulers of the eighteenth century recognized the value of their highly trained soldiers and wanted them, if taken, returned as soon as possible. Moreover, protracted confinement could prove ruinously expensive. Custom derived from civilian carceral culture dictated that prisoners must pay for their own upkeep. This practice endured during the eighteenth century for captured officers, who possessed the means to provide for themselves, but European monarchs were expected to supply their captive enlisted men with food, clothing, and medicine or to reimburse their opponents for expenses incurred on behalf of their subjects. Rather than write their enemies a blank check, armies would appoint commissary officers to reside near the prisoners for the purpose of procuring their provisions. Predictably, savvy merchants and farmers took advantage of their enemy's predicament and charged exorbitant rates for the necessities of life. The need both to cut costs and to return veteran soldiers to their regiments induced European monarchs to establish elaborate treaties, known as cartels, for the exchange of prisoners.[7]

Cartels stipulated the terms of the exchange that bound belligerents throughout a conflict and outlined the minimum standard of prisoner treatment. Most eighteenth-century cartels forbade the abuse of prisoners, including forced labor, and guaranteed that captives received rations and accommodations equal to those enjoyed by the capturing army. The ultimate goal, though, was the prisoners' swift repatriation. Soldiers and sailors were exchanged according to mutually agreed rates based on their military rank— for example, privates for privates, sergeants for sergeants, and generals for generals—typically within a short period of the prisoners' capture. For instance, the cartel between Britain and France during the Seven Years' War promised to release all prisoners through exchange within fifteen days; the realities of a global war fought from North America to India often prevented such speedy exchanges. Nonetheless, the cartel system promised, even if it did not always deliver, relief and release from the hardship of prolonged captivity. With this system firmly in place, obtaining enemy prisoners became not only psychologically advantageous, by boosting the morale of the captors, but militarily beneficial as well.[8]

The social structure of the armies also played a part in the constraint of wartime violence. Eighteenth-century Europe was a deeply hierarchical society, and its armies reflected this system. At the bottom of the spectrum, soldiers in the rank and file came from among the working poor. While their motives for enlisting varied, all endured harsh discipline, intensive drill, and corporal punishment aimed at controlling their behavior. Armies instituted labyrinthine systems of regulations to distinguish between legitimate and illegitimate violence and established military courts to adjudicate infractions. The enforcement of these rules fell to officers who rose through the ranks by purchasing commissions from the Crown rather than by merit. Members of the aristocracy, the landed gentry, and the moneyed elite, these men flocked to their monarch's standard to preserve and perform their honor and gain royal favor. Although not all eighteenth-century officers were nobles, they were all products of a society, and members of an institution, that sanctified aristocratic values. This culture of honor among the officer corps was central to eighteenth-century Europeans' understanding of the proper treatment of prisoners of war.[9]

Honor was not a revolutionary concept; in fact, these men saw themselves as the lineal descendants of a proud medieval tradition of chivalry, service, and sacrifice for God and monarch. Like their medieval forbearers, elite Europeans understood honor to mean one's reputation in the eyes of others. But reputation could not be earned through piety, bravery, or loyalty alone—honor was inherited. They took for granted that those of elevated birth possessed honor because of their ancestors. Those of more humble origins had precious few means of elevating themselves to rank among the innately honorable. Although it could not be purchased, honor could very easily be lost. Any insult, reproach, or slight that was not answered could deprive a noble of it. Appearing honorable in the presence of peers was paramount, and social ostracism faced the gentleman who declined an invitation to cross blades or exchange shots on the field of honor.[10]

Although obsession with honor could lead a European officer to accept a challenge over a trivial affair or to engage in reckless abandon on the battlefield, this aristocratic attribute also had a limiting effect on the violence of war. Eighteenth-century nobles saw combat as unexceptional, unavoidable, and even natural, but they also recognized their opponents on the other side of a battlefield as members of a common culture and caste. Aristocracy, though it took slightly different forms throughout Europe, looked much the same in Paris as it did in Vienna. Even in England, where the hereditary nobility was comparatively small, the landed gentry aped the styles, manners, and behaviors of their more illustrious Continental peers. This pan-European aristocratic culture stressed rigorous standards of self-control. From the manner of their dress to their posture, poise, and prose, European nobles were exceedingly conformist: excess was rigidly curtailed. Their very emotions had to be tightly managed. Displaying anger was uncouth; rage was for the unreasoning masses, not the genteel elite. Any behavior seen to be untoward would invite censure and dishonor.[11]

These deeply held values of restraint and self-control translated naturally to warfare. The bloodlust that so characterized the religious wars was incompatible with eighteenth-century aristocratic culture. While the battlefield was their natural theater, noble officers could not be seen to enjoy their part too much. Death in the service of one's monarch was a glorious sacrifice, but the taking of a common soldier's life was beneath the dignity of an aristocrat. Officers carried flimsy, highly decorated swords and nearly useless pikes, known as spontoons, rather than firearms. They strove to set an example of personal bravery under fire but left the killing to the common men. It was also incumbent upon officers to restrain their soldiers from any excesses in the heat of battle or its aftermath. This rule applied doubly to the protection of wounded or captured enemy officers. Seeing their conquered foes as fellow gentlemen and nobles, European officers spared their lives and treated them with courtesies that came to be known as the "honors of war."[12]

Once captured, defeated officers who had behaved honorably in battle could expect from their captors every indulgence in proportion to their rank and social station. Upon offering their parole of honor not to escape or aid the enemy, these men would customarily be allowed to retain their swords and personal property. It was not uncommon for noble officers to entertain their prisoners as dinner guests. In the wake of the failed Franco-Spanish siege of Gibraltar in 1783, American-born painter Benjamin West portrayed just such a moment of gentlemanly hospitality in his portrait of a British officer and his Spanish captive. Despite deep-seated cultural, religious, and political differences, the two men appear to relish each other's company. Officers like West's Spaniard had little to fear from their gentlemen captors. Rather than face the rigors of confinement, once paroled, they could live as lavishly as their purses— or lines of credit—would allow until they could be honorably, if not always equitably, exchanged. Many were permitted to return to their homes to await either exchange or the cessation of hostilities in ease and comfort. The entire

Figure 1. Two officers and a groom in a landscape, untitled painting by
Benjamin West. Gift of the Forbes Collection. Courtesy Princeton
University Art Museum/Art Resource, NY.

system was predicated upon an officer's scrupulous adherence to his word
of honor.[13]

Officers who violated the norms of self-restraint or betrayed the confidence
of their peers faced public ridicule. Fear of ostracism and the constant need to
be seen as honorable prompted many to adopt a punctilious insistence on the
protocols of war. Form mattered as much as, if not more than, function. Negotiations between opponents required elaborate rituals that could drag out inter-
minably as each side acknowledged, praised, and saluted the other. The least
breach of etiquette evoked strong rebuke. When opposing officers entered into
conventions, treaties, or agreements, they understood that the terms were
inviolate. Refusing to accept offers of surrender, denying care to the wounded,

or reneging on treaties all reflected poorly on the perpetrators. With honor at stake, material advantage took a back seat to decorous conduct. For most eighteenth-century nobles, death was preferable to dishonor.[14]

Practical considerations also supported the moderation of war's violence. Given the relative ease with which European powers shifted their military alliances, officers who had served with one another in the past might easily be arrayed against each other in the future. Friendships that bridged the battle lines were commonplace, and officers who had been prisoners and well treated relished the opportunity to return the favor. Similarly, captive officers worked to arrange favorable treatment and speedy exchange for their enlisted men out of their own self-interest. For many, their commission, and its monetary value, depended on recruitment. Regiments without enough soldiers in their ranks for active service rarely received the king's favor or the most coveted duty stations; they might even be disbanded. European nobles recognized their best interests and readily adopted unwritten codes of conduct based on the principle of reciprocity.[15]

Predictably, the culture of war during the Enlightenment also had its intellectual influences. What is surprising is how unconcerned the great philosophes were with mitigating war's horrors. Instead, many imagined the dawn of an age without war—peace in perpetuity. Eighteenth-century soldiers and statesmen, however, did not share this grand vision. Most viewed war as inevitable, and they prepared accordingly. Part of this preparation entailed the diligent study of how warfare had been practiced in the past. In their quest to distill the lessons of history, Europe's elite warriors drew on a long-standing intellectual current, the laws of war.[16]

Laws governing both when to go to war, *jus ad bellum*, and how to conduct the process once war was declared, *jus in bello*, had existed in Europe since early Christian theologians struggled with the bellicosity of their secular rulers. These religious intellectuals, however, were principally interested in defining what constituted just war; the governing of war's practice they left to its practitioners. The intellectual tradition of the laws of war continued to evolve in Renaissance and early modern Europe—Dutch legal scholar Hugo Grotius's 1625 treatise, *On the Law of War and Peace*, being a signal example—but it was not until the mid-eighteenth century that Swiss jurist Emer de Vattel popularized a series of laws for the conduct of war.[17]

Vattel, like other European aristocrats, obsessed over decorous form and the appearance of propriety. His 1758 treatise, *The Law of Nations*, clearly reflected the values of the aristocratic culture around him. Although paying lip service to the standard justifications for going to war—he agreed with the framework established by Saint Augustine—Vattel devoted the bulk of his attention to describing how nations should conduct warfare once the conflict began. Throughout his work, Vattel argued that belligerents should prosecute hostilities with honor and restraint. When he considered the battlefields of Europe, he saw both virtues in evidence: "At present, the European nations generally carry on their wars with great moderation and generosity." While commendable, this customary practice required codification lest violators claim ignorance in exculpation of misbehavior. Vattel argued that such a code derived from the laws of nature and amounted to a series of "maxims of humanity, moderation, and honour."[18]

What exactly did this vision of moderate and generous war look like? Vattel began with the premise that "civilized" peoples shared a common humanity. Seemingly obvious, this simple assertion represented a seismic shift in how Europeans viewed one another. In what psychologist Steven Pinker has termed a "Humanitarian Revolution," the continent witnessed the emergence of a culture of "humanitarian sensibility" that celebrated the value of human life and condemned cruelty. Eighteenth-century Europeans, now sensible to the feelings of others, began to question the probity of slavery, torture, capital punishment, and the tendency of soldiers to dehumanize their enemies. Imbued with this sensibility, Vattel argued: "Let us never forget that our enemies are men. Though reduced to the disagreeable necessity of prosecuting our right by force of arms, let us not divest ourselves of that charity which connects us with all mankind." With common humanity established, enemies could no longer butcher one another indiscriminately. Civilians as well had "nothing to fear from the sword of the enemy" because "at present, war is carried on by regular troops: the people, the peasants, the citizens, take no part in it."[19]

Even in war conducted between regular armies, enemy soldiers faced capture; but they too merited generous and humane treatment, according to Vattel. He warned combatants, "As soon as your enemy has laid down his arms and surrendered his person, you have no longer any right over his life." Although he did not go as far as twentieth-century military jurists by suggesting that prisoners of war had any rights other than to their lives, Vattel asserted that the execution of prisoners had no place in contemporary warfare. For their habit of massacring the survivors of battles, he rebuked the ancient Greeks and Romans. By contrast, he lauded England and France as "generous nations" for their treatment of prisoners during the Seven Years' War. Prisoners of war, he reminded his readers, "are men, and unfortunate." European nations deserved praise because such captives were "seldom ill-treated among them." Vattel no doubt approved of the civilian committee established in England in 1758 to "relieve the wants of the French Prisoners of War" after the war-worn French Crown defaulted on its obligation to provide clothing to the captured men. The English intellectual Samuel Johnson summarized the widespread opinion of elite Europeans when he wrote in favor of the committee: "The relief of enemies has a tendency to unite mankind in fraternal affection; to soften the acrimony of adverse nations, and dispose them to peace and amity."[20]

Violence remained central to warfare, however, and retaliation played a key role in Vattel's system. He knew that the laws of nations meant little if they could not be enforced. Without an international court to adjudicate violations, Vattel authorized proportional reprisals to compel combatants "to observe the laws of war." But he cautioned readers to employ retaliation, what he declared a "dreadful extremity," only as a last resort. Because of its tendency to escalate a conflict's violence, Vattel stipulated that the reprisal must match the infraction. Here he agreed with the long-standing legal tradition of the *lex talionis*: an eye for an eye. Disproportionate retaliation committed for revenge, rather than as an inducement for future good behavior, was "a licentiousness condemned by the law of nature." Instead, he encouraged nations to embrace "generosity" toward their erring foes. A far cry from the largely unbounded violence of centuries past, war through Vattel's eyes looked restrained and dispassionate.[21]

There were caveats to these mitigating rules. Eighteenth-century soldiers and jurists agreed that the laws of war did not extend to political traitors, domestic rebels, or the "uncivilized," such as the indigenous populations of European empires. They based these exceptions on the presumption that rebels and non-Europeans existed beyond the pale of civilization and therefore would not themselves obey the laws of war. By this logic, European armies could not be expected to maintain a higher standard than that of their "savage" enemies. When fighting "the other," soldiers regularly burned towns and villages, plundered farmers' fields, and killed and enslaved enemy noncombatants. Some of the most horrific excesses in the history of warfare occurred in this age of limited war when European armies imposed their will upon the indigenous populations of America, Africa, and Asia and ruthlessly suppressed internal revolts and rebellions. In conflicts such as these, where the cultural restraints on war lapsed, violence begot more violence.[22]

While the unrestrained application of violence against non-Europeans required little justification, the issue of rebellion was more difficult. Rebellion proved particularly vexing for Vattel, who devoted considerable space to the subject. He maintained that "every citizen should even patiently endure evils, which are not insupportable, rather than disturb the public peace" by engaging in rebellion. In the case of armed revolt, Vattel defended the sovereign's right and "duty to repress those who unnecessarily disturb the public peace." The monarch's troops, who could consider rebels as criminals in arms, could deny them all of the protections of the laws of war. Once captured, rebels faced punishment under civilian laws against treason and sedition—almost certainly the death penalty. Yet Vattel also knew of historical instances in which monarchs had exceeded justification by ravaging rebellious provinces and executing rebel prisoners out of hand. These acts of severity troubled Vattel. He advised monarchs "to show clemency towards unfortunate persons" and to suppress a rebellion with moderation, especially if its supporters grew numerous and organized enough to field a regular-style army. In that case, the conflict became a civil war in which the sovereign must observe the laws of war lest the struggle devolve into a cycle of reprisal and revenge.[23]

In practice, few eighteenth-century monarchs heeded Vattel's advice. Rebellions, no matter how futile, struck at the very heart of a regime's legitimacy. A single victory might easily legitimize the rebel cause and destabilize the government. For monarchies, in which power rested on the ephemeral shoulders of a single life, revolts proved especially dangerous and their suppression notoriously brutal. When eighteenth-century North American colonists resorted to arms to obtain redress for their grievances with Britain's ministry and parliament, they knew of the Crown's record of crushing domestic uprisings. Lingering disputes over dynastic succession and confessional politics resulting from the English Civil Wars and the Glorious Revolution of the seventeenth century prompted numerous Irish and Scots to oppose the Hanoverian succession by force of arms. Although these rebellions appear reckless in hindsight, they had the very real potential of devolving into civil war, or worse yet, inviting an invasion by Catholic France or Spain.[24]

From the point of view of American colonists contemplating revolt, Britain's suppression of the 1745 Jacobite Rebellion offered a sobering precedent. That uprising began when Highland Scots under the command of Prince Charles Edward Stuart, the son of a pretender to the British throne, captured Scotland, brushed away a British army near Edinburgh, and marched on London. King George II's response to the exiled Stuart dynasty's last grasp at the throne was swift and harsh. When government forces brought the Jacobite rebels to battle at Culloden in April 1746, they ignored calls for quarter, and prisoners perished alongside unarmed civilians. British dragoons mercilessly cut down fleeing Scots without concern for age, sex, or dynastic allegiance. The king's son, William Augustus, the Duke of Cumberland, earned the macabre moniker of "the Butcher" in the weeks following Culloden by launching punitive expeditions into the Highlands. His orders were chillingly simple: "You will constantly have in mind to distress whatever country of rebels you may pass through, and to seize or destroy all persons you can find who have been in the rebellion or their abettors." No one who had supported the Stuart cause should escape punishment.[25]

The suppression of the Jacobite Rebellion did not, however, rise to the level of what came to be called in the twentieth century "genocide." Most former rebels escaped with their lives; their cause and culture perished instead. A series of laws aimed at remaking the Highlands into a loyal, docile, and above all Protestant region succeeded in drawing these Scots into the British imperial fold. Nevertheless, the British Army's terror campaign in the Highlands was so shocking to those on the receiving end that it has scarce been forgotten since. In England the press portrayed the violence as the swift justice of a righteous monarch. The virulence of the government response to the Jacobite challenge reflected not only the very real threat that Charles Stuart and his supporters posed to the Hanoverian dynasty but also the cultural, religious, and ethnic differences between the Highlanders and other Britons. Most early modern rebellions occurred within a single polity whose denizens shared similar conceptions about the practice of war, thus limiting the violence of their conflict. Yet when the ruling regime viewed the rebels as culturally distinct, as was the case in the rebellions on Britain's Celtic fringe, the laws and customs of war did not apply. The principal leaders of the rebellion, except Prince Charles, who narrowly escaped, stood trial, with many suffering the death penalty for "High treason and levying War." The precedent was set: rebel was synonymous with traitor, and traitors were hanged. For late eighteenth-century Britons, the Jacobites had made rebellion so odious that execution seemed the only fitting punishment.[26]

The suppression of this uprising is an instructive case for understanding the limits of cultural restraints of warfare during the eighteenth century. Because rebellions call into question the existing political order and undermine its monopoly on violence, European monarchs were loath to legitimize their conduct by observing the customs and conventions of "civilized" warfare. Such events presented monarchs, and the aristocrats and armies who defended them, with an existential problem. Unlike defeat at the hands of a neighboring monarchical state, which at its worst would redraw the map and shift the balance of power, failing to quell a rebellion could prove a regime's unmaking. Simply defeating the rebels was not enough; they had to be crushed, both to exterminate all life from the movement and to dissuade future uprisings. Although the modern descendants of the British regiments that fought at Culloden prefer not to remember their predecessors' part in suppressing the Jacobites, those who engaged in that campaign felt pride in their service and saw nothing incongruous about their behavior. The British suppression of the 1745 revolt reveals that eighteenth-century Europeans were capable of excessive cruelty and disregard for the humanity of their opponents when cultural differences compounded rebellion. The helpless—civilians and prisoners of war—suffered most of the horrors.[27]

Eighteenth-century warfare exemplified a curious duality: atrocity and restraint. The "butchers" and "hangmen" of Culloden were also capable of accepting a French officer's surrender, returning his sword, and inviting the unfortunate man to dine with them. These men internalized a culture of war that had developed over the previous century as a result of structural changes in European armies and states brought about by the "military revolution," the culture of honor shared by Europe's aristocracy, and the evolving legal traditions of the laws of war. In this culture of war, violence between "civilized" nations was largely limited to the bloody, though increasingly rare, confrontations between standing armies in battle. French military theorist Jacques de Guibert summarized the prevailing European opinion in his 1773 essay on tactics: "War is become less barbarous and cruel. When battles are finished, no longer is any blood shed; prisoners are well treated, towns not sacked, countries are not ravaged and laid waste."[28]

When British soldiers crossed the Atlantic to combat another rebellion in 1775, the memory of the Jacobite Rebellion was alive and well, though so too were Vattel's cautions and the customs of war among "civilized" nations. As historian Stephen Conway has noted, "The British Army that deployed to

America during the Revolutionary War was essentially European in character."
Their American opponents were not an alien or "savage" people, and they did
not pose an immediate threat to the stability of the Protestant succession or
the Hanoverian dynasty. How would the British military respond? The leaders
of the American resistance movement thought they knew. They not only saw
themselves as the just inheritors of the rights of freeborn Englishmen but also
shared with their British opponents the same set of deeply ingrained values
and expectations about the conduct of war. Men like Washington, Alexander
Hamilton, Henry Knox, and Richard Montgomery marched off to war confident
that their conduct, and that of their enemy, would conform to customs of
"Humanity and Politeness."[29]

Warfare in Colonial America

From the outset, warfare permeated colonial American life. English colonists
arrived in Virginia wearing armor, with swords drawn and muskets primed;
it is little wonder that more than one scholar has described European colonization as an armed "invasion." Much of their leadership had learned well the
lessons of unrestrained warfare on the Continent and in Ireland, steeped as
they were in the extirpative combat of the religious wars. Expecting violence,
their stockade settlements bristled with cannon, but preparation did not bring
peace. Over the next century and a half, English Americans faced the nearly
omnipresent threat of European rivals, in the form of Catholic Spanish and
French colonists, as well as hostile Native Americans. Much like their contemporaries in Europe, colonial Americans accepted war as unavoidable, even
necessary.[30]

The conduct of warfare in the North American colonies, however, diverged
quickly from the European model. The verdant open fields and gently undulat-
ing hills of the Low Countries, France, and Germany, which had facilitated
the rise to primacy of musket-armed infantry in the sixteenth century, were
nowhere to be seen in America. Densely packed forests prevented anything
close to the rigid discipline of the European battlefield from becoming a reality
in the New World until the eighteenth century. The absence of an established
infrastructure of roads, magazines, and cantonments hindered the movement
of troops. Starvation and new diseases decimated the population of available
men for the ranks. Consequently, military institutions in the colonies began

to deviate from their European counterparts. While seventeenth-century European monarchs increasingly depended on standing armies, American colonists relied on themselves for defense in the form of militias composed of all able-bodied free men.[31]

The concept of universal male military service was hardly an American innovation, its roots tracing back to the ancient world and carried to England through classical republican political thought. Protected by the "wooden walls" of its navy, Britain had little need for an established army on the scale of France or Spain and consequently boasted a strong militia tradition. Civilians as soldiers also made sound political sense to a people deeply suspicious of the power and prerogative of royalty unchecked by Parliament. A less-than-virtuous monarch might use his army to impose an alien religion or subvert civil liberties. While the kings of England might have aspired to a royal army on par with that of their French peers, Parliament's "power of the purse" prevented such excesses. When King Charles I, and later his son James II, attempted to circumvent the legislature by creating ever-larger peacetime armies, Parliament and its supporters responded with violence. King Charles lost his head, his son merely his crown. For seventeenth-century Englishmen, power and liberty were at odds, and nothing represented the corrupting influence of power more visibly than a standing army.[32]

Although ideally adapted to republican ideology, militias by their very nature were defensive organizations, incapable of waging the ever more complex and technologically sophisticated European practice of war. Thus, in the wake of the Glorious Revolution (1688), with their country's religious future firmly secured in the Protestant camp, Englishmen came to accept the expansion and regimentation of their armed forces as long as these soldiers submitted to parliamentary, rather than royal, supervision. Provided they campaigned on the Continent or in the colonies, these troops posed little threat to English liberties. With this, the militia system, England's bulwark against tyranny, slipped quietly into decline; militia musters soon became glorified village fairs with a martial veneer.[33]

In England's North American colonies, the trajectory was somewhat different. Although the deficiencies of a universal militia in offensive operations were manifest early on, the colonies individually lacked the resources necessary to maintain peacetime armies, and until the Seven Years' War, London failed to provide substantive numbers of regulars for colonial defense. Instead, the colonies developed what John Dederer calls a "bifurcated militia system." The colonial militia came to resemble its English counterpart as primarily a social and political organization, while a select group of contractually recruited volunteers did the actual soldiering. These loosely organized and poorly trained bands of volunteers, often called rangers because of their tendency to range far and wide, defended their colonies by launching preemptive strikes against Native American villages. The ferocity of these attacks shocked the Indians, whose own deeply embedded cultural norms about the practice of war were entirely at odds with those of their European adversaries. One historian has dubbed the resultant conflict a "collision of military cultures."[34]

Throughout the colonial period, cultural misunderstandings between colonists and Natives about what constituted legitimate warfare exacerbated tensions and escalated violence. Numerous scholars have analyzed Native American cultures of war, some even arguing for a monolithic "Indian way of war," but all agree that European practices were as foreign to the Native Americans as their methods appeared to Europeans. Wayne Lee has pointed to the cognitive dissonance created by these divergent conceptions of war and its practices as the primary cause of the rapid escalation of violence between Natives and colonists. Others have emphasized protoracial hierarchies in European thought, changing conceptions of Indian technologies and bodies, or prior European experience with extirpative war. Whatever the root cause or causes, just as Europeans began to embrace restricting war's cruelty, colonists and their Indian adversaries adopted increasingly horrific and deadly practices in their conflicts. Viewing their male captives as failed warriors, Native Americans often subjected their Anglo-American prisoners to ritualistic torture before a painful death. Rangers responded by attacking villages, massacring the inhabitants, enslaving the survivors, and burning crops. Many colonial governments even offered generous bounties to anyone who produced a Native scalp.[35]

In addition to Native American resistance, colonists also had to contend with the presence of the French in Canada. Colonial Americans viewed the French colonies as an intractable barrier to their expansion and a looming threat to English liberty, freedom of commerce, and the Protestant faith. Unsurprisingly, as Britain and France vied for control of the balance of power in Europe, their colonists fought for supremacy in North America. In the series of wars that erupted after 1689, Britain's American colonies were drawn ever further into the imperial fold and into the prevailing European culture of war, in part because the capture of Canada demanded more financial, logistical, and manpower resources than any one colony could provide. After numerous failed attempts to reduce the French colony by invasion, American colonists looked to Britain for help. The ensuing conflict, known in Europe as the Seven Years' War and in America as the French and Indian War, would decide the fate of the continent.[36]

The British army that campaigned in North America from 1755 to 1763 was a long-established force led by men who took seriously the art of war. Although "pre-professional" by political scientist Samuel Huntington's standards, the mid-eighteenth-century British Army showed signs of professionalization, most notably in the education of its officers. Before the widespread foundation of military academies, a young officer was expected to cultivate a modicum of knowledge of the history, theory, practice, and laws of war through independent study of both classic and contemporary European military treatises. These men favored the Continental experts, of whom Vattel was one, but Britain also boasted its own military scholars. One such authority, Lieutenant Colonel James Anderson, published an essay in 1761 that proved popular with officers on both sides of the Atlantic.[37]

Although much of his *Essay on the Art of War* concerns tactics, operations, and a lengthy discourse on the Roman militia, Anderson was very clear on how prisoners of war should be treated in contemporary conflict: "As the Chance of War is uncertain, Politics as well as Humanity oblige the different Powers to treat the *Prisoners* of *War* on both Sides with Gentleness." He argued that it was the commanding general's responsibility to "comfort the Officers who are taken, and furnish them with whatever is necessary." In order to accomplish this humane and politically savvy project, Anderson advised that a cartel be established between the belligerent powers so that "Officers and Soldiers are exchanged against each other according to their Rank." These men were not only valuable commodities of exchange but also "visible Marks of Victory." Much like captured flags and cannons, captured men could be displayed to the public as symbolic evidence of glorious triumph. A prudent general "ought to spare Blood," Anderson cautioned, "as it is much more glorious to make Prisoners . . . than to massacre Soldiers who surrender." On these points Anderson was merely repeating and reflecting the prevailing European sentiment, but it was a sentiment his fellow officers likely shared.[38]

While many Americans were put off by the haughty airs and condescension of the Crown's officers and by the coarse ways and unthinking submission of the rankers, they admired the redcoats' courage, discipline, and restraint in battle and began modeling their own military force on its metropolitan counterpart. The process of "Anglicization" that scholars of colonial America's consumer and political culture have observed in the decades immediately preceding the Revolution applied equally to the practice of war. British Americans accepted that a disciplined military force was necessary to meet the French threat, and each colony raised regiments of volunteer soldiers known as provincial regulars. The provincials adopted European weapons, uniforms, drill manuals, and codes of conduct, while their officers emulated their British colleagues by reading the classic European texts on warfare. One such provincial officer, Virginia colonel George Washington, hoped "to attain some knowledge on the Military Profession." In addition to serving under General Braddock as an aide-de-camp, Washington purchased a copy of Turpin de Crissé's *Essay on the Art of War*. Anderson's *Essay on the Art of War* would eventually find its way into his library as well. In 1758 the colonel advised his regiment's major "in the strongest terms" of "the necessity of qualifying yourself (by reading)." Many other American officers also heeded this advice and continued to devour European texts on war well into the Revolution. While pillaging a Continental officer's baggage, Hessian officer Johann Ewald was shocked "to see how every wretched knapsack, in which were only a few shirts and a pair of torn breeches, would be filled up with military books." These texts, primarily penned by European authors, were translated into English so that those not fluent in French, as indeed Washington himself was not, could benefit from their insights.[39]

While European treatises on tactics were of little use in the North American forests, the conventions of the laws of war penetrated deep into the interior. British officers and their American provincial auxiliaries never sanctioned the calculated mistreatment of captured French soldiers or sailors. Frenchmen, though Catholics and therefore perfidious, were Europeans and by extension civilized. New York general William Johnson was so proud of preventing one of his Haudenosaunee (Iroquois) allies from scalping a wounded French officer during the Battle of Lake George in 1755 that he had the moment immortalized on canvas by the American portraitist Benjamin West. Rather than portraying Johnson as a conquering hero on a white horse, West depicted the general as a gentleman of humanity, sensibility, and compassion. The French officer, General Jean-Armand, baron de Dieskau, would spend the remainder of his captivity in the English resort town of Bath, where according to Secretary at War Lord Barrington, he merited "a Claim to every Civility and assistance"

*Figure 2. General Johnson Saving a Wounded French Officer from the Tomahawk
of a North American Indian,* by Benjamin West, 1768. Courtesy Derby
Museum and Art Gallery.

from the town's mayor. Such luxuries were beyond the reach of captured French enlisted men, but their imprisonment was no more severe than that of their comrades captured in Europe. Most traveled to England where they were exchanged for British soldiers in French custody. Johnson and his colleagues in the Anglo-American officer corps assumed that their French opponents would operate under the same norms of conduct as themselves.[40]

As the example of General Johnson's humanitarian gesture demonstrates, the restraints of the culture of war proved difficult to enforce when Native Americans were involved. The warring European powers depended upon Indian support because of the paucity of regular troops in North America, but aristocratic officers held little sway over their allies once war began, nor could they control their colonial subjects, who often acted without official sanction. Atrocities on both sides were uncomfortably commonplace. Despite the prevalence of this cross-cultural violence, when French general Louis-Joseph, marquis de Montcalm's Indian allies attacked a column of British and provincial troops after the surrender of Fort William Henry in 1757, the American press cried "massacre." The attack on troops protected by the terms of the capitulation, which took the lives of as many as 185 soldiers and civilians, highlighted alleged "Gallic Perfidy" in contrast to British humanity in the minds of Anglo-Americans. According to the customs of war in Europe, the surrendered redcoats were Montcalm's responsibility, and his inability to protect them soiled not only his personal honor but also that of France's army and king.[41]

Montcalm, who had not sanctioned the attack, was horrified. With his personal honor at stake, he worked indefatigably to ransom the survivors from their Native American captors and argued for the imprisonment of the warriors who had taken part. Paying as much as 130 livres and thirty bottles of brandy per captive, the general succeeded in recovering most of the English prisoners, though not his reputation. When he perished on the Plains of Abraham during the climactic battle for Quebec in 1759, the stain of the "massacre" remained. It was the memory of this event, compounded by other lesser outrages, that prompted Lieutenant General Jeffery Amherst to deny the honors of war to the last remaining French garrison in North America in 1760; they would have to surrender without their flags waving or drums beating. According to the British commander, this symbolic slight was retribution for "the infamous part the troops of France had acted in exciting the savages to perpetrate the most horrid and unheard of barbarities in the whole progress of the war." The French soldiers' inability to control their Native allies negated their claim to an honorable defeat. The subjugated troops marched into captivity unmolested, with their personal property intact but under the cloud of shame of an army that had violated the norms of acceptable practice in war.[42]

For American colonists living in the borderlands between the two belligerent empires, symbolic retaliation was not enough; they sought vengeance. Throughout the war, French and Native war parties had raided colonial settlements along the Susquehanna River valley, spreading violence and terror. Neither colonial officials in Pennsylvania nor the British forces had been capable, or willing, to defend the settlers; British authorities had no monopoly on violence on the frontier. Thus, the inhabitants looked to themselves to satiate their desire for revenge. When rumors of another attack reached the denizens of Paxton in December 1763, a group of local men known to history as the Paxton Boys launched a punitive raid against the peaceful Conestoga people. The surprise attack left six dead, slaughtered without regard for age or gender. Colonial officials could not protect the survivors from the vigilantes, who murdered a further fourteen innocent individuals seeking sanctuary in the Lancaster jail. Their fury unabated, an assemblage of over two hundred armed settlers marched on Philadelphia to press the provincial government to destroy their Native neighbors. The impending arrival of British troops dispersed the Paxton Boys, but the perpetrators never stood trial or faced any consequences for their actions. Colonial elites like Edward Shippen decried the wanton violence and the "riotous behavior" of the Paxton Boys, but they could not stop such activities—killing Indians was too popular. While the Paxton crisis ended without bloodshed in the capital, it taught anxious leaders the futility of standing between an angry populace and the object of its revenge.[43]

Washington and his fellow provincial soldiers learned a very different lesson from the "Great War for Empire": the conduct of war matters as much as its outcome. They had stood shoulder to shoulder with British regulars in order to drive the French from North America, and this contact profoundly shaped their conceptions of legitimate and illegitimate practices in war. One New York veteran reported with pleasure that the French "Prisoners were used with the greatest Humanity, not the least Insult or Abuse was given to the meanest" after the capture of Fort Frontenac in 1758. His opinion was seconded by a New Englander who believed that the British officers' "Humanity and Politeness to the Prisoners" contributed more to the "greater Glory" of the "British Character" than victory in battle. Washington, who had learned the soldier's trade under the direction of General Braddock and Brigadier John Forbes, fully

Figure 3. Colonel George Washington of the Virginia Regiment, by Charles Willson Peale, 1772. Washington-Custis-Lee Collection. Courtesy Washington and Lee University.

internalized the norms of European warfare. In 1772, just three years before American militiamen would fire on British regulars at Lexington, Washington posed for his first portrait, proudly donning the uniform of the Virginia Regiment of Provincial Regulars, men who had served their king with discipline and restraint.[44]

When Washington was called upon by the Second Continental Congress to command the army at Cambridge for the defense of the colonies in 1775, he left his British uniform at home. But he brought with him an understanding of "civilized" war and how it should be conducted, derived entirely from his experience with the British Army and his exposure to contemporary European military culture. Many of the officers he found commanding the New Englanders had been provincial soldiers in the last war, and while most had probably not studied Vattel, they were products of a culture that understood war in only two ways: restrained and thus "civilized" or unbridled and therefore "savage." By 1775, the revengeful violence of the Paxton Boys was a distant memory. Those elite Americans who took up arms to defend their British liberties from ministerial tyranny envisioned that the ensuing contest would be polite, restrained, humane, and above all civilized. They were mistaken.[45]

The First Prisoners

Josiah Smith, a wealthy merchant from South Carolina, was no soldier. Like most elite colonial Americans, he had never seen a shot fired in anger when he received news of the fighting at Lexington and Concord. Wars were distant and peripheral in his imagination; they were fought in Europe, on the frontier, in Canada, or in the West Indies. As a savvy man of business, he was aware that conflicts held the potential for both financial windfall and bankruptcy, but they posed no immediate threat to his personal safety. Even though the colonial government required his participation in militia training, as a man of means, there was never any real likelihood of his being sent on campaign. During the Seven Years' War, Smith and his peers in Charleston society never left the comforts of home. The arrival of British regulars ensured that men like him never knew the horrors of combat. The years since the expulsion of the French from Canada and the subordination of the Native peoples to British rule had been peaceful. Smith and his contemporaries on the western banks of the Atlantic were largely unprepared for the events of April 19, 1775.[46]

Although for an eighteenth-century South Carolinian Boston must have seemed very far away, the outbreak of combat so near a major colonial port city struck Smith as too close to home. In his estimation the British soldiers who fired on the Massachusetts men had "committed most horrid Barbarities" that "caused the boiling of much blood" among Charlestonians. By attacking American militiamen who were merely attempting to defend hearth and home, the British troops had violated Smith's conception of acceptable and legitimate military conduct. He was not alone in his astonishment and rancor. Embellished accounts of British grenadiers firing on unarmed men, abusing women and children, and dispatching the wounded at the point of the bayonet circulated throughout the colonies in the aftermath of the battles. Conjuring images of Native Americans mutilating the bodies of their captives, the *Massachusetts Spy* published an account of "the savage barbarity exercised upon the bodies of our unfortunate brethren" by the British. For the author, these atrocities strained credulity. That soldiers could be guilty of "shooting down the unarmed, aged and infirm" and "mangling their bodies in the most shocking manner" was quite literally "incredible." In the days after the engagements, real atrocities were magnified and exaggerated by propagandists to elicit the ire of the populace. Israel Putnam, a veteran of the Seven Years' War and one of the premier soldiers in Massachusetts, claimed that the British "behaved in a very cruel and barbarous Manner; going into Houses and killing sick People ..., putting the Muzzle of the Gun into their mouths and blowing their Heads in Pieces. Some Children had their Brains beat out!" These titillating accounts had the desired effect. The reported conduct of the king's troops on that April morning was confirmation enough for thousands of Americans of the corruption of the British ministry and people. Along the Eastern Seaboard, Americans of varying ethnic, social, religious, and political backgrounds confronted the reality that "the Sword is now drawn." By June 1775, Smith could report with pride "that a very martial Spirit now reigns among Persons of all Ranks here."[47]

When the British column returned to Boston on the evening of April 19, they had lost 273 men killed, wounded, or captured. Three days later Lieutenant General Thomas Gage wrote Secretary at War Lord Barrington, reporting on the events of that day. In his opinion the conflict was "nothing to trouble your Lordship." There had been a small skirmish in which the king's troops had "behaved with their usual Intrepidity." Gage was perplexed by the vitriolic accounts in the American press of his men's conduct. In another letter to Barrington, he complained that the Americans had "Published the most false and inflammatory Accounts of the Skirmish on the 19th." Exaggerated though they certainly were, there was some truth to the atrocity stories. The British troops and their officers were unprepared for armed opposition, and most had never endured combat. In the chaos that ensued, these inexperienced soldiers often denied quarter to surrendering Americans. While some militiamen were undoubtedly less than restrained as well, descriptions of American atrocities were few. One Connecticut newspaper boasted "that notwithstanding the highest provocations given by the enemy, not one instance of cruelty that we have heard of was committed by our Militia; but, listening to the merciful dictates of the Christian religion, they breathed higher sentiments of humanity."[48]

While the revolutionary press was pleased to congratulate the militia for its restraint and to demonize Crown forces, the reality of the situation was that confusion and disorganization better characterized the Americans than piety or humanity. Throughout the day, hordes of militiamen poured into the fighting from around the countryside, with little sense of order or control. No individual officer possessed the authority and gravitas necessary to take command of the offensive operations, much less to restrain the men or give instructions for the care and treatment of prisoners. During the British retreat from Concord, a group of militiamen captured the son of a man known to be sympathetic to the Crown. Accusing him of guiding the redcoats to the town, the militiamen shot the boy while he attempted to escape. According to one Connecticut whig, the supposed informant's fate was "a death too honourable for such a villain!" This boy's well-known status within the community as a loyalist made him an easy target for those bent on revenge. For years, whig crowds had employed violence, both threatened and real, to cow their more loyal neighbors. Royal-leaning John Peters recalled that earlier that April, a "mob seized me and threatened to execute me as an enemy to Congress." When "news arrived that the British troops had marched out of Boston, and were murdering the inhabitants, both young and old," Peters was arrested, threatened with death, and "plundered... of most of [his] moveable effects." The chaos of conflict unleashed long-seething resentments and provided a convenient cover for cruelty. Similar spontaneous assaults on loyalists occurred throughout the colonies in the days following Lexington and Concord. As Thomas Jefferson observed, "a phrenzy of revenge seems to have seized all ranks of people."[49]

Unlike such notorious loyalists as Peters, British soldiers, who were protected by the legitimacy of their scarlet uniforms, fared better in American custody. Lieutenant Edward Gould of the 4th Regiment of Foot, who was wounded at the Concord bridge, noted that he was "treated with the greatest humanity, and taken all possible care of by the provincials at Medford." A similar sentiment was expressed by the wife of a captured private soldier in a letter to her siblings in England. She reported, "my husband was wounded and taken prisoner, but they use him well." The Americans had taken this wounded Briton, whose leg was broken, to a hospital in Cambridge.[50]

The future for unscathed prisoners was much less certain. In the days following the battle, militiamen struggled with how to treat their new captives. Who was responsible for these men? Where could they be confined? Were they prisoners of war? Was this even a war? Captain James Reed of Burlington arrived in Lexington after the main column of British troops had already moved on to Concord. Upon his arrival, he discovered a lone redcoat—likely a deserter or shirker in search of plunder—whom, with the assistance of a Woburn man, he made a prisoner. After seizing his arms and ammunition, Reed marched the soldier back to his own home. Word spread that Reed was guarding the captive, and soon thereafter several of his neighbors handed off their captured charges to his care. By afternoon, Reed had nine or ten redcoats under guard. "Towards evening, it was thought best to remove them from my house," Reed noted, and, with the assistance of his comrades, he marched the group of prisoners to Billerica and then to Chelmsford. The sight of captured British soldiers "much frightened" the townspeople, and Reed was hard-pressed to pass off responsibility for the men. Eventually, he was able to persuade the Committee of Safety of Chelmsford to take the prisoners, provided that his militia company left a guard for their security.[51]

Reed's experience was likely the norm, as no one was expecting to fight that day; there certainly had been no plan or provision provided for what might happen if British soldiers fell into American hands. Unsurprisingly, such prisoners were dispersed throughout Massachusetts: some in jails, others in barns, and the lucky ones in private domiciles. Realizing the importance of having them in custody, John Hancock frantically wrote the Massachusetts Committee of Safety, demanding to know "what has taken place, and what your plan is; what prisoners we have, and what they have of ours." The committee did not have an answer. Within days, however, the impropriety of holding British prisoners so close to a major Crown garrison dawned on the members, and on April 26 they ordered the fifteen prisoners held in Concord to be taken to the jail at Worcester and delivered to the care of the jail keeper, Ephraim Jones. Once there, they received "Blankets and other cloathing" courtesy of the Worcester Committee of Safety. The committee turned over one of these prisoners, who was by trade a papermaker, to a Mr. Boyce to work in his mills, a confinement likely more comfortable than the Worcester jail. Even those who remained incarcerated did not complain about their treatment. Reverend William Gordon of Roxbury, a man whose loyalties lay firmly with his king and Parliament, wrote to a friend in England: "The prisoners at *Worcester, Concord, and Lexington,* all agreed in their being exceedingly well used. The policy of the people would determine them thereto, if their humanity did not." Gordon, who had no reason to congratulate men he considered rebels, attributed the prisoners' good treatment to sound judgment on the part of the Americans in arms. In his mind the sins of April 19 were reversible if the sinners begged forgiveness. The king, in all his benevolent majesty, was merciful. Mistreating his soldiers would only serve to add insult to injury and ensure the king's wrath.[52]

Exactly how many British soldiers became prisoners that April day remains something of a mystery. The provincial council appointed a Mr. Dix, Dr. Taylor, and Mr. Bullen as a committee "to inquire into the conduct of the several Towns relative to the prisoners," but their report has not come to light. Israel Putnam's statement that "70 or 80" men were taken was almost certainly too optimistic. Years later, American militia officer William Heath recalled the capture of twenty-eight British prisoners. In the immediate aftermath of the battle, General Gage reported twenty-four of his men missing, at least fifteen of whom were the prisoners transferred from Concord to Worcester.[53]

Gage's troops had captured some Americans as well. According to Lieutenant Frederick Mackenzie, the British had "about ten prisoners, some of whom were taken in arms. One or two more were killed on the march while prisoners by the fire of their own people." When Gage wrote Barrington in early May, he noted "Five or Six Prisoners taken in Arms." The captured Americans, or provincials as the British called them, were transferred to a warship in Boston Harbor to await their fate. The Provincial Congress of Massachusetts immediately began contriving a method to obtain their release. A committee appointed to consider the issue recommended sending an appeal "to General *Gage,* signed by the wives or nearest relations of such prisoners," in the hopes that the general, whose own wife was an American, might be coaxed into releasing the men. Gage was unsure of how to respond, knowing that he could not do anything that might be seen to legitimize the resistance movement. While he attempted to sort matters out, the men remained in custody.[54]

Although firing on the king's troops, no matter how provoked, was unquestionably an act of rebellion, both the British and the Americans were hesitant to use the term "rebel" in the days following the fighting; they knew too well the consequences of applying that term. From the American perspective, their quarrel was not with the king but with his ministers and Parliament. They had taken up arms in his name to defend their customary liberties. The British leadership in America was equally reticent. Gage, who presumed that the resistance was isolated to New England, did not want to escalate the situation by labeling it a rebellion. According to former royal governor of Massachusetts and friend to America Thomas Pownall, "General Gage . . . does not call the Americans *Rebels*." Despite many of his officers' strongest suggestions, the general refused to declare martial law and forbade his troops from firing on the provincials who encircled Boston, effectively besieging the town.[55]

Gage then agreed to an exchange of prisoners. On June 6, American generals Israel Putnam and Dr. Joseph Warren met with British major Thomas Moncrief for the purpose of exchanging some of the men captured on April 19. The Americans were accompanied by Captain Chester's company of Wethersfield, Connecticut, militiamen, the only troops in the American forces besieging Boston to possess a uniform set of clothing, arms, and accoutrements. In an effort to display to British onlookers their martial mastery, and by extension the legitimacy of their cause, the Americans paraded in Charlestown, "marching slowly through it." Once they arrived at the designated site of exchange, the ritual that followed looked much the same as those carried out in Flanders during the last European war. According to an article in the *Norwich Packet*, "The meeting was truly cordial and affectionate." After the exchange of private soldiers had taken place, "Major Moncrief, and the other officers returned with General Putnam and Dr. Warren, to the house of Dr. Foster, where an entertainment was provided for them." Moncrief and Putnam had been friends prior to the conflict, and neither man saw the commencement of hostilities as reason to give up good cheer and convivial company. Both shared the same vision of how war should be conducted: violence restricted to the battlefield, prisoners well cared for, officers affording each other the courtesy due to their military and social rank, and parlays and truces meticulously upheld. The author of the article proudly reported, "The whole was conducted with the utmost decency and good humor; and the Wethersfield Company did honor to themselves, their officers, and their country." If the American author is to be believed, the British concurred in his assessment: "Those who had been prisoners politely acknowledged the genteel, kind treatment they had received from their captors." As the HMS *Lively* carried the newly liberated Britons back to Boston, all concerned would have agreed that the coming contest would be fought with moderation and humanity.[56]

Still, the seeds of a shift in British thinking had already been planted. When news of the Battles of Lexington and Concord reached England, most Britons were in disbelief. Had their American cousins really killed the king's troops? Domestic opinion was divided on how best to proceed. People in the peripheries of Britain—northern England, Scotland, and Wales—tended to see the actions of April 19 as nothing short of rebellion and treason, while central and southern Englishmen largely favored reconciliation. Some newspapers described the engagements as a "squabble" and spoke of Americans as "our oppressed Brethren on the other Side of the Atlantic." For the hardliners, however, the defiance in Massachusetts was just another in a long series of rebellions in British history, all of which had been successfully suppressed by the proper application of force. One Tory correspondent hoped that the British generals in America would "adopt the principles of the late Duke of Cumberland, which, with a few of the Prime Rebel Heads . . . , will have an admirable effect in again reducing those worst kind of Traitors to Reason." Executing the Jacobites' leadership had been a successful tactic of Cumberland's in 1746. Some commentators went so far as to suggest that all rebels deserve to suffer death. In the opinion of an English author writing under the pseudonym "Politicus," the people of Massachusetts were "rebel vermin" whose actions would "consign them to the gallows whenever they are taken." This was the constituency to whom Prime Minister Lord Frederick North and his advisors listened. Under British law, the Americans were rebels; firing on Crown troops was tantamount to firing on the king himself.[57]

Facing mounting pressure, on June 12 Gage declared the colony of Massachusetts in a state of "avowed Rebellion," proclaimed martial law, and began arresting "Rebels and Traitors." To Americans who believed that they had taken up arms in self-defense, "rebel" sat uneasily, well aware that the appellation was accompanied by the likely prospect of the hangman's noose. Pennsylvania delegate to the Continental Congress John Morton wrote to a friend in London early in June expressing his concern that the king's government had "declared the New England People Rebels . . . , this putting the Halter about

our Necks." He declared, "we may as well die by the Sword as be hang'd like
Rebels." John Leach, an English seaman then living in Boston, shared Morton's
resilient defiance when Gage's officers came to arrest him on June 29. Accused
of being a spy, Leach spent ninety-seven days in a filthy prison cell alongside
future Continental congressman James Lovell and three others. According to
Leach, the American prisoners were "very close confined." Anyone who openly
challenged royal authority or questioned the general's actions could expect a
similar fate. Seeing the power of print to advance the rebel cause, Gage ordered
the arrest of Peter Edes, the son of *Boston Gazette* publisher Benjamin Edes,
to guarantee the cooperation of his more illustrious father. Imprisoned with
Leach, Edes recorded that the prisoners were "daily treated with Fresh insults
and abuses."[58]

Militiamen soon joined their civilian counterparts in Boston's jail. These
soldiers suffered a more rigorous confinement than did their civilian compatriots. A corporal named Walter Cruise was kept "close confined, and allowed
nothing but bread and water" in the dungeon. After the Battle of Bunker Hill
on June 17, the jail overflowed with American prisoners. The wounded suffered
grievously in the cramped cells, blanketed by humid, stagnant air. Few captives
received medical attention. Those fortunate enough to see a British surgeon
fared little better; Edes claimed that "not one survived amputation." Compounding their woes, the prisoners had to contend with the cruel hand of the
British provost officer, who used their status as "Damned Rebel[s]" to justify
his sadism. Horror stories emanating from the prison outraged Americans
across the colonies. Elite whigs, such as Joseph Reed of Pennsylvania, found
the harsh treatment of the officers, who as gentlemen should have been protected by their parole of honor, particularly alarming. In a letter to a British
prisoner held in Philadelphia, he expressed his contempt for the conditions of
confinement in Boston: "General Gage's Treatment of our Officers even of the
most respectable Rank would justify a severe Retaliation—They have perished
in a common Goal under the Hands of a Wretch." While men died from the
neglect or malpractice of surgeons "never before . . . employ'd but in the Diseases
of Horses," the provost regularly indulged his caprice by humiliating the
inmates. On one occasion he forced a prisoner to "get down on his knees in
the yard and say, God bless the King" before locking him in the solitary confinement of the dungeon. Denied the status of either civil or military prisoners,
captive Americans endured constant privation and abuse at the hands of their

captors. To many in the British Army, American rebels had forfeited any claim to humane treatment.[59]

General Washington, now firmly ensconced as commander in chief of the ragtag assemblage of citizen-soldiers besieging Boston, protested the "unworthy Treatment shewn to the Officers, and Citizens of America" in his letter to Gage. He was furious. Reminding the British general that his own "Officers, and Soldiers have been treated with a Tenderness due to Fellow Citizens, & Brethren" and that even loyalist demagogues, whom the American commander referred to as "execrable Parricides," had "been protected from the Fury of a justly enraged People," Washington bid farewell to his old comrade, "perhaps forever," with a defiant threat: "If your Officers who are our prisoners receive a Treatment from me, different from what I wish'd to [be] shewn them, they, & you, will remember the Occasion of it." Well accustomed to the norms and conventions of European warfare, he felt assured that the mere hint of retaliation would suffice to change the position of the British government and ensure that this conflict would be carried on with moderation and humanity. When his rebuke failed to achieve the desired effect, Washington, "very Contrary to his Disposition," ordered captive British officers on parole in Watertown and Cape Ann "to be confined in Northampton Gaol." But the Virginian was too much the European officer to carry out this retaliation in earnest. Instead, he "indulged" the officers "with the Liberty of walking about . . . Town." In a straightforward expression of his vision of war, Washington requested that the prisoners be shown "every other Indulgence & Civility consistent with their Security." The general hoped that these privileges would lead the prisoners, and Britons in general, to conclude "that Americans are equally merciful as brave."[60]

* * *

For colonial British Americans in 1775, war was either "civilized" or "savage." This dichotomy was a reflection of both the systemic changes to the European practice of war over the preceding century, which had combined to limit war's violence, and the colonists' practical experience of war with the Native peoples of North America. It was the former vision of war, one in which conflict was carried out by nation-states with standing armies, regulated by discipline, and officered by gentlemen of honor who restrained the use of violence to the field of battle and humanely treated prisoners of war in its aftermath, that the

American elite brought to the dispute with Great Britain in 1775. Seeing themselves not as rebels or traitors to the Crown but as virtuous and civilized freeborn Englishmen duty bound to oppose tyranny by force, these men were determined to scrupulously uphold the conventions of European warfare. At Lexington, Concord, and Bunker Hill, the British had violated these conventions by denying quarter and mistreating prisoners. Although outraged, Americans responded not by retaliating in kind but by further committing themselves to conducting war with humanity and moderation. Lurking under the surface, however, was the memory of another type of war, one in which humanity had no place. In the summer of 1775, the potential for "savage" retaliatory warfare was obscured by a vision of generosity, magnanimity, and humanity in the American prosecution of the conflict. Just how long this vision could endure remained to be seen.

Chapter 2

The Novelty of War

Ethan Allen did not look the part of a conquering hero as he sat chained, both hands and feet, in the bowels of HMS *Gaspé* in late September 1775. Only months before, the colonel and his Green Mountain Boys, a hardened band of militiamen from the border region between New York and New Hampshire, had captured the famed Fort Ticonderoga on Lake Champlain without losing a single man. Overnight he became the first victorious American commander of the conflict. Now the tables were turned. His British captors shackled Allen and his men together in pairs and "treated [them] with the greatest severity, nay as criminals." Upon hearing that one of the prisoners was the audacious victor of Ticonderoga, the British officer commanding Montreal, Brigadier Richard Prescott, "put himself in a great rage" and promised Allen that he would "grace a halter at Tyburn." In Prescott's opinion, Allen was a rebel of the worst sort: a successful one. Rather than accepting his surrender, proffering him a lenient parole, and entertaining him at his table, Prescott ordered the American "put into the lowest and most wretched part of" a ship of war with weighty leg irons "close upon [his] ancles [sic]." According to Allen, the brigadier instructed the *Gaspé*'s captain to treat his prisoners with "severity" and allowed his officers to amuse themselves by regularly mocking and insulting the American at their pleasure. Allen vociferously protested Prescott's "injustice and ungentleman [sic] like usage" and demanded "an honourable and humane treatment as an officer of my rank and merit should have," but his cries fell on deaf ears. Three months later the colonel and his comrades crossed the Atlantic in chains to face the fury of the British government.[1]

By the fall of 1775, the British military had made it abundantly clear to the American colonists that resistance constituted rebellion and rebels would be punished. Yet revolutionary leaders not only continued to insist that their opponents respect European conventions but also assiduously maintained them themselves. Confronted by the novelty of a war unlike any in past experience, these men clung to an idealized vision of restrained, limited, and humane warfare between "civilized" peoples. In order to prosecute this new conflict, the Continental Congress naturally relied on the handful of European-trained soldiers in the colonies to steer its military policy and practice. These veteran officers believed that they could conduct operations according to European norms, tempering the struggle's violence; this would be nothing like the brutal borderlands conflicts of the last century. To their horror, the actions of Crown armed forces and their Native American allies, as well as the reactions of their own citizens in demanding retribution, soon complicated this vision of moderate and humane warfare. Faced with widespread reports of the British abuse of American prisoners, how would the United Colonies' fledgling government respond?

During the first significant campaign of the war, the American invasion of Canada (1775–76), revolutionary forces captured hundreds of enemy soldiers, forcing the movement's political and military leadership to improvise a system for prisoner administration. No longer able to depend on the British military bureaucracy to guide, supervise, and regulate the minutiae of war, Congress nonetheless created a system of prisoner management largely consonant with European norms. Throughout the campaign, Congress's representatives diligently strove to treat their captured enemies humanely, and in accordance with the prevailing social hierarchy, in order to demonstrate the legitimacy of their cause to the king, Parliament, metropolitan subjects, and fellow colonists at home and abroad. Through their treatment of British soldiers captured in Canada, American leaders conveyed a powerful message to both their antagonists and each other: though reduced to the necessity of taking up arms to obtain redress for their grievances, *how* they fought would reflect *why* they fought. "The Glorious cause of liberty" had to be defended with honor and propriety. When confronted with British violations of the customs of "civilized" warfare, American commanders threatened retaliation but declined to follow through time and again. Instead, the revolutionaries' military and civilian leadership, as well as whig propagandists, delighted in contrasting American humanity with British savagery. Major General Philip Schuyler, one of the architects of the Canadian invasion, summarized the American stance: "It has been the invariable rule of Congress, and that of all its officers, to treat prisoners with the greatest humanity, and to pay all due deference to rank." By the conclusion of the campaign, the revolutionaries would have ample reason to reconsider that position.[2]

Invasion

Early in the summer of 1775, the ambitious Allen parlayed his reputation earned at Ticonderoga into a position in the hierarchy of the Continentals' Northern Army. Though many senior American officers considered him brash and reckless, Allen's popularity and aggressive spirit made him ideally suited for the revolutionaries' next move. While Washington contended with Gage in Boston, Americans in Connecticut and New York saw a golden opportunity in Voltaire's "few acres of snow." With Ticonderoga (and thus Lake Champlain) in their hands, the path to Canada lay open. The Americans wasted little time in organizing an expedition to secure their exposed northern flank and to bring the former French colony into the revolutionary fold.[3]

Attempts to invade Canada were hardly novel in 1775. In virtually every preceding conflict of the previous century, American provincial forces had attempted a two-pronged invasion of the Saint Lawrence River valley by both land and sea. Lacking the resources and unanimity necessary to subdue so vast a domain, the colonists had failed monumentally each time. It was not until Britain threw the weight of its fiscal-military state at New France in 1759 that Canada was finally coupled to the British Empire.[4]

In 1775 Canada once again posed a threat to American security. As a point of embarkation for a New York invasion force, a location rich with potential Native American allies and adversaries, and a vital base of supply for the Royal Navy, British-held Canada imperiled the future of the revolutionary cause. Believing that the native French-speaking population would rally to their side, the revolutionaries launched a simultaneous assault on Montreal and Quebec under Brigadier General Richard Montgomery and Colonel Benedict Arnold, respectively. Arnold's force struggled overland through the Maine wilderness, while Montgomery's troops advanced via Lake Champlain.[5]

An Irishman and former British officer who had taken part in the conquest of New France in 1759, Montgomery was an obvious choice to command the bold and intricate assault. Yet despite his experience, the general had no shortage of difficulties controlling an army of headstrong New Yorkers and New

Englanders; neither group was particularly fond of the other, and both were suspicious of Allen and the Green Mountain Boys. Allen, not one to be impressed by claims of rank, was especially insubordinate. Hoping to augment the laurels of Ticonderoga by capturing Montreal, he set out northward with a small force, planning to supplement his command by recruiting Canadian volunteers along the way. The element of surprise, he believed, would ensure success. Unfortunately for the upstart colonel, instead of an easy victory, he became the first senior American officer to fall into enemy hands.[6]

While Allen languished in captivity aboard the *Gaspé*, Montgomery's troops laid siege to the British garrison at Fort Saint John's, guarding the southern approach to Montreal via the Richelieu River. The earthen fortress was formidable, boasting forty pieces of artillery and a garrison of nearly six hundred men commanded by Major Charles Preston, a former acquaintance of Montgomery's. Had the Americans bypassed the fort and marched directly on Montreal, their interior lines would have been compromised and their route of retreat cut off. To capture Canada, Saint John's had to fall. Without either the heavy artillery or well-disciplined troops necessary to reduce the fortification by storm, Montgomery had to rely on a lengthy and costly siege. American victory now turned on preventing the fort's resupply or relief.[7]

The garrison's best hope for support lay with Major Joseph Stopford of the 7th Regiment of Foot and the British supply depot at Fort Chambly six miles to the north. Montgomery quickly dispatched Major John Brown with a small force to capture the post. The antiquated stone fortress was in no position to withstand a siege, and Stopford knew it. On October 18, after only two days of light bombardment, Stopford proposed terms for the surrender of his eighty-three-man garrison at Chambly. In accordance with European custom, the major sought the most favorable terms possible for his soldiers, suggesting that "the garrison, officers, and men, [were] not to be made prisoners, but to march unmolested . . . drums beating, colours flying," to Montreal. With that city's own garrison severely depleted, these regulars would have been invaluable to its defense. Stopford's terms were unacceptable. Major Brown countered that Stopford and his men were to "surrender [as] prisoners of war," but the soldiers would be allowed to keep their personal baggage while the women and children at Chambly would be permitted to leave unharmed.[8]

Considering Stopford's paltry defense of his post, the American terms were lenient. Perhaps Brown thought the stain on his opponent's honor was punishment enough. Much to the disgrace of the proud heritage of the 7th Foot, known as the Royal Fusiliers, Stopford surrendered the fort, his regiment's colors, and the entire garrison without even bothering to destroy his magazine and other military stores. The fusiliers' flags were sent to Congress to adorn the walls of the Pennsylvania State House, and the powder and ball were forwarded to Montgomery, sealing the fate of Fort Saint John's. The king's munitions were soon returned to the British via the muzzles of Montgomery's cannon.[9]

When news of Fort Chambly's fall reached Montgomery, he was overjoyed. But the general now had a problem. The British prisoners, their families, and all of their baggage were six miles upriver, and Fort Saint John's guarded the passage south. Major Preston, without much trouble, could have obstructed the movement of the prisoners, perhaps even intercepting the column and liberating Stopford's men. As a European officer, however, Preston could not violate the terms of Stopford's agreement with Brown, despite the shameful circumstances of their creation, without dishonoring himself and British arms. Montgomery sent one of his officers to negotiate the passage of the prisoners around Saint John's. In his report to General Schuyler, Montgomery, clearly relieved, observed that "the commanding officer at St. John's has been so polite as to let our batteaus pass to the head of the rapids in order to take in the baggage of the Chambly garrison." He was pleased that Preston had "behaved very genteelly" to his negotiating officer. As a former captain in the British Army, the American commander naturally sought to return the favor by entertaining the officers from among his new prisoners. He was particularly impressed with Stopford, whom he described to Schuyler as "a man of Family in Ireland." Stopford's officers, who were "genteel men" in Montgomery's opinion, were welcome additions to the general's evening soirées. Montgomery admitted that he felt "great pleasure in shewing them all the attention in my power."[10]

While the captured enlisted men were immediately hurried south to confinement in Connecticut, the officers were proffered lenient paroles and allowed to remain in Canada until their families could join them. Bound by their word of honor, they were under no further "restraint" while in Montgomery's custody. These gentlemen were "to be accommodated with refreshments Etc at the Public expence" and loaned the ready cash needed for their trip southward. Once prepared for travel, the officers were given their choice of lodgings in New Jersey or Pennsylvania. Ever the gallant, Montgomery even released several women who had been captured at Fort Chambly to join their husbands at Fort Saint John's, demonstrating to Preston and his besieged garrison that he understood the conventions of European warfare. Given the ramshackle appearance of the American forces and their haphazard conduct of the siege, the men of the garrison were likely concerned about their fate should the fort fall. Would the rebels grant them quarter and the honors of war? Irish and Scottish Jacobite rebels had rarely observed the niceties of European warfare. Montgomery, however, did not imagine himself as a rebel. He was a quintessential European officer; it would never have occurred to him to have behaved otherwise.[11]

To Major General Sir Guy Carleton, the governor of Canada, the American general was nothing more than a traitorous rebel. A fellow Irishman and comrade of Montgomery's from both the Louisbourg and Havana campaigns of the Seven Years' War, Carleton had no sympathy for a man who compounded rebellion with the betrayal of his brother officers and native land. Unable to punish Montgomery directly, the governor vented his anger on the closest surrogate: Ethan Allen. Following the colonel's capture, Carleton had the American paraded through the streets of Montreal in chains to impress upon the Canadian population the gravity of defying the king's authority. Despite the unease of a number of his own officers at this treatment, Carleton did not countermand Prescott's orders and allowed Allen and his men to remain chained in the *Gaspé*'s hold. Like the brigadier, the governor rebuffed the prisoner's pleas for relief.[12]

Prior to his capture, Allen's relationship with Montgomery was already strained. To Montgomery, an Irish gentleman who had held a king's commission, Allen appeared uncouth, untrustworthy, and unabashed in his appetite for fame. Upon learning of the New Englander's misfortune, he wrote Schuyler: "I have to lament Mr. Allen's imprudence & ambition." Nevertheless, he was an officer in the American army and Montgomery's subordinate. According to the norms of European warfare so familiar to the general, he had a responsibility to ensure that the colonel was treated according to his rank as an officer, even if he did not measure up to Montgomery's standards as a gentleman. Carleton's treatment of the captive Americans was a direct assault on the legitimacy of their army and Montgomery's authority. If the general could not protect his men, how could he expect them to follow him into harm's way?[13]

In Montgomery's view, the British commander required a reminder of the principle of reciprocity that undergirded Europe's culture of war. He instructed one of his officers to communicate to Carleton "that if Mr. *Allen* or any other prisoner of our troops . . . are treated with cruelty, or more severity than is necessary for their security, I must, much against my inclination, retaliate on those who already are or may fall into my hands." After the capture of Fort Chambly, Montgomery had plenty of suitable subjects for retribution. Much as Washington had threatened Gage with retaliation for the treatment of the Bunker Hill prisoners, Montgomery was confident that the mere suggestion of retaliation would suffice to alleviate the colonel's sufferings. In a report to Schuyler, Montgomery revealed his intention to "endeavour by means of the Chambly garrison to obtain better treatment for Allen & the other prisoners." He was equally concerned for the Canadians who had been captured with Allen. These men, who were direct subjects of Governor Carleton, were more likely to face summary judgment than were the Americans, who would probably be transferred to England for trial. If Montgomery did nothing to stop Carleton from hanging the Canadians, any hope of recruiting further allies from among France's former subjects would be at an end.[14]

But his threat did not produce the desired result as Carleton ignored him. Growing desperate, Montgomery asked Major Stopford to inform the governor of "the fatal consequences which must attend the carrying on so barbarous a war." In his opinion, treating "unfortunate prisoners with the most cruel severity, [and] loading them with irons" was beneath the dignity of so estimable an officer as Carleton. Writing the governor personally on October 22, Montgomery referred to him as "one of the most respectable officers of the Crown" and lamented "the melancholy and fatal necessity" of remonstrating against his treatment of American prisoners. This was no false flattery. Carleton had led the British assault against Morro Castle in Cuba in 1762, and young Lieutenant Montgomery had seen firsthand his bravery under fire.[15]

As governor of Canada, however, Carleton no longer looked the part of the brave and honorable officer of Montgomery's memory. He obviated not only his humanity but also his prudence by treating Allen and his men so severely. Did he not fear retaliation? Montgomery now possessed far more British prisoners than Carleton had Americans, and the entire garrison of Fort Saint John's was poised to fall into his hands as well. As a gentleman and man of sensibility, he admitted feeling "the most painful reluctance on this melancholy occasion," but his duty to his own troops demanded retaliation in kind. Carleton's treatment of Allen was a "shocking indignity" that required Montgomery to "execute with rigour the just and necessary law of retaliation" upon the Fort Chambly prisoners. Far exceeding the *lex talionis*, or law of retaliation, Montgomery threatened that if he did not receive a response in six days, he would interpret

Carlton's silence as "a declaration of a barbarous war" in which no quarter would be asked or given. Carleton, unwilling to negotiate with rebels and traitors, remained mute. In a letter to the secretary of state for the colonies, the Earl of Dartmouth, the governor vented, "I shall treat all their threats with silent contempt, and in this persevere, were I certain of falling into their hands the following week." Such bravado stemmed from his firm belief that he was not "at liberty to treat otherwise those who are traitors to the King." This was not a war between rival European dynasties, and Montgomery was no longer a fellow officer and gentleman. Rebellion had to be stamped out violently.[16]

Despite the vehemence of his official stance and Carleton's recalcitrance, Montgomery had no intention of eschewing the restraints of "civilized" warfare. He was well aware that the legitimacy of the Americans' cause in general, as well as their claim to be "liberating" Canada, depended upon the rigid adherence to European customs. Instead of retaliating on the prisoners at his disposal, Montgomery did nothing. He knew that if Fort Saint John's fell, Montreal would be indefensible; Carleton would have to surrender, and Allen and his men would be liberated. Thus, Montgomery disregarded retaliation and concentrated on the siege of Saint John's. When the Americans opened a new battery on the fort's flank in late October, Preston had little choice but to seek the best terms possible for his men. On November 1 Montgomery demanded the fort's surrender.[17]

Unlike Stopford, Preston had resisted the siege diligently, and he attempted to parlay the strength of that defense into a convention rather than a capitulation. The distinction between a convention and a capitulation was an important one in European warfare. A convention was a binding agreement between two armies that temporarily suspended hostilities, thereby sparing the defeated troops and their commander the shame of surrender. Instead of becoming prisoners of war, Preston proposed that his men would "embark for *Great Britain*" on the condition that they not serve in America again. Montgomery was sympathetic to the major's position. He had skillfully defended his post, maintaining his honor as a gentleman and that of his regiment under extremely adverse conditions. But the prize of over six hundred British prisoners was too great for the general to relinquish. Preston's position was hopeless, and under the conventions of European warfare, he was in no position to negotiate. As Montgomery phrased it, "if you do not surrender this day, it will be unnecessary to make any future proposals; the garrison shall be prisoners of war, without the honours of war, and I cannot ensure the officers their baggage." Had Preston rejected this ultimatum, the Americans would have stormed the fort under no obligation to grant the garrison quarter. Preston acquiesced.[18]

After a siege of forty-eight days, on the morning of November 3, Preston and his men marched out of the battered fortress "with the honours of war . . . due to their fortitude and perseverance" and grounded their arms in front of a roughhewn and patchwork parade of American soldiers. This armed assemblage of farmers, tradesmen, apprentices, and servants now possessed as prisoners nearly all of the regular British soldiers in Canada. The official articles of capitulation signed by Preston and Montgomery boasted that British "prisoners have been constantly treated with a brotherly affection" and promised that "the effects of the garrison shall not be withheld from them." The officers were allowed to keep their swords (and presumably their regimental colors as no mention was made of them in the articles of capitulation or in the records of the Continental Congress). At the conclusion of the ceremony, the prisoners embarked for confinement in Connecticut, "there to remain till our unhappy differences shall be compromised, or till they are exchanged." Quite contrary to his earlier show of bravado to Carleton, Montgomery relished extending gentlemanly courtesies to the captured officers, even releasing one "or two to go to their families . . . at *Montreal*" on parole. He explained his reasoning to Schuyler: "They cannot do us any harm, and there would have been a degree of inhumanity in refusing them." Although the general had been quick to invoke the law of retaliation in his protestations to Carleton, when faced with an opportunity for revenge, he did just the opposite. Seeing fellow officers and gentlemen in distress, Montgomery offered them every indulgence. The rank and file of the Fort Saint John's garrison were treated with respect, allowed to keep their personal property, and promised a lenient confinement until they could be exchanged. Montgomery's actions accorded perfectly with the law of nations as articulated by Vattel, the customs of war in eighteenth-century Europe, and the social hierarchy of the late eighteenth-century Atlantic world.[19]

General Schuyler, a veteran of New York's provincial forces and a scion of one of the wealthiest and most politically connected families in the colony, was equally concerned with displaying his gentility and upholding his colony's honor in front of his new captives. He acquainted Governor Jonathan Trumbull of Connecticut of his past relationships with the garrison's officers: "From Major Preston, and the officers of the Twenty-Sixth Regiment, I have experienced the most polite and friendly attentions when I was a stranger and traveller in *Ireland*." Remembering their gentlemanly courtesy and sociability, Schuyler recommended them to the governor's "notice" and requested that "if there is any choice in the quarters which you shall destine to them, that theirs were the best." On their route southward, the prisoners were "to be Entertained at the Publick expence" and "treated with the utmost attention and politeness." He warned the officer of the guards conveying the captives to "be particularly attentive that no person, who may have forgot the rights of mankind and the principles of Englishmen offer the least insult to any of the Gentlemen, the Soldiers, their Wives, or Children." Still imagining himself as a British gentleman, the general insisted that his subordinate officers conduct themselves likewise. Montgomery and Schuyler were not men prepared to exercise the *lex talionis,* instead endeavoring to ensure their comfort in provisions and lodgings by forwarding the captured Britons and Canadians to New York and Connecticut.[20]

As the transports carried Preston's men down the Richelieu toward confinement, Carleton began preparations to abandon Montreal. Knowing that he could not possibly hold the city with his meager garrison, the governor fled rather than contest Montgomery's advance. Before he decamped to Quebec, Carleton conveyed Allen and his fellow prisoners to the capital, where they were confined aboard a ship in the Saint Lawrence so that they would not fall into American hands. In a letter to Dartmouth, he admitted that the men were confined in irons, a security measure far too stringent for traditional prisoners of war. Carleton explained, "We have neither prisons to hold, nor troops to guard them." Nevertheless, he asserted that "they have been treated with as much humanity as our own safety would permit." These justifications aside, Allen's confinement was neither humane nor safe. With Colonel Arnold's column nearing Quebec, the city's commander, Lieutenant Governor Hector Cramahé, made the strategic decision to send Allen and the other Americans to England. Lacking suitable jails and the manpower necessary to guard them, Cramahé was ecstatic to be rid of so many useless mouths to feed.[21]

Word of his departure terrified Colonel Allen. Any chance of escape or rescue was at an end. Instead, he and his men endured the transatlantic passage under the stewardship of a captain named Brook Watson, described by Allen as "a man of malicious and cruel disposition." Watson ordered all thirty-four prisoners confined in a purpose-built pen in the hold of the ship, where they were forced to both "eat and perform the office of evacuation, during the voyage to England." According to Allen, Watson claimed "the place was good enough for a rebel" and "that anything short of a halter was too good for" him and the others. Every league the ship drew nearer to England, the captain's threat grew closer to reality. In Canada the absence of any official policy for how to treat revolutionary prisoners had preserved his life, though it ensured the severity of his captivity. In England Allen would be subject to civil law, and he knew well the punishment for treason. Prescott's prophesy of a halter at Tyburn Hill now looked like a very near reality.[22]

As Allen approached his fate, American forces under Montgomery pried Montreal from the grasp of the British Empire. In a reverse of the 1759 campaign that subdued New France, Canada's second-most-populous city surrendered before the capital was even attacked, exposing the Saint Lawrence valley to American incursions and dooming Quebec if not relieved by sea. Along with the city and its 150-man garrison, Montgomery also captured the infamous Brigadier Prescott. The man who had ordered Allen in chains, Prescott was beneath Montgomery's contempt, having violated the customary norms of war between "civilized" peoples by treating the colonel as a common criminal instead of as an officer and gentleman. The general described Prescott as a "cruel rascal" who deserved to be treated "with the sovereign contempt his inhumanity and barbarity merit[ed]." His dislike of the brigadier was such that he confessed to Schuyler that should anything happen to Allen, "I hope *Prescott* will fall a sacrifice to his manes." Despite this imprecation, Montgomery did little to punish the officer beyond banishing the Briton from his dinner table. Passing him on to Schuyler at Ticonderoga, Prescott was then sent into Connecticut with the other officers of his regiment. Montgomery's actions, or inactions, should come as no surprise. While outraged by Prescott's behavior, Montgomery could not punish him without further escalating the conflict's violence and sullying his own honor and that of American arms.[23]

For some of Montgomery's junior officers, less versed in contemporary European customs, the general's treatment of British prisoners looked more like weakness than humanity. Their only experience of war was the present conflict, in which the British were not observing such niceties. Why was Montgomery holding American troops to a higher standard? Grumbling escalated to an official complaint in which the general was accused of endangering "the publick safety" by allowing British officers to remain at liberty in the city. As Montgomery explained to Schuyler, "A number of officers presumed to remonstrate against the indulgence I had given some of the officers of the King's troops." Schuyler, who was deeply concerned with maintaining the army's disciplined appearance in the eyes of his antagonists and superiors alike, was concerned that "this turbulent and mutinous spirit will tend to the ruin of our cause" if Montgomery did not quell it at once. Infuriated by his officers' temerity and insubordination, the general resigned on the spot. His officers, soon realizing their error, begged him to resume command. Montgomery was the only senior officer in the Northern Army with substantive knowledge of European tactics and siege operations; though they disagreed with his policies, they were cognizant of his indispensability. Having made his point, Montgomery immediately returned to his duties as the army's commander. The officers would never again question his vision of the proper conduct of war.[24]

The common soldiers of the Northern Army, however, were less easily mollified. Many viewed the captured Britons as spoils of war and considered themselves entitled to their possessions. In the aftermath of the fall of Montreal, New York soldiers pillaged British troops of their personal clothing and effects. Not one to take his responsibility toward enemy prisoners lightly, Montgomery interceded and returned their clothing, much to the dissatisfaction of the New Yorkers. The general explained to Schuyler, "I would not have sullied my own reputation nor disgraced the Continental arms by such a breach of Capitulation." As an officer and a gentleman, as well as a representative of the Continental Congress, Montgomery was honor bound to protect his prisoners and maintain the terms of the articles of capitulation. That his men disagreed is a telling reminder of just how tenuous and elite focused the European culture of war was on the other side of the Atlantic.[25]

News of the American victories in Canada electrified revolutionaries across the colonies. As fort after fort fell, the press painted an image of an unstoppable American juggernaut in their readers' imaginations. The manner in which the campaign was conducted was a point of particular pride. American troops had not adopted the "skulking way of war" so derided by British officers in the last conflict, and they were no longer hiding behind defensive works awaiting Crown assaults. Newspapers from Philadelphia to Boston printed the articles of capitulation for Fort Chambly, Fort Saint John's, and Montreal, crafting a potent picture of Continental forces on the offensive, reducing Britain's northern bastions one by one according to conventional European modes. Along with a copy of Marshal Maurice de Saxe's *Reveries*, Montgomery had brought with him a vision of "civilized" warfare developed over years of experience and study, which induced him to humanely handle his captured enemies according to their social station. While not everyone in his army shared this vision, the general successfully imposed the European culture of war on the American volunteers.[26]

Away from the front, revolutionary Americans took pride that their army conducted itself with "humanity and benevolence." When Arnold captured the British fort at Crown Point in July, he received an address from the "principal Inhabitants" of the region complimenting him on his "tenderness and polite treatment" of his prisoners. Expressing a sentiment commonly held by elites throughout the colonies, the men declared, "The humane and polite manner with which you treated your prisoners, insures to you the applause of all." Montgomery, who looked the part of the virtuous and benevolent officer in the European mold, received even more adulation than the rustic Arnold. Revolutionary Americans praised him as the paragon of martial glory and "civilized" sensibility. After the capture of Montreal, John Hancock complimented Montgomery not just for his victory but also for the manner in which it was achieved. Commenting on his treatment of prisoners, Hancock applauded: "Nor are the humanity and politeness with which you have treated those in your power less illustrious instances of magnanimity than the valour by which you reduced them to it." Courage was inseparable from benevolence in the Massachusetts delegate's idealized European conception of warfare. In his panegyric Hancock promised that Congress, "utterly abhorrent from every species of cruelty to prisoners," would continue to support Montgomery's vision of war and "ever applaud their officers for beautifully blending the Christian with the conqueror."[27]

The Canadian Prisoners

While the Northern Army shifted its attention to the capital city of Quebec, the British prisoners from Fort Saint John's, Fort Chambly, and Montreal began their march southward. When they reached Fort Ticonderoga, General Schuyler made the decision to foist them upon the governments of New York and Connecticut. These were ideal locations: far enough from the enemy's main force in Boston that rescue was unlikely but close enough to both Washington's and Schuyler's headquarters that orders could easily be relayed. Both colonies also had experience housing French prisoners during the last war. Because Connecticut was the only colony whose governor embraced the revolutionary effort, it still maintained many of its prewar governmental institutions and was thus better prepared to receive large numbers of captives than was New York. Moreover, the colony already had British prisoners in its care. After seizing Ticonderoga, Allen had sent the captured garrison to Hartford, where a committee of the colonial assembly oversaw their confinement. Informing Governor Trumbull of his newest wards, Schuyler instructed him to "dispose of them as your Honour shall direct." The Connecticut Assembly, realizing that Congress had failed to make any provision for the detention or support of the captives, asked the governor to write and inquire "in what manner the officers and soldiers who are prisoners . . . shall be provided for and supported, and how and in what manner the expence incurred thereby shall be defrayed." According to the customs of European warfare, the British Army was responsible for forwarding provisions, clothing, and medicines for the captured men, but in the meantime the assembly wondered, who would pay? Until directions from Congress could be had, Connecticut legislators ordered that the prisoners be administered in the same manner as the garrison of Fort Ticonderoga.[28]

Unlike the British soldiers captured at Lexington and Concord, who were often confined in cramped local jails, the Connecticut Assembly allowed the enlisted prisoners from Canada, along with the previously captured redcoats, the privilege of seeking employment among the local population. This option was beneficial not only to the prisoners, who were allowed to keep their earnings, but also to the colony by successfully outsourcing their wards' lodging and provisioning. Ezekiel Williams, a member of the committee appointed by the assembly to care for the prisoners from Fort Chambly, later reported that the men were sent "out into the several Towns near about Hartford and hire[d] . . . [and] Boarded in Families in the best manner we could." Williams "appointed and engaged some of the respectable Men in the several towns to take care & have the oversight of them" because he lacked any "regulation of Congress concerning them." The enlisted men captured at Fort Saint John's were "put out in like manner" in Litchfield County.[29]

The hiring-out system, however, could not be used to accommodate officers, whose status as gentlemen protected them from manual labor. Drawing upon the European customs for the treatment of enemy officers, the assembly granted the commissioned prisoners their freedom of movement, within certain geographic parameters, upon signing a parole of honor neither to escape nor to oppose in word or deed the United Colonies. They were expected to live peaceably and quietly until Congress and the British government arranged a treaty of exchange, known as a cartel, to release the men in return for captured American officers of equal rank. Prescott, Preston, and their junior officers readily acceded to the terms of the parole. In return for their good behavior, the officers could expect to be accorded all the privileges of their exalted status.[30]

The New York Provincial Congress followed Connecticut's lead in its treatment of the British prisoners captured in Canada, ordering the Albany Committee of Correspondence to "provide them with Lodgings & Board at the public expense." Although the officers could reasonably be expected to sustain themselves by drawing lines of credit, the congressmen considered it their "Duty to alleviate as much as possible the Evils of their Confinement" by furnishing them the necessities of life. They even released two British enlisted men on their parole, who were "permitted to remain peaceable and unmolested in the City of *New-York*." This would never have transpired in a European conflict. Common soldiers, unlike their officers, were not considered innately honorable and thus were ineligible for parole. So concerned with treating their enemy captives with generosity, thereby performing their legitimacy as a governmental institution, the provincial congress effectively released men who were unconstrained by the strictures of gentlemanly honor. Novices in the conduct of war, these civilian representatives applied the European custom of parole further than it was ever intended.[31]

Not everyone agreed that British prisoners, especially common soldiers, should be allowed to roam freely. During the summer of 1775, the Albany Committee requested permission to put prisoners from Canada "in close Confinement" because its members believed the "prisoners from St Johns have it in their Power to be of disservice to the public Cause." In the opinion of the committee, the prisoners took "more Liberty than Consistent with the Station they were in." Enlisted prisoners loitering about taverns and inns in relative freedom and luxury did little to motivate potential recruits or boost morale. The provincial congress overruled the request, but these concerns did not disappear.[32]

The situation in Connecticut was little better. The inhabitants of Farmington reported that some of the prisoners captured at Fort Chambly were "turbulent and disorderly" and likely to escape. Rather than imprison the men, the Connecticut Committee of Safety suggested that the townspeople keep "a special and vigilant watch over those persons, so as to prevent their escape, even if some extra expense should be incurred thereby." The committee members knew that if they confined the soldiers, "they may complain of hard usage," a propaganda coup the British might use to justify their harsh treatment of American prisoners. Connecticut's leaders were unwilling to throw away the moral high ground Montgomery had won in Canada. Nevertheless, their patience for disorderly, prone-to-escape, and expensive prisoners was running out quickly.[33]

To many ordinary Americans, his majesty's captured officers were equally as wearisome. Although welcomed at first as gentlemen of refinement, erudition, and sensibility, as the fall of 1775 slipped into winter, the burden of the British officers began to take its toll on the communities that housed them. Philip Skene, the former lieutenant governor of Forts Ticonderoga and Crown Point, apparently made himself quite unpopular in Hartford. When news reached that community that Lieutenant General Gage refused to countenance an exchange of prisoners, one exasperated Hartford resident sardonically quipped, "In all Probability we shall have the Honour of his Excellency Governor Skeen's [sic] residence among us—God knows how long." This refusal surprised both townspeople and prisoners alike, who assumed that the captives' confinement would be only temporary. They had believed that Washington and Gage would establish a formal cartel specifying how and when the men would be exchanged; such agreements had been commonplace in European warfare for over a century. When Gage was recalled to England, the new British commander, Major General William Howe, followed his predecessor's lead by refusing to negotiate with Washington. The two men severed all communication in late August 1775 and did not resume contact until the end of December. Without communication, there could be no compromise and no exchange. The officers would remain prisoners.[34]

While most were content to while away their captivity at cards, in drink, or at play, some officers chafed under the conditions of their paroles. One particularly obstreperous officer, Major Christopher French, pestered his captors with a catalog of complaints and insults. Paroled to Hartford, the major was at liberty to come and go as he pleased throughout the town. He spent his days, according to Hartford Committee of Safety chairman Thomas Seymour, haranguing every passerby "in high Tone" on the evils of rebellion and promised to "act vigorously against the Country, & do every thing in his Power to reduce it." Seymour informed General Washington that French "talkd in so high a Strain that the People veiwd him as a most determined Foe." Popular animus against the officer ran high, but rather than confine him in Hartford's jail, where he could do no harm, the committee merely forbade him the privilege of wearing his sword in public. In Seymour's opinion, the people of Hartford "would not bare with his wearing Arms at any Rate." A seemingly innocuous punishment, this disarmament was no "mere Punctilio" to French.[35]

The symbol of an officer—as much a badge of rank and social status as a weapon—the sword was vested with dense meaning in Europe's culture of war. For an eighteenth-century European nobleman, the sword was not only a tool to defend his sovereign as well as his own honor but also an inseparable part of his social and gender identity. Wearing a sword denoted gentlemanly status. The common law of England even forbade the practice for any who were not entitled to do so by birth or military position. Although by 1775 swords had fallen out of fashion among gentlemen in England and its colonies, the tradition and its cultural significance remained strong with military men. Major French, already deprived of his liberty by men he considered to be traitors and criminals, was aghast that the committee sought to rob him of the visible trappings of his martial identity as well. In his remonstrance to Washington, the major disparaged the "lower Class of Townspeople [who] took umbrage at" his strolling about the city armed and appealed to the general as a brother officer. After all, in Europe "it was customary for Officers (& Volunteers, being Gentlemen,) on their Paroles to be allow'd to wear their Swords." French was quite certain that Washington's "long Service & intimate acquaintance with Military Rules & Customs" would induce him to overrule the committee. The Virginia gentleman would clearly understand that a European officer should "not be insulted by being oblig'd to surrender [his sword] . . . merely to gratify the Populace."[36]

But French failed to grasp what Washington knew all too well: the revolutionary cause rested upon the support of the population. The American general could not so easily dismiss the townspeople's complaint. Nevertheless, Washington was unwilling to abandon his vision of "civilized" warfare. He assured French that the Americans had "shewn on our Part the Strongest Disposition to observe" the European customs of war and that his "Disposition" did not allow him "to follow the unworthy Example set me by General Gage," who had refused to treat captured American officers according to their rank. No matter the civilian pressure, he would not knowingly violate the laws of war. In his response to the Hartford Committee of Safety, Washington recommended "a Gentleness even to Forbearance with Persons so intirely in our Power. We know not what the Chance of War may be." The golden rule of reciprocity, as much as humanity, required a temperate response.[37]

Washington was under no obligation, however, to exceed the customary European practice in such cases. After reviewing the military literature available to him, the general concluded that "the Rule with Regard to the Indulgence in Question is, that Prisoners do not wear their Swords. I therefore cannot approve of it." European military custom, not New World vengeance, dictated the case's outcome. Hardly mollified, French continued to badger Governor Trumbull and the Hartford Committee of Safety with a litany of complaints his captors deemed trivial.[38]

For Congress, the problems of prisoner management exceeded the cavils of nettlesome officers. British prisoners were spread throughout Connecticut, New York, and New Jersey, and the expense of their upkeep began to mount. Committees of safety, often the only governmental bodies capable of administering the captives, petitioned Congress for instructions, regulations, and reimbursement. Even Washington did not know how the delegates wanted to proceed. In late October he put together a list of urgent questions for Congress, several having to do with prisoners of war: "In what manner are prisoners to be treated? What allowance made them and how are they to be Cloathed?" In conference with delegates who traveled to Cambridge to meet with him, Washington received his answer. They concurred with the general that captured enemy soldiers should "be treated as Prisoners of War but with Humanity" and provided an "Allowance of Provisions" equal to that of the Continental Army. The individual colonies would have to front the money until reimbursement arrived from the British. Presumably, each colony would also provide clothing and other necessaries for the common prisoners, while "officers being in Pay should supply themselves with Cloathes." The delegates also suggested that Washington attempt to establish a cartel of exchange with General Howe. In an effort to discourage the British from arresting prominent civilian Bostonians in order to exchange them for the officers captured in Canada, they declared that Congress "agreed that the Exchange will be proper, Citizens for Citizens, but not Officers & Soldiers of the regular Army for Citizens." Any exchange that might occur would be conducted according to customary European practice: officers for officers of equal rank, soldiers for soldiers of equal rank, and civilians for civilians according to their social station. British sailors, soldiers, marines, merchant mariners, and civilians captured at sea were to "be deemed Prisoners at the Disposal of the General." Washington finally had a set of guidelines for the administration of enemy prisoners. As an officer well informed of the customs of war in Europe, none of these instructions would have been unfamiliar. But how could he apply them with little authority beyond his own army and even less ready capital?[39]

Washington's first suggestion was to move the prisoners farther from the seat of war. In his opinion, Connecticut's exposed shores were too vulnerable to enemy raids. The Royal Navy ruled the waves, and nothing was stopping Howe from sallying forth out of Boston and landing within striking distance of Hartford before Washington could mobilize any sort of resistance. The general submitted "to the Wisdom of Congress, whether, some convenient Inland Towns—remote from the Post Roads—ought not to be assign'd" for the reception of enemy prisoners. General Schuyler agreed. In a missive to the president of Congress, John Hancock, he wondered, "As the Ministry seem determined to carry on the war with spirit, would it not be advisable, as soon as there is good sledding, to remove all the prisoners from *Connecticut* to some of the interior Towns in *Pennsylvania*." Such locales would be safe from British maritime incursions and likely better able to supply the prisoners than Connecticut or New York, both of which had the added responsibility of contributing provisions for the sustenance of Continental forces around Boston.[40]

Realizing that the number of British prisoners was likely to increase, Washington also proposed that "a Commissary or Agent [be] appointed to see that justice is done both to [the prisoners] and to the publick." He cautioned, "Without a mode of this sort is adopted, I fear there will be sad confusion hereafter." In his opinion, disorganization would lead only to graft and wastage. Well aware that European armies customarily established departments, or commissariats, to see to the provision, lodging, parole, and exchange of enemy prisoners, Washington impressed upon Congress the need for such a bureaucracy in the American army. The general's entreaties went unanswered, as the delegates were too preoccupied with the business of forming a government to systematically develop a prisoner-of-war policy. Washington was on his own for the time being.[41]

Congress, however, did acquiesce to the general's request to move the prisoners inland. Facing mounting complaints from the Connecticut Assembly, the delegates resolved "that the prisoners taken at Chambly and St. John's, be sent to, and kept in, the towns of Reading, Lancaster, and York, in the colony of Pennsylvania." Nearby Carlisle was added to the list a few weeks later. These locations were both far enough from the primary theater of operations in New

England and close enough to each other that prisoners could be rotated relatively easily if any one community were overburdened and incapable of providing for the soldiers and their families. Lancaster, with its large barracks complex
built during the Seven Years' War, was an especially suitable location for
prisoner detention. All three communities also boasted thriving local economies and demonstrative zeal for the revolutionary effort; Lancaster County
alone provided eleven battalions in the summer of 1775. Surrounded by verdant
farms, these communities would have no difficulty feeding the British prisoners.
From the position of delegates in Philadelphia, the Pennsylvania interior
appeared to be an ideal location to house the captured men while General
Washington negotiated their exchange.[42]

Local officials were less certain. With most of the militarily eligible men
serving elsewhere and a small but vocal loyalist community in their midst, the
committees of safety of Lancaster, Reading, York, and Carlisle were uncertain
about housing and guarding hundreds of ravenous, roughshod, and recalcitrant
redcoats. In the words of the Lancaster committee, "We are at a loss what kind
of conduct to pursue." Before the prisoners began their trek southward, Hancock instructed the Continental commissary general of issues "to supply them
agreeably to the Rations given to the Continental Army," but he made no
provision for supplying the men once they reached their destinations. The
prisoners slated for Pennsylvania were not inconsiderable. Those from the 7th
Regiment numbered 242 officers and men as well as 60 women and children,
while the 26th Regiment had 257 officers and soldiers and an additional 186
women and children. Although the population of Lancaster at the time
exceeded 3,000, the arrival of nearly 750 new mouths to feed and backs to clothe
was not a welcome sight. When the prisoners reached Bethlehem, Pennsylvania,
on their way to Lancaster in early December, the inhabitants "found much
trouble to provide for and lodge them."[43]

Understandably, the Lancaster Committee of Safety was nonplussed to
learn that the Continental officer commanding the detainees, Egbert Dumont,
had "no particular orders relative to them then than to conduct them to this
place." On behalf of Congress, the officer requested "the Committee to take
such measures with respect to the said Prisoners as they may think most conducive to the Publick Service." Dumont's advice was little comfort to the
committeemen, who knew "of no person or persons here who are appointed
to supply these people with Provisions." Much like those in Connecticut, the
committees of safety in Lancaster, York, Reading, and Carlisle were composed

of civilians with little knowledge of military affairs. They were utterly at a loss for what to do. What was the customary subsistence for prisoners of war? Who would provide it? The Reading Committee of Safety confessed that its members "were much Surprised at so large a party [of prisoners] being ordered here, without any provision, notice, & without any person attending them to supply them with necessaries." Beyond the simple obligation of feeding the men, the Lancaster committee wanted to know "whether it is expected [the prisoners] shall be kept constantly confined to the Barracks" and "whether the Officers . . . may be permitted to take private Lodgings in the Town." If the men needed to be confined to the barracks, a guard would be necessary to secure them properly. But how would a guard be raised, and who would pay their wages? The committee wanted answers.[44]

With winter setting in, there was no time to wait for a response. Fortuitously, Matthais Slough, a member of the committee and an innkeeper in Lancaster, volunteered "to furnish the necessary articles for the support of the prisoners" until Congress's orders on the matter could be known. A similar temporary solution was hit upon by the board in Reading. Committeeman Henry Haller was asked "to provide Houses, Firewood & provisions for the party, who must have otherwise suffered much at this severe season."[45]

Throughout Pennsylvania, housing the prisoners proved difficult. Unlike Reading, Lancaster was fortunate to possess barracks that could be pressed into service to lodge the enlisted men. The accommodations were far too scanty for gentlemen, so the committee allowed the officers to take rooms "in a public House." Nor were the barracks an ideal detention center for the common soldiers. Built to quarter British and provincial troops, not prisoners of war, the stone edifices were not enclosed. The committee members had no means of securing the men unless funds could be acquired to fence in the barracks. Emphasizing the tenuous situation to a subcommittee of Congress tasked with contracting for the prisoners' supply, the Lancaster committee asserted, "The Peace of this Borough & good order of the Troops, we are firmly persuaded, would be much better preserved by such a Partition." The only hope to prevent escape, or worse yet insurrection, was to ensure that the prisoners were entirely separated from the local populace.[46]

Given the lamentable condition of the prisoners' clothing and quarters, keeping them away from locals inclined toward generosity was no small order. To many members of the congregations and pious communities of central Pennsylvania, the captives appeared to be fitting subjects for Christian charity.

In Bethlehem the Moravian community took pity on the "poor women & children" of the "Royal prisoners from Canada" by assisting them as best they could. The enlisted men were in similar need; their uniforms were in utter disrepair, and they were almost entirely devoid of winter clothing and heavy blankets. The Lancaster committee wrote Congress "that the Captive Soldiers here are in great Distress for want of Breeches, shoes & stockings.... [T]heir other cloathing is bad." The prisoners had endured a precipitous trek of over five hundred miles without resupply. When confined at Trenton, New Jersey, before being transferred to Pennsylvania, nineteen men of the 7th Regiment reported having lost eighteen pairs of breeches, twenty-six shirts, thirty pairs of shoes, and thirty-three pairs of stockings on the march. Facing a Pennsylvania winter without warm clothing, their fate looked bleak. The Lancaster committee reported to Congress that the barracks only had "about 165 old Blankets, almost worn out." Although they were able to scrounge "72 new ones" at the public expense, the committee assured Congress that "the whole serve as a scanty covering for the soldiers against the Rigours & Inclemency of the Season." Something had to be done, or the men and their families might not survive the winter.[47]

Pressed by committees of safety in Pennsylvania, New Jersey, and Connecticut for a standardized method to supply the prisoners, Congress looked to Old World precedent for guidance. As Washington had earlier advised, European countries at war customarily appointed commissary officers and assistants to see to the provisioning and lodging of their captured enemies. A statement of the expenses of their upkeep would then be presented to their opponent's commissary for reimbursement. Very often, opposing armies would task contractors—usually successful merchants—to reside near detention sites in order to best victual their incarcerated troops. Much like the treatment of prisoners of war more broadly, this informal system was predicated upon the principle of reciprocity. Shorting enemy prisoners of their allotted provisions and necessaries was not only dishonorable but also unwise. Retaliation in kind would likely follow. Armies insisted on fastidious record keeping to guarantee equitability and to prevent graft. With no prospect of an exchange on the horizon, Congress resolved on December 1 to allow David Franks of Philadelphia "to supply the troops, who are prisoners in this Colony, with provisions and other necessaries, at the expence of the crown." Franks had risen to prominence among Philadelphia's merchants for his role in provisioning British and provincial troops during the Seven Years' War. In light of his previous experience working with British quartermaster officers, he was the logical choice.[48]

Washington was relieved to hear of Franks's appointment, noting that "it will Save me much time & much trouble." As commander in chief of Continental forces, the general was constantly petitioned by enemy prisoners with requests for favors, exchanges, and provisions. Exasperated, he informed Hancock, "I am applied to and wearied by their repeated requests." Without an established commissary of prisoners, however, all Washington could do was ask the various local committees to do their best to meet the prisoners' needs. Franks's employment as agent-contractor to the British prisoners was a step in the right direction, though only one man could not be responsible for the growing numbers of prisoners in American hands. The general once again strongly suggested that Congress adopt the European mode of appointing an overall commissary of prisoners. This time Washington pointed out that such an officer would reduce the expense of prisoner management by preventing "many exorbitant charges" and ensuring that greedy farmers or war profiteers did not take pecuniary advantage of the prisoners' distressed situation. Evincing a lack of foresight unremarkable for a collection of novices, Congress demurred.[49]

The British, on the other hand, were surprisingly cooperative. Washington was not the only general who had received countless complaints and petitions for redress; Howe was equally perturbed by the prisoners. The British general was under strict orders from Lord Germain, secretary of state for the American Department, not to "enter into any treaty or agreement with Rebels for a regular cartel for exchange of prisoners," but he was likewise requested "to procure the release of such of His Majesty's officers and loyal subjects as are in the disgraceful situation of being prisoners to the Rebels." Provided he did not impugn "the King's dignity and honour" by invoking his name in communication with rebels, Howe was free to negotiate for the relief or release of British prisoners. The general acquiesced to Franks's appointment as contractor and ordered his own commissary general of stores and provisions to issue instructions for the provisioning of the troops captured in Canada. The arrival of British foodstuffs and other necessaries must have been a welcome sight in the Pennsylvania interior.[50]

Yet Howe did not make provision for the prisoners' families also in confinement. His position surprised not only the American committees tasked with their care but also the women and children, who were customarily entitled to half rations as civilians "on the strength" of their regiments. In the eighteenth century, wherever British troops marched, women and children followed. By 1775, soldiers' wives, known as camp followers, were an integral part of the military machine, providing essential support services and logistics. In return for their labor as laundresses, seamstresses, sutlers, and nurses, they and their children were entitled to join their husbands' messes and draw half rations from the regiment. Hardly the rowdy trollops of popular imagination, these women toiled side by side their uniformed husbands and were equally subject to martial law. Quite rightly, they were appalled that Franks refused to feed them. According to the Lancaster committee, Franks gave "express orders not to deliver out any allowance of meat or Bread to the soldiers wives or children for the future." His contract with the British quartermaster stipulated that he supply the prisoners from the 7th Regiment, the 26th Regiment, the Royal Highland Emigrant Regiment, and the Royal Artillery. Strictly interpreting his orders lest he should be stuck with a bill that the British government refused to reimburse, Franks denied the women's request for provisions.[51]

The Pennsylvania committees now had over two hundred women and children in custody and entirely dependent upon their captors for sustenance. In a letter to Congress justifying their decision to supply the soldiers' families "at the Expense of this country," the Lancaster committee invoked the European principle of humanity in warfare. "Being mindful that Humanity ought ever to distinguish the Sons of America & that Cruelty should find no admission amongst a free People, we could not avoid considering the situation of the Women & Children as pitiable indeed." Positioning themselves as compassionate, in stark contrast to the cruelty of British indifference, the people of Lancaster reaffirmed their commitment to conducting war with moderation and humanity.[52]

Their conduct met with the approbation of both Congress and the captured British officers. The prisoners praised the committee's "humanity" for assisting the distressed women and children as well as "other civilities." Hancock fully approved "of those humane sentiments which induced [the committee] to provide for [the women and children] in their distress" and promised reimbursement. Reiterating Congress's position on the treatment of prisoners of war, he lauded the committee for rendering "the situation of our prisoners as comfortable as possible.... As men, they have a claim to all the rights of humanity; as countrymen, though enemies, they claim something more." The law of nations, in his opinion, protected any "civilized" soldier from the violence of unrestrained warfare, but these prisoners were not French, Spanish, or

Dutch—they were brother Englishmen. Hancock was adamant that the revolutionaries should go out of their way to perform the customs of "civilized" warfare in order to prevent the conflict from devolving into the barbarism of civil war. As long as the Americans stridently maintained the appearance of legitimacy, the British would eventually see the justice of their grievances, and a peaceful settlement would be within reach. In Hancock's opinion, this required a rigorous attention to the customs of war.[53]

Many of the captive officers sought to capitalize on Congress's goodwill and exploit American inexperience at war to their advantage. Hoping to catch the civilian legislators unaware of the finer points of military capitulations, they asserted that the Pennsylvania committees had violated the terms of surrender for Fort Chambly, Fort Saint John's, and Montreal by billeting them away from their enlisted men. The Lancaster committee reported to Congress that the officers "complain greatly of a Separation from their Soldiers as Breach of Genl. Schuyler's solemn Engagement." As justification for their remonstrance, the officers argued that they had to remain in close proximity to their men in order to superintend the distribution of clothing and salary, claiming that "Justice cannot be done to the Privates . . . unless the officers are upon the spot." Lancaster, however, lacked suitable accommodations for all of the officers. In order to ease the burden on the town's inhabitants, Congress resolved "that the officers be distributed in such places as are most agreeable to themselves . . . , officers and privates be not stationed in the same places."[54]

This resolution was hardly agreeable to the officers, but not simply because of the reasons they outlined. Ever since the prisoners had arrived in Pennsylvania, Continental Army recruiters had covetously eyed the expertly drilled and disciplined redcoats. Not at a loss for recruits that winter—Pennsylvania, like the other colonies, was in the throes of what Charles Royster has called a *rage militaire*—the army was in dire need of experienced noncommissioned officers who could transform farmers, apprentices, and shopkeepers into disciplined regulars. Colonel Arthur St. Clair admitted to President Hancock that one of his officers had enlisted a sergeant and a drummer belonging to the 26th Regiment. He explained, "It is rather my sentiment that the inlisting [of] the prisoners is improper; but as we were much in want of sergeants and drums," the men were allowed to join the Continentals. The officers of the 26th were furious. They feared that if they were removed from their men, American recruiters would abscond with their entire regiment. Claiming that the articles of capitulation had been violated, the officers of the 7th and 26th regiments refused to sign their paroles. By asserting that the Americans had violated the terms, they hoped to bully Congress into obtaining quarters for them close to their soldiers in the comparatively more cosmopolitan Lancaster.[55]

Amateurs though they were, the American delegates were in the right. Only the terms for the capitulation of Fort Chambly included an article that stipulated that "the men [were] not to be decoyed from their Regiment." The soldiers of the 7th Regiment who surrendered with Major Stopford were thus off limits to American recruiters, but the men of the 26th and those soldiers of the Royal Artillery, the Royal Highland Emigrants, and members of the 7th captured with General Prescott were all fair game. Perhaps unwittingly, St. Clair had enlisted only members of the 26th Regiment captured at Fort Saint John's. Recruiting enemy prisoners was a commonplace practice in European warfare and, unless specifically forbidden in articles of capitulation, was condoned and expected. Enlisting prisoners obviated the need to confine and subsist nonproductive soldiers, swelled the ranks of one's own army with trained troops, and denied the enemy that manpower. Over one-fifth of the French and Bavarian prisoners captured at Blenheim in 1704 joined the British and allied forces in the aftermath of that battle. Similarly, in 1756 Frederick the Great recruited 18,000 Saxon troops into his army upon their defeat. Fully aware that their arguments were not based in European precedent, the British officers hoped nevertheless that Congress would defer to their superior knowledge and experience in military affairs without question.[56]

Congress was not intimidated. President Hancock informed the Lancaster committee that the officers' "complaint, that a separation from the soldiers is a breach of General Schuyler's solemn engagement, we apprehend not to be well-founded." While he agreed that "all stipulations of a capitulation ought, undoubtedly, to be held sacred, and faithfully fulfilled . . . , no such stipulation is found in the capitulations upon which those gentlemen surrendered." Had their complaints been legitimate, Congress would have complied eagerly with their requests, but the revolutionaries would not be browbeaten into disadvantage. As in any "civilized" conflict, the articles of capitulation would be enforced. Nevertheless, Hancock placated the prisoners by permitting "two or more of the officers to come, at proper times, from their places of residence to *Lancaster*, for the purpose of settling with, and paying, their soldiers." Congress would hear of no further challenge to its authority. If the officers did not want to submit to the terms of their parole, Congress "shall be extremely sorry to be reduced to the necessity of confining them in prison." Predictably, the Britons backed down.[57]

Cowed but not appeased, the officers remained dissatisfied. With few diversions other than food, drink, or amorous companionship, they quickly exhausted their ready cash in the pursuit of pleasure and began accruing ruinous debts. Initially, Congress promised to reimburse the innkeepers and tavern owners for the officers' expenses, but the prisoners' "exceedingly extravagant" lifestyle quickly became untenable. Shocked by the mounting bills, the delegates resolved to allot the men two dollars per week to defray the costs of their room and board on the condition that the sum was repaid upon their release. Blaming the Americans for their financial woes, the Britons complained that because they were quartered in taverns on their march to Pennsylvania, they were "under the necessity of living in a more expensive manner than they otherwise would have done." Although they appreciated Congress's gesture, two dollars a week was "inadequate to the manner which they, as gentlemen and *British* officers, have been accustomed to live in."[58]

Even in captivity, European officers were expected to maintain the trappings of gentility. The prisoners entertained generously and frequently, each trying to outdo the other. Such lavish lifestyles were unsustainable for many. The more impecunious officers lived in fear "of being turned out of doors" by their creditors. Although they agreed to draw bills of exchange in the hope that the British government would cover their expenses, they were not sanguine. The Lancaster committee took pity on the poverty-stricken captives and induced "some of the inhabitants to afford them private lodgings ..., where they lodged and breakfasted." Justifying such actions to Congress, the committee invoked the prisoners' social status: "To gentlemen in that delicate situation, though enemies, we could not avoid rendering every service in our power.... We could not be idle spectators of the distresses these gentlemen were reduced to." Congress was unmoved. The legislated allotment was generous; the officers could "refuse it or add to it on their own account, as they please."[59]

Disgruntled, haughty, and expensive, the officers soon wore out their welcome. When some quartered in Connecticut appeared to celebrate an American defeat in January 1776, a crowd of townspeople gathered with the intention of punishing the officers for "mak[ing] merry and rejoic[ing] at their Misfortune." As the crowd grew more agitated, the Britons, including the ever-aggrieved Major French, feared for their lives. Thankfully, Continental captain John Sedgwick managed to convince the agitators to disperse, "happily without Blood Shed." Later that winter, however, these officers and several townsmen exchanged "some Blows" because the Britons refused to abandon their riotous singing and cavorting. Enraged revolutionaries felt little constrained by the customs of war in Europe. Fortunately, several American officers interceded and prevented the brawl from escalating.[60]

Although vexing, the captive officers posed little actual threat to the revolutionary effort or to the communities that housed them; the common soldiers, on the other hand, proved dangerous. Confined to their quarters, unable to engage in either work or drill, the idle soldiers were "active, restless, and uneasy," in the estimation of one Lancaster resident. Were they to band together, even unarmed, the enlisted prisoners might easily overwhelm the county's meager collection of soldiers. By early January 1776, the Lancaster committee found it "absolutely impossible to preserve the Peace & good Order of this Borough" without the assistance of Congress in the form of more specific regulations for the management and security of the captives. Lacking such instructions and fearing insurrection, the members appointed "a Serjeant & 12 Privates to mount Guard at the public Magazine every Evening" to prevent powder and arms from falling into the hands of the prisoners. The watchmen were instructed to patrol "the Street every two Hours in the Night to prevent Disorders." Despite their precautions, "disturbances" between the British prisoners and local civilians could not be avoided. When Congress did reply, it was that no troops or funds could be spared for the Pennsylvania committees. The best the delegates could do was to authorize the committees to confine unruly prisoners "in cases of gross misbehavior."[61]

The situation in Reading was even more serious than in Lancaster due to the lack of suitable barracks; the prisoners had to be lodged in private homes. Residents implored the Pennsylvania Assembly to remove their burden by constructing secure barracks for the captives, fearing that "from the idleness of the said Prisoners' manner of living, they will probably become disorderly." Similarly, the Pennsylvania Committee of Safety worried that "the kind Treatment given them [the prisoners] meets with a very improper & indecent Return." The men "often express themselves in most disrespectful & offensive Terms and openly threaten Revenge whenever opportunity shall present." Drawing on the experience of the prisoners during their captivity in Connecticut, the Pennsylvania committee suggested that the British soldiers be "dispersed among the Farmers, in the Country where their opportunities of doing Mischief will less correspond with their inclinations." Spread out through the countryside and industriously engaged, they would be neutralized as both a threat and a drain on Continental coffers. Congress concurred.[62]

Many of its constituents, however, balked at the liberal conditions of the Britons' confinement. As lurid accounts of Ethan Allen's treatment at Carleton's hands circulated through the colonies, popular outrage began to focus on prisoners of war. Despite having been treated "more like friends than prisoners" by the "genteel families" of Trenton, Lieutenant John Shuttleworth of the 7th Regiment lamented "the repeated insults and illiberal behaviour we daily met with from the inhabitants." This abuse took the form of threats and even physical violence. Lieutenant John André claimed, "Several of us have been fired at, and we have more than once been waylaid by men determined to assassinate us." Similarly, a group of officers at Carlisle reported that they had "been insulted in the most gross terms, pelted with stones, hatchets have been brandish'd over our heads, fire Arms presented at us, nay fir'd and more than one plan concerted for way-laying and murdering us." Instead of the "brotherly Affection" they had earlier experienced from their captors, the officers received "a treatment we had no reason to expect in a civiliz'd Country." The prisoners attributed the alteration in their treatment to the "defamatory papers spread about the town to render us odious to the people."[63]

The committees, possessing neither firm orders from Congress nor the troops to enforce them, could do little to protect the prisoners from the rage of their respective townspeople. When Captain W. Home complained of his treatment at Lebanon, a member of the local committee apologized but admitted that he "durst not interfere, least he himself should be treated in the same manner." Many Americans were unimpressed by the revolutionary leadership's vision of war. Instead of seeing gentlemen officers who deserved to be accorded respect, politeness, and deference during their captivity, they saw tangible evidence of British tyranny and corruption. In their eyes, advocating for enemy prisoners when brave Americans like Colonel Allen wasted in British jails smacked of treason.[64]

Allen's treatment was so egregious that even some revolutionary elites added their voices to the mounting chorus demanding retribution. Benjamin Franklin warned a friend in England that the colonel's harsh confinement and other "Barbarities" had "fix[ed] us in a rooted Hatred of your Nation" and a willingness to see "these Mischiefs . . . revenged." Treating British prisoners "with the utmost Kindness and Humanity" was clearly not working. After hearing that Carleton had sent Allen and "the unhappy prisoners, it is said, in irons" to England, Governor Trumbull wondered, "Is it not time to retaliate?" By December 1775, even General Washington was inclined to agree with his civilian colleagues. He warned General Howe "that whatever Treatment Colonel Allen receives—whatever fate he undergoes—such exactly shall be the treatment & Fate of Brigadier Prescot [sic], now in our hands."[65]

Notwithstanding this hard stance, Washington had great respect for his British counterpart, and he loathed the prospect of retaliation. Howe's politics were known to lean decidedly whiggish, and his courage in combat at the siege of Louisbourg and on the Plains of Abraham during the Seven Years' War was the stuff of legend. Appealing to the general as "a man of Honour, Gentleman & Soldier," Washington was confident that he would release the prisoners whom Carleton had "treated without regard to decency, humanity, or the rules of War." If Howe ignored his pleas, the Virginian reiterated his intention to invoke "The Law of retaliation," which was "not only justifiable in the Eyes of God & man, but absolutely a duty which in our present circumstances we owe to our Relations Friends & fellow Citizens." In the past the British had ignored Washington's threats, which in turn had proved empty. They did so again now.[66]

With the tide of public opinion turning against the British prisoners, the delegates in Philadelphia reassured their constituents that "whenever retaliation may be necessary, or tend to their security, this Congress will undertake the disagreeable task." However, they cautioned against confusing retaliation with vengeance. The law of retaliation might justifiably be invoked to ease the sufferings of their captured comrades, but Americans must continue to be "mindful that humanity ought to distinguish the brave; that cruelty should find no admission among a free people." The previous year's fighting suggested that British "enormities" in the conduct of the war reflected the kingdom's "execrable barbarity." But rather than stoop to their level, Congress argued, the revolutionaries must "take care that no page in the annals of *America* be stained by a recital of any action which justice or Christianity may condemn." Ever concerned with the opinion of posterity and the still-present possibility of reconciliation with Britain, leaders continued to insist upon generosity toward enemy prisoners. Perhaps more important, they hoped that contrasting British barbarity with American humanity would induce the undecided to embrace the common cause and maybe even turn public opinion in Britain against continued hostilities. The delegates' resolves were published by the *Pennsylvania Evening Post* on January 4, 1776.[67]

To Ethan Allen, awaiting the vengeance of the British Crown in a prison cell in Pendennis Castle, the king's subjects seemed unmoved. The colonel believed that they were determined to crush the rebellion by force. Curious visitors to the prison were all of the opinion that he would soon be hanged. Although his jail keeper "was very generous," Allen was still a criminal in the eyes of his captors. He and his men "continued in irons" while they awaited their fate. In a letter to Congress, which he hoped would fall into the hands of the British ministry, the colonel urged the delegates to embrace retaliation on British prisoners, "not according to the smallness of my character in America, but in proportion to the importance of the cause for which I suffered." Fear of retaliation, he hoped, might just save his neck. Fortunately for Allen, because he was not considered a prisoner of war, he was subject not only to the penalties of English civil law but also to the protections. Several members of Parliament, inclined toward sympathy with the American cause, obtained a writ of habeas corpus demanding formal charges be levied against him. Uninterested in the expense, time, and negative publicity of trying every American rebel who fell into their hands, the British ministry shipped Allen back across the Atlantic beyond the grasp of sympathetic lawyers.[68]

Allen's fortuitous escape from the hangman's noose did little to conciliate the revolutionaries who called for retribution. If British prisoners were not brought to account for the transgressions of their government, what would prevent the Crown from continually violating the customs of war? A petitioner to Congress, writing in the *Connecticut Gazette* under the apt pseudonym "Justice," begged the delegates to "retaliate for the barbarous injuries which any of your officers or men (who fell into the hands of the enemy) might receive in the present war." Pointing to Allen's treatment by Brigadier Prescott, the petitioner suggested that Congress "make retaliation on Prescot [*sic*] and others, that those Americans in their hands may be treated better by them." Such a just retaliation would serve as "evidence that the American Congress holds faith with their people." A columnist for the *New-England Chronicle* enunciated the prevailing opinion among irate revolutionaries: "How different the situation of ALLEN and Prescott;—the First, taken fighting for Life, Liberty and Property, is treated as a villain; while the other, taken fighting to support the cruel edicts of a tyrannical ministry, whose aim is to rob and enslave, is lodged at a first rate tavern in this city, and fed with the best the markets afford.—Oh! George! who is the savage?—After this, can any man blame the Americans should they retaliate?" Facing rising pressure for decisive action, Congress had little choice but to investigate the charges of Prescott's complicity in Allen's treatment.[69]

After a thorough inquiry by a committee tasked with the issue, Congress concluded that Prescott was guilty of "great Malevolence and bad Behavior to our People." After a vote of eight delegations to two, Congress ordered the brigadier securely confined in the Philadelphia jail. Prescott's treatment of Allen and other prisoners violated the revolutionaries' conception of the legitimate practice of warfare, unjustified violence that warranted punishment. On January 29, 1776, the British officer was turned over to the custody of the keeper of Philadelphia's new jail. With evident glee, a Philadelphia newspaper reported Prescott's removal "from his apartments in the city tavern" to the stark surroundings of the jailhouse.[70]

On the surface Congress's resolve appeared to be just the sort of retaliation the hardliners called for, but in reality Prescott's confinement was hardly stringent. Congress granted him "the attendance of his servant, and in case his health requires it, that he be allowed the attendance of a physician." Although he was denied freedom of the jail yard, Prescott was permitted "to receive Visits from his Bror. Officers and to have Pen Ink and Paper." On February 5, after seven nights in confinement, Congress ordered the brigadier removed "from the jail of this city to some private lodgings" on account of a recommendation from his surgeon that the prison was not conducive to his health. Congress "indulged" Prescott with the "Liberty to take Lodgings in the City Tavern" among the company of several of his officers. Upon recovering his health, Prescott was sent to the Pennsylvania interior along with the rest of the Canadian prisoners. The delegates had evidently lost their taste for retaliation—if they had ever had the stomach for it in the first place.[71]

Despite numerous allegations that Prescott had mistreated American prisoners, the British officer continued to enjoy a lenient captivity. One of his former captives, Thomas Walker, journeyed to Philadelphia from Montreal for the express purpose of obtaining "some satisfaction" for the brigadier's "inhuman violence." Walker hoped to see him pay for the "indignity and sufferings" he had caused. Instead of finding Prescott confined in irons in a dank cell, he witnessed "Mr. *Prescott* lodged in the best tavern of the place, walking or riding at large through *Philadelphia* and *Bucks* Counties . . . , feasting with gentlemen of the first rank in the Province." Congress offered Walker no redress. Prescott and several other officers rented a house near Reading, where they were allowed to stay despite orders to remove the British officers to Carlisle. The Lancaster committee did not want "to put them to any unnecessary hardship."[72]

Those revolutionaries who pressed for a prisoner-of-war policy that reflected British outrages must have been displeased by the congressional response. On May 21, 1776, Congress officially codified the practices of the Connecticut and Pennsylvania committees by establishing a formal set of regulations for the administration of enemy prisoners. These regulations, which were based on their knowledge of "the Custom in England and France" for the treatment of prisoners, would remain on the books for the remainder of the conflict. All captured enemy soldiers were "to be treated as prisoners-of-war, but with humanity." While in captivity, common soldiers would be "allowed the same rations as the troops in the service of the United Colonies" and "permitted to exercise their trades, and to labour, in order to support themselves and families." Officers, as gentlemen and men of honor, were entitled to "be put on their parole" and to draw two dollars a week for their subsistence and lodging. In addition to the congressional loan, they were permitted to sell their bills of exchange so that they might live as comfortably as their credit would allow. Not keen to be stuck with a bill for the prisoners' support, Congress officially placed the responsibility for provisioning the soldiers on British contractor Franks. In the event of his refusal to comply, the delegates agreed to supply both the men and "the women and children belonging to the prisoners" with "subsistence . . . and other things absolutely necessary for their support." Surprisingly, they stipulated that "no prisoners be inlisted in the Continental Army." Either out of deference to the articles of capitulation for Fort Chambly or from the realization that British prisoners were more likely to abscond with their bounty money than face the very real chance of execution if they ever fell into their countrymen's custody, Congress officially forbade the army from indulging in this customary European practice.[73]

Perhaps most important, Congress empowered local authorities, in the form of assemblies, conventions, committees, or councils, to "remove such prisoners from place to place, within the same Colonies, as often as . . . it shall seem proper." Here Congress diverged from customary European practice (again). Because the revolutionaries were ideologically constrained from establishing a centralized government with the power to raise revenue through taxation, Congress was forced to rely on individual colonies to supervise the prisoners. Had the United Colonies been able to fund a highly developed military bureaucracy such as Britain's War Office, they might have established permanent prisoner-of-war detention facilities far from the seat of conflict. As it was, Congress had to depend on the generosity and loyalty of small communities to support the captives. Given this reliance, delegates had little choice but to allow the individual colonies autonomy over the location of confinement. If the prisoners became too burdensome on the people of Lancaster, for instance, Pennsylvania could remove them to Carlisle or York, provided that they paid attention to the "former Resolutions of Congress concerning Prisoners" that guaranteed their humane and uniform treatment. This provision, though unavoidable, opened the door to infraction, neglect, and maltreatment. Although Congress appointed a commissary for each of its three military departments "to superintend and take the Direction and supplying of such Prisoners . . . as nearly conformable as the Circumstances of this Country will admit of, to the custom of other civilized Nations," with the prisoners' management in the hands of the individual colonies, it was powerless to prevent local conditions from trumping national policy. As the war progressed, these shortcomings had a profoundly deleterious effect on the treatment of enemy prisoners. The dictates of humanity did not always accord with local self-interest.[74]

The Cedars

Unlike the British prisoners who enjoyed warm bunks in the barracks, taverns, and dwelling houses of central Pennsylvania, the American Northern Army passed the winter of 1775–76 in the ardent, and often futile, pursuit of survival. After the initial victories over the British positions at Fort Chambly, Fort Saint John's, and Montreal, the American advance stalled at the gates of Quebec. In early December 1775 Montgomery's army joined up with the smaller force under Arnold that had advanced up the Kennebec and Chaudière rivers to descend on the capital city from the east. Carleton's position looked desperate. Without reinforcements from Britain, his trifling force of remaining regulars and Canadian militia would soon share the fate of Montreal's garrison. Montgomery, however, was less confident of his own success. Arnold's force had suffered severe losses on the trek northward, and many of his own soldiers' enlistments would expire at the end of the year. Fearing the arrival of British troops in the spring and the disintegration of their own command, Montgomery and Arnold launched an abortive assault on the city on the snow-covered evening of December 31, 1775. Before morning, Montgomery lay dead, Arnold was severely wounded, and over four hundred American soldiers were killed or captured. The remaining revolutionary troops fled to their encampments in disarray. Stubborn to the point of obstinacy, Arnold refused to abandon the quest for Canada. The American forces continued a half-hearted and ineffectual siege of Quebec throughout the winter.[75]

While recovering from his wound, Arnold was gravely concerned about the fate of his captured men. He had earlier attempted to establish formal communication with the garrison to negotiate the exchange of prisoners of war. In mid-November Arnold had sent an officer to treat with Lieutenant Governor Cramahé on the issue. Assuming that his envoy would be protected by a flag of truce, Arnold dispatched the officer to the city's gates, according to European custom, with a drummer beating the parlay. Cramahé scoffed at the rebels' show of martial etiquette and ordered his soldiers to fire on the men, who only "narrowly escaped being killed." Fulminating, Arnold declared these actions "contrary to humanity and the laws of nations" and demanded to know if the prisoners were being held in "irons." The colonel reminded the lieutenant governor that he had several British prisoners, "who now feed at my own table," and threatened that they "will be treated in the same manner, in future, as you treat mine." According to the laws of war in Europe, proportional retaliation was not only sanctioned but also required in such instances. To Cramahé, Arnold and his men were rebels; negotiating with them would have legitimated that rebellion. There would be no further discussion.[76]

Now, in the aftermath of the December 31 assault, Arnold could ill afford to be so bold. When the smoke of battle cleared, Carleton possessed "the Flower of the rebel army" in his custody. How would the governor treat these men? Would they be confined in irons and shipped to England to suffer the judgment of British justice? Perhaps remembering Montgomery and Arnold's former threats of retaliation, or moved by the sight of the poorly clothed, malnourished, and exhausted soldiers, the governor confined the men in the relative luxury of the capital's seminary. The officers were quartered separately in the upper floor of the building, while the enlisted men were confined in the monastery, the first time the British had acknowledged distinctions of rank among their American prisoners. Both officers and men received ample supplies of bread, cheese, and even porter from local merchants. According to one prisoner, wounded Americans were placed under the care of British surgeons: "To the great honor of general Carleton, they were all, whether friends or enemies, treated with like attention and humanity." The governor even ordered his men to bury the American dead with the honors of war. General Montgomery, as befitting the commander of an opposing army and a former British officer, was interred in an elaborate ceremony following a formal procession through the city. An American prisoner remembered shedding "tears of thankfulness, towards general Carleton" for his show of respect. Despite his continued insistence "that no message, nor shou'd any letters be receiv'd thro the Channel of the Rebels," Carleton did allow Arnold to send in five sleighs "loaden with baggage," winter clothing, personal effects, and "a little money for the Prisoners." Upon hearing of Montgomery's defeat, John Hancock took solace in the knowledge that "the prisoners are treated with humanity."[77]

Notwithstanding Carleton's apparent kindness to the prisoners, their fate remained uncertain—after all, he might have been preserving them for the gallows. An American prisoner remembered that soon after their capture, a Scottish officer informed them that the officers "may be sent to England, and there be tried for treason" because they were "in rebellion." The Americans were well aware that Ethan Allen had been sent overseas, and they were consumed by "doubt and uncertainty." Ninety-four prisoners enlisted in a loyalist regiment, the Royal Highland Emigrants, in return for exoneration, fresh provisions, and the king's shilling. Their change of heart provoked skepticism from some of Carleton's officers. Captain Thomas Ainslie reported, "Many wagers were laid that the greatest part of them will take the very first opportunity to desert." Their prognostications proved valid; desertions were incessant.[78]

Those unconvinced by British promises and unable to escape continued in their benevolent confinement until the evening of March 31, 1776, when guards uncovered a plot to escape from the barracks. Captain Ainslie claimed that the enlisted prisoners had concocted "a plan to join their friends without the walls" by surprising the guards, seizing their arms, and opening the gates of the city to Arnold's forces. Carleton's kindness was betrayed; he would not make that mistake again. As Ainslie recorded, "The greatest part of those concern'd in this plot were put in irons; many of them behav'd very insolently on this occasion." Although some of the prisoners surreptitiously removed their fetters, others spent the remainder of the winter chained to the floor, "attached to a monstrous bar, the weight of which was above their strength to carry," in the "frigid weather." Several American officers, unbound by a parole of honor, plotted their own jailbreak in April. When discovered, Carleton ordered the men confined, as Allen had been, in the dank hold of a British warship. Scurvy and "a violent diarhoea" soon appeared among the men both afloat and ashore. Far from the leniency of their initial confinement, "wailings, groanings and death" characterized the experience of the prisoners after their escape attempts.[79]

Carleton's change of heart did not go unnoticed in the American camp, but Arnold had neither the time nor the means to relieve the prisoners' suffering. As the Canadian snows abated and the frozen Saint Lawrence thawed, both Carleton and Arnold anxiously awaited the arrival of British reinforcements. On May 7, American hopes were dashed when two ships were spotted approaching the city, creating a "great joy in town." With no prospect of defeating the now-reinforced garrison, American forces began "their disorderly retreat." Seeing that his prisoners now posed little threat to the city's security with the American army on the run, Carleton ordered their chains removed. Nonetheless, one American officer claimed, "we have been worse used since our people removed, than formerly.... [O]ur situation [is] truly miserable." Although the outlook turned bleak, Arnold and the Northern Army still occupied Montreal. If they could hold that city and its environs until their own reinforcements arrived, the quest for Canada might survive another season.[80]

The success of the campaign now hinged on the actions, or inactions, of Canada's indigenous population. The American commanders had initially hoped for a profitable Indian alliance, but the prospect of cooperation was greatly hindered by their decision to interdict the lucrative fur trade between the Saint Lawrence valley and the Great Lakes, fearing that it might support western British garrisons such as Detroit. This policy alienated Indians and French Canadian merchants alike. Although Congress dispatched a delegation to appease these populations, their arrival proved too little, too late. Only the Caughnawagas—Iroquoian people who had converted to Christianity under French influence—resisted the British call to arms. In order to defend against Indian incursions from the west, the revolutionaries established a fortified stockade forty miles upriver from Montreal at a strategic point commanding the Saint Lawrence known as the Cedars (Les Cèdres). By April 26, 1776, Colonel Timothy Bedel, with four hundred troops and two pieces of field artillery, occupied the site and began constructing a fort. Arnold described the post as "well entrenched." Montreal's western flank appeared secure.[81]

British officials, however, knew the American position to be tenuous. Short on supplies; reduced by death, disease, and desertion; and disheartened by the failure to capture Quebec, the Northern Army was a shadow of its former strength. Recent reinforcements were poorly trained and, in the opinion of Zephaniah Shepardson, a private soldier at the Cedars, were "not very well disciplined, being young in the military art." Even Arnold, now a brigadier general, admitted that his men were "Raw Troops, badly cloathed and fed, & worse paid, & without Dicipline." Their officers were not much better. Shepardson referred to his commanders as "ignorant of the art and policy of war." Colonel Bedel himself seemed to personify this assessment. Uninterested in garrisoning an isolated outpost, he ventured into the countryside to recruit Native allies, turning over responsibilities to his second in command, Major Isaac Butterfield.[82]

As the garrison idled, the British descended. Captain George Forster of the 8th Regiment of Foot led a combined force of 36 regulars, 11 Canadian volunteers, and 160 Native warriors—a multinational contingent including Mohawks—to surprise the post on May 18. Rather than assault Butterfield's entrenched artillery, Forster demanded that the major surrender, threatening that if he did not yield, "the savages could not be restrained." Fearing a massacre, Butterfield capitulated after a perfunctory exchange of fire. In the opinion of one of the American prisoners confined in Quebec, the paltry defense put up by the troops at the Cedars ensured "their eternal disgrace." To Maryland congressman John Carroll, Butterfield's surrender was "a disgraceful capitulation."[83]

Under the articles of capitulation, the Americans were required to turn over their foodstuffs, powder, cannon, and small arms, for which Captain Forster promised them their "lives and the clothes which you have on." With the ceremony of surrender complete, Forster's Native allies proceeded to strip the garrison of their knapsacks, watches, money, hats, and other personal effects. The ritual plundering of prisoners was a customary component of Native American warfare. Forster could do nothing to restrain his allies lest they decide to massacre the prisoners or turn on his own men. Undoubtedly against his will, the captain nonetheless violated the articles of capitulation much as Montcalm had twenty years earlier. To their horror if not their surprise, the Americans realized that European customs of war were not easily upheld in the borderlands of the British Empire.[84]

A relief column under the command of Major Henry Sherburne en route to the Cedars met a similar fate on May 20. Unlike Butterfield's garrison, Sherburne's 140 men put up a staunch resistance but, when finally surrounded by Native warriors, agreed to lay down their arms. As at the Cedars but to a greater degree, the Indians divested the Americans of most of their possessions. The wounded were not so fortunate. Sherburne recalled that as soon as the guns fell silent, several warriors began "tomahawking and scalping my wounded men, some of whom were butchered in my presence." The major was immediately seized by a warrior, who was on the point of scalping the American when a Canadian officer interceded. According to the Canadian, the Indian proposed sharing Sherburne's remains—the officer could have the American's body, the warrior only desired his scalp. Aware of the potential for retaliation, the Canadian forcibly interceded on Sherburne's behalf, grabbing the warrior by the neck and lecturing him: "You Dog, you want to kill a man who could be the cause of the death of four of our own prisoners—on the contrary, we will exchange these prisoners so that we might see our friends again." The officer placated his ally by allowing him to strip the major of his finery. Soon devoid of shirt and breeches, Sherburne must have been a pitiful sight. The Canadian officer covered the major with his cloak and afterward succeeded in conveying the majority of the American prisoners back to the Cedars alive, if humiliated.[85]

As far as Captain Forster was concerned, Sherburne and his men had no cause for complaint. They had surrendered to "savages" commanded by Canadians, not British regulars, and they had done so "without any stipulation" for their treatment. One of Forster's officers excused the abuse of Sherburne's command by pointing to the Natives' culture of war: "savages ever deem their prisoners as the private property of those who take them, and have generally, in former wars, sacrificed their prisoners to the manes of their deceased friends." In his opinion, this practice, known to historians as "mourning war," was not to be condoned, but it was also impossible to avoid. Forster could not impose his vision of war on his Indian allies, who "had been very unruly," but nevertheless tirelessly cajoled, bribed, begged, and implored them to spare prisoners' lives. Despite his best efforts, several Americans were hurried away into the Canadian interior to face certain torture followed by death or adoption by their Native captors. Forster's men were equally unable to prevent the warriors from entering the barracks at the Cedars and pillaging "the prisoners indiscriminately." For hungry men in tattered uniforms, this must have been particularly burdensome. According to Sherburne, "The barbarity with which we were treated by the savages, together with our sufferings for want of provisions and clothes, is beyond anything which can be imagined or described."[86]

Although pleased with his victories, Captain Forster was anxious to divest himself of his prisoners and return westward before American reinforcements could arrive. He now possessed more than five hundred captives, with only a handful of regulars to guard them. Supplying the prisoners with anything resembling adequate provisions or shelter was out of the question. The British marched them to the village of Quinze Chênes, where they were billeted in the open. One American remembered: "We lay on the ground for our bed.... Nothing but mud and mire for our downy feather'd beds; clouds to cover us, with wind, hail and rain. We had no fires ... nor meat to cook nor bread to eat." In the still frigid and damp Canadian air, the prisoners suffered grievously. Forster had to act or they would perish. He approached the captured American officers about signing a cartel of exchange. In conference, both sides agreed to an equitable swap of prisoners: officers for officers, soldiers for soldiers. Forster demanded, however, that the released Americans "shall not, on any pretext whatsoever, hereafter take up arms against the Government of Great Britain." The British prisoners would not be so constrained, upon their release able to rejoin their regiments in suppressing the rebellion.[87]

When word of the cartel reached Arnold, who with a force of about six hundred men was advancing on Forster's position to rescue the prisoners and secure Montreal's flank, he was livid. The general dismissed the cartel of exchange out of hand "on account of the inequality of the second article" forbidding American soldiers to serve once released. Firing back a vehement response, he demanded the "surrender of our prisoners" and warned that if "any of them were murdered, I would sacrifice every *Indian* who fell into my hands." Not satisfied with the threat of cold-blooded murder, Arnold promised Forster that he "would follow [the warriors] to their towns, and destroy them by fire and sword." To the American commander, the Native warriors were barbarians who violated the norms of war as he understood them; Forster was their accomplice. The captain was not easily rattled. Forster threatened to "immediately kill every prisoner, and give no quarter to any who should fall" into his hands in the future if the Americans attacked his position. Arnold had a difficult decision to make. His troops were "raging for action" and "ample revenge," but their captured countrymen were "on the point of being sacrificed if our vengeance was not delayed." The general, who was "torn by conflicting passions of revenge and humanity," agreed to accept the articles of exchange provided that the offending stipulation was removed. Forster was relieved and immediately acceded to Arnold's conditions "as the only means to avoid the destruction of the prisoners."[88]

The preamble to the new exchange agreement proposed by Forster revealed his uneasiness with his Native allies' culture of war. In his opinion, "the Customs and manners of the Savages in War" were "opposite and contrary to the humane disposition of the British Government, and to all civilized Nations." Induced by "the dictates of Humanity" to consider the prisoners' lamentable position, he "thought fit to enter into the following Articles of Agreement with General Arnold" for their exchange. Under the terms of the agreement, the Americans were released immediately and permitted to "return to their own Country" on the condition that an equal number of British prisoners of the same rank were sent to Canada "within the space of two months." Not wholly trusting his rebellious adversaries, Forster demanded that "Hostages be delivered for the performance of the Articles." The general allowed four captains to "be sent to Quebec as Hostages [to] remain there until the Prisoners are exchanged."[89]

Arnold had every intention of scrupulously maintaining the agreement, but he did not forget his lust for vengeance. Prior to the establishment of the cartel, his forces came upon five prisoners left behind during Forster's precipitous retreat. Arnold described the "five unhappy wretches" as "naked and almost starved." They informed him that one or two of their fellow prisoners, "being unwell, were inhumanely butchered." The general's indignation at the "base hypocritical conduct of the King's officers, their employing savages to screen them in their butcheries, [and] their suffering their prisoners to be killed in cool blood" knew no bounds. Nevertheless, Arnold was cognizant that his actions had weighty repercussions for the American war effort. As a congressionally appointed officer and a gentleman, he represented the justice and legitimacy of the American cause and thus was bound to conduct himself with honor. On May 27 he instructed Colonel John De Haas of Pennsylvania to "keep strick [sic] Discipline among the Troops you will be Governed by the Articles respecting an Exchange of Prisoners." As long as the British upheld their end of the bargain, so too would Arnold.[90]

De Haas had the unenviable responsibility of ferrying the exchanged Americans down the Saint Lawrence to Montreal while under the suspicious

glare of Forster's Native allies. High winds and the many wounded men complicated the process and delayed their embarkation. Watching the spoils of
their victories slip away, the warriors grew restless. Forster warned De Haas
that he must hurry because "it is Intirely out of my Power to put a stop to the
Ravages the Savages committ against the prisoners." As the men were ferried
back to the American position, a party of "savages amusing themselves by the
water side, did fire several muskets" at the unarmed soldiers, but their shots
fell short. A British witness maintained that the Indians did not have "the least
intention to injure them, nor were any of them injured." From the perspective
of a frightened American, the Natives' intentions appeared less lighthearted.
Private Shepardson remembered "a host of Indians with all there weapons of
cruelty and the most horrid noise of war" who appeared and "attempted to
rush upon us but were hindered by there superiors." In Shepardson's version
of the events, the warriors "threaten'd us with there tomahawks, spears, knives
and fire arms, showing the skalps they took off five of my mates, whom they
killed after they were made prisoners." Once the warriors commenced firing,
the Americans no longer considered themselves "bound to perform our part
of the Capitulation."[91]

In Arnold's opinion, the British were guilty of this flagrant violation of the
customs and norms of war. Arnold felt that Captain Forster only "pretended
it was not in his power" to command and restrain his Native allies. The American general could not be seen to tolerate such enormities without invaliding
his own claim to the authority and legitimacy of a gentleman soldier. His
officers and men wanted revenge, and unlike Montgomery, Arnold, who was
relatively inexperienced in European-style warfare, agreed with them. Although
he would not violate the terms of the cartel, the general fully intended "to take
ample vengeance" on the "savages, and still more savage British troops." Forster's
Native allies were obvious choices for retaliation, but Arnold would not be
sated by Indian blood alone. In his opinion, the British negated any innate
civility they might have possessed by failing to restrain their auxiliaries. Forgetting his instructions from General Washington at the outset of the campaign
to restrain "not only your own Troops but the Indians from all Acts of Cruelty
& Insult which will disgrace American Arms," Arnold ordered De Haas to
attack the village of Conosadaga "and give no Quarter to the Savages white or
Brown." He hoped to obtain justice "for the Cruel and inhuman murder of our
unhappy Countrymen." His instructions were chillingly simple: "Surround
the Town at the Break of Day you will attack them and kill, Burn and Destroy,

the whole, leave not one store . . . or give Quarter to any one." For Arnold, burning the village and killing enemy combatants and noncombatants alike was "no more than a Just retaliation for the many murders they have Committed on our unhappy Countrymen (in cold Blood)." He intended to send Carleton, Forster, and their Native allies a clear message: if the British wanted a barbarous war, they would get one.[92]

Colonel De Haas, however, was unready and unwilling to abandon the restraints of "civilized" warfare. Indian warriors might legitimately be denied quarter, as had been the case in the colonial wars of the past century, but their women, children, and, most importantly, white Britons and Canadians could not be slaughtered out of hand. In conference with his officers, De Haas decided to ignore Arnold's instructions. He justified his insubordination by claiming to have "confident assurance of the Enemies being reinforced," but his opponents were clear on his true motivation: mercy. British lieutenant Andrew Parke commended the colonel on his "honourable" and "manly" conduct in sparing the village. He was also pleasantly surprised by the disciplined and restrained behavior of the common soldiers throughout the campaign, which was much more "than could reasonably have been expected from men under such unprincipled leaders" like Arnold.[93]

Arnold had little time to dispute the matter with De Haas; he now faced the advance of over eight thousand recently arrived British and German troops under the command of veteran general John Burgoyne. In early June Carleton, with Burgoyne's fresh troops in the van, began his advance toward Montreal. Confronted by such a host, the revolutionaries had no prospect of holding on to the city or to any of their Canadian possessions; the best they could hope for was "an orderly retreat out of Canada." Withdrawing southward on Lake Champlain to Crown Point, New York, Arnold's army abandoned Canada to Carleton. On June 17 British forces entered Montreal in triumph. The American quest for a fourteenth colony was over.[94]

With Canada no longer under siege, Governor Carleton eased the rigor of his prisoners' confinement. No doubt moved by the sight of the "distorted, bloated, and blackened limbs" of the scurvy-ridden captives, Carleton gifted a fresh linen shirt to each of the nearly naked men. The Americans were elated by the clothing and by the promise of improved nourishment. In June the British commissaries, recently resupplied by sea, were finally able to provide the prisoners with fruits and vegetables to combat the effects of the disease. Satiating their "voracious appetite[s]" with "scurvy grass, in many varieties, eschalots, small onions, onion tops and garlic," the Americans began to regain their strength. Those with the familial connections or social status necessary to establish lines of credit purchased "cheese, sugar, tea, coffee," and even tobacco. In August, when the prisoners were healthy enough to travel, Carleton dispatched them to New York under parole "for the purpose of being exchanged." The governor hoped that by releasing the men, he would "convince all His Majesty's unhappy subjects, that the King's mercy and Benevolence were still open to them."[95]

When news of the "unfortunate affair at the Cedars" reached Congress, the members were in no mood for benevolence. Their campaign to conquer Canada was in ruins, and Carleton and Burgoyne appeared poised to strike south down Lake Champlain into New York. Compounding their woes, the delegates had to contend with Captain Forster's alleged violation of the first official prisoner-exchange cartel of the conflict. If the reports were true, Forster's actions, or rather inactions, might portend a large-scale Indian war, something delegates had hoped to avoid. In that case Congress would have to reject the Arnold-Forster cartel, which in turn might imperil future exchange negotiations. But overturning the agreement might have some salutary consequences as well. By highlighting Britain's decision to involve Native Americans in the colonial dispute, revolutionary leaders could play on their constituents' fear of Indian incursions to build support for the lagging war effort. Congress appointed a committee to investigate.[96]

After perusing numerous eyewitness depositions and the correspondence between Forster and Arnold, the committee concluded that the captain had violated not only the cartel of exchange but also the articles of capitulation of the Cedars. Forster was culpable for permitting his Native allies to plunder the prisoners, failing to prevent the murder of several of their number, and allowing others to die of exposure and hunger while in captivity. Based on this information, Congress resolved that the British officer had acted "contrary to good faith, the laws of nature, [and] the customs of civilized nations." The delegates condemned "the murder of the prisoners of war" and demanded that the perpetrators be brought to "condign punishment." Because Arnold served at the pleasure of Congress, any agreement he entered into with Forster was subject to congressional approval, which would never be granted unless the British turned over the perpetrators of the crimes and made proper indemnification for their plundering. By attaching stipulations that British leaders would never allow, Congress effectively nullified the cartel.[97]

The committee made its report just six days after Congress had voted on the issue of independence. The declaration to which the delegates pledged their lives, fortunes, and sacred honor was as much a timely political manifesto as it was a timeless statement of inalienable human rights. At its center was a fiery invective aimed at their king for his "repeated injuries and usurpations." The final five accusations laid at the monarch's feet concerned the laws of war. As Robert Parkinson has argued, these last five grievances were the document's crescendo, hammering home the necessity of an immediate independency. Brimming with indignation, Jefferson (and the committee that revised his prose) accused King George of plundering, ravaging, burning, and destroying his subjects. The conduct of his forces during the war was "scarcely paralleled in the most barbarous Ages, and totally unworthy the Head of a civilized Nation." The section's closing stanza excoriates the king for inciting "the merciless Indian Savages whose known rule of warfare, is an undistinguished destruction." A contemporary audience would have recognized the prisoners taken at the Cedars being at the very heart of America's founding document.[98]

By enshrining the laws of war in the Declaration of Independence, Congress made its position on the treatment of prisoners abundantly clear. The newly independent United States of America was a "civilized" nation that deserved and demanded the accordance of the customary protections of war between European powers. Through their prosecution of the conflict, the British demonstrated their barbarity and by extension the justice of the American cause. Reconciliation with the Crown, once longed for by many revolutionaries, was now impossible. They could no longer envision themselves as subjects of an empire capable of such savagery—irrevocable independency was the only option. No longer subjects of the Crown, as citizens of an independent and sovereign republic, Jefferson and his compatriots in Congress believed it their duty to teach the British "to respect the violated rights of nations." In the future, Congress would inflict "punishments of the same kinds and degree . . . on an equal number of the captives from them in our possession" as the only means of "stopping the progress of human butchery." The Americans had threatened retaliation in the past to no effect. Would they now carry through on their threats?[99]

* * *

Congress's quest to capture Canada was an unmitigated failure, but its commitment to Europe's culture of restrained warfare, and consequently the

Chapter 3

The Realities of War

While serving as one of the Massachusetts delegates to the Continental Congress in March 1776, John Adams reflected upon human nature. "Resentment is a Passion, implanted by Nature for the Preservation of the Individual," he mused. The British Army's conduct of the war in Canada, as well as in his native Massachusetts, had excited such a passion in his breast "as naturally and necessarily as Frost and Ice excite the feeling of cold." For Adams, resentment was a necessary emotion. An injured man "ought, for his own Security and Honour, and for the public good to punish those who injure him." So too should "communities." But resentment was not revenge. The staunch New England Calvinist knew well that "Revenge is unlawfull." He opined to his wife, Abigail, "In a Time of Warr, and especially a War like this, one may see the Necessity and Utility, of the divine Prohibitions of Revenge." Revolutionary Americans might justifiably punish their British antagonists for violations of the laws of war, but they could not abandon those very rules in favor of unrestrained vengeance lest they themselves become "Devils." Abigail agreed. News of the "the recital of the inhumane and Brutal Treatment of those poor creatures who have fallen into their Hands, Freazes me with Horrour," she confessed. Nevertheless, she too hoped that Americans would never be provoked "to retaliate their cruelties."[1]

Over the coming year, as British forces fought to capture and subdue New York City and its environs, the Adamses had cause to rethink their position on revenge. The New York Campaign witnessed a significant intensification in wartime violence as the revolutionary struggle devolved into a civil war that rent not just the British Empire but also communities, friends, and even families. Repeated British atrocities, amplified and exaggerated by the prolific revolutionary press; large-scale armed loyalist opposition; and the limitations of republican government unleashed an internecine conflict in which cruelty and misery characterized the plight of prisoners on both sides. By the New York Campaign's culmination, thousands of Americans wasted in noisome British prisons without hope of release or exchange, while thousands of others had taken up arms against the new nation. The Continental Congress was powerless to prevent either circumstance. Confronted by the threat of loyalist uprisings at every turn and by vivid accounts of the suffering of American prisoners, revolutionaries from across the social spectrum began to view their British opponents as barbarians rather than cousins and American loyalists as rebels and traitors rather than neighbors and brothers. Both groups no longer merited the protections of "civilized" warfare. Crown decisions to employ foreign troops, confine captured Americans in floating prisons, and arm loyalists to oppose the revolutionary movement galvanized ordinary Americans, who took to arms in the quest for retribution. This combustible combination, which occurred wherever British forces ranged, launched the conflict on a path of escalating violence.

Nevertheless, Americans' deeply ingrained vision of "civilized" warfare was not so easily degraded or jettisoned. Restraint in wartime violence had significant cultural resonance in early America, and much of the revolutionary leadership continued to insist upon rigid adherence to the customs and practices of warfare among European powers. Without a centralized government or military bureaucracy empowered to organize, administer, and direct the war effort, however, standards for the treatment of captured enemies could not easily be enforced. Thus, the day-to-day operations of the conflict increasingly fell upon individual state (no longer colonial) governments, each of which conducted the war with varying degrees of severity; those in closest proximity to British forces were most likely to react with the greatest violence. While the states waged their own terror campaigns, Washington continued to insist upon the restrained behavior of the Continental Army, but the decentralized nature of the American war effort—in conjunction with the widespread dissemination of accounts of British misconduct in the press and the pervasive threat of loyalist insurrection, both real and imagined—ensured that much of the conflict's conduct was beyond his control. Consequently, the Continental commissary general of prisoners, Elias Boudinot, could boast in the summer of 1777 without the least insincerity that "humanity to Prisoners of War has ever been the peculiar Characteristic of the american [sic] Army" while enemy prisoners in New York, New Jersey, Pennsylvania, and Connecticut suffered in squalor aboard American prison ships and overcrowded jails and others perished at the gallows for treason against a country they never claimed.[2]

American Prisoners in New York

Perched on the highest point on Manhattan Island overlooking the Hudson River, in November 1776 Fort Washington was an impressive feat of military engineering. Named in honor of the American commander, the pentagonal fortification was the Continental Army's last hope to prevent the island from falling into British hands. Despite assiduous preparation that past summer, American forces had been unable to stop a Crown armada from landing nearly twenty-five thousand British and Hessian troops on Long Island in August. The long-feared "Armies of foreign Mercenaries" that Jefferson had decried in the Declaration of Independence had arrived. Executing a virtually textbook example of envelopment, Major General Howe defeated the Continentals on August 27 at the Battle of Brooklyn, capturing over a thousand prisoners. Washington, who had bloodlessly driven the British from Boston in March, now fled in turn. Fortunate to escape with any of his troops, the Virginian retreated the length of Manhattan, losing men, materiel, and most of his mettle at Kip's Bay, Harlem Heights, and White Plains. The British were unimpressed with their adversary's haphazard and unsoldierly defense of New York. One Hessian described the American officers as "nothing but mechanics, tailors, shoemakers, wig-makers, [and] barbers," hardly the stalwarts who had bloodied the regulars at Concord and Bunker Hill. Victory was almost too easy. Perhaps the formidable entrenchments of Fort Washington would at last offer worthy opposition.[3]

To the horror of the American commander in chief, observing from the other side of the Hudson, they did not. Shortly before dawn on November 16, British land batteries and naval artillery erupted in "a violent Cannonade," engulfing Fort Washington in a haze of acrid smoke punctuated by blinding illumination. Out of the fog emerged the leveled bayonets of the Hessian grenadiers, English light infantry, and Scottish Highlanders. In the face of such a martial onslaught, the American outer works were quickly abandoned, rendering the fort's position desperate. Should the enemy breach the walls, there would be little hope for quarter for the defenders within. According to a British officer present at the attack, General Howe insisted that the Americans "surrender immediately, without any other terms than a promise of their lives, and their baggage." The American commander, Colonel Robert Magaw of Pennsylvania, "pled for the Honors of War," but Howe would have none of it. The fort would fall; only the garrison's fate was in question.[4]

The defenders lost their appetite for resistance at the sight of the oncoming Hessians. These rented soldiers had earned a reputation for brutality since their arrival that August. In the aftermath of the Battle of Brooklyn, rumors abounded throughout the Continental Army that they had refused to spare surrendering Americans. One Pennsylvania officer recalled that he was determined "to run any risk rather than fall into their hands." The rumors carried more than a shred of truth. A Hessian officer admitted that the American riflemen killed in that battle "were mostly pitted to the trees with bayonets." He attributed the actions of his countrymen not to any innate Germanic cruelty but to the fact that "the English did not give much quarter, and constantly urged our people to do the like." A Scottish officer corroborated his Hessian ally's explanation: "We took care to tell the *Hessians* that the Rebels had resolved to give no quarters to them in particular, which made them fight desperately, and put all to death that fell into their hands." Because the Americans were rebels and "vile enemies to their King and country," the Scot rejoiced that "the *Hessians* and our brave *Highlanders* gave no quarters; and it was a fine sight to see with what alacrity they dispatched the Rebels with their bayonets." Magaw's troops knew that the officers commanding the assault on Fort Washington were unlikely to intercede on behalf of men they considered to be "damned rebels." They waited anxiously while the Continental colonel and his subordinate officers considered the British proposition.[5]

Rather than consign his men to death, Magaw capitulated. By early afternoon, the fort's guns fell silent, and 2,837 American soldiers laid down their arms in surrender. The garrison marched out of the fort, flanked on either side by the Hessian troops who had led the assault; exhausted and enraged at the carnage, they were in no mood for niceties. A Hessian chaplain who witnessed the surrender admitted that "despite the strictest orders, the prisoners received a number of blows." Most of these were delivered with the butt end of a musket as the prisoners filed out of the works, but John Adlum, a Pennsylvania militiaman and survivor of the battle, remembered hearing "that some of our soldiers, was [sic] severely cut with the swords of the Hessians." All suffered blistering insults and unabated plundering at the hands of their captors, the guarantees for their personal property in the articles of capitulation notwithstanding. British officers present at the scene did nothing to restrain their allies. At least one, General Howe's adjutant Stephen Kemble, was shocked by the breach of the articles. "To our shame, tho' they Capitulated for the Safety of their Baggage, they were stripped of their Wearing Apparel as they [were] Marched out by Hessians."[6]

Other British officers were less than apologetic. Captain Frederick Mackenzie thought the Americans "had no right to expect the mild treatment they met with." After all, the men were "Rebels taken in arms" and thus "forfeit their lives by the laws of all Countries." Although he was pleased to boast that "Humanity is the characteristic of the British troops," Mackenzie expressed the prevailing opinion among his fellow officers that "we act with too much lenity and humanity towards the Rebels." Fear of British violence should bring the upstart Americans to heel.[7]

The Fort Washington prisoners had plenty to fear as they marched toward captivity. The specter of the hangman still loomed large in their imaginations. According to one Connecticut soldier, William Slade, their guards referred to the Americans as "Yankee Rebbels a going to the gallows." In the aftermath of Brooklyn, the captives had been similarly accosted by British "officers, soldiers and camp-ladies" in "the most scurrilous and abusive language," demanding to know why they had not been "put to the bayonet or hanged." No one knew what was in store for the prisoners once they reached New York City.[8]

To compound their woes, the prisoners trudged southward with empty stomachs and bare backs. The British failed to supply them with any provisions on their march, and most had been plundered of what little warm clothing they owned. William Slade spent the day after the battle "in sorrow and hunger, having no mercy showed." In their affidavit to Congress, prisoners Samuel Young and William Houston reported that "they had no victuals given them of any kind" for three days after the surrender. Far from eliciting the sympathy of their captors, these starving, exhausted, and dejected men "excited the laughter of our Soldiers," according to Captain Mackenzie. Many Britons, protected from the cold by their watch coats, regimentals, and woolen breeches, appeared to delight in the suffering of their prisoners, who "were in general but very indifferently clothed; few of them appeared to have a Second shirt." The Americans were understandably less jocose. Slade aptly summarized their predicament: "These four days we spent in hunger and sorrow being decried by every one and calld [sic] Rebs." Unless they were resupplied and properly quartered, they might have more to "dread than the common sufferings of prisoners of war." Prayers for a speedy exchange were on everyone's lips.[9]

For his part, General Howe was equally anxious to divest himself of the captured troops. When Fort Washington fell, the British lacked the infrastructure necessary to maintain the prisoners they already possessed. The addition of almost three thousand more men proved vexing. With winter approaching, Howe was responsible for quartering and provisioning a massive array of British and Hessian soldiers on an island devastated by warfare. Most of the inhabitable buildings in lower Manhattan had been destroyed by fire shortly after the British arrived, and Howe was now greeted by an influx of loyalist refugees fleeing rebel lines. Most having lost their homes, businesses, and property for their support of the king, they justifiably demanded shelter and sustenance. Under the circumstances, Howe had no intention of holding a ravenous and ill-clad army of prisoners in captivity for long. He appointed Massachusetts loyalist Joshua Loring as his commissary of prisoners to attend to the men's wants and negotiate their release. In early December 1776 Howe informed Lord George Germain that, although he was "under the necessity of detaining [the prisoners] . . . at a very great expence and inconvenience," he was confident that he would soon be rid "of the remaining incumbrance." Until then, Loring would see to their needs.[10]

Despite almost a century of intermittent warfare with the great Catholic powers of Europe, the British Army was surprisingly unprepared for such an influx of prisoners. In prior conflicts prisoners of war had been administered by a civilian board under the auspices of the Lords Commissioners of the Admiralty known as the Commission for Sick and Hurt Seamen and the Exchange of Prisoners. Since 1740, this commission had become a permanent component of the British war machine, tasked with not only the care of enemy prisoners, both terrestrial and maritime, but also their swift and efficient repatriation. Prisoners awaiting exchange were housed in castles and local jails and aboard decommissioned warships, known as hulks. The commission provided the captives with clothing and provisions at the expense of their home governments and paid for the supply of British prisoners in enemy custody. The key to the success of the British method was the rigid adherence to cartels of exchange established with their French and Spanish counterparts. While imperfect, this system was largely successful at returning prisoners before the stark conditions of eighteenth-century captivity began to take a toll on their health. But Howe's prisoners were not European soldiers; they were rebels in arms. As such, the general was under strict orders not to acknowledge the United States or its representatives through a formal exchange of prisoners.[11]

Unable to establish a formal cartel with the United States, Howe appealed to Washington as a gentleman and brother officer to arrange a system of informal exchanges. The two men had entered negotiations in July when Washington suggested that an "exchange of prisoners will be attended with mutual convenience and pleasure to both parties." Acting with congressional approval, the Virginian proposed that officers be exchanged for those of equal rank and that soldiers, sailors, and civilians be exchanged equally for their respective counterparts. Constantly pestered by captured British officers requesting preferential exchange, Howe was elated to learn that the Americans were willing to conduct informal exchanges. Not only would such an exchange rid him of the nuisance of constant petitions, but he would also recoup valuable officers and veteran troops captured in Canada for his subsequent campaigns in return for ill-trained and hungry novices. "Wishing sincerely to give Relief to the Distresses of all Prisoners," he informed Washington in August that he would "readily consent to the Mode of Exchange You are pleased to propose."[12]

Not all of Howe's subordinates agreed with their general. Captain Mackenzie thought it "rather extraordinary that under the present circumstances we should treat with them as if on an equality." The Americans were no better than criminals; even an informal exchange would implicitly acknowledge that they were beyond the jurisdiction of British civil law. In Mackenzie's opinion, it was wiser to keep "all the Rebel prisoners taken in arms, without any immediate hope of release, and in a state of uncertainty with respect to their fate" in order to "strike great terror into their army." Morale in Howe's command was high after the successes around New York, and many officers felt that total victory was close at hand. One more vigorous assault would "crush the Rebel Colonies" and ensure that all the king's men would "return covered with *American* laurels."[13]

Desirous and hopeful for reconciliation, however, Howe viewed the exchange as an opportunity to demonstrate the magnanimity and lenience of the Crown. The bayonets of his men had already given the enemy ample evidence of Britain's determination to suppress the rebellion; now was the time for conciliation. Unlike the American general, who threatened retaliation for alleged British atrocities, Howe firmly believed that "Examples of Moderation will ever be the sharpest reproach to those who violate the Laws of Honor &

Humanity." Despite the thinly veiled reproach, Howe knew Washington to be a man of honor, a fellow gentleman with whom he could negotiate. Provided the two men maintained a regular and honest correspondence, peace must surely follow. Clearly skeptical of the likelihood of a negotiated end to the war, Elbridge Gerry told John Adams that "General Howe is desirous of keeping open a Communication with our General and thinks he has made the *first Advances to an Accomodation* [*sic*]." From Howe's perspective, that accommodation hinged on mutual trust between the two commanding generals.[14]

In the weeks following his victory at Brooklyn, Howe sought to establish that trust by orchestrating several high-level prisoner exchanges as a demonstration of his good faith. He was pleased to trade the popular American general John Sullivan for the irascible Brigadier Prescott, whom the Americans had accused of mistreating Ethan Allen at Montreal. Although he could not acquiesce to Washington's request for the release of Brigadier General William Alexander in exchange for brevet Brigadier Donald MacDonald because of the disparity between their commissioned ranks, Howe generously accepted the captured British governor of the Bahamas, Montfort Browne, instead. Because Governor Browne had not been acting in a military capacity when an American naval force under the command of Commodore Esek Hopkins made him a prisoner, and he did not possess a commission in the regular army, Howe's proposal was exceedingly generous; under European conventions, Browne should have been exchanged only for a civilian prisoner of equal political stature. The British general even ordered the immediate exchange of the prominent whig and future member of the Continental Congress James Lovell for Governor Philip Skene, an exchange that Howe had earlier refused on the grounds that Lovell had carried on "a prohibited Correspondence" during his captivity. With New York in his hands and empowered by King George to seek a peaceful resolution to the conflict, Howe could now negotiate from a position of strength. Washington was in no position to haggle; he jumped at the opportunity to regain two of his most trusted lieutenants as well as a respected, influential, and long-suffering civilian.[15]

Word that the British were finally willing to conduct an exchange of prisoners reverberated throughout the states. Newspapers sang the praises of an alteration in the treatment of American prisoners. While some like Colonel Allen had been treated with "the utmost barbarity" in the past, they were now afforded the privileges of their rank and station. Crown policy had "softened." For those in American custody, the change in British attitude seemed to presage their release. Major Christopher French, who had so vexed Washington and Hancock through his constant petitions and imperious style, noted that all of the officers in Hartford, whose "Scituation [sic] (in close Goal) could not be . . . more irksome," took "great pleasure" in the promise of an imminent exchange. Howe's lenient approach to the formerly thorny issue of treating captured Americans as prisoners of war also met with the approval of the authorities in London. Lord Barrington, Britain's secretary at war, was pleased to learn "that an opportunity may offer for your getting those Officers and Men exchanged who were made Prisoners at Chamble [sic] & St John's." The ministry's experiment with holding Americans in perpetuity had proven cumbersome, expensive, and politically unsound; now all they hoped for was a fair swap.[16]

A general exchange, however, remained elusive. Congress had vested each of its departmental commanders with the authority to conduct exchanges in July 1776, but unlike Howe, who had sole custody of his prisoners, Washington had little actual authority over the captured Britons. The prisoners from Canada were dispersed in isolated communities between Connecticut and Virginia, and even Massachusetts boasted a sizable number of Scottish prisoners who had mistakenly sailed into Boston Harbor in June, unaware that Howe had already evacuated the town. All of these prisoners were technically under the jurisdiction and care of the newly created Board of War, headed by John Adams, but in reality they were in the hands of local committees of safety that were loath to surrender them without any guarantee of reimbursement or the promise of preferential exchange for captured community members. Despite numerous requests, the Board of War could not obtain accurate lists of the number and character of British prisoners in state custody. Confusion reigned.[17]

Dispersing the prisoners had spared Washington the nuisance of their accommodation and had prevented the British from attempting any rescue operations, but now the general wanted them back. Desperately concerned with personal propriety and soldierly decorum, he worried to Hancock about "the difficulty that will attend the proposed exchange on account of the dispersed and scattered state of the prisoners in our Hands." If he failed to uphold his end of the bargain, his personal honor and reputation, as well as that of the Continental Army, would be impugned. All Washington could do was urge Congress "more than once" to establish a European-style commissary "to superintend & conduct in such instances" the exchange of the prisoners. His pleas went unanswered. In September the Continental commander explained his situation to Howe: "The exchange of privates, I shall take the earliest oppertunity [sic] in my power to carry into execution but they being greatly dispersed through the New England governments, in order to their better accomodation [sic], will prevent it for some time."[18]

Occupying a burned-out, pestilence-infested ruin of a city bulging at the seams with soldiers, sailors, refugees, and the flotsam and jetsam of prostitutes, vagabonds, and ne'er-do-wells who thrived in the company of early modern armies, Howe did not have the luxury of time. Where would he house his American captives, how would they be fed, and who would tend their wounds? Even before the capture of Fort Washington, he chastised the Virginian for his apparent torpor: "I beg Leave to take this Opportunity of remonstrating against the Delay on your Part in the Exchange of Prisoners." Howe was particularly anxious because he had received reports that "many Officers in your Power are still exposed to the Confinement of common Goals." Given Washington's earlier acquiescence to their agreement for the exchange of prisoners, such behavior was contrary to "the Custom of War" in Howe's mind. Here the British general knew he had leverage over Washington. By suggesting that the American had violated European customs of war, he highlighted the amateurism that his counterpart had tried so hard to efface. Howe hoped that his reproof would prod the Americans to action before overcrowding and disease claimed the lives of the prisoners.[19]

The British commander had struck a nerve. Washington was insulted, but any feeling of indignation was overcome by shame. Howe was in the right. As the commanding general, Washington was responsible for the actions of his subordinates, and his inability to produce the prisoners in a timely fashion advertised his impotency to a man he highly esteemed. In an apologetic letter on November 9, Washington regretted "that it has not been in my power to effect the proposed Exchange of Prisoners before this time," assuring Howe that "it has not arisen Sir from any design on my part. . . . [T]heir disperresed [sic] situation for their better accommodation [sic] has been the reason of the delay." He would later confess to Hancock that he had felt "much embarrassed on the Subject of Exchanges." Washington was not entirely forthcoming in his mea culpa, however. The truth of the matter was that the prisoners had become a valuable commodity to the places that housed them. With many of their agricultural laborers and tradesmen doing duty with the army or the militia, these communities desperately needed their manpower to reap the harvest and to maintain their struggling economies. Local committees of safety were also under tremendous pressure to obtain the release of their constituents captured during Howe's rush through New York. If they simply handed the prisoners over to Washington, he would likely exchange them for men who had been longest in captivity rather than for their friends and relations.[20]

To complicate matters, Congress had also created a loophole in its policy by allowing individual states to conduct independent trades with the British. Although they were theoretically only allowed to exchange prisoners captured by their state forces or militia, the temptation to swap some congressional prisoners was real. In the absence of a Continental commissary of prisoners to keep track of how many there were and under whose jurisdiction they belonged, state governments in Rhode Island, Connecticut, and Massachusetts regularly and eagerly bargained with the British without congressional oversight.[21]

Saddled with a Congress that was overburdened, ineffectual, untutored in the customs of war, and deeply suspicious of consolidated power, as well as state governments that appeared to be conducting their own individual wars with the Crown, Washington was forced to face the reality that this conflict was not living up to his expectations of restrained, efficient, and "civilized" warfare. Nonetheless, he dashed off numerous letters to the governors, committee members, and councilmen of the surrounding states imploring them "to have all the Continental prisoners of War, (belonging to the Land Service) in the different Towns in your State, collected and brought together to some convenient place, from whence they may be removed hither when a Cartel is fully settled." Cajoling Connecticut's governor, the general pleaded that the return of the "prisoners as early as possible will much oblige me." Although Trumbull was pleased to comply with Washington's wishes, he wondered whether "such of the Privates as are Mechanicks, & some Others who have a strong Inclination to Abide & remain in the Country, must be forced & Obliged to return & be exchanged." He also wanted some assurance "that the Charge & expence Attending the keeping [of] the prisoners" would be reimbursed. Again, Washington was powerless to do anything other than request the opinion of Congress on the matter. He knew that allowing some of the prisoners—the skilled tradesmen useful to the war effort and those disinclined to return to the drudgery of army life—to remain unexchanged was a breach of the articles of capitulation "on the part of General Montgomery for those that were taken in Canada," but the final decision lay with Congress. While the delegates procrastinated, all Washington could do was wait, exactly what the American prisoners in New York feared most.[22]

When the Fort Washington prisoners arrived in lower Manhattan on November 18, they were immediately confined in the abandoned churches, meetinghouses, and sugar refineries that dotted the tip of the island. There they discovered the sunken faces and emaciated bodies of comrades captured at Brooklyn and Kip's Bay as well as in Canada; imagine their horror at seeing the physical embodiment of the fate that awaited them. British captain Mackenzie found the prisoners' "desponding appearance enough to shock one." Just days before the new prisoners arrived, captured colonels Samuel Miles and Samuel Atlee alerted Washington of the men's "truly deplorable" situation. Although the British had accepted the American officers' parole and allowed them to draw lines of credit for their subsistence and suitable housing, the common soldiers were closely confined and inadequately provisioned. In the colonels' dire appraisal of the men's circumstances, only "Death must relieeve them from their present misserable Situation." The disparity between the officers' confinement and that of their men could not have been starker. American general Charles Lee, a former British officer who knew Howe personally, penned a concerned missive to his old comrade on November 26 informing him that "the Americans whom chance has thrown into your hands, are as We are assured, confined closely in Prison" and allowed only "short allowance," while "those of yours who fall into our hands have the full liberty of the Towns or villages allotted to em [sic] and credit for a comfortable and ample subsistence." In disbelief Lee remarked: "If this mode can be approved of by Mr. Howe, He is strangely altered. It is neither consonant to humanity nor the eternal rules of Justice." The American was hopeful that "the fact is exaggerated."[23]

The accounts were no exaggeration; the enlisted soldiers were starving. Major General Nathanael Greene received intelligence of their condition on November 11 and immediately informed Washington, "our prisoners in the City are Perishing for want of sustinance—having only half allowance of bread and Water—They are reduced to the necessity to beg and instead of receiveing any Charity are called damn Rebbels and told their fare is good enough." That fare officially consisted of a two-thirds portion of the rations provided to British soldiers on active duty, but in reality Greene's estimate was not far off. William Slade's prison diary is a litany of hunger, "sorrow, and sadness." When lucky, Slade received three-fourths of a pound of pork and two pounds of bread, intended to last two days—an amount well below the two-thirds allotment. At other times he and his comrades had only "1/2 lb of pork a man, 3/4 of bisd [hardtack biscuits], a little peas and rice, and butter" to carry them through three days of confinement. On the second day Slade reported having "verry [*sic*] little to eat"; day three was "spent in hunger." Howe would later claim that "the Allowance of Provisions to prisoners, from the Beginning of my Command, has been equal in Quantity and Quality to what is given to our own Troops not on Service," but even he must have known that graft, thievery, and spoilage ensured that the men rarely, if ever, saw their entitled allotment.[24]

Contrary to what the American press (and latter-day historians) alleged, the prisoners' deplorable situation was not the result of premeditated cruelty; Howe was operating within customary parameters for the treatment of enemy prisoners in Britain. Regrettably for the captured Americans, the British Army policy of allowing prisoners only two-thirds rations was predicated on faulty logic. Policymakers presumed that a soldier could live on a diet of seven pounds of beef and seven pounds of bread a week, augmented by a smaller quantity of butter or cheese, oatmeal, and peas. Soldiers who were expected to march upward of fifteen miles a day carrying sixty pounds of arms, accoutrements, powder, and ball would not last for long on such a paltry portion. Even in peacetime, the British soldier's diet was notoriously inadequate. The dearth of leafy greens and fresh citrus regularly resulted in cases of malnutrition and scurvy. To counteract this predicament, the army permitted—and indeed expected—soldiers to augment their provisions through either independent labor in peacetime or foraging in times of war. Pilfering civilian property was officially discouraged, perpetrators occasionally suffering capital punishment for their actions, but British officers often turned a blind eye to a little creative procurement on the part of their men. In garrison, officers actively encouraged their soldiers to tend their own gardens in order to provide the nutrients their bodies required. Confined to their prisons, the American soldiers had no such opportunity for supplementation. Under these conditions, historian Edwin Burrows estimates that most of the prisoners would have lost a pound of body weight per week of captivity.[25]

By the time the Fort Washington prisoners arrived in the city, the situation in New York's jails had grown desperate. Captain Mackenzie described the prisoners as "very Sickly, owing to their want of Clothing and necessaries, salt provisions, confinement, foul air, & little exercise." Evincing characteristic metropolitan disdain for all things provincial, the British officer described these men as "such low spirited creatures, particularly the [native-born] Americans, that if once they are taken sick they seldom recover." The only anodyne for "their dirty, unhealthy, and desponding appearance" was a fresh supply of clothing and provisions. Perhaps aware that his Hessian auxiliaries were at least partly responsible for the lamentable condition of the prisoners' wardrobes, Howe presented each man with a fresh linen shirt. Much like Carleton's earlier gift to the Americans captured in Canada, the shirts were much appreciated, but a single layer of thin cloth would do little to keep out the coming winter cold. Had Howe been able to swiftly exchange the prisoners, as would have been the case in Europe, their nutritional and sartorial deficiencies, though uncomfortable, would have been innocuous. Instead, the men languished in the vain hope that Washington would expedite their release.[26]

Surprisingly, neither Washington nor the prisoners blamed Howe for their predicament; Congress was clearly not doing its part. The British supply lines stretched over three thousand miles across the Atlantic. Washington, who knew too well the challenges of feeding an army in a devastated environment while conducting an active campaign, acknowledged that the prisoners' allowance was likely "as good as the situation of General How's [sic] Stores will admit." The British commander was doing the best he could under the circumstances; Congress's inaction, on the other hand, was bordering on negligence. Upon seeing "the horrid dismal situation of our poor privates in the Hospitals in Newyork [sic]," Joseph Webb of Connecticut expressed the common sentiment that "the Country does too much neglect something to be done for 'em." After all, the British, through the auspices of David Franks, had provided their captured troops with "provisions and other necessaries" at the expense of the Crown for nearly a year. As was European custom, Howe expected the American authorities to either supply the prisoners or provide sufficient reimbursement. On this point the two generals agreed. But without Congress's intervention, how could Washington provision these prisoners when he could barely afford to provide for his own army? Colonels Atlee and Miles had the solution. Congress should appoint an agent, such as Franks, to open a line of credit with British merchants in New York to furnish the prisoners with the necessary supplies. The suggestion was consistent with Washington's understanding of European practice, and he dutifully forwarded it to Philadelphia, insisting that "Humanity and the good of the service require it." The delegates predictably ignored it.[27]

Unlike Congress, Howe could not afford to remain aloof from his prisoners' suffering. On December 8 a group of American officers, who were enjoying the freedom of their paroles, alerted the general that "the State of the Sick & wounded Prisoners is of too melancholy a kind for Recital; and the consequences of a General Contagion to be dreaded." Both smallpox and typhus were present among the confined men. Fearing the spread of the diseases among his own troops on a densely populated island, Howe dispatched Colonel Miles to Congress in order to "expedite the Exchange of prisoners." Howe's adjutant assured Miles that "the General has every Disposition to promote" the exchange. Perhaps an eyewitness to the consequences of congressional indifference would persuade the delegates to act.[28]

In their defense, the members of the Board of War were doing everything in their limited power to collect the British prisoners from the various states for exchange, but their march north was hampered by delay after delay. Contrary to congressional instructions, several states had already enlisted these men and were unwilling to return them to face execution for desertion. Two such prisoners, Robert Colefox and Richards Williams, claimed to prefer "perpetual imprisonment, rather than to be exchanged & returned to the British Army or Navy." Captain Rowland Chambers of the Somerset Militia hoped that Governor William Livingston of New Jersey might be able to prevent their exchange on the grounds that they would "undoubtedly" join the state's forces, despite the two being "considered as Continental Prisoners & Wholey at the disposal of the Congress." Livingston interceded, and the men were not sent forward for exchange. Others were delayed by weather, impassable roads, or misunderstandings.[29]

With no immediate prospect of an exchange on the horizon, Howe opted to confine 750 prisoners on board the troop-transport ships *Whitby* and *Grosvenor* in an effort to relieve the city's overcrowded prisons. The vessels were emptied, cleaned, and prepared for the reception of the prisoners. William Slade was among the Fort Washington captives who shivered in the cold while waiting to enter the *Grosvenor* in early December. He reported "much confusion" as the over five hundred prisoners clamored to claim a berth below decks. Once aboard, Slade and his comrades spent a "verry long" night in hunger and sorrow. This was just the beginning of their suffering. While British officers and soldiers celebrated Christmas 1776 with fine repasts and orotund toasts, the Americans aboard the *Whitby* endured a night "spent in dying grones [*sic*] and cries." By the time Slade was finally released, as many as two-thirds of his companions may have perished from disease, exposure, and starvation.[30]

Although Howe could never have imagined the repercussions of his actions, his decision to transform the transports into floating prisons set the precedent for a system of confinement that Edwin Burrows estimates accounted for roughly half of all American fatalities during the eight-year conflict. A single hulk, the decommissioned ship of the line *Jersey*, may have claimed the lives of as many as 11,000 men, primarily merchant sailors and privateers. Packed into "the putrefied stagnated air of the hold of a vessel crowded with vermin," American seamen had to survive on two-thirds the subsistence allotted to British sailors. By September 1780, British commissary for naval prisoners David Sproat was forced to admit that "contagion, and death" were likely in store for the American seamen on board "the crowded Prison ships" were they not released soon. According to Colonel Thomas Hartley of Pennsylvania, few survived to tell the "doleful Story of their Captivity and Distress."[31]

Prison ships were not novel examples of Crown sadism intended to punish refractory rebels; the British had employed them to house French and Spanish prisoners in the past to great effect. Although less salubrious than their land-based equivalents, the hulks anchored in the Thames and in the coastal towns of Portsmouth, Yarmouth, Plymouth, and Chatham during the Seven Years' War were well supplied, frequently cleaned, and rarely overcrowded. Sheldon Cohen has suggested that the death rate of prisoners on board those vessels only slightly exceeded that of conventional prisons. The conditions in the New York prison ships deteriorated so rapidly because of the sheer numbers of prisoners the British possessed (over 4,500), the cold climate, local farmers' hesitation to trade with the invading army, and Congress's inability (or unwillingness) to adequately supply the men or remunerate the Crown for their upkeep. When it came to handing out Howe's few available resources, the cries and lamentations of the American captives were drowned out by those of the 14,000 soldiers and 11,000 civilians clamoring for the general's attention; the prisoners were Washington's problem. Unfortunately for the British, that was not how most Americans viewed the situation.[32]

It did not take long for news of the hulks and the suffering men they contained to spread beyond New York. Timothy Parker of Connecticut managed to secret a letter out of the *Whitby* in early December to inform Governor Trumbull that "there are more than two Hundred and fifty prisoners of us on board this Ship (some of which are Sick & without the least assistance from

Figure 4. The Prison Ship "Jersey," engraving by P. Meeder, 1906. Courtesy
Library of Congress (LC-USZ62-124949).

Physician Drugg or Medicine) all fed on two thirds allowance of salt provisions and all Crowded promiscuously together without Distinction or Respect to person office or Colour in the Small room of a Ship Between Decks." In his opinion, these "Miserable Circumstances" would lead to "a kind of lingering Inevitable death, Unless we obtain a timely and Sensible Release." Not only had the British imperiled the officers' health, but they also had undermined their racial and class identities by suffering gentlemen to share their confinement with those they deemed beneath them. The *Pennsylvania Evening Post* quickly picked up the story and stunned its readers with an account of "Captains and Lieutenants in the Continental service . . . huddled together between decks in a prison-ship, with Indians, Mallattoes, Negroes, &c." After enumerating a litany of abuses and insults, the article's author concluded that British "inhumanity has extended beyond this life, for the dead have been thrown out upon the highway and open fields, with this impious and horrid expression, 'D——n the rebel, he's not worth a grave.'" The moral of the story was apparent to all: the British considered Americans, even officers possessing commissions from Congress, to be rebels unworthy of the protections of "civilized" warfare. A protracted and painful death from starvation, dehydration, or disease awaited all those who opposed their lawful monarch. This was just the type of story the revolutionary press needed to inflame the fury of a war-weary population. By his decision to utilize prison ships, occasioned by the honest intention to relieve the overcrowded conditions of New York's improvised prisons until Congress and Washington could fulfill their side of the exchange, Howe unwittingly assumed the culpability for a situation not of his making.[33]

Colonel Miles, who knew too well the prisoners' misfortune, continued to maintain that Congress was the primary author of their suffering. He expressed his frustration to Elias Boudinot in July 1777: "Notwithstanding the reasonableness of the purposal I brought from Genl Howe for an exchange of Officers, & Genl Washingtons sentiments concerning there with, the Congress have to my great surprise refused to comply with it." The colonel did not seem to appreciate that it was the very republican principles for which he and his comrades had gone to war that now circumscribed the delegates' actions. If individual states privileged their own best interests over the common good, how could Congress order them to do otherwise without risking the charge of tyranny? What he saw as a "mark of their injustice & want of common Humanity" was just a republic at work. A veteran of the Seven Years' War, Miles believed that debates and committees had no place in warfare. He and his officers had been "treated as genteely by the Hessian & highland officers as we could expect or have wished," and General Howe had been "kind enough" to allow the men as much of their personal "Bagage as is necessary for our health & comfort." The same could not be said for Congress. Despondent, Miles wondered to a friend in Pennsylvania, "God knows what your people in power [Congress] think of us if they think of us at all." In a scathing critique of congressional inaction, the colonel raged, "I do believe that no prisoners ever were treated with more inhuman Cruelty than our's have been by their Employers."[34]

Miles's indictment of the republican government's war management was muffled by the deluge of propagandistic accounts castigating the British as barbarians and butchers that permeated American newspapers, pamphlets, and periodicals that winter. By the spring of 1777, revolutionary Americans had seen enough of the realities of this war to know who their enemies were and of what they were capable. Governor Livingston summarized the common opinion when, in a fiery fit of rhetorical hyperbole, he accused Crown forces of having "butchered the wounded, asking for quarter; mangled the dying, weltering in their blood; refused to the dead the rights of sepulture; suffered prisoners to perish for want of sustenance [and] violated the chastity of women." In the war of words, the Americans held the high ground, a position that would have dire consequences for how the revolutionaries came to envision the enemy in their hands.[35]

Tory Hunting

Away from the fury of the fighting around New York and the frenetic debates of congressional committee rooms in Philadelphia, American communities from Georgia to Massachusetts grappled with their own local foes and struggled in their own "internal wars." While the conflict had been a civil war within the British Empire from its outset, for most of its first year, Americans had mercifully avoided war among themselves. Nonetheless, the revolutionaries were under no illusion that their cause enjoyed unanimous support. Throughout the imperial crisis, revolutionary sympathizers confronted members of their communities who opposed the resistance movement with violence. Derogatively termed "tories," a label that carried the taint of Stuart absolutism and Jacobite rebellion, these men and women of all social orders were targeted by crowds brandishing clubs, destroying property, burning effigies, and doling out tar and feathers. As T. H. Breen and others have observed, such mass actions could become exceedingly violent, spreading terror among friend and foe alike.[36]

Nevertheless, much of the revolutionary leadership believed that the loyalists posed little imminent threat to the "glorious cause." A decade of marginalization, insult, and abuse had degraded the probability of a cohesive loyalist community in all but a few locales. Within the first months of fighting, local militias throughout the colonies had purged suspected Crown supporters from the apparatus of government. Congress soon followed up by instructing local committees of safety to disarm all those suspected of "disaffection," though disenfranchisement and disarmament should not escalate to assault or widespread imprisonment. As long as such people remained placid, they were to be unharmed. Delegates further resolved in early January 1776 that all "friends to American liberty" should treat suspected loyalists "with kindness and attention." To the revolutionary elites who sought to mold the resistance movement into a European-style army, offering violence to those deceived by corrupt ministers' promises and prevarications was cruelty not to be countenanced; war was no time for personal vendettas or the settlement of petty scores. Upon assuming the command of the army at Cambridge, Massachusetts, General Washington issued a proclamation making it criminal to "molest any of those people commonly called Tories." If convicted, officers would forfeit their commissions and soldiers would "suffer corporeal punishment." When John Lovell, the master of the Public Grammar School in Boston, was seized by American officers who entered his house "with all the ravings of dogs just up with the game," Washington ordered him released and allowed to walk the streets of Boston "as a free subject of the King of Britain." Elite revolutionaries and their subordinates in the reconfigured colonial governments sought to contain popular violence against loyalists such as Lovell.[37]

Armed with muskets and on the march, loyalists looked less pitiable to the revolutionary governments in Virginia and North Carolina. During the fall of 1775 and winter of 1776, Royal Governors John Murray, 4th Earl of Dunmore and Josiah Martin raised the king's standard and called all loyal and able-bodied men to arms. By promising freedom to slaves belonging to rebel masters in return for military service, Dunmore augmented his force of British regulars, recent Scottish immigrants, and a small party of loyal Virginians. The outpouring of white loyalist support the earl hoped for, however, never materialized. Defeated at the Battle of Great Bridge on December 9, 1775, Dunmore was forced to decamp to a British warship in Chesapeake Bay. In the aftermath of the engagement, the American commander, Colonel William Woodford, captured several "disaffected persons and Negroes." Although his "Instructions Mention[d] proceeding against Slaves taken in arms, according to the rules of War," he and his officers were of the "Unanimous Opinion" that they should be summarily executed "to make an Immediate Example of them." Accountable to the collective wisdom of the colony's civilian leadership, however, Woodford requested further instructions. While awaiting commands from the Virginia Committee of Safety, the colonel did order one Scottish loyalist named Hamilton "to be coupled to one of his Black Brother Soldiers with a pair of Handcuffs" as a punishment. He proudly declared that such treatment "shall be the fate of all those Cattle" captured in the future. Virginia's revolutionary leadership, keen to expose Dunmore as the sole violator of "the practices of war among civilized nations," would not allow white men, no matter how misguided, to be shackled to slaves. They overruled Woodford, ordering the exchange of the regulars and the loyalists and returning the slaves to their masters. With Dunmore's threatened slave insurrection neutralized, his white followers could be pardoned, his black ones returned to their servile station, and the status quo reestablished.[38]

The situation was much the same in North Carolina. Despite Governor Martin's confidence that loyal North Carolinians would rally to his assistance in droves, fewer than a thousand took up arms. This meager force was easily defeated at the Battle of Moore's Creek Bridge in February 1776. In the tense moments following the loyalists' initial abortive assault, American officers promised the men that "they should meet with no bad treatment" provided they laid down their arms. The revolutionaries were good for their word, for the most part. One loyalist recorded, "our private men were all sett [sic] at liberty." Upon taking an oath to "Bear true Allegiance to the State of North Carolina," the men were granted "free Pardon and Protection" from their captors. In an inversion of the traditional European rules of war, the loyalist officers, whose influence was too great to be allowed to remain in the colony, were less fortunate. Confined in nearby Halifax's "cold dirty jail without fire or even a seat to rest upon," these men endured "almost all the inconveniences inseparable from the state of prison." Within a few weeks, however, they were paroled within the Halifax town limits. Twenty-six of the principal officers were then dispatched to Philadelphia to prevent their involvement in any future disturbances, but all were eventually paroled and exchanged. The North

Carolina Provincial Congress assured their prisoners and their constituents alike "that every indulgence which humanity and compassion can give . . . shall be extended to those whom we have in our power." Provided the men adhered to their parole, the revolutionaries would "hail their reformation with increasing pleasure, and receive them to us with open arms." After their decisive defeat, the loyalists posed little threat to the stability of the colony (later state). North Carolina's revolutionary leadership hoped that the overt demonstration of compassion and clemency would suffice to maintain loyalist docility in the future.[39]

Some loyalists, however, were past pardoning. Acting under the congressional resolution of October 6, 1775, allowing each colony to arrest anyone who might "endanger the safety of the colony, or the liberties of America," local committees and councils of safety imprisoned suspected spies and saboteurs at will. From the outset of hostilities, Philadelphia's "old goal" was crowded with men and women the Pennsylvania Council of Safety deemed too "dangerous" to stay at large. Nevertheless, most suspected Crown supporters experienced relatively benign treatment during the first year of the war. William Judd recorded being "Treated very Civilly by the Magistrates" in Philadelphia and "Kindly used by the Sheriff" in October 1775. In early January 1776 Judd even accompanied his jailer, Thomas Dewees, "to the City Tavern," where the two men "drank plentifully of Excellent wine at his Expense" before being returned "back to the Goal." The Reverend Jonathan Odell was similarly well used. Arrested on orders from the New Jersey Provincial Congress in October 1775, his Anglican parishioners quickly arranged for his release.[40]

Not all political prisoners received such generous treatment, of course, but the postwar loyalist claims suggest that confinement was temporary. Suspected loyalists with deep pockets or close community connections could obtain their freedom by posting a financial security for their future good behavior. John Peters, who would go on to command the Queen's Loyal Rangers, remembered being "seized by three mobs" and "ill-treated" in 1775, but he was eventually liberated "under bonds," having only suffered "some ill language from the mob." Others were simply released to ease overcrowding in primitive colonial jails. Local whig officials kept close tabs on suspected internal enemies, but as long as all Americans were nominally "loyal" to the king, the simple expression of that fidelity was not a crime. Those who opposed the American war effort could be considered "disaffected" or "inimical" to the cause of liberty, but until Congress declared the colonies free and independent of Great Britain,

the revolutionaries did not perceive their loyalist opposition as traitors, insur-
rectionists, or, worse yet, rebels. Some were certainly "dangerous" and deserv-
ing of "close confinement," but none posed an existential threat to the cause.[41]

The revolutionaries' lenient response to armed loyalism in late 1775 and
early 1776 would likely have endured had that challenge remained unsupported
and attenuated. But the British had other plans. Based on inflated estimates of
loyalist support in the Carolinas, General Sir Henry Clinton led a major expeditionary force to the South carrying ten thousand muskets to arm southern
Americans who had not forsaken their rightful sovereign. This loyalist host
never materialized, however, and the British fleet was battered and repulsed
at Charleston in June 1776. Nevertheless, Crown policy did not change. When
General Howe arrived at New York in late June, he brought arms, munitions,
and the promise of royal commissions to those who could rally loyalist support.
Throughout the war, the British continually overestimated that support, but
unfortunately for the loyalists, so too did the Americans.[42]

Given the results of the Charleston expedition, the revolutionaries might
have breathed a sigh of relief. The few southern loyalists who had mobilized
were easily swept aside. Instead, they panicked. Brandishing British-supplied
bayonets, the real and imagined loyalists came to occupy a place of prominence
in the minds of revolutionaries; their treachery and conspiracy seemed to lurk
in every part of the continent. Aware that New York was the intended target
of Howe's armada, crowds of alarmed residents there took to the streets to
locate and punish suspected Crown supporters. One Continental officer in
the city was "disagreeably surprised" by the "very tumultuous noise" of a "mob"
dragging a man to jail merely "on suspicion of being a Tory." His commanding
officer, Major General Israel Putnam, complained "of the riotous and disorderly
conduct of numbers of the inhabitants" that led to "acts of violence towards
some disaffected persons." Fearing unchecked vigilante justice and not content
to rely on crowd action alone, the New York Provincial Congress established
a "secret committee" in mid-June to uncover the loyalists involved in "dangerous Designs and treasonable Conspiracies." Under orders from the committee,
a detachment of General Greene's brigade roused David Matthews, the city's
mayor, from his slumber and made him a prisoner. The secret committee had
received intelligence that Matthews and several other "dangerous persons"
were involved in a plot to enlist Continental soldiers in the British Army, but
a search of his papers revealed no evidence of such a loyalist conspiracy. Hardly
placated, the council locked the mayor in the city's jail for two months before

sending him to Connecticut for confinement. His alleged coconspirator Thomas Hickey, a soldier in Washington's bodyguard, was less fortunate. Unshielded by social status and subject to martial law, he was found guilty of "Sedition and mutiny, and also of holding treach'rous correspondence with the enemy." On June 28, 1776, Private Hickey was executed for betraying a country that would not come into existence for six more days.[43]

With rumors of loyalist plots circulating widely and the British on the cusp of capturing New York, Congress acted to criminalize internal opposition. Even without a formal declaration of independence, the delegates resolved on June 24 that anyone "abiding within any of the United Colonies" who professed allegiance "to the king of Great Britain" was "guilty of treason." Without the power or authority to legislate for all, Congress was constrained from enunciating an overarching rubric for determining and punishing sedition, suggesting only that each colony "pass laws for punishing" the king's friends. Joseph Hawley, a lawyer from Massachusetts, believed that the loyalist threat was too great to be checked at the local level. He implored his congressman, Elbridge Gerry, for a continental treason law: "Did any state ever subsist without exterminating traitors? . . . It is amazingly wonderful, that having no capital punishment for our intestine enemies, we have not been utterly ruined before now. . . . High treason ought to be the same in all the United States." Hawley did not get his way, but soon after the Declaration of Independence, each state did enact its own version of a treason law and began to prosecute offenders. By 1778, every state had established "tests" to determine the loyalties of its inhabitants.[44]

Because of its proximity to British forces in New York, Connecticut was among the first to try loyalists for treason. Loyalists there had long suffered at the hands of revolutionary crowds, but with a congressional resolution in hand, local authorities began rounding up suspected persons in earnest. On July 7 Major Christopher French, still a prisoner in Hartford, received word that "Mr. M.cNeal Mr. Seaman & Mr. Fairchild were committed to Simsbury Mines for two years . . . having been found guilty of being Friends to Government—*and good order.*" Connecticut officials confined these men nearly seventy feet below ground in an abandoned copper mine at Simsbury known as Newgate Prison. Connecticut loyalist Reverend Samuel Peters described the prisoners' ordeal: they were "let down on a windlass into this dismal cavern, through a hole which answers the triple purpose of conveying them food, air and—I was going to say light, but that scarcely reaches them." Often with over a hundred inmates crowded into Newgate, sanitary conditions deteriorated precipitously. Peters sarcastically claimed that "in a few months the prisoners are released by death and the colony rejoices in her great humanity and the mildness of her laws." Loyalist John Short, imprisoned in the mines on General Washington's orders, succumbed after a mere three days. An early nineteenth-century account of the trial and confinement of Edward Huntington confirms the prisoners' plight. At his trial Huntington claimed to be "a British subject" and "prisoner of war" who deserved "such treatment as the laws of civilized warfare dictate." The court ignored his protestations. Bowing to pressure from members of the crowd who cried, "Away with the traitor—to the mines with the tory," the court found him guilty of high treason and condemned him to "perpetual imprisonment in the Mines." Confined in the "dark abyss," where "at noon only a gloomy twilight" illuminated "the squalid forms of the miserable wretches here incarcerated," Huntington languished "in the midst of sorrow." Months before the British ever housed an American soldier on board a prison ship, the revolutionary government of Connecticut banished men beneath the earth for defending what had been their lawful government just the previous year.[45]

All the states agreed that the overt act of "leveling war" against the United States constituted treason, but there was much variance about less explicit seditious acts. Radical revolutionaries in Pennsylvania pushed for a catholic definition of treason: loyalty to the king was disloyalty to the United States. The state's new convention, charged with creating a constitution, did not go so far, however. In September its delegates passed an ordinance defining treason as armed opposition and anything less as "misprision of treason." Both crimes carried sentences of imprisonment "not exceeding the duration of the present war," though only convicted traitors suffered forfeiture of all their lands and property. In December 1776 Joseph Stansbury, a merchant from Philadelphia, was "made prisoner in [his] dwelling house, by some armed men," who accused him of having "sung God save the King, or joined in the chorus." After a brief examination, he was thrown in the city's new jail "without the least shadow of Reason whatever." In a petition to the Council of Safety, Stansbury appealed to the English Bill of Rights and demanded to know why he was "wantonly deprived of his Liberty." Congress's June 24 resolution had nullified English law, and as a suspected loyalist Stansbury had no claim for redress. He remained in prison until the British occupied Philadelphia in 1777 and was not cleared of the charge until June 1779.[46]

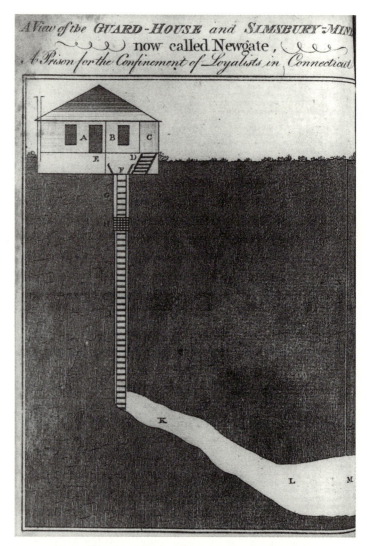

Figure 5. *A View of the Guard House and Simsbury Mines, now called Newgate, a Prison for the Confinement of Loyalists in Connecticut,* engraving by J. Bew, 1781. Courtesy Library of Congress (LC-USZ62-50390).

New Yorkers were not so lenient. With the British fleet anchored off Staten Island, the New York Provincial Convention resolved unanimously to declare any "adherent to the King" within the state guilty of treason and punishable by the *pains and penalties of* DEATH!" The proclamation was ordered to be read aloud in Manhattan so that no one in the city might claim ignorance. To add teeth to the resolution, the convention established a committee for "detecting and defeating the designs of the internal enemies of this State," even authorizing the formation of a company of 220 officers and men to suppress loyalist opposition. This force must have been insufficient because Washington dispatched elements of his own army to Staten Island in early July to arrest all "Such persons as from their Conduct had shewn themselves inimical" or "gave just Cause of Suspicion." He confided to Brigadier General William Livingston, soon to be governor of New Jersey, "I would suggest to you that my Tenderness has been often abused & I have had Reason to repent the Indulgences shewn them [the loyalists]." The pressures of civil war were trying Washington's patience.[47]

For many loyalists, the moment for patient endurance in the face of insult and injury was equally at an end. With British troops securely ensconced on Manhattan by October 1776, the king's friends flocked to the island: some for relief, others for revenge. Aware that the loyalists were facing increased persecution, New York's royal governor, William Tryon, was confident that "a great number would join the King's troops as soon as they saw them land." He was not disappointed. Crown supporters from across the social, religious, ethnic, and racial spectrum volunteered to suppress the rebellion in droves. In early September Howe authorized Oliver De Lancey, a veteran of the Seven Years' War, "to raise a Brigade of Provincials ... to reestablish Order, and Government ... [and] to Apprehend or drive all Concealed Rebels from among his Majesties well Affected Subjects." In short order De Lancey succeeded in fielding three battalions of loyalist infantry, uniformed and equipped by the Crown. De Lancey's counterpart in New Jersey, Cortland Skinner, was even more successful. In the early winter of 1776, the brigadier's New Jersey Volunteers boasted six battalions numbering over 2,500 men in arms.[48]

Because of their alleged familiarity with local geography, loyalist units often received orders to conduct reconnaissance, skirmishing, and other special operations known to contemporary theorists as "petit guerre." Some regiments, such as the Queen's American Rangers, would go on to earn plaudits for their discipline and tactical acumen, but many provincial recruits saw military service as an opportunity for rampage, rapine, and revenge. Operating "between the lines of the two armies," ill-disciplined loyalists committed "every kind of crime—robbery, house burning, murder &c," according to one Connecticut officer. The revolutionary press, keen to exploit any chink in the Crown's armor, circulated exaggerated accounts of these depredations that compounded stories of Hessian atrocities, Indian raids, and slave uprisings, fueling animosity and eliciting demands for retaliation. American troops were hardly innocent of plunder and worse, but the loyalist press had yet to organize an effective counteroffensive. To the reading public, "the internal enemies of America" were guilty of aiding "an army of foreigners" engaged in "indiscriminately murdering, plundering, and ravishing" without concern for "humanity and the practices of civilized nations." Unsurprisingly, these "war stories" turned many neutrals into furious revolutionaries.[49]

Notwithstanding their own rebellion against the Crown, in the months following independence, revolutionary leaders began to envision any homegrown opposition as rebellion that had to be violently suppressed. State and Continental forces waged a brutal campaign to quell both real and alleged loyalist "rebellions." Only days after the fall of Fort Washington, the "danger of an Insurrection of Tories in the County of Monmouth" forced General Washington to send a Continental regiment "to apprehend all such persons ... concerned in any plot or design against the liberty or safety of the United States." These troops were augmented by state militia in December, when the New York Committee of Safety tasked Brigadier General George Clinton (later a Continental officer) with the responsibility of "Overawing and Curbing the disaffected or Revolted Subjects of that State." Although not immediately successful, Clinton was confident that he "shou'd be able to drive the Rebels out of this Quarter of the Country"; a shortage of artillery was all that prevented him from attacking "those Parricides with Success." To ardent revolutionaries like Clinton, loyalists were no longer misguided malcontents or rowdy reactionaries but rebels against their country. The president pro tempore of New York, Leonard Gansevoort, pithily summarized the shift in American opinion: "The Disaffected or rather the Rebels throughout America have hitherto been treated with a Degree of Indulgence which neither the Regard due to the Country or their merits can justify—without Vigour, firmness and Decision few Revolutions succeed."[50]

In New Jersey such vigor and firmness fell on those merely suspected of loyalism. Early in 1777, revolutionary militias acting "under the Pretext of

Inlisting condign punishment on the Internal Enemies of our Country" targeted potential loyalists in their midst. "The rage of tory-hunting," Quaker Margaret Morris noted, gripped the state. She recorded that "parties of armed men rudely entered the town, and diligent search was made for tories." Sympathetic to the loyalist plight, Morris successfully concealed one "refugee" from the "tory hunters." Archibald Kennedy, a retired Royal Navy officer living peaceably in New Jersey, was not so lucky. He was "dragged out of his Bed in the Night & carried a Prisoner to Morris Town," where he endured a three-year confinement. His case was far from unique. Governor Livingston decried this state of affairs, which he attributed to the militiamen's desire to plunder "their Fellow Inhabitants on [the] Pretence that . . . [they] were inimicable to the Liberties of America." He instructed his troops "to desist for the future from all such Depredations & Violence" but was clear that "Traitors and Disaffected persons" would be punished.[51]

By criminalizing fidelity to the king, the revolutionaries denied loyalists prisoner-of-war status. Ineligible for exchange, men and women, soldiers and civilians, were all subject to revolutionary tribunals. Mary Quin and Elisabeth Brewer were tried by a Continental Army "Court of inquiry" for "suspicion of being an Enemy to their country." Quin was released on the grounds of insufficient evidence, but Brewer was sentenced "to be confined during the war." Loyalist soldiers might face even harsher punishments. In the fall of 1777, Lieutenant James Iliff was taken while recruiting for the New Jersey Volunteers. He and his men were tried for treason against the state of New Jersey. While the enlisted men were pardoned, "on the Express Condition of their Inlisting in the Continental Army," the lieutenant was sentenced to death. He and John Mee, a former British soldier who had taken an oath of allegiance to the state to avoid imprisonment only to be captured with Iliff's loyalist volunteers, were executed on December 2, 1777. According to Peter Dubois, who witnessed the execution, Iliff "behaved with Great Calmness and fortitude, Declaring that He had Acted from a principle of Duty to His King." Dubois informed British general Sir Henry Clinton that "the Corps[es] of ILIFF & MEE were drawn on a Sled from under the Gallows & thrown Into the Room in which [other loyalists] are confined in Irons. And the Gallows was placed before their prison window." New Jersey revolutionaries hoped to make an example of Iliff: treason would not be tolerated.[52]

Moses Dunbar of Connecticut suffered a similar fate. Captured while attempting to enlist men for his loyalist regiment in January 1777, Dunbar was put on trial for holding a captain's commission from General Howe. As an officer of the British Army, he should have been paroled to await exchange. Instead, the Superior Court of Connecticut sentenced him "to suffer death" for holding a commission that in a European context would have guaranteed his safety and benign treatment while in captivity. Connecticut revolutionaries were so blinded by the dual threat of external invasion and internal rebellion that the very document intended to invest his conduct with cultural legitimacy and legality had become evidence of the unpardonable crime of treason. With no legal recourse, Dunbar took solace that he would "soon be delivered from all the pains and troubles of this wicked mortal state." He did not have long to wait. Captain Dunbar was hanged at Hartford in front of "a prodigious concourse of people" on March 19, 1777.[53]

Judicial executions were rare, however; most convicted counterrevolutionaries faced the jail cell, not the gallows. When Major Richard Stockton of the New Jersey Volunteers was captured in February 1777, he and his men were paraded through the streets of Philadelphia in irons, "a drum going before him beating the rogue's march." For months, Pennsylvania authorities shuttled the prisoners between jails across the state. According to Stockton, the jail at Carlisle "really surpasses every thing that was ever heard of in a Christian Land, we are mixt with ruffians and criminals who are thrown into goal, sick and well all together." By October 1777, their situation had grown desperate. "We have no glasses to the windows seven of us are obliged to sleep in one room without anything but most of us each one Blankett." The officers pleaded with Congress to be released on parole as prisoners of war, reminding the legislators of "the Law of Nations and the Rules of War." But the delegates could do little to help the officers since they were state prisoners. Stockton and his comrades were found "guilty of high Treason, for having joined the Royal Army." While their lands and property were confiscated, they themselves were eventually exchanged in April 1778. The soldiers' status as provincial regulars likely shielded Stockton's group from the sentence Will Frish received for being a "trecherious" person. After seven months' confinement, Frish was "condemned & sold" as a servant for the duration of the war, a common method of easing overcrowding in the primitive community jails of New England.[54]

Overwhelmed with convicted "traitors," officials in New York were reduced to the necessity of fitting out three prison ships in the Hudson River in early May 1777. Anchored off Kingston, the state's new capital, these floating prisons, known collectively as the Fleet Prison, were fetid cesspits of disease, suffering, and privation. Within days of their establishment, there were already 175 loyal-ists confined on board, with more pouring in all summer. Unlike the Americans aboard the hulks in New York Harbor, who were at least nominally provided with two-thirds rations, the loyalists in Kingston were required to pay for their own provisions. As if to add insult to injury, the Council of Safety soon decided that the provisions being sold to the prisoners were "too great" and ordered their daily intake reduced to "one quarter of a pound of beef, pork or mutton . . . and one pound and a half of flour" per day, a ration considerably less than what the American prisoners in New York were entitled to receive. In the opinion of contemporary historian Thomas Jones, the loyalists' treatment was "an instance of that rebel humanity of which they made such a boast during the war, while they were perpetually taxing the British with carrying it on with a barbarity peculiar to savages only."[55]

Because the loyalists were "rebels" against their country, revolutionaries increasingly came to imagine them as beyond the jurisdiction of civil law. Death rather than capture was the likely fate for armed loyalists in areas threat-ened by British forces. Without even the pretense of legal due process, the New York Convention instructed the state's militia in May 1777 to uncover all "Emissaries of the Enemy" and "immediately execute them in Terrorem." In an effort to "prevent[,] suppress & quell all Insurrections Revolts & Disaffection within their respective Counties," all who opposed the militia were to be "destroyed." Apparently, these militiamen were successful. An officer with Continental forces at Morristown reported that month that "a number of Tory traitors have been hanged in these States southward of New England." Express-ing the opinion of many, he hoped that such tactics would "clear the land of such pests to human society."[56]

Similar terror campaigns occurred wherever rumors of an impending British attack circulated. When a fleet threatened the Chesapeake in winter 1777, the Maryland General Assembly ordered James Campbell to apprehend loyalists and "all other suspected persons." He warned Crown supporters there that he would "imideatly hang up every person that I Catch holding any Cor-respondence with or giving succor to the enemy." The loyalists' plight was no better in Pennsylvania, which would soon be the target of British designs. In April 1777 Sarah Shepherd notified her husband, who had fled the state because of his royalist leanings, that an acquaintance of theirs was "no more[,] he was hanged on the Commons last Monday." She feared that she might be next. Revolutionary forces already had ransacked her house in a futile attempt to locate her husband. In a furtive letter to him, Shepherd confessed: "I never met with so hard [a] Tryal as this Unhappy Affair has been. . . . God knows what I have suffer'd." Like countless other loyalists, the Revolution had turned the Shepherds' life upside down for the crime of following the laws under which they were born. Speaking for all those who suffered under the heavy hand of revolutionary justice, the *New-York Gazette* enunciated the prevailing loyalist reaction to their treatment: "Instead of Humanity, which the News-papers are filled with . . . , [the prisoners] have barely enough to keep Life and Soul together in Goals, and many left to shift for themselves or starve. Men, Women, and Children, suffer the same Fate. . . . [W]hat Services they do are at the Risque of their Lives and Fortunes." For many, fidelity to King George came at far too heavy a cost.[57]

By the autumn of 1777, American civil and military forces were embattled in a sanguinary and vicious internecine conflict that bore little resemblance to their prewar vision of "civilized warfare." That violence was most widespread in areas where the British Army was in close-enough proximity to support, or at least encourage, a loyalist insurrection. Bands of armed loyalists, some wearing the uniform of the king and others not, committed outrages and murders on a scale proportional to that of their revolutionary counterparts. But unlike the revolutionaries, who often relied on the preexisting legal mechanism of the court system to persecute their adversaries, the "king's friends" acted without official sanction. With the stability and future of their infant state on the line, few revolutionaries had any scruples about using every means at their disposal to suppress the counterrevolutionaries.

Some Americans, however, did maintain that the violence of the conflict could be restrained and the cause of independence preserved unsullied. In their opinion, Americans did not have to stoop to their enemy's level. When Maryland Continental troops captured, tried, and executed a loyalist "by Hanging the Poor fellow from a Limb of a Sycamore Bush," Washington was disheartened—this was not how officers and gentlemen were supposed to conduct a war between "civilized" peoples. Though he admitted that the man's treason "was heinous enough to deserve the fate he met with," the general lectured the officer responsible that "the whole proceeding was irregular and illegal, and will have a tendency to excite discontent, jealousy and murmurs among the people." The Maryland troops had only emulated the practices of countless state militias, but Washington insisted that, as Continentals, they represented the Continental Congress and were subject to "our articles of war," which did not "justify your inflicting a *capital* punishment, even on a soldier much less on a citizen." Revealing his belief that the legitimacy of the United States as a sovereign country rested on its army's scrupulous attention to the customs of war among "civilized nations" and his hope that Americans would rise above British barbarism, Washington concluded, "The temper of the Americans and the principles on which the present contest turns will not countenance proceedings of this nature."[58]

Washington overestimated the people's patience for treason. The imprisonment and execution of loyalists continued throughout the war, notwithstanding the grim irony that the British never tried a single American for treason, sedition, or rebellion. Taking up arms for their king had transformed the loyalists into rebels in the eyes of their neighbors, and as General Gage had warned Washington in 1775, rebels were "destined to the cord." While the persecution of the loyalists never approached that committed by the French revolutionaries on their opponents during the Terror, the feelings of fear and insecurity that ignited the violence of the latter were present in the former. By arming the loyalists, the British had unwittingly invited the worst type of war—a civil war. As Emer de Vattel warned, civil wars tend to "become cruel, horrible, and every day more destructive."[59]

The Hessians

In December 1776, while state forces throughout the former colonies were mired in increasingly violent and chaotic internal conflicts, Washington and the remnants of his army faced a British force entrenched in New York and poised to occupy most of New Jersey. Come spring, Howe intended to march south, capture Philadelphia, arrest the Congress, and declare the rebellion at an end. The only thing standing in his way was a threadbare contingent of Continentals whose enlistments were soon to expire. For those adherents to the revolutionary cause in New Jersey, the situation was dire. British and Hessian forces occupied posts as far south as Trenton and Bordentown on the Delaware River—within striking distance of Philadelphia. In what many historians consider to be his greatest, if not his only, strategic coup, Washington surprised Colonel Johann Rall's brigade of Hessian troops at Trenton on the morning of December 26, 1776. Surrounded and stunned, more than eight hundred soldiers surrendered in defeat. Colonel Rall and twenty-one of his men suffered mortal wounds.[60]

News of the resounding success at Trenton leapfrogged the length of the continent, elating revolutionary sympathizers and demoralizing loyalists. A letter published in the *Independent Chronicle* boasted that "three Regiments of Hessians . . . were obliged to throw down their Arms, and are now harmless two-legged Animals in the back Counties of Pennsylvania." The once-menacing minions of a despotic prince sent to deprive peaceful Americans of their liberties were transformed overnight into objects of derision, mockery, and amusement. Revolutionaries everywhere could hardly contain their jubilation. Loyalist John Lovell noted that the defeat of the Hessians "electricized the drooping hearts of the whole Continent." Another loyalist, who managed to get a copy of a New York paper by way of "Antigua or Grenada," was aghast at how word of the victory induced "some of the violent scoundrels in the City, stilling [*sic*] themselves patriots [to] hold up their Heads." The revolutionary cause, which a month earlier had appeared to be at the end of its tether, was rejuvenated. Any success would have been welcomed, but the crowning achievement of Washington's bold stroke was the capture of so many enemy soldiers. Visible evidence of American triumph, the prisoners were more than just spoils of war; they were symbols of revolutionary endurance.[61]

Washington was keen to exploit the Hessian prisoners for all their propagandistic potential. After hurriedly shuttling the men across the Delaware to prevent their rescue, the general triumphantly paraded them through the streets of Philadelphia on December 30. According to one eyewitness, the Hessians "made a poor, despicable appearance." Envisioning superhuman myrmidons, many Americans were shocked by their fallible forms. After having "the pleasure to see the Hessian prisoners paraded in Front Street," members of the Executive Committee of Congress informed Hancock that "most people seemed very angry they should ever think of running away from such a set of vagabonds." Nonetheless, massive crowds turned out to witness the triumphal parade. Sara Fisher, a Philadelphia loyalist, observed "a multitude of people going to see the Hessian prisoners." In her opinion, they "looked poorly clad . . . their outside clothes appeared to be dirty." As one captive officer phrased it, the Americans "had come to see strange animals and found in their disgust, that we looked like human beings. It seems comical, but it is true, that they had formed such an idea of the Hessians." Hardly the bogeymen of their nightmares, the Hessians were humans after all.[62]

While loyalists like Fisher empathized with the prisoners, other Americans called for vengeance. After all, these were the very men who had plundered and burned their way through New York and New Jersey. One English officer noted that "ever since their first landing on *Long-Island*, the Provincials have borne them [the Hessians] a grudge, and they in return have not been backward in showing their dislike." Those feelings now manifested themselves in the form of taunts, insults, and abuses. One Hessian officer, Lieutenant Jakob Piel, reported being greeted in Philadelphia by "a great confluence of people whose catcalls were not complimentary." As they were marched through the streets, "old women who were present screamed and scolded at us in a terrible manner and wanted to strangle us because we had come to America to steal their freedom," according to Johannes Reuber, a Hessian grenadier. In his evaluation of the situation, "the people were so angry and so threatening toward us" that they "nearly overpowered the guard." For many Americans, justice required that these prisoners be punished for their crimes.[63]

But Washington had other plans. With neither commitment to parliamentary supremacy nor vested interest in the outcome of the conflict, the Hessians were not only potential recruits for the Continental Army but also potent political weapons. Once exchanged, these prisoners, provided they were civilly treated and shown the benefits of American citizenship, might destabilize the British war machine by spreading disaffection among their comrades. Were Howe's Hessian host to be significantly depleted by desertion, the British treasury would suffer and Howe's offensive capability would diminish. In the aftermath of Trenton, Washington ordered that "the [Hessian] Officers and Men should be separated. I wish the former may be well treated, and that the latter may have such principles instilled into them during their Confinement, that when they return, they may open the Eyes of their Countrymen." The Virginian had earlier concocted a plan to spread disloyalty and dissension among their ranks. One prisoner had apprised the general in October that much of the Hessian force had been recruited by threat of violence or worse and that if assured of good treatment by the Americans, they "would all lay down their Arms—[they] have no desire to return to thier [*sic*] Ridgments [Regiments] again."[64]

Hoping to capitalize on the Hessians' distressed situation, Congress offered "all such foreigners" who agreed to become citizens of the United States "the rights, privileges and immunities of natives." To sweeten the deal, it promised to "provide, for every such person, fifty acres of unappropriated lands in some of these States, to be held by him and his heirs in absolute property." Washington hoped that this enticing offer would ensure that the Hessians' release would "be attended with many salutary consequences." Material advantage thus amplified his commitment to the European tradition of humane treatment of prisoners. He must have been pleased that Congress acquiesced to his suggestion, advising that "both the officers & men shou'd be well treated." Washington's subordinates listened as well. Lieutenant Piel gratefully recorded the "friendly treatment" he received from Colonel George Weedon in the wake of the battle. With his army convinced, Washington now had the unenviable task of changing the citizenry's opinion of the Hessian prisoners.[65]

By marching the poorly clad and dejected men through Philadelphia, Washington and the revolutionary leadership hoped that the populace might come to pity the prisoners and treat them with kindness. Instead of bloodthirsty mercenaries, "these miserable creatures now justly excite our compassion— They have no Enmity with us," the Pennsylvania Council of Safety proclaimed. It was the British, not the Hessians, who were responsible for the atrocious conduct of the war around New York. Summarizing the desired alteration in American opinion, the council argued: "We ought no longer to regard them as our Enemies. . . . 'Tis Britain alone that is our Enemy." Apparently, this missive had the desired effect. One Hessian prisoner recorded that "everyday people came from the city with food for us. Old, young, rich and poor, and all treated us in a friendly manner." While not everyone agreed with the council, Washington's propaganda campaign, combined with actual experience with the prisoners, served to expose the Hessians for what they really were: mere pawns in the British imperial project.[66]

The general knew, however, that compassion would become revulsion if the prisoners were not properly supplied and quartered in short order. He ordered Deputy Quartermaster General Clement Biddle to forward the men to Lancaster, where they could be more easily housed and fed. In a letter to the Council of Safety, Biddle suggested that the state appoint a commissary of prisoners "to furnish Provisions [and] have Charge of them." In the absence of a commissary, the Lancaster Committee of Safety ordered "that the Barracks here may be put-in a Condition to receive them [the Hessians] immediately." The town had already housed British prisoners, and its barracks were well appointed to receive new occupants. To that end, the enlisted soldiers marched out of Philadelphia on January 8, 1777, "under escort of an American detachment." The prisoners were quartered in churches "for security" during the march.[67]

Once arrived in Lancaster, the men were housed in the barracks, where "everything was peaceful and calm," according to one of them. The stone building had seventy-six rooms of approximately 263 square feet, each with a fireplace and windows. Surrounded by a fifteen-foot-high wooden palisade, the barracks were thus a secure and commodious place of confinement. Because Washington hoped to lure the rank-and-file prisoners away from the British, he ordered their officers sent to Baltimore, where they could do little to enforce the loyalty of the men; the enlisted prisoners do not seem to have regretted the lack of supervision. There was no dearth of provisions. Grenadier Reuber noted that he "received one pound of bread and as much meat and such wood as necessary for cooking and heating, and everything which we needed for conducting our households was delivered to us." Pennsylvania authorities soon permitted the men to hire themselves out to local farmers or tradesmen. Welcomed by the prisoners, this practice had the added benefit of relieving "the public of the burthern of maintaining them." According to Reuber, prospective employers were required to "provide food and drink and pay a wage of fifteen stiver daily" for their services. Some prisoners received quite a bit more for their work. Those Hessians working in the public buildings near Lancaster earned two shillings, or twenty-four pence, a day for their labor in August 1777, an extraordinary sum when compared to the eight pence a day British soldiers received for serving the Crown. The captives had little cause for complaint. As Grenadier Reuber put it, "So far so good."[68]

British prisoners, however, did not share their Hessian colleagues' good fortune. In the past they had proven obstinately loyal to king and country, so there was little for the revolutionaries to gain by coddling them. Congress made no provision to offer land to British deserters, and the soldiers who were captured at Princeton in early January 1777 were not shielded from the anger of the populace. While the Hessians were immediately dispatched to Lancaster, the "British Prisoners and Tories" were "sent to the State Prison" in Philadelphia. Only overcrowding and fear of a jailbreak persuaded their captors to send the Britons to the backcountry.[69]

Unsurprisingly, the British prisoners grew restive. Local officials at inland detention centers reported that the recently arrived men "behav'd execeding[ly] bad coming from Philadelphia" and continued to "behave Ill here," in contrast to the Hessians, who "behave well." Consequently, instead of being permitted to hire out their services, the Britons were confined to the barracks or the local jail. A party of twenty-seven captive dragoons begged the Philadelphia Committee of Safety for "the liberty of walking about to take a little fresh air" because they were "in a very indifferent state of health, three of them being very ill."

The committee did nothing to relieve their suffering. Despondent, several British prisoners in early May 1777 asked the Committee of Safety why they were "Confin'd to goal as Criminals?" Although there is no record of an official response to their petition, the men must have known that, unlike their Hessian comrades, in the eyes of their American captors, they no longer deserved humane and mild treatment. Lancaster residents were well aware of the deplorable conditions of American prisoners, many of them from their own community, confined aboard the prison ships in New York Harbor. To them, in light of such reports, a cramped and damp jail cell was more than the British enlisted men deserved. Even if Congress had wanted to relieve their plight, the prisoners were in the hands of the local authorities, and without a Continental commissary of prisoners to enforce a national policy, the delegates could do nothing.[70]

The British prisoners' confinement in Lancaster was mild when compared to the plight of African Americans captured acting against the revolutionary cause. A "Negro man nam'd Tom," who had fled enslavement to enlist with the Hessian troops in the fall of 1776, was dragged from his confinement as a prisoner of war and returned to his master, Samuel Henry of Trenton, in February 1777. Hessian regiments actively recruited runaway slaves as musicians, and Tom was likely serving in that capacity when he was captured at the Battle of Trenton. Though he was initially treated as a prisoner of war, his captors reported that "he was not in Arms"; nonetheless, under European conventions, field musicians were entitled to the same privileges as their armed comrades. Both Hessian and British prisoners could be confident of their eventual release, if not by exchange then at the end of the war, but Tom had no such prospect. Unless British forces marched near his master's abode once more, he would likely remain a slave for the rest of his life.[71]

Throughout the war, both state and congressional forces refused to acknowledge blacks as legitimate combatants. In the aftermath of Dunmore's proclamation, the Virginia Convention resolved to transport any slave "taken in arms against this colony" to "any of the foreign West India islands, there to be disposed of by sale." The proceeds were to be used to purchase arms and ammunition. At least one black prisoner, called Tom by his master, was sold into slavery in the West Indies in return for powder. With the British navy patrolling the coastline, this must have been a risky endeavor. The convention changed its policy in May 1776, resolving instead to consign black prisoners to labor in lead mines in the western part of the state. Virginia was not alone in denying

Figure 6. Drittes Regiment Garde (detail), by J. H. Carl, circa 1784. Courtesy
Anne S. K. Brown Military Collection, Brown University Library.

captured African Americans the protections of prisoner-of-war status. When
New Jersey militiamen captured an escaped slave who had gone "over to the
enemy" in July 1777, Washington gave instructions "to deliver him to his owner."
If an individual's master could not be determined, or if he were a free man, his
captors often deemed him their own personal property. Similarly, black sailors
could be auctioned off with the rest of a captured ship's assets. Either returned
to their masters, forced to serve as privateers or laborers for the revolutionary
forces, or sold into slavery, captured black soldiers and sailors were segregated
from their white comrades and deemed ineligible for the "many indulgences"
white prisoners received.[72]

    Although likely preferable to enslavement in the West Indies, the situation
in the Lancaster barracks was growing desperate by the summer of 1777.

Overcrowding and food shortages galled the British prisoners. The men had earlier been confined to the barracks for their "unruly & threatening conduct," which had made the inhabitants of the town "uneasy." Celebrating the king's birthday on June 4 with a bonfire in the barracks' courtyard, the inebriated prisoners became raucous, according to Reuber creating "such a disturbance." When American troops tried to put an end to the proceedings, the Britons "attacked the fifteen men of the American guard, took their weapons, broke them into pieces, and threw them into the fire." Panicked by their prisoners' insubordination, the guards called for reinforcements. From Reuber's vantage point, it looked as if "an entire regiment with two cannon marched into the barracks courtyard." Leveling their muskets, the Americans "delivered a fire against the English. Some were initially killed and some wounded." The surviving ringleaders were identified and sent in irons to the town's jail. American authorities were pleased that the Hessians had not taken part in the riot and rewarded them accordingly. Reuber noted that they "received much better treatment than the English"; they were "prospering."[73]

The ability of the prisoners to launch a riot, and the extreme violence of the local authorities' reaction to it, highlighted to Congress the deficiencies in the decentralized American system of prisoner administration as well as the pressing need for an expedited exchange. Even prior to the disturbance, the secretary of the Board of War, Richard Peters, lamented that "there have been many Enormities committed both by the Persons having the Care of them [the prisoners] and the Prisoners themselves." He explained: "Sometimes the Comittees have been unreasonably rigorous & other Times so culpably lax & inattentive that the most flagrant & dangerous Abuses & treasonable Practices have been committed & carried on by Prisoners." Congress had attempted to rectify the problem by permitting Washington to appoint a Continental commissary general in April 1777, but as the events of the June riot suggest, simply creating the position was no solution. Nonetheless, Washington was hopeful that all prisoner affairs could be centralized and an official cartel established. Failing to secure his first choice for the post—Colonel Cornelius Cox of Pennsylvania thought a desk job inglorious—the general hit upon the thirty-seven-year-old New Jersey lawyer Elias Boudinot. The prominent attorney was no soldier, but he had clout in Congress and a predilection for lists, ledgers, and letters. After some hesitation, Boudinot accepted the post of commissary general and began the monumental task of administering enemy prisoners and relieving the distress of Americans in British custody. He had his work cut out

for him. Boudinot would later recall, "soon after I had entered on my department, the applications of the Prisoners were so numerous and their distress
[was] so urgent" that it was difficult to know where to begin. As the pleading
letters from prisoners on both sides poured in, Boudinot must have had second
thoughts about accepting so much responsibility with so little power.[74]

From the outset, Boudinot was at a distinct disadvantage. Unlike his British
counterpart, Joshua Loring, Boudinot did not have the authority to direct
individual state officials in matters of prisoner administration. Congress had
already permitted each state to establish its own commissariat of prisoners to
oversee the care and management of both prisoners of war and "state" prisoners,
or loyalists. Boudinot confessed his frustration to Secretary Peters in mid-June:
"I have lately rec'd from the Clerk of the Congress, Copies of the Resolutions
made since the Commencement of the War relating to my department, among
wch. is one requesting each State to appoint a Commissary of Prisoners of
War—This resolution militates directly agt. my Appointment." Already aware
that local interests would invariably clash with Continental ones, he was firmly
of the opinion "that the Office should finally center in one Man." Congress
could not easily undo its own resolutions, however, and the states jealously
guarded their prerogatives. To mollify Boudinot, the Board of War ordered
that he be allowed "to appoint three Deputies under him" and instructed "that
all Commissaries . . . be obliged at any time when required by the Commissary
General of Prisoners . . . to deliver over to him . . . all such Prisoners of war as
are or shall be in their care" for exchange. Notwithstanding this official expansion of his powers, Boudinot was vexed that "no clear chain of authority was
outlined." He could not issue orders, only recommendations, concerning the
lodging, provisioning, or funding of prisoners in state custody. Moreover, he
was financially constrained by a Congress with more pressing concerns—paying, feeding, lodging, supplying, and arming the Continental Army and Navy.
Hoping to build additional barracks to house prisoners, Boudinot failed time
and again to obtain sufficient appropriations from the delegates.[75]

Boudinot was more successful, however, at investigating and relieving the
distressed conditions of American prisoners in British hands. Flooded with
"complaints of the cruel Treatment of a number of our Prisoners, taken by the
Enemy & confined in the Goals of the City of New York," he conducted "an
Inquiry into the Truth of the Facts alleged." Communicating with not only
the American commissary residing in New York, Lewis Pintard, but also with
his British counterpart, Commissary Loring, Boudinot concluded that "there

is Evidence of the greatest Cruelty being used towards several of our unhappy Prisoners." He learned that "several of our Officers who have lately had the small Pox in the Goals, have been suffered to languish (one of whom died) with out the least aid either as to Physick, Provision or other necessaries—That in general the daily Rations are not sufficient more than barely to keep the Prisoners from starving." To combat their privation, Boudinot worked with Pintard to supply the men out of his own pocket. When Congress finally acquiesced to his repeated requests for funds, they provided him with a meager £600, hardly enough to reimburse the British for the expenses the prisoners had already incurred. Although Boudinot would later describe his efforts as "very small & very indifferent," to the prisoners, the supply of clothing and provisions he provided was often the difference between life and death. Despite Boudinot's best efforts, Pintard reported that the prisoners "all want more Exceedingly and are very pressing for it."[76]

The only thing that would have effectively relieved the prisoners' distress was beyond Boudinot's control: an exchange. Although Howe had neither reconsidered nor abandoned his earlier desire to effect a cartel, Washington was determined to "send in no more prisoners" until the British commander agreed to exchange them in the order of their capture. Concerned with the equity of the swap, the Virginian wanted those men who had been longest in British custody, such as Colonel Allen, released first. Howe, on the other hand, maintained that their original agreement stipulated only that the exchange be conducted based on equity of rank, not length of captivity; he did not have the time, ability, or inclination to search the city for the specific prisoners Washington might request. The American general was determined to stand his ground. As he informed Governor Trumbull, "General Howe, without paying any regard to my request, sent out such [prisoners] as best pleased him." Unless Howe agreed "to send out such only as I name," Washington would "not send any more of his prisoners in."[77]

To complicate matters, in late December 1776 British forces captured Major General Charles Lee and immediately conveyed him to confinement in New York. Congress's darling, Lee was everything Washington was not: brash, mercurial, unkempt, radical, and, most important, an experienced European officer. Both men had seen battle under General Braddock in 1755, but only Lee, born in Cheshire as the son of a British officer, had possessed a king's commission. A veteran of both the American and European theaters of the war, Lee immigrated to Virginia on the eve of the Revolution after alienating most of his former colleagues and resigning his commission. Not one to eschew the limelight or shirk the quest for glory, he offered his services to Congress in 1775 and was one of the first generals commissioned.[78]

Although Washington referred to him as "the first officer in Military knowledge and experience we have in the whole army," there was little camaraderie between the two men, with more than a little envy and competition on both sides. Many in Congress believed that Lee, not Washington, should be in command of Continental forces. In July 1775 Abigail Adams had notified her husband that his appointment to the army gave "universal satisfaction. The people have the highest opinion of Lees [sic] abilities." In contrast to Washington's meticulous attention to dress and decorum, Lee looked to Mrs. Adams "like a careless hardy Veteran" who brought to mind images of Sweden's warrior king, Charles XII. With the death of Richard Montgomery during the Canadian campaign, many in Congress agreed with her, seeing Lee as an invaluably experienced officer they could not afford to lose. When word of his capture reached Philadelphia, Hancock instructed Washington to send an officer under flag of truce "to Genl Howe to know in what Manner Genl Lee is treated." Congress even managed to appropriate "one Hundred Half Johannes . . . to render the Situation of that Gentleman as easy as possible during his Captivity." Hancock echoed most revolutionaries when he confided to Washington that Lee's "loss must be extremely regretted by every Friend to this Country."[79]

To General Howe, Lee was no friend to his country—he was a deserter. For a man who had been born and bred in England and honored with a commission from his king, to command a parcel of rebels was not only disgraceful but also treasonous. In the opinion of one British officer, Lee was an "atrocious Monster" who was "as perfect in Treachery as if he had been an American born." Cries of treason resounded across the Atlantic. One English lyricist recorded his disdain by imagining the general's execution in verse: "On the bare earth Charles Lee shall kneel, Young Harcourt [the arresting officer] draws the shining steel, and bids the party—fire!" From the vantage point of many Britons, Lee, even more so than Ethan Allen, looked like a suitable subject for summary justice.[80]

Although Lee informed Howe that he had resigned his commission, the British general was unsure of how to proceed. The hardliners in his army and at home were calling for Lee's head; were Howe to release the man on parole, he would appear weak and soft on rebellion and treason. Aware that many of his junior officers were suspicious of his own whig politics, his connections to

America, and his apparent inability to isolate and destroy Washington's army, Howe could not afford to be seen as overly generous. Consequently, he denied Lee parole and ordered the American general confined in the city hall pending instructions from London. Hardly the stark surroundings of the improvised jails, sugarhouses, or prison ships that other American prisoners endured, Lee's cell was "one of the genteelest public rooms in the City," according to loyalist historian Thomas Jones. Notwithstanding this finery, the general was still a man in limbo. One word from the British ministry, which had no reason to look favorably upon him, would send Lee to the gallows.[81]

American printers soon took up the story of Lee's capture and disseminated inflated and exaggerated accounts of his treatment. The reading public, who by now had little reason to doubt accounts of British atrocity, were outraged to learn that Lee was treated "with every other Marks of Indignity" and confined "in a small mean looking house." Congress received word in early February 1777 that "General Lee hath, since his captivity, been committed to custody of the provost, instead of being enlarged upon his parole, according to the humane practice that has taken place with officers of the enemy who have fallen into the hands of the American troops." Sharing their countrymen's indignation, the delegates invoked "the principles of retaliation." Should Howe refuse to accept the immediate exchange for Lee of "six Hessian field officers" who had been captured at Trenton, "the same treatment which General Lee shall receive, may be exactly inflicted upon" those men. In case the British commander was immune to threats against foreign officers, Congress substituted Lieutenant Colonel Archibald Campbell for one of the Hessians. The Council of Massachusetts was ordered "to detain Lieutenant Colonel Campbell," who had been enjoying a lenient parole, until Howe had the opportunity to respond.[82]

Without orders from his superiors, Howe could do little to appease Congress in this matter; he could, however, release other American prisoners under the terms of his agreement with Washington. Early in the new year, Commissary Loring, at Howe's behest, opened the doors of the makeshift prisons and the hatches of the hulks to send many of the Fort Washington prisoners on their way. While Howe did not free all his prisoners, historians estimate that over 1,800 of the men captured during the New York Campaign were released during the winter of 1776–77. The gesture was not simply a mark of the general's humanity, however; he was aware that smallpox and typhus were rampant in his prisons, and most of these men would not survive the winter. By returning the prisoners before disease could claim their lives, he could demand an equal number of healthy British prisoners under the terms of his agreement with Washington. Not surprisingly, on their trek homeward the men perished in droves, the effects of malnutrition, close confinement, and disease taking their toll. Washington was horrified by "the miserable emaciated Countenances of those poor Creatures who have lately been released." Those who made it home alive were perfect vectors for the pestilence they carried. Governor Trumbull feared that "our returning Soldiers have spread the Infection into almost every Town in the State." If Howe had hoped that releasing the men would guarantee good treatment toward Lieutenant Colonel Campbell and the Hessian field officers, he would be disappointed.[83]

On February 20, 1777, the Board of War received instructions "to order the five Hessian field officers and Lieutenant Colonel Campbell into safe and close custody; it being the unalterable resolution of Congress to retaliate on them the same punishment as may be inflicted on the person of General Lee." This was not a decision lightly made. Cognizant that their actions were scrutinized by foreign powers and aware of the judgmental glare of posterity, the delegates nevertheless believed the measure necessary and justified to "teach our cruel enemies to regard the laws of nations and the rights of humanity." The Board of War did not delay in carrying out Congress's orders. Lieutenant Piel, quartered in Baltimore, recorded that the local committee of safety "notified our staff officers of their arrest and placed sentries before their quarters" in early March. Although he had already been committed to "the common goal of Concord" on February 1, when Congress's order reached the Council of Massachusetts, Lieutenant Colonel Campbell reported that he was "lodged in a dungeon of about 12 or 13 feet square whose sides are black with the grease and Litter of successive Criminals. Two doors with double locks and Bolts shut me up from the yard." His cell contained only "two small windows strongly grated with Iron," which only served to let in the "frost and snow" of the New England winter.[84]

Campbell was at a loss to explain his treatment. He informed Howe that upon his capture he had received "every mark of humanity, and treatment suitable to my Rank" from "the Controlling Power at Boston." He now found himself "stripped of half my private property[,] the very necessaries of life," in "a lothsome [sic] black Hole" still redolent of the "very excrement" of the prior occupant. Campbell's only companions were his "little friends the mice." He wished the "*Yankees* were so honest & humane as those little urchins." If this was Congress's idea of "humanity and kindness," then those once-lauded virtues were now "crimes more atrocious than oppression and cruelty." While General Lee slept warm in his bed, attended by an Italian servant and with his beloved dog as company, Campbell wasted away in a stone cell, open to the elements, without heat, and accompanied only by the prison rats who shared his meager meals.[85]

Washington and many of his officers were ill at ease with such a heavy response. The general had received intelligence that Lee's confinement was considerably milder than Congress imagined. Even if the reports of mistreatment were true, to retaliate on six men for the hardships endured by one seemed to be a flagrant misuse of the *lex talionis* and a violation of the laws of nations and customs of war. Washington had been prepared to exact "the most severe and adequate Retaliation" when rumors of Lee's rigorous confinement and impending trial for desertion and treason seemed valid, but with fresh intelligence in hand, he now believed that Congress had erred. Always deferential to his civilian masters, Washington nonetheless informed Hancock that the resolutions were "founded in impolicy, and will, if adhered to, produce consequences of an extensive, and melancholy nature." He argued that retaliation would only lead to the escalation of violence on the part of the British. "Can we imagine that our Enemies will not mete the same punishments—the same indignities—the same cruelties to those belonging to us in their possession, that we impose on theirs in our power?" Moreover, Congress's decision to retaliate primarily on Hessian officers would only serve to undo the effects of his efforts to seduce the foreign soldiers away from British service. In short, Washington felt that "the mischeifs which may & must innevitably flow from the execution of the Resolves, appear to be endless & innumerable." Nathanael Greene was equally frank in his remonstrance to the president of the Board of War, John Adams: "I cannot help thinking the sacrafice you are makeing for General Lee is impolitick as it respects the Hessians, and unjust as it respects our prisoners with General How[e]." Notwithstanding the logic of their own generals' arguments, Congress refused to budge. As long as Lee remained in close custody with the prospect of execution looming, so too would Campbell and the Hessian officers.[86]

Congress did, however, empower Washington to negotiate with Howe for Lee's release. If the British general agreed to treat Lee as a prisoner of war, Washington was free to carry out the exchange. On March 10, 1777, envoys sent by Howe and Washington—Lieutenant Colonels William Walcott and Henry Harrison, respectively—met at Brunswick, New Jersey, to negotiate the terms. Walcott demanded that Washington return an equal number of British prisoners for the sickly Americans already released. For his part, Harrison refused to consider any proposal until the British agreed to treat Lee as a gentleman officer eligible for parole and exchange. Walcott believed it his duty to "adhere strictly & literally to the Terms of the Original Agreement" and declined to comment on Lee's status. Harrison could not exchange healthy British soldiers for the ghosts of "many of [the prisoners who] died on their Return . . . owing to their close & rigorous Confinement." They were at an impasse. After a nine-hour meeting, negotiations broke down, and both sides returned to their commanders empty-handed.[87]

Although informal negotiations continued all summer, no agreement was reached. Lord Germain instructed Howe "to put an immediate end to a fruitless Negotiation" in September 1777. Without a cartel, American prisoners continued to suffer aboard British prison hulks and in makeshift jails in New York, while the tide of popular resentment continued to turn against British and loyalist prisoners in American custody. The aggrieved father of one Connecticut soldier who had perished alongside all but six of his company aboard a prison ship spoke for many when he urged his brother to "Execute justice" on the British for the "Savage Barbarity" of "murdering in Cool blood thousands of our friends." He hoped that no American would shirk the responsibility of retribution. The time for talk was over. Only a reversal in the fortunes of war would bring both parties to the table again.[88]

* * *

On the surface, the New York Campaign looks like a textbook example of eighteenth-century European warfare. British forces engaged and defeated their foes in several pitched battles, occupied one of the enemy's most populous and prosperous cities, and opened peace negotiations with representatives of their opponent's government. Only a brilliant tactical coup de main on the part of the Continental commander in chief forestalled a resounding British victory. Viewing the campaign from this angle, as its principal historians have done, obscures the very real transition in the conflict's character that had transpired: the onset of civil warfare in America. To capture and pacify New York, the British relied on hired Hessians and armed loyalists to bolster their forces. The Hessian penchant for plunder and the loyalist quest for retribution resulted in very real crimes and atrocities that horrified ardent and lukewarm Americans alike. In this context the revolutionaries came to envision loyalists not simply as deluded neighbors but rather as traitorous rebels against the United States. The realities of this expanding civil war looked nothing like the revolutionary leadership's idealized original vision of "civilized" combat.

Throughout the campaign, Congress and the revolutionary press martialed stories of British cruelty to bolster support for the cause, flagging after the loss of New York. When reports of the "poor, sick, dying prisoners" on the hulks circulated, Americans had little trouble believing their enemies responsible for willful murder. Notwithstanding the prisoners' complaints that Congress, in its inability to provide for the captives or effect their exchange, was the true author of their misfortune, Americans could see only British barbarity. While matters of policy ensured the generous treatment of the Hessians captured at Trenton, Congress embraced retaliation against enemy prisoners for the first time, and communities under British threat sought vengeance for the mistreatment of their citizens in Crown custody. By the summer of 1777, even John Adams, who had denounced revenge as "unlawfull" in the winter of 1776, admitted that "there is something sweet and delicious in the Contemplation of it." He was not the only one in the revolutionary leadership to realize that this was a new type of war—a *revolutionary* war. The old rules might not apply.[89]

Washington, for his part, remained critical of the escalating violence. But he had come to realize that in this war the mere threat of retaliatory action was not always enough. As he told Admiral Richard, 1st Earl Howe (the general's brother): "You may call us Rebels and say that we deserve no better treatment. But remember my Lord that supposing us Rebels we still have feelings equally as keen & sensible as Loyalists and will if forced to it most assuredly retaliate upon those upon whom we look as the unjust invaders of our Rights Liberties and properties." This time Washington was in earnest.[90]

Chapter 4

The Fortune of War

In the midmorning hours of October 17, 1777, a fifty-five-year-old playwright, sometime actor, gambler, socialite, bon vivant, and general in the British Army recited what must have been the most agonizing lines of his storied career: "The fortune of war, General Gates, has made me your prisoner." Dapperly clad in his finest scarlet coat, with a profusion of feathers protruding from his cocked hat, John Burgoyne, known to posterity as "Gentleman Johnny," proffered his sword to the diminutive, bespectacled, and balding American major general Horatio Gates. In contrast to the British peacock standing before him, Gates, whose own soldiers called him "Granny," looked the part of the ascetic republican, clothed in a plain blue frock. The two men's respective appearances, however, belied their similarities. Both were native-born Englishmen who had held a king's commission. Unsurprising for men who had belonged to the exclusive fraternity that was the eighteenth-century British officer corps, Gates and Burgoyne had known each other for thirty-two years. Each had begun his military career as a lieutenant in the 20th Regiment of Foot. Although privilege, patronage, and more than a fair share of luck had catapulted Burgoyne to the highest echelons of Britain's military and civil society, while Gates had languished in obscurity, both were products of Europe's culture of war, and each knew exactly how the surrender would play out.[1]

Over the previous few days, Burgoyne and Gates, through their respective intermediaries, had hammered out the details of an agreement that would bring hostilities in the northern theater to a close. Taking a ritualistic form that would have been well known to William of Orange and Marshal Turenne in the seventeenth century or to Maurice de Saxe and the Duke of Cumberland in the last major European war, the negotiations proceeded from Gates's initial demand for an unconditional surrender to his eventual offer of the "honors of war": Officers were to keep their swords, the men their personal effects.

Influenced by both his regard for Burgoyne and intelligence of an approaching British relief column, Gates agreed to allow the general and his army of nearly six thousand men to march to Boston, the nearest major American port, and take ship home to England, the only proscription being that they not bear arms in North America for the remainder of the conflict. Most important, under the terms of the accord, the men were not to be considered prisoners of war. Gates even consented to term the surrender a "convention" rather than a "capitulation."[2]

In contemporary European warfare, a convention was a negotiated treaty for a cessation of hostilities, not a surrender agreement. Victorious generals would offer these generous terms as a demonstration of respect for an enemy force that had conducted itself with honor. That is exactly how Burgoyne's officers interpreted the agreement. According to Ensign Thomas Anburey, General Gates was "fully sensible of the mortification attending our reverse of fortune" and had no wish "to add any circumstance that might aggravate our present calamity." Anburey was pleased that the Americans agreed to uphold "the authorized maxims and practices of war" by behaving with "civil deport-ment to a captured enemy." Burgoyne's defeated men had every reason to expect that their adversaries would abide by European customs and uphold their end of the bargain.[3]

When Burgoyne's proud troops filed out of their entrenchments to pile their arms, no one on either side could have known that they would spend the next five and a half years in captivity—longer than any other contingent of British prisoners. By the time their ordeal was over, the soldiers and their civilian followers, who became known as the Convention Army, had marched over 1,100 miles, enduring confinement in overcrowded and rotting barracks, jails, and prison ships in eight different states and losing roughly 85 percent of their number to disease, desertion, starvation, and fatigue. Theirs is a painful story to tell. At one of the army's bleakest hours, Ensign Anburey took comfort in the belief that, "from the cruelty and ill usage they have continually expe-rienced, since they became prisoners," the convention troops would prove the bravest in the British Army, willing to "fight to desperation" to avenge their mistreatment. Few among them would ever get that chance.[4]

The revocation of the Convention of Saratoga was a watershed moment in the course of the Revolution. By nullifying the compact, Congress openly flouted the norms of the European culture of war that the revolutionary leadership had held sacrosanct since the commencement of hostilities. Unlike

Figure 7. Horatio Gates at Saratoga, by James Peale, circa 1800. Courtesy
Maryland Historical Society.

prior acts of congressional retaliation, which were aimed at redressing specific examples of prisoner abuse on the part of the British and improving the plight of American prisoners, the decision to invalidate the convention was an acknowledgment that the rules by which the revolutionaries had conducted the war had changed. The time had come for a new policy—a policy of retribution.

In resolving to suspend the convention indefinitely, the delegates had not foreseen, nor did they desire, the absolute destruction of the Convention Army. They were not sadists motivated by bloodlust. They were, however, deeply troubled by the treaty's ramifications. Gates's victory had electrified the revolutionary movement at a moment when it was approaching its nadir. But by agreeing to such generous terms, the general had squandered the revolutionaries' best chance to turn the tide of the conflict not only militarily but also symbolically. Many Americans, aggrieved by British abuses and loyalist insurrections, hoped to make an example of Burgoyne's army. Hewing closely to the norms of "civilized" warfare as they understood them had done the revolutionaries precious little good in the past. To the British they were still rebels, no matter how decorous their behavior. Unless the British could be persuaded that their actions had severe consequences, the cycle of abuse would never end. To the outraged American populace, the nullification of the Convention of Saratoga looked like the just vengeance of a wronged people.

From the perspective of the Crown prisoners, Congress's motivation for negating the convention did not matter; the results were the same. By refusing to exchange the men, even when it would have been militarily advantageous, while failing to provide for their support and subsistence, Congress set the Convention Army on a march to its demise. Once the decision to suspend the embarkation was made, there was little option but to foist the prisoners upon state officials and local communities. In doing so, Congress unwittingly relinquished control of the captives. Time after time the men exhausted the resources and the welcome of the communities that housed them. As the prisoners learned too well, ongoing neglect can be just as devastating as deliberate cruelty. Rather than reassessing its obdurate position, however, Congress only entrenched further. To parole the men to England or release them through exchange would be to repudiate its hardline stance, destroying congressional creditability with most Americans, who, after years of hearing and reading about British atrocities, thirsted for retribution. By negating the Saratoga Convention and relegating the prisoners to indefinite confinement, Congress sent both the British and its constituents a powerful message: Americans would turn the other cheek no longer.[5]

Unwelcome near Boston

Rumors of Burgoyne's battlefield defeats at Freeman's Farm and Bemis Heights reached Congress in mid-October, but as the month drew to a close, no one had heard from General Gates. Because they had received no official notice, Congressman Henry Laurens lamented that "some people begin to doubt the truth of the accounts" of Burgoyne's defeat. Colonel James Wilkinson, tasked by Gates with informing Congress of the victory, was in no hurry to do so. He relished being the bearer of good news and took full advantage of the many open tables and bottomless glasses to which the welcome word afforded him along his route. By the time he finally reached Congress (now assembled at York, Pennsylvania) on October 31, the vague reports of Burgoyne's surrender had already been confirmed. A week earlier the *Massachusetts Spy* had reported that "Gen. Burgoyne had delivered himself and army [as] prisoners of war into the hands of General Gates." The news exhilarated the population of Worcester, many of whom rushed to the common to see "thirteen discharges of cannon" and to drink thirteen toasts to the success of American arms. Camped at White Marsh on the outskirts of occupied Philadelphia, Washington informed his army on the eighteenth that "G. Burgoyne and his whole Army surrendered prisoners of war." He hoped that "every heart [would] expand with grateful joy to the supreme disposer of all events who has granted us this signal success." Congress went even further, designating December 18 as a day "for solemn thanksgiving and praise" and ordering "a medal of gold be struck" for General Gates in commemoration of "this great event." The revolutionaries had much to be thankful for—never before had their forces captured an entire army of European regulars.[6]

Americans throughout the continent rejoiced that the proud and pompous Burgoyne was now their prisoner. With Philadelphia, New York, and Newport in British hands, independence was teetering on the edge of extinction when the two armies joined battle at Saratoga. Unsurprisingly, word of Gates's conquest exhilarated ardent revolutionaries. Aware from the initial reports that Burgoyne's position was untenable—he was surrounded with his line of retreat cut off—most Americans expected a total victory. In their opinion, the enemy deserved no better terms than those offered to the American garrison at Fort Washington: unconditional surrender. Even members of Gates's command who witnessed the ceremony thought that the Britons were now prisoners of war. Ralph Cross, a soldier under Gates, reported that "the Grand Army of Gen Burgoin Capittelated & agreed to bee all Prisoners of Warr." One of Cross's superiors, Henry Dearborn, recorded that "Mister Burgouyn with his whole army surrendered themselves as Prisoners of War." He called the victory the "greatest Conquest ever known."[7]

Although Congress initially shared Dearborn's enthusiasm, when Wilkinson's copy of the articles of convention began to circulate, the mood in the room quickly soured. The colonel remembered that several delegates began to "derogate from Gen. Gates's triumph." As the general's representative, Wilkinson was subjected to a barrage of caustic questions. How had Gates allowed Burgoyne to talk himself out of unconditional surrender? Would it not have been preferable to allow Burgoyne to retreat to Canada, where his battered army could do little harm? Wilkinson did his best to defend his commander, but the tenor of the conversation was decidedly critical of Gates and his convention.[8]

The congressional debate was fruitless; under the terms of the agreement, Burgoyne and his army were not prisoners. Although they could not serve in America unless exchanged, nothing in the terms prohibited the soldiers' service elsewhere. The return of the troops to Britain under the Convention of Saratoga would free regiments tasked with garrison duty in Europe for the fight in America. Rather than exchanging the Crown soldiers for American prisoners suffering in New York and Philadelphia, Gates had simply let them go, practically ensuring that an army of fresh British troops would arrive on American shores in the spring. Unwilling to sacrifice the popular enthusiasm for the victory, Congress publicly praised Gates, but many members remained deeply displeased with his convention.[9]

To some Americans, Gates's generosity verged on treachery. The Reverend Samuel Cooper, a fiery Congressionalist minister in Boston, confided in John Adams that his "Joy is damp'd by the Concessions G[ates] has made, considering how totally Burgoyne was in our Power." Cooper attributed the terms of "this unaccountable Treaty" to Gates's "Infatuation" with Burgoyne and his old employers, "or something worse." Gates should have seen such a critique coming. The general's admiration for Burgoyne was well known. In a public and widely circulated letter to the British general before the capitulation, he had complimented "the famous Lieutenant-general Burgoyne, in whom the fine gentleman is united with the soldier and the scholar." Cooper, like many zealous revolutionaries, feared that perhaps Gates, who after all was an Englishman by birth, had traded his adopted country for British favor. Even if he was not guilty of treason with the generous terms, it was easy to imagine his prior connections clouding his judgment. Laurens, now the newly elected president of Congress, thought Gates had been "a little captivated" by Burgoyne's flattery and "too polite" in his terms. Major General Arnold, who bore little love for his former commander, apparently referred to Gates as "*the greatest poltroon in the world*."[10]

Washington shared his colleagues' dismay over the articles of convention. The commander in chief could not "help complaining, most bitterly" to Richard Henry Lee "that this event will not equal our expectations; and that, without great precaution, and very delicate management, we shall have all these men, if not the officers, opposed to us in the spring." Experienced with British chicanery, Washington imagined that the ministry in London might "justify, a breach of the Covenant on their part" on the grounds "that no faith is to be held with Rebels." The general was not alone in his concerns. One of his aides, Colonel Samuel Webb, noted the mood of the army upon learning of Gates's terms: "We have this day the articles of treaty between Lt. Genl. Burgoyne and Major Genl. Gates, & 'tis the general opinion that Gates has given him much better terms than he need have done, which causes much uneasiness."[11]

Revolutionary Americans found the convention particularly galling because of the methods Burgoyne had used in his invasion of New York. Reverend Cooper decried the terms as "large and generous considering . . . the manner in which they have carried on the War." Similarly, Edward Stevens queried Alexander Hamilton to know why Gates had granted such "favorable Terms" to "*the Savage*" Burgoyne. This was not mere whig bombast. In July 1777 Burgoyne had promised Americans that he would bring "the vengeance of the state" against anyone who opposed him by spreading "devastation, famine, and every concomitant horror." He kept his word. British forces, including their loyalist and Native American allies, felt little compunction at pillaging, plundering, and burning rebel property on their march southward. Colonel Wilkinson claimed that "the hostile Indians" who "were let loose by the British commander" were guilty of "committing murders and spreading terror over the country." Although Burgoyne had not ordered or condoned murder, he had done little to restrain his loyalist and Native American auxiliaries. When a scouting party of British-allied Wyandot warriors allegedly scalped and murdered Jane McCrea, a young loyalist woman who was engaged to be married to one of Burgoyne's officers, the general issued a "very severe" reproach but did not punish the culprits for fear of losing the allies. This incident instantly became a propaganda sensation for the revolutionary cause. The American press painted McCrea as the virtuous victim of British depravity. Enraged by stories of "unmanly acts of murder upon women & Children," Laurens claimed that had he been in Burgoyne's position, he would "have Surrendered my Self to a pistol Ball in preference to becoming the prisoner of those people whom I had reviled by the Epithet of Rebels."[12]

As exaggerated accounts of her death proliferated, American animosity soared. The revolutionaries denounced Burgoyne as "the chief director of the King of Great Britain's band of thieves, robers [sic], cut throats, scalpers, and murderers." In the opinion of one concerned citizen, the general was a latter-day Duke of Cumberland, willing to "put to death in cold blood, without form of trial," all who opposed him. Because the British had evinced "barbarian Inhumanity" by violating "those Rules according to which civilized nations usually prosecute Wars," the New York Council of Safety petitioned Congress to demand that Burgoyne's army be kept as "Hostages for the future good Behavior of the Enemy." Congress had a duty to its citizens, who were "already ruined by their [British] Ravages," to "retard the Embarkation" of the troops. With a sizable army in American custody for the first time, the long-awaited opportunity for retribution on a grand scale had at last arrived. As the New York council phrased it: "We have long borne with their Inhumanity—Our Threats of Retaliation have hitherto been considered as Safe Words—it is Time to give them Efficacy—the Juncture is favorable. A brave People should dare to execute what they have thought it just to Threaten."[13]

Fear of retaliation was the last thing on the minds of Burgoyne's ragged and weary men as they trudged toward Boston; the troops were amazed by the generous terms of the accord and by the kind treatment they received from their erstwhile foes. Gates was adamant that from the moment they laid down their arms, the Crown troops would be treated with civility and respect. Under the articles of the convention, the Americans could not search the surrendered soldiers' personal baggage. Gates even agreed to provision the men "at the same rate of rations as the troops" of his own army until British transports arrived to carry them to Europe. Unlike the Americans captured at Fort Washington, Burgoyne's men did not endure taunts, beatings, or robberies in the aftermath of the surrender. British lieutenant William Digby was so impressed by the Americans' "decent behaviour" that he felt they "merited the utmost approbation and praise." The Germans were even more complimentary of their captors. According to one officer from the Brunswick Regiment Specht, the Americans "competed with each other to show us all possible niceties." While the captive officers dined with their American counterparts, the ravenous enlisted men enjoyed "good wheat flour and fresh meat" from American supplies, and their wounded countrymen received "tea, sugar, chocolate and wine" to ease their suffering. One of Burgoyne's German surgeons, who had been captured prior to the convention, was so pleased by his treatment that he admonished his countrymen to "learn to treat your friends as well as the inhabitants of New England treat their enemies!" In her postwar history, Mercy Otis Warren summarized the initial American response to the convention troops: "They were every where treated with such humanity, and even delicacy, that they were overwhelmed with astonishment and gratitude. Not one insult was offered, not an opprobrious reflection cast." The captured men could take comfort that, though defeated, they were entitled to all the privileges due to an army that had acquitted itself honorably.[14]

Despite Gates's best efforts to facilitate the march of the convention troops, Boston, and the prospect of a speedy passage home, lay at the end of an arduous three-week trek of over two hundred miles across the Green Mountains. The men already were exhausted. They had endured a grueling summer campaign, cutting their way through the New York forests from Canada while constantly pestered by American forces and, at times more vexing, American mosquitoes. Because revolutionary privateers had intercepted the army's 1777 clothing issue, their threadbare uniforms were literally disintegrating. To add to their distress, the weather turned colder as soon as the men began their march. One German officer reported that "the weather at night" was "so disagreeable" and included "not only rain but also snow and hail." Another complained that "our wet clothes froze as stiff as iron." Snow blanketed the soldiers as they slept. A Massachusetts militiaman feared that "many of the Hessians will die" before their arrival in Boston. When the column of troops reached the Green Mountains, "the roads across them were almost impassible." Ensign Anburey described the bedlam that ensued: "carts breaking down, others sticking fast, some oversetting, horses tumbling with their loads of baggage, men cursing, women shrieking, and children squalling!" In the laconic understatement of one German officer, "we made a very troublesome march."[15]

The trip was not nearly so arduous for General Burgoyne and his senior officers. Gates and his subordinate Major General Schuyler delighted in showing their European adversaries every courtesy and comfort. The Baroness Frederika von Riedesel, wife of the commander of Burgoyne's German allies, Major General Friedrich Adolf von Riedesel, observed that Gates and Burgoyne "were on very friendly terms" with one another. Schuyler invited the British commander and his entourage to join him in Albany, where they were welcomed "not as enemies, but in the friendliest manner possible." Traveling by coach, Burgoyne's party stopped frequently to sate the curiosity of American onlookers and to enjoy their hospitality. While the enlisted men and junior officers regularly bivouacked in the open, exposed to the elements, Burgoyne, Riedesel, and the other senior officers and their families were housed either by elite Americans along their route or in local inns and taverns. Closely mimicking European custom, the officers were feted and feasted all the way to Boston.[16]

When news of the impending arrival of Burgoyne's army reached Boston, the celebratory atmosphere soon subsided. The prospect of providing provisions and quarters for nearly six thousand famished and bone-chilled men plus their dependents sent residents into a frenzy. Where would they obtain flour, firewood, and beef in sufficient quantity at such a time of year? With a substantial British army and fleet ensconced at Newport, trade into and out of Boston was severely curtailed. Scarcity combined with the continual depreciation of Continental currency had driven the price of household necessities through the roof. Flour was in particularly short supply. To compound matters, Boston had yet to recover from Washington's protracted siege. The surrounding area had been completely deforested by his troops, forcing local inhabitants to depend on spotty and insufficient imports of fuel from Maine. Even before the troops arrived near town, the price of wood was fourteen dollars per cord. Hannah Winthrop, a resident of Cambridge, estimated that the Convention Army would consume more than 250 cords per week. She wondered rhetorically to Mercy Otis Warren, "Is there not a degree of unkindness in loading poor Cambridge, almost ruined before this great army seemed to be let loose upon us?" The president of the Massachusetts Council, Jeremiah Powell, echoed her sentiments when he informed John Hancock, "it will be very distressing to us, under our present Circumstances, as well as dangerous to the United States to have those Troops Continued here for any time." He worried that the presence of such a large body of enemy soldiers would serve "to poison the minds of our People and to divide them." Powell hoped that Congress would use its

"Authority & Influence" to see that the troops were dispatched to England "with all possible Expedition."[17]

Fortunately for the government of Massachusetts, the convention troops were at least nominally wards of the Continental Army, thus their immediate direction fell to the military commander of the Eastern Department, Major General William Heath. More farmer than soldier, the Massachusetts native had failed to capture British-occupied Fort Independence in January 1777, staining his military reputation. Viewed by Washington as more suited for an administrative rather than a combat role, Heath was transferred to Boston and out of harm's way. Rising to the command of the Eastern Department when Major General Artemas Ward retired in March 1777, Heath was utterly unprepared for the myriad challenges before him. Gates had forwarded enough provisions to get the conventioners to Boston, but once arrived, they were Heath's problem. The general bemoaned to Washington the "wide and difficult Field" he faced: "to provide Quarters, provisions, Fuel &c. for Five or Six Thousand Men will be no small Task." Although he was determined to "treat them [on the one hand] with politeness & humanity and on the other with precaution and strict Order," Heath begged the Virginian "to facilitate their removal as soon as possible, as their continuance for any considerable time will greatly distress the Inhabitants both as to provisions and Fuel." In the meantime, he appealed to the civilian authorities in the Massachusetts Assembly for whatever assistance they could provide.[18]

Inclined to help but loath to accept any added responsibility, the assembly, in characteristic republican form, appointed a committee "to consider what Provision etc. is necessary to be made for the Reception of the Prisoners." The committee concluded that Burgoyne's army could not be properly subsisted in Boston—the town simply lacked the necessary infrastructure to house and feed so many people. Aware that the fourth article of the Saratoga Convention required the men to be quartered "in, near, or as convenient as possible to Boston," the assembly could not disperse the troops throughout the countryside to work for their subsistence, as was the standard American procedure for prisoners of war at the time. Compromising, state authorities allowed General Heath to house the men outside of Cambridge in barracks on Prospect Hill and Winter Hill, which had the added benefit of being sufficiently isolated from the bulk of Boston's population to discourage fraternization. Only the senior officers, who presumably were less likely to escape, were to be quartered within the Cambridge town limits, though even they were debarred from visiting Boston. Isolated on their hilltop barracks, the conquered troops could be more easily provisioned and supervised, and Boston would be spared the invariable disorder that would result from soldiers roaming the streets at will. To enforce their orders, the assemblymen authorized Heath, who possessed only a skeleton garrison of Continentals, to raise "one thousand men, including officers . . . , from such parts of the militia of this State" to serve as guards under the general's direct command. He requested 1,200 men, but even finding 1,000 to do guard duty proved difficult because Bostonians were in no mood to be cooperative.[19]

The arrival in their midst of throngs of filthy and malodorous enemy soldiers—men the revolutionary press had portrayed as wanton murderers, plunderers, and rapists—incensed area residents. To the wary whigs of Boston, these men were not only godless mercenaries who had pillaged and plagued the frontiers of New England, but as vectors of the twin contagions of smallpox and royalism, they also were a direct threat to the health, economy, and political stability of the region. Winthrop described the November 7 arrival of Burgoyne's German troops at Winter Hill, about a mile and a half outside of Cambridge, as "truly astonishing." She could not believe that "creation produced such a sordid set of creatures in human figure—poor, dirty, emaciated men" accompanied by "great numbers of women, who seemed to be beasts of burden . . . , barefoot, [and] clothed in dirty rags." The stench must have been arresting. According to Winthrop, "effluvia filled the air while they were passing." Only their constant smoking allayed her fears of being contaminated.[20]

At least the Germans looked like prisoners and objects of pity; the British were proudly "prancing and patrolling in every corner of the town, ornamented with their glittering side-arms—weapons of destruction," even insisting that the residents "ought not to look on them as Prisoners." Winthrop feared that Burgoyne's officers, who lived in "the most Luxurious manner possible, rioting on the Fat of the Land, Stalking at Large with the Self-importance of Lords of the Soil," would prove a corrupting influence on the town's population. Her concerns must have been commonplace. Roger Lamb, a corporal in the Convention Army, remembered "the general unwillingness of the people [of Cambridge] to administer the least civility" to the troops. In his opinion, "the people of New England appeared to indulge a deadly hatred against the British prisoners." A far cry from the kindness and civility they had received from Gates and his officers, the troops encountered only antipathy from the inhabitants, who like Winthrop believed that the Convention Army would leave only "insults, famine, and a train of evils" in their wake. Both sides agreed that the transport ships that would carry the soldiers to England could not arrive soon enough.[21]

The vessels were nowhere to be seen when the men marched into the dilapidated ruins of barracks that dotted the barren and exposed hills outside of Boston. These makeshift shelters had been constructed in the second half of 1775 to house Washington's besieging troops, but no one had bothered to see to their upkeep after the army departed for New York in the spring of 1776. Briefly used to house smallpox victims who were beyond hope of recovery, the bulk of the buildings were now entirely unsuitable for human habitation. As one of Burgoyne's Brunswick grenadiers, Johann Bense, described: "The barracks were only put together with boards. The gables were open; there were no windows but just open holes. We had neither wood nor straw to lie on. . . . [I]n short, we were the most wretched people." Each "small, miserable, open hut" housed "thirty, or forty persons, men, women and children . . . indiscriminately crowded together," according to Corporal Lamb. All endured "the chill peltings" of the November rain and snow, "which the wind drifted" into the open barracks. Gnawing hunger occasioned by food shortages compounded their predicament. In late November Heath's adjutant reported that the troops on Winter Hill were "entirely destitute of vegetables, Poultry, Roots &c." The results were predictable: disease and malnutrition began to take a toll on the captives. Grenadier Bense noted that "many died of scurvy" during their confinement outside Boston. But at least the survivors could take solace in the knowledge that their confinement was temporary. Surely, the transports would arrive before the Massachusetts winter made their embarkation impracticable.[22]

Barracks life was little better for Burgoyne's officers. Anburey was horrified by his quarters. In his opinion, they were "in the worst condition imaginable for the reception of troops, being so much out of repair." According to one of the ensign's German colleagues: "The barracks are without foundations, and built of boards, through which the rain and snow penetrate from all sides. . . . [O]ur people have to endure a great deal of hardship while in them, as they afford not the least protection against the cold." The officers, who were accustomed to a certain level of comfort and privacy even while on active duty, were disgusted to learn that they would live six to a room "not twelve feet square" inside the barracks. Sharing common bunks that one German officer characterized as "holes in which it is impossible to turn one's self" at night, the men struggled to keep warm. With threadbare blankets and no wood for the fireplaces, shared body heat alone prevented the onset of hypothermia. The colonel commanding the American guards, William Raymond Lee, informed Heath that he discovered "Field Officers & some Others walking by their Barracks to keep themselves from perishing with cold; not one stick of Wood to put into the Fire." Lee believed that "if some other method cannot be found to supply them they must either perish or burn all the Publick buildings." One forlorn German summarized the prevailing mood in the barracks: "we are now living in misery."[23]

The officers had every right to grumble. Heath knew that under the seventh article of the convention, they were entitled to be "quartered according to rank." As the departmental commander, it was the general's responsibility to see to the comfort and entertainment of the captured officers and to the health and provision of the enlisted men. When their quarters and provisions failed to live up to their expectations, Heath became the object of the officers' indignation. Attempting to ameliorate their plight, he dashed off a frenetic series of letters to the Massachusetts Council, the governors of neighboring states, Congress, and General Washington—all to no avail. Even Commissary General Joseph Trumbull refused to supply the captives with flour without a direct order from Congress, which he knew would not be forthcoming. Incensed by the terms of the Saratoga Convention, Congress was not about to share valuable provisions, which were so badly needed by its own soldiers, with an enemy army on the verge of embarkation. The people of Cambridge proved equally obstinate. Landlords banded together to refuse housing to Burgoyne's senior officers except at ruinous rates, well beyond the means of all but the general himself. From their perspective, they had not been party to the negotiations between Gates and Burgoyne and therefore had no qualms about profiting from the captives. Unsurprisingly, the city's merchants were also keen to exploit the enemy consumers. Prices soared. Anburey recorded that "every species of provisions was very dear." He regularly traversed over a mile in the snow to procure enough milk for his breakfast. This was hardly the lap of luxury that Hannah Winthrop had feared would erode the virtuous republican spirit of Boston.[24]

Witnessing his army's distress, Burgoyne fumed. Gates had led him to expect that Bostonians would accord his troops the respect due to honorable foes. He could not sit idly by and submit to such indignities, which sullied not only the royal cause but also his personal honor. Upon inspecting the officers' barracks and noting that "the quarters allotted to them would be held unfit for gentlemen in their situation in any part of the world," Burgoyne informed Heath that he and his men believed "that the Convention [was] infringed in several circumstances." He was aghast that neither Heath nor the members of the Massachusetts Council were willing to impress private property for the officers' use, as was the custom in European conflicts. Not fully grasping the limitations of republican government, the British general suspected that their intransigence stemmed from a sinister plan to break the Saratoga Convention and consign his troops to indefinite captivity. In protest, Burgoyne instructed his officers to refuse signing their paroles until their grievances were redressed.[25]

In his public letters to Burgoyne, Heath denied any infraction of the convention, but privately he worried that his inability to properly quarter the troops might besmirch the "Honor and Dignity of Congress and of the United States." He sought guidance from Congress, reminding President Laurens that the convention was "the first made by these rising States which will be nicely review'd by all the polite States in Europe, and the World." The general knew that, according to Vattel, "all promises made to an enemy in the course of a war are obligatory." If he could not enforce the terms of the convention, the reputation of the United States would suffer, as would the quest for European allies. Heath needed money or at least direct orders from Congress granting him permission to bypass the Massachusetts Council and requisition the supplies and buildings he so desperately required. While awaiting instructions, all the general could do was assure Burgoyne that "no Endeavors of mine shall be wanting to fulfill the Convention."[26]

Heath's best efforts were simply not good enough. Congress had saddled him with the thankless task of upholding Gates's agreement without the funds, manpower, or authority to do so. Bostonians had made it abundantly clear that they either wanted nothing to do with the convention troops or intended to profit from their distress; the Massachusetts Council refused to deviate from the desires of its constituents. In a desperate letter to the council, Heath exclaimed, "Every principle of interest and policy calls for our attention to the fulfillment of the Convention." But no one listened. The general had done everything in his limited purview to prevent any infraction of the terms that might reflect poorly on the honor of his country and person, but without a sizable influx of capital, all was for naught. On November 23 an exasperated Heath confessed to Washington that he was "not a little embarrassed in obtaining Quarters for the Officers" and "much embarrassed in the Commissary's

Department." Determined to play the part of the professional officer in the
European mold, he could not help but take this failure personally.[27]

As the weeks passed and the oft-promised support failed to materialize,
both Heath and his captive guests anxiously awaited the only viable solution
to their problems: the embarkation of the troops for Britain. Although sailing to
Boston so late in the year was precarious at best, and Congress had refused to
change the departure point to the more easily accessible British-occupied
Newport, both parties held out hope that the transports would arrive before
the new year. As far as Heath was concerned, the sooner the conventioners
departed, the better. He informed Laurens that they were consuming nearly
$20,000 of provisions and fuel a week just to maintain basic subsistence, and
they were escaping in droves. Because Congress had failed to provide him with
a suitable supply of sufficiently trained guards, Heath could do little to stem
the tide. By Christmas, the situation had grown untenable, Heath reporting,
"my situation [is] truly disagreeable." Word of the arrival of the British transports at Newport lifted his spirits, however. As he told Laurens, with any luck,
"the Continuance of the Troops of the Convention here will be but short."
Regrettably for Burgoyne's ill-fated army, Congress had other plans.[28]

Congressional Retaliation

When Burgoyne sat down at his rented desk in a Cambridge tavern to apprise
his former colleague turned capturer of his army's predicament, he could
never have imagined the ramifications of his prose. In what General Heath
would later call "a very serious entanglement," Burgoyne complained to Gates
of the "very unexpected treatment" he and his army had received from the
people of the Boston area. While acquitting Heath and his officers of any
wrongdoing, the general alleged that the Massachusetts Council's inability—
or unwillingness—to provide adequate quarters for his soldiers constituted
a violation of the Saratoga Convention. As he informed Gates, "the public
faith is broke; & we are the immediate sufferers." The American did not dispute
his old comrade's critique; Brigadier General John Glover, the American
officer who had overseen the march of the convention troops to Boston, had
already informed him of the housing crisis. Gates was mortified. The two men
had pledged their word of honor as gentlemen to uphold all the articles of the
accord. He had no proof of any violation on Burgoyne's part, and the evidence

of American infractions was voluminous. But Gates was no longer in charge of the army's fate. All the "Hero of Saratoga" could do was forward Burgoyne's concerns to Congress.[29]

Far from serving its intended purpose of improving his army's plight, Burgoyne's remonstrance convinced President Laurens that the British general intended to violate the convention himself. He reasoned that by alleging an American breach of faith, Burgoyne might justify repudiating the agreement as soon as he and his army were safely aboard British ships. Laurens had already suspected that the general had not been entirely straightforward in his dealings with Gates. A committee of Congress had reported in late November that Burgoyne had turned over an insufficient quantity of arms and military stores. What had happened to the regimental flags and the army's pay chest? Why had these not been relinquished as well? In the opinion of the committee, "the whole return seems very inadequate to a well appointed army." Most likely, the report speculated, the Crown troops had destroyed much of their arms and ammunition and secreted away their currency and colors prior to their march to Boston. Given this apparent disingenuous behavior, Laurens could not believe Burgoyne's audacity in insinuating that Congress had violated the agreement. Fulminating, the president advised Heath that "it will be impossible to part with [Burgoyne] before an eclaircissement is had on this important charge." Congress had previously resolved that the investigation would in no way delay the embarkation of the troops, but in the aftermath of Burgoyne's letter to Gates, Laurens had no intention of allowing the general to depart until he retracted his allegation and allowed Heath to conduct a full accounting of the captured army's strength and remaining military stores.[30]

Although lacking substantive evidence, there was some truth to Laurens's suspicions. At the time of the convention, Burgoyne had assured Gates that he had deliberately left his regimental flags in Canada and thus could not surrender them. The American had accepted his word of honor as a gentleman and had pursued the issue no further. But Burgoyne had not been truthful—his army had marched to Saratoga with its colors. Surrendering the flags, which the men had carried throughout the campaign, would have destroyed the morale of his army and obviated his claim that his troops were not in fact prisoners. The proud Briton was not about to hand them over to a parcel of rebellious traitors. What happened to the flags is not entirely clear. Once the convention was agreed upon, Burgoyne's German troops burned their flag-staffs but saved their colors by sewing them into Baroness von Riedesel's mattress. These "badges of honor" were later smuggled into New York and eventually returned to the regiments stationed in Canada. One bold British officer was so determined to preserve his unit's colors that he risked carrying them throughout his captivity in his personal baggage. When he later presented them to the king, his bravery was rewarded with a colonel's commission. As for the other British flags, presumably they were either similarly preserved or at the very least destroyed. None of Burgoyne's colors were surrendered as trophies of war to be hung on the walls of Congress.[31]

Notwithstanding Burgoyne's duplicity concerning the flags, Congress's other critiques were unsubstantiated. In his letter to Laurens, Gates assured the president that he possessed no evidence "to justify our Charge of their having violated the Convention." If there were fewer muskets and bayonets than might be expected for such a large army, the only culprits were "Our own Men" who augmented their paltry supply from the pile of weapons the Britons left behind. As for the money and medical supplies, Burgoyne had exhausted both prior to signing the convention. Gates did admit that he should have stipulated that the troops surrender their cartridge pouches, but he had not included this proviso in the terms and to do so now would constitute a severe breach of faith. Given his knowledge of Burgoyne's actions, Gates was unwilling to placate the president by adding his voice to the growing number of revolutionaries calling for a suspension of the compact. This was not what Laurens wanted to hear. Even if Burgoyne had not directly infringed the agreement, his charge that the "public faith is broke" was too serious to ignore. Laurens appointed a committee to investigate the claim and to determine a suitable response. After considering the charges "with mature attention," the committee offered its opinion on December 27, 1777.[32]

Officially, the report reiterated the accusations about missing military stores and Burgoyne's intransigence; unofficially, it toyed with revenge. One member's notes listed "the Unprecedented Cruelties to which the Subjects of the US, prisoners in N.Y. & Philada. are, continually Exposed" alongside "General Burgoyne's Letter" as reasons to detain the Crown troops. These charges of British mistreatment of American prisoners never made it into the final report. More than likely, the committee realized that such allegations were insufficient grounds to negate the convention under the laws of war. Members felt that they were on firmer ground when it came to Burgoyne himself. "The apprehensions of General Burgoyne's future intentions" to disregard the accord were warranted and the general's "personal honor . . .

hereby destroyed." The army's departure should be delayed until the "King of Great Britain shall on his part cause his ratification of the said agreement to be properly notified to these States." But those on the committee and in Congress knew all too well that the king would never ratify a formal agreement with rebels—to do so would be to acknowledge the United States as a sovereign power.[33]

The recommendation was a bold departure from previous policy. It is true that Congress had overturned the treaty of capitulation of the Cedars, as well as Arnold's cartel of exchange with Captain Forster in the summer of 1776, though not before conducting extensive eyewitness interviews and concluding that the British had openly violated each agreement by abusing American prisoners. Burgoyne had done no such thing. If delegates voted to approve the committee's resolution, they would be openly invalidating the first international accord in which a senior congressional representative pledged the honor and faith of the United States. Doing so would be a clear violation of the laws of war and nations as enunciated by Vattel and an absolute rejection of the norms of the European culture of limited warfare. Richard Henry Lee feared that the British would use even "the appearance of infraction on our part" to "totally ruin the reputation" of the young nation in the eyes of the world. Unsurprisingly, the mood in the chamber was tense. Rather than make a hasty decision, the delegates resolved to suspend discussion until a later date.[34]

Almost a week elapsed before Congress again addressed the issue of the Saratoga Convention. The members had had plenty of time to consider the committee's recommendations and to imagine the implications of their actions. Looking out at his colleagues from the president's chair, Laurens must have sensed their uncertainty. Everyone in the room knew where the president stood on the issue, but did he have enough votes to suspend the embarkation? Before the vote was called, a portly delegate from New Jersey, the Scottish Presbyterian cleric John Witherspoon, addressed his assembled colleagues.[35]

As Congress's chaplain and a member of the Board of War, Witherspoon was an ideal advocate for Laurens's position. He began his speech by calming the more conservative delegates, admitting that "the convention is not so broken, on the part of General Burgoyne, as to entitle us to refuse compliance with it on ours, and detain him and his army as prisoners of war." It was imperative, Witherspoon maintained, for an infant state like theirs to "preserve its faith and honour in solemn contracts." Yet it was also the "indispensable duty" of every member to see that "justice be done to the American States." The reverend eschewed recourse to the scholarly works on the laws of nations; instead, he asked his colleagues to use their powers of reason. Burgoyne's letter of November 14 was "of the most alarming nature" because by alleging "that the convention is broken on our part, he will not hold to it on his." To this logic, Witherspoon added a discourse on Burgoyne's character and career. As one of the British commanders during the siege of Boston, the general had called the burning of Charlestown "a glorious light." During his march from Canada, he had issued a "lofty and sonorous proclamation" promising violence and destruction to all who opposed him. By his actions, Burgoyne had shown himself to be "showy, vain, impetuous, and rash." In short, he was not to be trusted. On these grounds—and these grounds alone—Congress should impede his departure until it was clear that he could do the people of the United States no more harm.[36]

Debate ensued for several more days, but Witherspoon had been convincing. On January 8, 1778, after what Laurens characterized as "a long time on the Anvil," he called for a vote on the recommendation to suspend the embarkation of the troops until the Saratoga Convention was ratified by the court of Great Britain. Enraged by alleged Crown atrocities and duplicities, fourteen members chose to forsake the norms of "civilized" warfare that they had so assiduously guarded since the conflict began. Only four dared to oppose the measure. Lacking any legitimate evidence of wrongdoing on Burgoyne's part, or even the pretense of proportional retaliation, Congress thus resolved to hold the conventioners for the foreseeable future. Clearly satisfied, Laurens sent orders to General Heath "to detain the said Lieutenant General Burgoyne[,] his Officers[,] Troops[,] and other persons and to suspend their intended embarkation until you shall be further Instructed."[37]

Little did Laurens know, but his assessment of Burgoyne's intentions was correct. On November 16 Howe had written the general in secret with a plan to free the convention troops from the Americans. The previous winter he had released nearly two thousand sickly American prisoners from captivity under an agreement with Washington that an equal number of captured Britons would be returned in their stead. Washington was not about to release thousands of largely healthy British and German soldiers in exchange for the specters Howe had sent him. In the convention troops, though, the Crown commander saw an opportunity to recoup his losses. He therefore instructed Burgoyne that when the troops were "embarked, he is to proceed with the British Artillery men and Infantry to New York, my Design being to exchange the officers for those of the Rebels in my Possession, and the soldiers for the 2,220 Prisoners of the Enemy, that I sent in last Winter." Howe justified his decision by assuring the general that he intended "only to repair an Injury in which Mr. Washington so obstinately persists." Knowing that Congress and Washington would not agree with his logic, he ordered Burgoyne "to use every possible Precaution to keep the Enemy ignorant of my Intentions." Without ever learning of Howe's plan, however, Laurens and his followers had thwarted the British commander, leaving the convention troops in limbo: not quite prisoners, but certainly not free.[38]

When news of the resolution leaked, fervent revolutionaries everywhere rejoiced. President Laurens was pleased to learn that his diligent efforts "for effecting the determination of Congress for suspending the embarkation of Mr. Burgoyne" met with the approbation of "the most sensible [civilians] and by all the officers in the Army." John Thaxter, a congressional clerk, was convinced that it was Burgoyne, not Congress, who had violated the agreement. He assured Abigail Adams that "the treaty has not been violated by us," and therefore Congress was "determined not to recede from their resolution of 8th of Jany." Radical Pennsylvania delegate Daniel Roberdeau knew the real cause for the resolution. He informed John Adams that Congress had passed "a lex talionis" for British cruelties that were "unheared [sic] of among Nations called civilized." The "cruel usage and whippings" American prisoners endured at British hands "coroborates [sic] the reasons for suspending the Convention at Saratoga." Roberdeau closed his missive with biblical verse: "Vengeance is mine I will repay saith the Lord."[39]

For furious revolutionaries like Roberdeau, the issue of who had violated the convention first mattered not at all; the British had long since demonstrated their cruelty and perfidy. Scarcely a day went by without an account in the newspapers of another atrocity. To irate whigs everywhere, it looked as if Congress had finally acted to obtain justice for the long-suffering American prisoners in New York. Governor Livingston, writing in the New-Jersey Gazette under the pseudonym "Adolphus," proudly proclaimed: "The detention of Burgoyne and his army, until the Convention of Saratoga is ratified by the Court of Great Britain, is a measure founded on the truest policy and strictest justice." His rationale had nothing to do with missing munitions or hidden standards but was instead predicated upon the repeated mistreatment of American prisoners. Reminding his readers of the plight of the Fort Washington garrison, Livingston asked how they could trust the British to uphold the

Saratoga Convention when "three thousand freemen capitulate on condition of being treated as *prisoners of war*—but the moment their arms are out of their hands, they are treated as *rebels*, crowded together in the holds of transports, or amidst the unwholesome damps of churches, and suffered to perish with hunger and cold." The answer was simple—they could not. From the outset of the conflict, "Adolphus" argued, Americans had treated British prisoners "generously while they [the British] violated every principle of justice—we treated them kindly while they outraged every sentiment of humanity— . . . we have born their cruelty and frauds with a patience unparalleled in history." The only recourse Americans now possessed was to treat the British as they deserved, "as robbers and murderers when they presume to treat us as rebels."[40]

Some revolutionaries, however, were less inclined to discard their vision of the normative practice of warfare between "civilized" peoples. To them, the resolution compromised the reputation of the United States and insulted General Gates. Hamilton, who aspired to be the very model of a European gentleman officer, was horrified. He accused Congress of having "embraced a system of infidelity." As he complained to the governor of New York, George Clinton, "they have violated the convention of Saratoga; and I have reason to believe the ostensible motives for it were little better than pretences, that had no foundation." Even President Laurens's own son John, an officer in the Continental Army who supported the resolution, cautioned his father: "It might have been better perhaps if a little more republican laconism had been used in explaining the reasons for it." In his opinion, it would have been preferable to offer no justification at all; the evidence of bad faith on Burgoyne's part was simply not there. James Wilkinson, the officer tasked by Gates to inform Congress of the convention, felt "equally hurt and alarmed" by the news. He confessed to Gates: "I consider [the conventioners'] detention inadmissible in the spirit of the treaty. I fear a timorous circumspection has sullied our reputation, and injured our cause." Years later, long after victory in the war was assured, Wilkinson still maintained that Congress's actions were "unworthy [of] the representatives of a free people." He would gladly have "fought over the campaign again, sooner than suffer the national honour to be tarnished."[41]

Surprisingly, Washington was silent on the issue. Given his oft-repeated insistence on the humane treatment of prisoners of war and his prior diligent observance of the laws of nations, Congress's resolution could not have sat

easily with him. By the winter of 1777–78, the general was no stranger to proportional retaliation, but to suspend a treaty agreed upon by two senior officers
on the mere pretense of a violation was something else. On January 9 Washington notified Laurens that the resolution would undoubtedly much "chagrine"
Burgoyne, but he passed no judgment on the proceedings of Congress. The
Virginian imagined himself as that body's servant, and although he did not
always agree with its actions, he could not publicly criticize his civilian masters.
He was also cognizant of the manifold benefits of delaying the troops' embarkation. Howe had had the better of Washington's army during the previous
campaign, and the remnants of that tattered force were suffering in the cold at
Valley Forge. With Philadelphia, New York, and Newport in British hands, the
addition of six thousand fresh troops in the spring might be enough to anni-
hilate the decimated Continental forces—and with them, the Revolution.[42]

Above all, Washington, like most of his countrymen, was furious about
the frequent accounts of the mistreatment of American prisoners. Only twelve
days after the resolution passed, and long before his British counterpart had
learned of the suspension of Burgoyne's embarkation, the general warned
Howe that "Americans have the feelings of Sympathy, as well as Other men—A
series of injuries may exhaust their patience—and it is natural that the Sufferings of their Friends in captivity should at length irritate them into resentment
and to acts of retaliation." It seems probable that even Washington, the exemplar
of revolutionary America's commitment to the European culture of war, had
simply had enough. On Laurens's advice he agreed to keep the resolution secret
until General Burgoyne could be officially notified and General Heath's garrison strengthened lest the British attempt to liberate the troops by force.
Despite the best efforts of Congress, it did not take long for the news to reach
Boston. Even before the final version was approved, Burgoyne was aware of its
contents.[43]

The congressional resolution was the last thing that Heath and his beleaguered garrison of guards needed that winter. Tensions between the British
troops and their American captors were already elevated before rumors of the
measure circulated. According to a German officer, "there is tremendous
animosity between the American and the English soldiers, and there have been
many vexatious occurrences." Resentment escalated precipitously when stories
of the pending suspension reached Prospect Hill. The American commandant
of the British barracks, Colonel David Henley, whom Heath would later characterize as "warm and quick in his natural temper," reported that "the prisoners

have been mutinous, their Behavior insolent and outrageous." One soldier
threw a stone at an American sentry, "which deprived him of his reason and
near his life." Others "arm'd themselves with clubs &c," daring the guards to
fire. The Americans dispersed the mob "with firelocks club'd," but the next
day a larger contingent of furious Britons challenged them. Henley assembled
his guards, leading them against the rioters with sword in hand. Seeing the
futility of opposing a battalion of armed men, the captives began to disband,
though not with enough alacrity to placate the colonel. His temper soaring,
Henley ran "a British soldier through the body [with his sword] and push[ed]
with such force" that it proved fatal. Standing over the dying man, he had no
regrets, firmly believing that "lenity is often constru'd as timidity and . . . more
vigorous exertions necessary." Rounding up about forty conventioners who
had participated in the unrest, Henley sent them under guard to a prison ship
in Boston Harbor. Unlike the British hulks at New York and Newport, which
were the only viable option for housing enemy prisoners on those densely
populated occupied islands, the prison ships in Boston existed solely for vengeful incarceration.[44]

Retaliation had now come to dominate the American discourse on prisoner
treatment. Through the tireless efforts of the revolutionary press, readers
throughout the continent were exposed to a barrage of articles enumerating
British abuses of American prisoners, many of them New England privateers,
in New York, Newport, and Philadelphia. One New England columnist contrasted the fate of "our countrymen perishing with cold or hunger in the goals
[sic] of our enemies" to the experience of "the British and Hessian soldiers now
among us, [who] enjoy plenty, warm fires, and the benefits arising from their
labour." Why were these enemy captives allowed to roam about Cambridge
seemingly at will, when American prisoners were dying by the day? The correspondent enjoined his countrymen: "Do not heaven and earth call upon us
to put a stop to this pitiful milk and water kind of humanity, and to comepll
[sic] our enemies to act justly, by Retaliation?" Like many of his colleagues,
Connecticut general Israel Putnam thought "the Treatment which the Enemy
have given to the unfortunate officers and soldiers of our Army who have fallen
into their hands makes some step for Retaliation absolutely necessary." He
believed that all British prisoners should be exiled to the subterranean Newgate
Prison at the Simsbury mines. Upon hearing of the alleged massacre of some
American dragoons in October 1778, John Beatty, who by then had replaced
Boudinot as the Continental commissary general of prisoners, suggested

executing two conventioners for every American slain in the action. Proportional retaliation had not worked; "no other method" but excessive force would "reach their sensibility," he declared. Massachusetts-born Major Jonathan Rice preferred a more moderate plan. If the British were going to use prison ships, so too should the Americans. As he confided to one of Heath's aides in August 1778, "I wish every Briton now on Prospect-Hill was on board ye Guard-Ship."[45]

Although unwilling to consign the entire Convention Army to nautical confinement in the winter of 1777–78, Commissary General of Prisoners Boudinot authorized his deputy commissaries in Connecticut and Boston to outfit prison ships in their states for the purpose of retaliation. Prison ships were hardly novel weapons in the revolutionary arsenal, several states already using them to confine convicted loyalists. But with British prisoners now targets of retaliation, the revolutionaries needed more such vessels. Deputy Commissary of Prisoners Joshua Mersereau informed Boudinot that Connecticut planned to purchase a 500-ton Dutch ship that could hold "4 or 500" men; authorities began filling that vessel with British prisoners in April 1778. Those not protected by the convention would be the first so incarcerated, but in the likely event that some of Burgoyne's men proved rowdy or felonious, they too should face imprisonment aboard a hulk.[46]

Boudinot's prison-ship orders came as no surprise to Massachusetts commissary of prisoners Robert Pierpont, who had been confining enemy prisoners aboard ship in Boston Harbor for months. When Ensign Thomas Hughes arrived as a prisoner in Boston in early October 1777, he and six fellow officers "were crowded into a hole" of a prison ship where "every crevice is full of vermin." In addition to the officers, Massachusetts authorities relegated over two hundred enlisted prisoners, "with countenances the pictures of famine," to that ship's hold. Because of congestion, poor sanitation, and insufficient rations, disease spread rapidly. Hughes suffered from "violent dysentery," while his captain was afflicted by "fever." Several hundred Canadian loyalists and Brunswick troops, captured at the Battle of Bennington and thus not included in the Saratoga Convention, experienced a similar fate aboard the prison ships. In November the captives petitioned Commissary Pierpont, explaining "that our situation is too disagreeable to continue long, the farther we go the worse we are; being reduced to lay one upon the other, the vermin devouring us." When their pleas fell on deaf ears, they then begged Burgoyne to intercede on their behalf, for if he did not, "more than half will never live to see spring." The general could do little to help the men without compromising his argument that a firm distinction be made between traditional prisoners of war and the convention troops. He knew that if Henley had his way, his entire army might be destined for the prison ships.[47]

When Burgoyne received intelligence of the riot and its violent suppression, it looked as if his fears had come to fruition. He was indignant. Under the terms of the convention, his men were not prisoners and thus were not subject to American military justice. If his soldiers were guilty of misbehavior, it was his prerogative, not Henley's, to discipline them. On January 9, 1778, Burgoyne admonished Heath for allowing the colonel's "heinously criminal" behavior to go unpunished. In his strongly worded reproach, the general accused Henley "of the most indecent, violent, vindictive severity against unarmed men, and of intentional murder." Not only did he demand that Heath release the conventioners aboard the prison ships, but he also called for "a proper tribunal" to try Henley for murder. Only "prompt and satisfactory justice" would suffice.[48]

Heath was in a difficult position. He knew of the rumors that Congress intended to delay the troops' departure, but he remained under orders to uphold the terms of Gates's convention to the best of his abilities. Unwilling to abandon the charade without positive instructions from Laurens to the contrary, Heath politely acknowledged Burgoyne's letter and promptly removed Henley from his post pending an investigation. The general was unwilling, however, to deny the right of American authorities to punish disorderly or criminal members of the Convention Army. He assured Burgoyne that "it is my fixed Determination, to Enquire into all abuses, whether Committed by my own Troops or those of the Convention." While this assertion of absolute American authority over the conventioners likely irked Burgoyne, he was mollified by the swift response to his complaint. Heath even allowed Burgoyne to act as a de facto prosecutor at Henley's trial.[49]

No stranger to the public stage, Burgoyne, who possessed both the legal erudition of a long-standing member of Parliament and the dramatic flair of a passionate devotee of the theatrical arts, thrived during the proceedings. He was so persuasive in his denunciation of Henley that the American judge advocate, whose duty it was to prosecute the case, took on the mantle of defense attorney to give the colonel a fighting chance. As it turned out, Henley had little to fear from the court itself. Were the judges to rule in Burgoyne's favor, they would be repudiating Heath's, and by extension Congress's, claim of jurisdiction over the convention troops. Predictably, Henley was cleared of all wrongdoing and was officially reinstated to his post. Heath soon transferred the colonel back to his regiment and away from Burgoyne, an acknowledgment of the British general's herculean defense of his soldiers.[50]

Although he did not know it at the time, Burgoyne's performance at Colonel Henley's trial was the final act in his American saga. On February 4, 1778, Heath formally notified the general of Congress's resolution to suspend the troops' embarkation. Burgoyne was despondent; sadness rather than outrage characterized his response. Upholding the Saratoga Convention, and thereby returning his men to active service, was the only means of repairing his shattered reputation in England. With this prospect extinguished, Burgoyne finally surrendered. The vim and vigor that once characterized his correspondence evaporated. Fearing that the general would attempt to escape, Washington had authorized Heath to increase his garrison of guards, but that was entirely unnecessary. The formerly fortunate gamester had played his last card, and now all he desired was to retire to England on his parole. With Washington's support, Congress resolved in March to allow him to proceed home by way of Rhode Island. The general sailed for England in April, never again to return to the continent that he had aspired to conquer.[51]

Not all Britons shared Burgoyne's quiet resignation. His officers believed that Congress had no right to suspend the terms of the treaty. After all, the convention had been established between two military officers based on their personal honor and reputations. To an eighteenth-century European officer, such contracts were inviolate. Ensign Anburey believed that only Americans could "be base enough to evade and break the articles of capitulation." In his opinion, "the Conduct of Congress upon this extraordinary transaction, is extremely visible." Anburey and his comrades indicted the delegates for doing the unthinkable, failing to honor the norms of European warfare. For the ensign, the Americans had chosen "to sacrifice their faith and reputation . . . by an act never excusable." A British officer in New York seconded Anburey's indignation: "the congress have acted unworthy of themselves and shewen the world what a nest of villians [sic] they are by the detention of General Burgoin and his troops in breach of the convention." In Parliament, even staunch whigs who had opposed the war expressed "their Abhorrence of Congress" and demanded that Americans "be treated as savages for Shamefully violating the Convention of Saratoga." For Britons on both sides of the Atlantic, Congress had obliterated any claim to legitimacy. France and other potential allies would finally see the Americans for who they really were: rebels and rank amateurs.[52]

With their embarkation suspended indefinitely, the enlisted men no longer felt bound by the terms of the treaty. In Corporal Lamb's opinion, he and his comrades were "under no tie of honour" since "Congress had no intention of allowing the British troops to return to England." Due to this duplicity, Lamb believed it was his duty to escape to New York to rejoin the fight. British officers, who had previously discouraged desertion when the troops were slated for departure, now agreed with Lamb and openly encouraged their men to flee. Deputy Commissary Mersereau reported that "above 200" Britons escaped to New York that winter, blaming the desertions on poor discipline among the guards and the illicit practice of recruiting conventioners whose sole motive was to escape and return to British service. Heath was embarrassed, but he could do nothing "to prevent the troops from dispersing" except appeal to Congress and the Massachusetts Council for more men and more money, neither of which was forthcoming.[53]

For General Heath, Congress's decision to detain the convention troops proved an onerous burden. The resolution had not been accompanied by a vast appropriation of capital to his department or the authority to requisition civilian property for housing the captives. He had begged and borrowed enough food-stuffs and necessities to keep the men from starving that winter, but by the spring of 1778, the general was absolutely at the end of his tether. In March Heath explained to Laurens that the "troops of the Convention [are] suffering for fuel" and the "creditors will supply us no longer." From Congress's perspective, provisioning the troops was not an American problem. Under the terms of the convention, the British were supposed to repay or replenish the supplies consumed by the prisoners. Heath had received some support from General Howe that winter, but Congress had resolved in December 1777 that the British repay their debts in specie rather than Continental dollars on the grounds that they were guilty of counterfeiting Continentals for the purpose of devaluing the currency.[54]

Burgoyne managed to repay most of his debt with a combination of coin and provisions before he departed, but after the resolution to suspend the troops' embarkation, the British were in no hurry to continue funneling money into rebel coffers. One British officer in Rhode Island even believed that the Americans were detaining the conventioners to drain the royal treasury and reinvigorate their stagnant economy. When Congress requested that local merchants be granted passage into and out of Boston Harbor free of molestation by the Royal Navy for the purpose of supplying the troops, Howe refused, hoping that if the Americans could not feed the men, they would be forced to release them.[55]

Exacerbating Heath's predicament, Burgoyne's successor in command, the irascible Major General William Phillips, was determined to oppose the American at every turn. From the beginning of his tenure as commander of the conventioners, Phillips refused to acknowledge that, for all intents and purposes, his men were prisoners of war. After the promulgation of the January 8 resolution, many Americans, as well as the revolutionary press, began to refer to the conventioners as prisoners. As Phillips explained to British general Sir Henry Clinton, "the American Congress, as well as many others of the Americans have industriously use[d] the word 'prisoner,'" while "we have considered ourselves as passengers under the sanction and virtue of a treaty, not as prisoners." There was some truth to his claim; after all, the convention itself was not suspended, only the embarkation of the troops for England. But by the spring of 1778, Phillips's insistence on the distinction had begun to grate on Heath. When the Briton pedantically lectured the American general on "the customs of Armies" in May 1778, Heath fired back, "notwithstanding your Knowledge and age in soldiering[,] you are much mistaken." Although Heath had been a farmer when Phillips had learned the soldier's trade on the battlefields of Europe during the Seven Years' War, Congress had entrusted the New Englander to superintend the convention troops, and he would brook no insubordination from one of his wards, no matter how exalted the man's rank, status, or experience.[56]

The tension between the two men detonated in June 1778 when one of Heath's sentries killed a British officer. Lieutenant Richard Brown of the 21st Regiment was on a carriage ride around Prospect Hill, accompanied by two young ladies, when he was challenged by a fourteen-year-old American soldier. Having difficulty controlling his chaise, the lieutenant failed to stop when hailed by the sentry—prompting the young American to discharge his firelock. Brown did not survive his wound. Possessed of all of Burgoyne's pomposity but none of his charm, Phillips accused the sentry of deliberate murder and the American people of possessing a "Bloody disposition which has joined itself to Rebellion." Excoriating Heath, he raged, "I do not ask for Justice for I believe every principle of it is fled from this Province." Heath realized at once that the British general intended to capitalize on the horrible accident for propagandistic purposes by linking Brown's death to the continued detention of the army. But he would not allow such blatant opportunism, refusing Phillips's request to send an officer with the news to the British commander in New York and placing the general under house arrest. While apprising Laurens of his actions, Heath noted the mood of the people of Boston after the incident. In his opinion, Phillips had "given almost universal disgust here and I am happy to say that the steps which I have taken meet a general approbation." Surrounded by American guards and unable to visit his troops, even Phillips was forced to admit that he was finally a prisoner.[57]

The general's confinement did not go far enough for most Bostonians, however—they wanted the British gone. While Boston merchants and Cambridge landlords had prospered from the British presence, most residents resented the hauteur of the convention officers and the relatively lax confinement of the enlisted men. Cavorting about the taverns of Cambridge, the paroled officers offended the piety and probity of many Bostonians, while enlisted conventioners escaped from the barracks were a constant source of frustration for American magistrates. As their detention dragged on, the soldiers suffered from the twin plagues of early modern armies: boredom and alcohol abuse. Vice, indiscipline, and malefaction were the invariable result. Typifying the infractions committed by the conventioners, George Gilbert was confined on board a prison ship for "drinking damnation to the Congress." At his trial the soldier was contrite, confessing that "he was so much disguised with Liquour that he is not able to give any acct. of the matter himself." More seriously, James Fill Gerald stood trial for "a general abuse to the Inhabitants, threatening to Kill men and women & children and burn their houses." Though no witnesses stepped forward, the court of inquiry ordered him "confined in the Guard house."[58]

Even law-abiding conventioners could be a threat to the civilian population. Smallpox and typhus were present among the troops; the former disease claimed the lives of over three hundred conventioners in the spring of 1778, while the latter took an additional forty-eight that summer. Cambridge authorities were so concerned about the potential for an outbreak that they canceled Harvard College's commencement exercises. With Boston's jails and prison ships overflowing with unruly redcoats and its hospitals crowded with contagious men, it is little wonder that James Warren felt that it was "a misfortune to us that this State was pitched upon as the place of their captivity, especially as they were detained here so much longer than was at first expected." The conventioners had worn out their welcome.[59]

Washington, Heath, and the Massachusetts Council all agreed that the obvious solution to the problem was to exchange the convention troops for Americans in British captivity. Article three of the convention stipulated that the soldiers were eligible for exchange under a general cartel. Washington had been in negotiations with Howe on the subject of a large-scale prisoner exchange throughout the winter, and ever since it had become clear that Congress intended to retard the troops' embarkation, his British counterpart had been eager to settle an accord. Congress, however, refused to budge on its insistence that the prisoners' accounts be discharged in solid coin. Fearing that the British might agree to the proposition, delegates further resolved that any loyalist captured in arms against the United States would be sent to his respective state to be tried as a traitor; the penalty for treason in most states was death by hanging. With a significant part of his army composed of uniformed loyalist troops, this was a stipulation to which Howe would never agree. Governor Trumbull thought such intransigence justified considering the "barbarous Treatment of our Prisoners by our Enemies," but he suggested that "a future spirited Retaliation" would be more effective than "any Obstruction of the Cartel." The Connecticut governor knew that his country lacked the resources "to secure the prisoners we have on Hand." Congress disagreed. The detention of the convention troops was a symbolic gesture, a very visible protest against the enemy's continued practice of atrocity and abuse.[60]

Moreover, the delegates were aware that any large-scale exchange of prisoners was simply not in the national interest at the time. While Howe primarily possessed American officers and sailors, having already released most of the enlisted soldiers captured during the New York Campaign, the Americans now had an entire British army in their custody. Were Congress to exchange those troops for the officers in the customary proportion based on rank, the British would instantly recoup a veteran field army for the ensuing campaign. Washington was not immune to this logic, but he had pledged "the public, as well as my own personal Honor and faith" to General Howe. If he were to rescind the offer, "it would be difficult to prevent our being generally accused with a Breach of good Faith." The delegates had heard that indictment before, and Washington was no more persuasive than Burgoyne had been. With Congress unwilling to countenance the slightest compromise, the exchange negotiations, like those that preceded them, ended in stalemate. The best the negotiators could arrange was a partial exchange of fewer than one hundred men, including the long-suffering Ethan Allen, who was swapped for the equally misfortunate Archibald Campbell, and the pampered Charles Lee for the once-again-captured Richard Prescott. Washington, who believed Congress acted "on the principle of retaliation," admitted feeling "extremely embarrassed"; his "sensibility [was] not a little wounded."[61]

Unwilling either to release the prisoners per the terms of the Saratoga Convention or to exchange them, and aware that Heath could no longer maintain the men in Massachusetts, Congress proposed its own solution to the problem: relocation. To better accommodate the troops, the delegates had earlier authorized Heath to transport several hundred conventioners from the British light infantry and artillery fifty-five miles farther inland to the town of Rutland. Though a minor infraction of the convention, which stipulated that the troops be quartered "as convenient as possible" to Boston, neither Burgoyne nor Phillips protested the move in hopes of providing more commodious quarters for their soldiers.[62]

Unfortunately for the troops, the housing situation in Rutland proved even more problematic than in Cambridge. Landlords demanded exorbitant rates, and the local committee of safety refused either manpower or material support to the American commissaries struggling to erect barracks. In September Deputy Commissary Isaac Tuckerman pleaded with Heath's aide Jonathan Chase to stem the tide of relocation. "I have not the least prospect of procuring Quarters for the officers[.] [I]t was with grate difficulty that the officers already here is quartered." Town officials had ignored Heath's pleas for assistance, and Tuckerman feared that if any more conventioners arrived, "we shall be in grate confusion as we have not Barracks to receive them."[63]

There was little love lost between the inland local population and the prisoners, who just a year earlier had threatened to wreak havoc on the Massachusetts backcountry. Because he was "too much respected by the British and German officers," Commissary Mersereau confessed in August, "There are some in this Country would have Mob'd me long ago (but they know I have good pistols)." Another American commissary, a Mr. Speakman of Brookfield, was horrified by the caprice of the local committees. He reported that two innocent conventioners were "taken up by the Committee" and flogged "with an Horsewhip ... in direct opposition to all Law." In light of this "Shameful sketch of Power," it is little wonder that Ensign Anburey believed that the troops were "treated with great severity, [and] very badly supplied with provisions" by the committee at Rutland. In his opinion, both officers and soldiers were "treated worse at Rutland" than at Cambridge. Despite the Continentals' best efforts, Rutland was not the solution for which Heath had hoped. Thankfully for the exhausted general, Congress had a more ambitious plan.[64]

On September 11, 1778, Congress resolved to send Sir Henry Clinton, who had replaced Howe as the Crown commander in chief in America, an ultimatum. If the British general did not immediately discharge his debt in hard currency, Congress would relocate the Convention Army to a place of its choosing, negating the Saratoga Convention in all but name. By the delegates' reckoning, the king's government owed the people of the United States £103,000 for the troops' upkeep since March. A British officer in New York estimated that at that rate, the Crown would be in arrears "upwards of £200,000 sterling for the year." Naturally, neither Phillips nor Clinton agreed with Congress's calculation of the "pretended debt." Jonathan Clarke, the assistant commissary general of the Convention Army, warned Clinton that "upon refusing the Payment of the Accounts . . . , the Congress will declare the Convention at an end, and the Army Prisoners of War." Given that "the prospect of their release [was] so distant," Clarke suggested that Clinton should consider giving up on the convention altogether. Phillips concurred. If Congress intended to infringe the agreement, then it should pay for the army's upkeep. Emboldened by Phillips's advice, Clinton ignored the American demand.[65]

At long last the delegates had their smoking gun. By refusing to pay Burgoyne's debt, Clinton provided Congress with just enough justification to shirk its obligations to the Saratoga Convention once and for all. Since receiving word of Gates's negotiations, the mood in Congress had been against the convention, and now with the French alliance secured, the assembled members voted on October 16, 1778, to nullify it, consigning the conventioners to indefinite confinement in Albemarle County, Virginia, just shy of one year since they had laid down their arms. Largely spared from the ravages of war, far removed from any British army, and already utilized to detain loyalist and Hessian prisoners, the interior of Virginia seemed to be an ideal location to confine and supply the conventioners. There, delegates reasoned, the men could be held until the British reformed their barbaric ways or a favorable opportunity for exchange presented itself. If the convention troops still harbored any doubts about the status of their captivity, they could now rest assured that they were in fact prisoners of war.[66]

Destruction

When he received his orders from Congress, General Heath was wracked by competing emotions. On the one hand, he was relieved to be rid of the onerous burden; the convention prisoners and all their complaints, peccadilloes, and misdemeanors were now somebody else's problem. "The trouble & difficulty which I have had with the troops of the Convention," he told Washington, "are almost inconceivable." Yet he could not hide his surprise at the decision. It was one thing to delay the troops' embarkation; it was another thing altogether to dismiss the convention outright, sending the men on an arduous trek of over six hundred miles so late in the year. The general knew that many of the conventioners would not survive the march. Moreover, despite his dislike of General Phillips, Heath had grown fond of many of the senior officers of the Convention Army, having treated the Roxbury farmer with the respect due to his rank. He may have failed as a battlefield commander, but Heath had managed to keep Burgoyne's army largely intact with very little support from either local or congressional authorities. And yet in one stroke, Congress had erased the greatest achievement of his military career. But like so many good soldiers before and since, Heath followed his orders.[67]

The officers and soldiers of the Convention Army were equally shocked by the news. According to Ensign Anburey, "when this resolve of Congress was made known, every one was struck with amazement." Corporal Lamb believed the orders for relocation were "universally considered by the privates as a very great hardship, and by the officers as a shameful violation" of the convention. Not only had the Americans abandoned any pretense of upholding the treaty, but Anburey thought that they also intended to destroy the army by "marching the men eight hundred miles in the depth of winter." The senior officers pleaded with Heath to delay the march until the weather improved, or at least until they had had an opportunity to convey their desperation to General Clinton in New York. All he could do, however, was pass on their lamentations to his superiors. The general apprised Laurens that "they appear much affected at this order to remove so great a distance.... [T]he Germans in particular appear much dejected." Compounding their distress, the men still had not received their yearly issue of clothing. In the late fall of 1778, the prisoners were still wearing the threadbare, patched, and cut-down coats of 1776. As if to torment the prisoners further, a British ship carrying a fresh supply of clothing from New York arrived just as the men prepared to march. Under strict orders not to delay, Heath had no choice but to deny the prisoners' request to reclothe; the uniforms would have to be sent to Virginia by sea. One German officer despaired, "we shall have to make this wearisome march in our rags and find our uniforms in a climate where on account of the heat we may make little use of them." Grasping for a silver lining, Anburey consoled himself, "after the cruelties and barbarities the troops have experienced since our arrival, that we are quitting such an inhospitable country."[68]

On November 9, 1778, the Convention Army—2,263 British and 1,882 German troops—departed Massachusetts on a march that proved every bit as arduous as the prisoners had feared. Having lost, or left behind, over eleven hundred men due to desertion, disease, or death at the hands of American guards during its captivity near Boston, Burgoyne's army was a shell of its former self when the march began. As the prisoners progressed southward toward British-occupied New York at the blistering pace of twenty-seven miles per day, the "siren call" of freedom pulled many conventioners away from their regiments. Because Washington could spare few Continental troops to serve as guards, Congress was forced to rely on the individual states through which the column passed to provide security. Unsurprisingly, those who reported for guard duty were seldom the most fervent or fit revolutionaries, and any prisoner bent on escape rarely encountered difficulty accomplishing his ends. Corporal Lamb was among the 579 British and German troops who decamped along the line of march to Virginia in November and December.[69]

In making good his escape to New York, Lamb evaded a harrowing ordeal. Those who remained with the army were not so lucky. Throughout the march, the men suffered "abusive treatment from the Militia" who guarded them as well as from the inhabitants of the communities through which they passed. If their human tormentors were not enough, nature soon conspired against them. Alexander King, a Connecticut man who witnessed the prisoners cross the Connecticut River in mid-November, noted that "they lost 2 of theirs on passing the River[,] the wind being high drove them over the falls." Those who survived "suffered terribly from the cold and, what was even worse, from lack of food," according to the Baroness von Riedesel. When they were fortunate, the men spent the evenings "in goals or Churchers [sic]," but the bulk of the time they bivouacked under the stars. Soon after beginning their journey, the snow set in, covering the soldiers as they slept "1/2 yd deep." Braving the weather, the prisoners pressed on, with the first division arriving in Charlottesville in early January amid what Thomas Jefferson referred to as "the worst spell of weather ever known within the memory of man." By mid-February 1779, roughly three months after they had commenced the journey, the remnants of Burgoyne's army had all arrived, footsore and shivering, in Virginia.[70]

Despite ample time between the prisoners' departure and their arrival in Charlottesville, revolutionary officials in Virginia were entirely unprepared to house and feed the weary troops. In settling on Albemarle County, Congress had listened to one of the Virginia delegates, John Harvie, who had offered to allow the prisoners the use of his personal property rent free. Hardly a philanthropist—he was in dire financial straits—Harvie realized that the prisoners would undoubtedly improve the land, thus increasing its resale value after their departure. His colleagues jumped on the opportunity. Dispatching Virginia-born commissary officer Captain George Rice with $23,000 to build barracks on Harvie's land, Congress thought it had solved the problem of accommodating the men. With government cash lining his pockets, Rice departed for Charlottesville in little hurry to begin construction. To their horror, "instead of comfortable barracks," the prisoners found "a few log huts [that] were just begun to be built, the most part not covered over, and all of them full of snow." According to Brunswick grenadier Johann Bense, he and his comrades had survived a "long, difficult march" only to discover that the barracks "were not even half finished. . . . All walls were open; there were neither fire places nor sleeping places, no door and a miserable roof." The men, "in order to protect . . . against rain, snow, and cold," immediately began improving the shanties into something resembling habitable quarters. British corporal George Fox reported that their progress was impeded because Rice had failed to provide them with a sufficient supply of nails.[71]

Of even greater concern, the Continental commissary officers in Virginia had failed to secure adequate provisions for the prisoners upon their arrival. When Congress ordered the Convention Army to Charlottesville, the Board of War had allotted an extra $7,000 over the cost of constructing the barracks to cover the immediate needs of the men, but the intended provisions were nowhere to be seen. Anburey blamed Harvie, suggesting that the Virginia delegate "misguided and duped" his colleagues and absconded with the money. In reality, the Continental deputy commissary general for purchases, Colonel William Aylett, had misjudged the speed at which the prisoners would march so that the provisions he purchased spoiled. The results were the same, however. According to Anburey, "for Six days they [the conventioners] subsisted on the meal of Indian corn made into cakes." If the prisoners had hoped that their relocation would bring improved provisions and accommodation, they could not have been more disappointed. Although the commander of the American guards, Colonel Theodorick Bland, had assured General Phillips in December, "as I ever feel for the misfortunes of the brave, so shall it always be my study to alleviate their distress when in my power," it was simply not in his power to feed the men once they arrived at Charlottesville. Bland had done his job; now it was Virginia's turn to provide for the prisoners.[72]

Governor Patrick Henry was dismayed by the prisoners' arrival. Deeply embroiled in his own war against British lieutenant governor Henry Hamilton in the west, Henry had neither the resources nor the manpower to support the Convention Army. Congress, through its delegation of responsibilities to Harvie, Rice, and Aylett, had evidently botched the job, and the governor now feared that he would have to pick up the pieces. Moreover, he believed that Charlottesville was entirely unsuited for the reception of prisoners of war. The inland hamlet was over seventy miles away from the nearest navigable river, thus impeding the movement of supplies from the coast. Upon visiting the camp in late January 1779, the governor's deputy quartermaster, William Finnie, observed that the barracks were "ill provided, and but very little Water near them." The supply wagons were easily bogged down on the dirt roads in wet weather, and the "troops cannot be regularly supplied." Finnie also believed that the price of grain in the region was "enormous!" Apprised of this information, Henry concluded that "the Troops cannot, by any Means, be supported in that Part of the Country." Jefferson disagreed. Seeking to maintain the influx of capital and consumers into his beloved Albemarle County, Jefferson reasoned that Congress had already spent close to $25,000 building and guarding the barracks; to abandon them now would be wasteful. Furthermore, which state was better suited to provide for the prisoners? Away from the fury of the battlefield, Virginia was the ideal location. A more efficient commissary officer was all that was required to improve the prisoners' predicament. Jefferson's friends in Congress agreed with their former colleague. The conventioners would stay put, and Virginia would pay for them.[73]

Although the confinement of the senior officers improved with time—many of them enjoyed frequent visits to Monticello—the situation in the barracks continued to deteriorate. Through their labor, the troops had rendered the buildings habitable, but food remained scarce. According to Anburey, "the men have been exceedingly ill supplied with provisions in general, having meat only twice or thrice a week, and for some weeks none, what they get is scarcely wholesome, this is at present what the poor fellows term a fast." The winter thaw did not bring much improvement. It was not long before the pleasant spring air turned sultry and heavy with the heat and humidity. Insects, snakes, rats, and bats descended on the camp, tormenting the prisoners. Termites and grubs began demolishing their wooden barracks and decimating the gardens the soldiers had planted to supplement their diets and prevent the onset of scurvy. Provisions remained inadequate throughout the summer. Anburey noted, "For the greatest part of the summer they have been thirty and forty days, at different periods, without any other provision delivered to them than the meal of Indian corn." Even the salted provisions were tainted. Attempting to save a quantity of salted meat, the American commissary had buried the food "in the earth for a few days" before serving it to the troops so that it was "swarming with vermin."[74]

Predictably, a new wave of desertion, disease, and death inundated the camp. Corporal Fox recalled helping fence in an acre of land "to prevent the wild beasts from breaking in" and devouring the bodies of his deceased comrades. According to a British return compiled in August 1779, only 1,495 British and 1,533 German prisoners remained alive in Charlottesville. Since leaving Massachusetts, the British and Germans had lost 34 percent and 18.5 percent of their number, respectively. Hardly one for hyperbole, Baroness von Riedesel enunciated the prevailing sentiment in the barracks when she confessed feeling "more dead than alive" that summer.[75]

Back in Massachusetts, roughly 150 infirmed and diseased convention prisoners, along with their comrades who had been captured before the agreement was signed, were in equally dire straits. Congress had completely forgotten about them after the bulk of the captives had marched southward. Upon turning over command of the Eastern Department to General Gates in November 1778, Heath informed his successor that the prisoners at Rutland were "in great distress." Without assistance from Congress, however, Gates could do little to better their plight. In April 1779 Commissary Mersereau pleaded with Heath to exert his influence on the captives' behalf. "We are in a Deplorable situation here—the flour almost gone. . . . I shall not know how to provide for the prisoners, I cannot make bricks without straw." By the end of May, Mersereau assured the general that "many of the prisoners have not had a mouthful of Bread, this 3 days." Describing the result of their starvation diet, he wrote only: "Women and children crying, prisoners murmuring for Bread." If adequate provisions could not be had, Mersereau suggested the obvious solution—an equitable exchange. As he told Heath, "I think it would be best to rid the Country of all the British [prisoners]." Gates had other plans. Afraid of being seen by Congress as overly lenient to the convention prisoners, he instructed Heath to "order every one of the Conventioners now in Confinement [at Rutland] . . . to be brought to Boston, where it will undoubtedly be right to secure them in the Prison ship." There they would languish until Congress saw fit to exchange them.[76]

While Congress had acquiesced to the exchange of numerous convention officers for their American counterparts in British custody throughout 1778 and 1779, revolutionary America's political leadership remained reluctant to establish a general cartel. Washington, unwilling to impinge upon the congressional prerogative, nonetheless hoped that the delegates would consent to such an exchange. After all, desertion and death were depleting the Convention Army at an alarming rate. If a cartel were not soon agreed upon, there would be no one left to exchange. Washington, Gates, and Phillips entered discussions during the first months of 1779.[77]

Their efforts were for naught. Congress was unwilling to part with the convention troops. As both the physical embodiment of the Revolution's greatest triumph and the most suitable subjects for retaliation, the Convention Army was far more valuable to the revolutionary effort than the parcel of privateers and Continental officers Clinton held in New York. The long-suffering American prisoners failed to see the logic. Brigadier General William Thompson, who had been captured in Canada in 1776, reportedly exclaimed "in a great passion" that "he was obliged to General Clinton, but not to Congress, they had used him *damned rascally.*" The British high command was similarly disappointed, though not surprised. Lord Germain concluded that Congress was up to its usual "chicane." Phillips took the news the hardest. Convinced that he had done his best to obtain his army's release, the general, like his predecessor Burgoyne, finally gave up. Pleased to be rid of him, Congress granted his request to go to New York on parole in June 1779.[78]

Unlike their former commander, the conventioners who remained in Virginia faced increasing hostility from the local population. Far from being a boon to Charlottesville's economy, by 1780, the prisoners had become a heavy burden to the community. Neither officers nor enlisted men could afford to discharge their debts. They were so far in arrears that Virginia civil authorities prohibited local merchants and farmers from selling them "flour or meal" on credit. Ravenous redcoats elicited little sympathy from their revolutionary neighbors. Aggravating these financial tensions was the omnipresent fear of invasion. With a British army occupying coastal Georgia and South Carolina, Virginians had cause for concern. Were North Carolina to fall, their state would be next. White residents had not forgotten Governor Dunmore's 1775 proclamation: A British invasion portended slave insurrection. As rumors of Crown depredations and manumissions trickled northward, revolutionaries of all social orders panicked. When Continental brigadier general Anthony Wayne heard of "the horrid devastation committed by the enemy to the Southward," he declared the age of conducting war with "liberality" at an end. From now on, he hoped, the Continental Army would "adopt the alternative of neither giving nor receiving quarter." Wayne's plan did not pass muster with the commander in chief, but ordinary Virginians, unhindered by rules and regulations, were free to target their foes as they saw fit.[79]

The inhabitants of Fluvanna County found just such a target in convention prisoner Jonas Parker. A subaltern officer in the 62nd Regiment of Foot, Parker rented lodgings outside of the barracks. It was there in early May 1780 that he encountered "six or seven Men" who "greatly insulted and struck" him with sticks. The Virginians demanded that he and his comrades leave the county or "stand to the consequences." Parker claimed never to have seen the men before, "having had no connection or even conversation with any one in the Country"; his scarlet uniform was enough to engender enmity among the locals. The aggrieved officer complained to the American commander at the barracks to no avail, for the Continental Army did not have jurisdiction over Virginia's citizens. Similar attacks occurred in Albemarle County. According to Anburey, ordinary Virginians enjoyed "quarrelling with the officers" so much that he feared for his life. When convention officers protested their treatment, Virginia authorities confessed that "the civil power was of little use ... among the back-woods men." All they could do was advise the Britons to "not quit the barracks." Furious, the ensign attributed their mistreatment to "the spirit of equality or levelling principle," which "since the war ... seems to have gained great ground in Virginia." While pleased by the "politeness" and "hospitality" of the local gentry, the elitist Briton decried the "savage and revengeful" behavior of the "lower people." He could not wait to be free of their "barbarity."[80]

Confined to the barracks and debarred from exchange by Congress, the rank and file of the Convention Army experienced even more hardship than their officers throughout the spring and summer of 1780. Anburey believed that "the soldiers fare little better than on their first arrival." The Continental commissary officer charged with provisioning the troops, Francis Tate, described the difficult task he faced in March: "Description falls short of my distressful situation[,] some of the Convention troops have been without bread fourteen days, their melancholy complaints & pleys [*sic*] (although an enemy) makes me perfectly Miserable." He begged his superior in Philadelphia, Major Robert Forsyth, to "have such steps taken as will prevent our being quite starved." It was not long before the prisoners exhibited "violent symptoms of scurvy," according to the new Continental commander of the barracks, Colonel James Wood. In late August 1780 the prisoners had not received any meat for seventy days. Realizing that the situation was untenable, Wood appealed to the Assembly of Virginia for aid. He requested any assistance the assembly could grant him, reminding the legislators that "Congress had made a resolution to the Executive of the State of Virginia to supply the said Troops in future." The assemblymen sympathized with Wood, but they could not help. The prisoners were the governor's problem.[81]

Replacing Henry as governor of Virginia in June 1779, Thomas Jefferson had reversed his stance on the continuance of the convention prisoners in his state since coming to office. The prospect of feeding and guarding so many enemy troops without any support from Congress, all while threatened by British raids on the coast and by invasion from the south, was too much for any state to bear. Jefferson wanted the prisoners gone. In September 1780 Congress answered his pleas by resolving "to march the Convention troops from Albemarle barracks, by way of Winchester, to fort Frederick, in the state of Maryland." The governor's enthusiasm was tempered, however, by the added proviso that Virginia and Maryland would split the expense of provisioning the prisoners equally. The resolution was a bitter pill to swallow, but at least Virginia would be free of the troublesome captives.[82]

Relocation to Maryland was even more alarming to the conventioners. The British prisoners had worked tirelessly to make their quarters at Charlottesville habitable, while the Germans, whom the revolutionaries deemed less of a flight risk, had enjoyed the freedom of working and lodging with local farmers. The officers, who were required to pay their own expenses, were particularly aggrieved by the prospect of another removal. Anburey observed that "the murmurs of the officers were great. . . . [M]any had laid out considerable sums to render their log huts comfortable against the approaching winter." Compounding their concerns, the officers had little ready cash to remunerate their creditors and pay travel expenses. Several German officers pleaded with General Clinton to provide them with a moving stipend because they had "experienced in the painful course of three years captivity considerable losses of different kinds, occasioned particularly by expensive removals from place to place at our own expense." The British government disagreed on the grounds that refunding such expenses would set a bad precedent for other prisoners of war. The officers would have to make do with what Congress provided. Despite their grievances, the convention prisoners began their march northward in November 1780—the third winter march since their captivity began—once again hopeful that new environs would bring a reversal of their fortunes.[83]

Regrettably for the conventioners, Maryland was hardly a panacea. With a much smaller tax base than its neighbor to the south, the state did not have the resources or the infrastructure in place to absorb the prisoners. The new commander of the Convention Army, Brigadier James Hamilton, reported to Clinton in December that the troops "were with much difficulty received by the States of this Province." His laconic description belied the horrors the men suffered. When they arrived at Fort Frederick, a ruin of a Seven Years' War–era post, there were not enough barracks to even house the British prisoners. Thankfully, Jefferson was willing to keep the Germans at Winchester while Maryland authorities scrambled to find quarters for them. In early December Maryland's commissary of prisoners, Lieutenant Colonel Moses Rawlings, told its governor, Thomas Sim Lee, "my Situation here is Truly alarming, for the prisoners realy [sic] suffer for water as well as meat, for the wells Both in & out of the fort are Dry."[84]

The conventioners grew restive. Rawlings had to resort to force to quell an insurrection of the starving prisoners, who nearly overpowered his guards. Sending a contingent of Britons to the barracks and the "poor House" in the town of Frederick eased Rawlings's predicament somewhat, but he still lacked the means to adequately feed the men. In late January 1781 Brigadier Hamilton, exasperated by Rawlings's empty promises, lodged a formal complaint with Governor Lee on behalf of his beleaguered soldiers. "The Troops have received no Meat for these five Days past[,] this Day included, & that the ration in that Specie has been considerably diminished of late." In addition, Hamilton complained "of the irregular & scanty manner that fuel is served out" and of the dearth of nails and boards with which to improve the barracks. The Council of Maryland responded by promising boards and nails, but they could do little about provisions because Jefferson had not been forthcoming with Virginia's share. In Jefferson's opinion, the necessity of feeding the American southern army superseded his responsibility to the prisoners. Unable to meet such demands, Jefferson appealed to the Board of War for "a revisal of this requisition."[85]

With neither Virginia nor Maryland capable of sustaining the Convention Army, Congress had to reevaluate its stance. The initial decision was just more of the same—relocation. On March 3, 1781, Congress resolved to send the remaining 819 British officers and men to the prisoner-of-war depot at York, Pennsylvania; the Germans would be interned in Lancaster. The delegates instructed the president of Pennsylvania to "make the necessary preparations for the reception of the prisoners," but they promised that once the men arrived, the Board of War would "take order for their future security and supply." Many in Congress, however, realized that moving the prisoners to Pennsylvania would not solve the root problem: continuing to hold the men was too expensive. The march was suspended while delegates debated a more comprehensive solution. Reviewing the history of the convention prisoners, a committee concluded that for years the troops had been subsisted, at least in theory, at the same rate of rations as Continental soldiers according to the fifth article of the convention, while other British prisoners of war received only a two-thirds allotment. Under the agreement, the British government should have reimbursed the Americans for all the expenses incurred by the troops, but General Clinton had no intention of paying for their upkeep as long as they were de facto prisoners. If Congress would have to foot the bill either way, the committee reasoned, why not declare the Saratoga Convention at an end and reduce the prisoners' rations?[86]

To a cash-strapped government, the logic was irresistible. The committee's report was amended to maintain a nominal distinction between the convention prisoners and other prisoners of war, but the results were the same. The conventioners were now prisoners of war in name as well as status. Per the resolve, the officers would be separated from their men and sent on their parole to Simsbury, Connecticut; and the enlisted soldiers would be closely confined and reduced to two-thirds rations. This decision had little immediate effect, however, because the prisoners had not been receiving anything close to two-thirds provisions for months, and there were not enough jails in all of Maryland to confine the whole army. According to a conventioner escaped from Frederick, the men were "treated with the greatest severity—being ill off for provisions— one pound of coarse Indian Meal & 10 ounces of flour is allowed them as a

Ration." Ensign Anburey feared that his men would be "forced from us into a prison, where experiencing every severity, perhaps famishing for want of food, and ready to perish with cold," they would have no one to advocate in their favor. He had learned well over the years that British prisoners had "little to expect from the humanity of Americans." Unfortunately for the enlisted conventioners, Anburey proved prophetic.[87]

In the summer of 1781, after a series of conflicting orders from Congress, the convention prisoners marched for Pennsylvania, where they would endure their most trying confinement yet. By the time the men arrived at Lancaster in early June 1781, there were scarcely six hundred Britons remaining. Because the troops were accompanied by "near five hundred Women & children"— many of the prisoners had married American women during their captivity in Virginia and Maryland—the commissary of prisoners in the town, William Atlee, could not find suitable housing for them; the hastily constructed stockade at Lancaster could barely contain the single men alone. Atlee had little option but to allow the married men and their families, whom he believed less prone to escape than their unattached comrades, to encamp outside of the prison's walls. But without a roof over their head, these prisoners were "badly shelter'd from the weather." Exacerbating an already perilous state of affairs, the Lancaster barracks had recently been used to house "near eight hundred Prisoners of War . . . , among them a great number sick of a putrid fever." Within days of their arrival, Atlee informed the state's executive, President Joseph Reed, that "this fatal disorder has gained ground & there are now at least a hundred & fifty sick in these greatly crouded Barracks without a prospect of its abating." Corporal Fox believed that the conventioners suffered from "yellow fever," introduced by other prisoners recently arrived from Philadelphia's notorious New Jail. Disease was certainly present in the jails of Philadelphia that summer. An escapee reported in April, "our Prisoners [in Philadelphia] are very sickly and many of them have died." Whatever its source or typology, the epidemic was virulent. "Not less than 4 to 6 are daily buried owing to their crowded situation," according to American colonel Adam Hubley. From the vantage point of Corporal Fox inside the barracks, it looked as if his comrades "died like rotten Sheep."[88]

Attempting to stem the contagion, Pennsylvania authorities moved the prisoners to York in mid-August, but their health continued to deteriorate. Neither Congress nor the state's revolutionary government had allocated any resources to refurbishing that town's barracks or to stockpiling provisions for the captives. Upon their arrival, they were forced once more to build their own prison. As soon as their "huts" were constructed, the healthy prisoners began laying out a cemetery and digging graves. Before the month was out, they had "Buried upwards of forty Men[,] women, and children." Although an attempt was made to erect a hospital, British surgeon's mate Benjamin Shield noted that the prisoners were "falling Sick so fast there was not Men enough to attend the Sick." Reporting on the camp's conditions to Brigadier Hamilton, Shield bemoaned, "I have often been at a loss to distinguish which most deserv'd to be lamented by their Country in whose cause they have and are still hourly suffering, the sickening, the dying, or the Dead." The entire army, in his opinion, was "at the very jaws of Death." Without fresh clothing, blankets, and medicines, the prisoners would never survive "the severity of a long Winter." By Shield's accounting, 196 men were suffering from the "Jailfever," fully one-third of the remaining British captives. In August General Clinton was informed by an escaped prisoner that the conventioners at Lancaster "die three or four a day." Nonetheless, Clinton, like Congress, was unwilling to sacrifice any political capital by appropriately supplying the men. If the Americans intended to keep the convention troops as prisoners, they would have to pay for them.[89]

The plight of the German conventioners was little better. Once they arrived in Pennsylvania in the summer of 1781, the men were forced to camp "on a meadow in the open air for 8 weeks and were plagued by the great heat during the day and by rain and cold during the night" because local authorities had nowhere to house them. When they were finally moved to Reading in mid-June, the American commissary there ordered the men to construct barracks. Vexed by the prospect of building another set of shelters that in all likelihood they would soon be forced to abandon, the German prisoners refused. According to Grenadier Bense, they insisted on constructing straw huts instead. For their noncompliance, the prisoners were "treated very severely" by the American guards and eventually forced to build more permanent housing.[90]

The Germans were equally frustrated by the paucity of their rations. President Reed refused to supply the men on the grounds that "the Prisoners are brought into Pennsylv. by order of Gen. Washington & Congress." In his opinion, it was "the superintending Continental officer" and the congressionally appointed contractor's responsibility to "keep good order" and "to supply them with Provisions." Though ostensibly agreeing with Reed, the Board of War had poorly calculated "the Numbers of Rations necessary" for both the German and British prisoners and thus had not provided a sufficient supply. When

Colonel Wood, still the Continental officer in charge of the Convention Army, appealed to Pennsylvania commissary William Scott for supplies, President Reed responded in no uncertain terms: "We do not conceive it incumbent on us to provide" provisions for the prisoners. While Congress, the Board of War, and the Council of Pennsylvania tried to sort out the issue of who was responsible for feeding the men, the prisoners went hungry. Only the congressional decision to allow the Germans to hire themselves to local farmers prevented the men from starving.[91]

While the convention prisoners suffered and died in overcrowded and disease-infested camps in Maryland and Pennsylvania, Congress remained steadfast in its refusal to exchange them. Even after the fall of Charleston in May 1780, when for the first time since Saratoga the British held more prisoners than the Americans, the delegates rebuffed Clinton's proposition for a cartel that would include the Saratoga troops. The Convention Army remained symbolically, financially, and politically too valuable to Congress to be traded for captured Americans whose enlistments were about to expire. Forlorn, Germain complained to Phillips, "It is not easy to imagine upon what grounds the Congress attempted to justify their refusal to exchange the privates of the Convention Troops in the same manner with other prisoners of war." He could not fathom why the Americans would not only deny the men the "benefit of [the] Convention" but also treat them "with more severity than" other prisoners; they were not following "any rules of reason." For Congress, reason had nothing to do with it. Long accused by their constituents of turning a blind eye to British violations of the customary norms of "civilized" warfare, the delegates had detained the convention prisoners as an act of retaliation, not for any specific British misdeed but for all of them. The miseries experienced by the conventioners would never make up for those endured by American captives, but the gesture was spectacularly popular among revolutionary Americans who no longer sought justice, only revenge. Prisoner-exchange negotiations continued for the remainder of the war, but Congress remained steadfast in its decision. As long as British troops sought to conquer America, the Convention Army would remain in captivity.[92]

When the preliminary articles of peace arrived in New York in 1783, the convention prisoners were exactly where Congress had left them two years earlier, either confined in the jails and prison camps of Pennsylvania or at work with local inhabitants. There were not many left. In the fall of 1782, Sergeant Major Samuel Vaupel of the Hesse Hanau Regiment reported to his commander

that only three hundred Hessian and Brunswick conventioners remained with
the army, dispersed between the barracks and jails of Reading and Lancaster.
Grenadier Bense was one of the forty-two unfortunate prisoners confined "in
the dungeon" of Lancaster. He described the remnants of the German contingent as "the most wretched and most miserable men." When he witnessed the
arrival of the German conventioners in New York after their release, Hessian
officer Johann Ewald observed that "they were not half clad, and misery and
hunger could be read in their faces." He believed that "on the whole, the Brunswick troops [of the Convention Army] have endured the most misfortune of
all the Germans" who served in the war. With the British prisoners at York,
Corporal George Fox was confined in a fenced barracks when he received news
of the peace. Fox was one of only 511 British conventioners, including large
numbers of recaptured escapees, still in American custody that May. Of the
over five thousand British and German soldiers who surrendered their arms
under the protection of the Convention of Saratoga in 1777, fewer than eight
hundred marched for New York at war's end. Many of the prisoners had already
escaped to British lines, and others had found new homes among the Americans.
Both American and British observers noted that desertion was widespread,
especially during the army's frequent marches to new places of confinement.
The identities of at least 315 British conventioners who either escaped or
attempted to escape their confinement are revealed by the historical record,
but there were certainly far more escapees. Although exactly how many convention prisoners escaped or how many perished in American hands remains
unknown, those who reached British lines in the spring and summer of 1783
were just thankful to be alive. None of the enlisted conventioners who left
journals or memoirs of their experiences in confinement recorded their emotions upon finally gaining their freedom after nearly six years of captivity, but
Ensign Anburey must have spoken for all when he recorded: "It is impossible
to describe the emotions of joy depicted in the countenance of every one; when
. . . we felt ourselves once more at liberty and safe out of the hands of
barbarians."[93]

* * *

Saratoga is commonly known as the turning point of the war, but it was also a
point of no return. Americans went to war in 1775 strong in the conviction that
their cause was righteous, even providentially sanctioned, and they were
adamant that their conduct during the conflict would reflect the nobility of

Chapter 5

The Vengeance of War

Surveying the besieged city of Charleston, South Carolina, in early May 1780, the British commander in chief in America was in the mood to be magnanimous. For weeks, General Sir Henry Clinton's army had slowly, methodically, but inexorably invested the American stronghold. An ardent student of the art of war and a veteran of the European theater of the Seven Years' War, Clinton, unlike his predecessor and rival Sir William Howe, was determined to conduct his operations by the book; he would not risk battle, even with rebels, if it could be avoided. Despite mutterings from many in his army critical of the torpidity of his advance on the city, Clinton's gradual and deliberate siege had worked. With their line of retreat now cut off and their food supply dwindling, the Americans had no choice but to give up the town. When he received word on May 11 that the American commander, the jocular and rotund Massachusetts militiaman turned major general Benjamin Lincoln, sought to surrender his army of nearly six thousand men, Clinton was relieved that he would not have to hurl his battalions of British and Hessian troops at the city's defenses. For the price of fewer than eighty British lives, Clinton had seized the most populous and prosperous city south of Philadelphia, captured the only American army between him and Washington, and erased the shame of his abortive 1776 attack. If his superiors in London were correct, this victory would pave the way for the complete subordination of the southern colonies to the king's will. Deprived of the wealth and resources of the South, the revolutionary cause would wither on the vine. With total victory in sight, it was not the time for pettiness or punishment; it was time to demonstrate British benevolence.[1]

Much to General Lincoln's surprise—he had twice rejected generous terms for capitulation—Clinton did not insist upon unconditional surrender. Instead, he allowed the Continental soldiers and sailors, "with their Baggage," to remain "Prisoners of War until exchanged." He even permitted the officers to keep and wear their swords. Unlike General Howe, who had denied the garrison of Fort Washington prisoner-of-war status, preferring to treat them as rebels in arms, Clinton promised that the American regulars would be afforded the customary European protections of that status. They would be "supplied with good and wholesome Provisions, in such Quantity as is served out to the Troops of his Britannic Majesty," while they awaited exchange for the soldiers of the Convention Army in American captivity.[2]

Lincoln's militia posed a thornier problem for the British commander. As citizens in arms they were not protected under the contemporary European laws of war. Nonetheless, in an unprecedented gesture of leniency for a British general during the American War, Clinton agreed to allow the militiamen "to return to their respective Homes, as Prisoners upon Parole." By pledging not to bear arms against the British government until exchanged, they were free to leave. Clinton even promised that their paroles would "secure them from being molested in their property by the British Troops." Unprepared for such generosity from an enemy who had consistently refused to treat Americans as legitimate combatants in the past, the former president of the Continental Congress, Henry Laurens, whose own son was a prisoner in the city, was perplexed by this apparent volte-face. The surrender agreement, which Laurens called "a strange kind of Capitulation," seemed too good to be true. Given the continued detention of the Convention Army and Lincoln's obstinate refusal to surrender even after Charleston had been surrounded, why would Clinton grant terms that were "full as good" as Laurens could ever have hoped?[3]

Clinton's actions were not merely the merciful caprice of a conqueror; they reflected his hope that the war in the South would be different. Believing that most southerners were war weary and open to reconciliation with Britain, Clinton was determined to wage the campaign with benevolence rather than brutality. As he explained to Lord Germain, "Whatever severe justice might dictate on such an occasion, we resolved not to press to unconditional submission a reduced army, whom we hoped clemency might yet reconcile to us." He enjoined his subordinates "from offering violence to innocent and inoffensive people" and ordered them to "protect the aged, infirm, the women, and children of every denomination from insult and outrage." Clinton had no desire to repeat Howe's mistakes. He would not abandon his loyalist supporters, but neither would he allow their personal grudges to interfere with his plans to bring peace to the province. Empowered by the king to offer a "free and general Pardon" to all former rebels, Clinton set out to pacify the South, not conquer it. His vision for the war in that region was nothing short of a repudiation of the policy and practice of his predecessor.[4]

Less than a year later, in February 1781, Moses Hall, a twenty-one-year-old militiaman, witnessed the murder of six loyalist prisoners of war in the North Carolina interior. The men, who had been captured by Continental troops earlier in the day, were "hewed to pieces with broadswords" by Hall's fellow militiamen. Although not officially sanctioned by the revolutionary government, their actions were consonant with the standing orders of the North Carolina Board of War issued October 17, 1780, to "treat them [loyalists] with the Severity they deserve." The sanguinary scene initially horrified Hall, who recalled feeling "overcome and unmanned by a distressing gloom" as he contemplated "the cruelties of war." Feelings of shock and regret "for the slaughter of the Tories" were soon subsumed by desire for further vengeance when he came upon the body of "a youth about sixteen" who had been bayoneted by loyalist troops and left for dead. Confronting the violence of civil war firsthand, Hall "desired nothing so much as the opportunity of participating in their [the loyalists'] destruction." His experience was far from unique during the waning years of the conflict. Hall's recollections of his military service during the campaigns of 1780 and 1781 are emblematic of the vehemence and violence with which both sides prosecuted the war after the fall of Charleston.[5]

Noting the violent character of the southern campaigns is hardly novel; historians and Hollywood have long recognized its destructiveness. Seeing it as an aberration, a peculiarly violent coda to an otherwise restrained conflict, scholars have pointed to the ethnic composition of the southern colonies, long-standing political disputes between the eastern planter elite and the backcountry yeomanry, the inherent violence of a social system predicated upon human bondage, the widespread use of Native American tactical practices, and even the cultural legitimacy of retributive justice to explain why the war in the South, to borrow historian Wayne Lee's phrase, "spiraled out of control."[6]

While not denying the violence of the southern campaigns, viewing the treatment of enemy prisoners in the South within the context of prior British and American practice reveals more continuity than disjuncture. Through this lens, the war in the South emerges not as a drastic departure from a limited European-style conflict but as the intense culmination of a process of escalating violence that had begun in the summer of 1776. Ordinary Americans, enraged by years of British abuses amplified by the revolutionary press and exacerbated by civil war, mobilized for a war of vengeance. While some members of the revolutionary elite, such as Generals Washington and Greene, strove to temper popular outrage, they were few and far between in the last years of the conflict. Congress, ever dependent on popular support to wage the war, would do little to mitigate its violence.

The internecine conflict that developed in the southern backcountry, which began with the breakdown of Clinton's policy of pacification, looked nothing like the revolutionaries' earlier vision of virtuous and limited war. Revenge, not proportional retaliation, was the order of the day. The horrors of the southern campaigns were not limited to the work of bands of ruffians possessed of malleable loyalties and a penchant for plunder. Regular Continental and British units were also marred by the murder and mistreatment of enemy prisoners. While officially discouraged, British and American military officials turned a blind eye to violations that would have elicited severe reproach at the war's commencement. The arrival of Washington's Continental forces and the French army of Lieutenant General Jean Baptiste Donatien de Vimeur, comte de Rochambeau in Virginia in the fall of 1781 reintroduced a veneer of restraint to the conflict. The allies granted Lieutenant General Charles, 2nd Earl Cornwallis and his army terms for capitulation at Yorktown that were every bit as generous as those Clinton proffered Lincoln at Charleston. These proved instantly unpopular with revolutionary southerners fixated on vengeance. With the forces of France eventually removed, Congress responded to its constituents' call and consigned the Yorktown prisoners to an arduous confinement in the Pennsylvania interior, where they suffered from deprivation, disease, and exposure for the remainder of the war. As with General Burgoyne's army, congressional delegates remained unwilling to consider an exchange; the prisoners' cries went unanswered. By war's end, Congress, like an anonymous correspondent in the *Boston Evening-Post*, had come to believe that "towards the nation of Britain, as citizens of America, you owe nothing but revenge."[7]

The Failure of Pacification

When Lincoln's Continental regiments filed out of their entrenchments on May 12 to lay down their arms and surrender their colors, their captors were shocked by the Americans' appearance. Their faces gaunt from months of deprivation and their uniforms soiled, threadbare, and torn, the prisoners nonetheless evinced "more appearance of discipline" than what one of Clinton's Scottish officers had "seen formerly" from American troops. These men were not the parcel of novices the British had confronted during the first years of the war; they were regulars who deserved to be treated as such. Though defeated, the Continentals had much for which to be proud. Having skillfully fortified Charleston and defended it against the combined might of Britain's army and navy for months, the soldiers could rest assured that they had done their duty and had surrendered with honor. Brigadier General William Moultrie remembered that the British officers congratulated their prisoners on having "made a gallant defence." Instead of the jeers and jabs endured by the garrison of Fort Washington, Charleston's defenders marched out unmolested, accompanied only by the shrill melodies of their field musicians. Impressed by the respectful silence of their adversaries, the troops returned to their barracks and the officers to their quarters, all prepared to enter captivity.[8]

General Clinton had two options when it came to the Continental prisoners. He could allow them to remain confined to their barracks, or he could order the men aboard troop transports bound for New York; the articles of capitulation had not specified the mode or location of their confinement. Were Clinton to send the prisoners to New York, the city's commander, Lieutenant General Wilhelm von Knyphausen, would have no choice but to confine them aboard prison ships. Clinton was aware of the insalubrious conditions on board the hulks, and he had no intention of sending his recent captives to their deaths; the prisoners were far too valuable. For years, Congress had refused to exchange the Convention Army for privateers in British custody, but now Clinton had enough American soldiers to redeem the survivors of Burgoyne's unfortunate force. The timing could not have been better. After France's entry into the war in 1778, Lord Germain had required the general to shift a significant percentage of his forces to the West Indies to protect Britain's lucrative sugar islands. London promised reinforcements, but none were yet forthcoming. Clinton needed more men. Augmenting his southern army with the Saratoga Convention troops would allow him to shift a sizable segment of his command to New York, where he could begin operations against Washington. While he prepared to negotiate the Continental prisoners' exchange, Clinton allowed them to remain in the comfort of their barracks. True to his word in the articles of capitulation, the British commander ordered the men provided with wholesome rations. After the war, an American surgeon with the prisoners, Dr. Peter

Fayssoux, claimed that the troops had no "material cause of complaint." No one in Charleston expected them to remain confined for long.[9]

Soon after the Continental troops surrendered, Clinton's officers began the arduous process of administering paroles to the city's militia. Composing over half of the garrison, the militiamen did not present as martial an appearance as their Continental brethren. One British officer described them as "*poor Creatures*" who "began to creep out of their Holes" following the capitulation. Eager to safeguard their possessions—the slave owners among the population were particularly anxious to keep their human property—thousands of civilians, both those who had been in arms and those who had refused to defend the city, came forward to claim their paroles. Moultrie recalled seeing "the aged, the timid, the disaffected, and the infirm, many of them who had never appeared during the whole siege," come forward "to enrol [*sic*] on a conqueror's list." The American general believed that the people were "tired of war" and keen to accept Clinton's "pleasing offers, in hopes they would have been suffered to remain peaceably and quietly at home with their families." It was a very tempting proposition, one that thousands of Charlestonians accepted. Clinton was overjoyed by the turnout, informing Germain, "with the greatest pleasure," that "there are few men in South Carolina who are not either our prisoners or in arms with us." It looked as if his policy of benevolence had worked. With their paroles in hand, most of the militiamen departed the city, pleased to be rid of war.[10]

Possessed of Charleston, the British general now sought to expand his reach into the countryside. Fearing that his "success at Charles Town—unless followed in the Back Country—will be of little avail," Clinton ordered his second in command, Lieutenant General Cornwallis, to consolidate royal authority in the colony by establishing fortified positions inland and by administering oaths of allegiance to the populace. Armed with promises of pardon, Cornwallis's troops fanned out into the South Carolina hinterlands. Clinton was confident that residents there were "not only friendly to Government" but also willing "to take up arms in its support."[11]

Clinton was not wholly mistaken. In the weeks following Charleston's fall, thousands of loyalists flocked to his troops for protection and for the opportunity to chastise their rebel neighbors. For years, they had endured persecution at the hands of the revolutionaries, but now the time had come for revenge. As one of Clinton's aides informed him, the loyalists were "clamorous for retributive Justice" and would not rest "until those People whose persecuting spirit hath caused such calamities to their fellow subjects shall receive the punishment their Inequities deserve." Seizing the opportunity, many Crown supporters took matters into their own hands. According to an officer in Clinton's army, a party of "friends to Government" rounded up "forty odd Rebels" to answer for seventy of their own who had been "condemned to be hanged" in 1779. The loyalists, who had been "obliged to hide in Swamps & Caves to keep from Prison themselves," now gladly embraced "the opportunity to retaliate." Frustrated, Clinton issued orders "to restrain the militia" from acts of wanton violence. His entire plan for pacifying the South rested on forgiveness for past transgressions. But clemency was not what South Carolina loyalists had in mind. The sight of unrepentant rebels going about their daily routines, protected in their person and property by British paroles, galled them. In their opinion, vengeance should be swift and merciless.[12]

Loyalists could take comfort at least from the knowledge that many in Clinton's army disagreed with their commander's policy of benevolent pacification. Paroling rebel officers was bad enough, but permitting common militiamen to return home on the bare promise of neutrality was egregious. These were not gentlemen who could be depended upon to keep their word. Scottish Captain John Peebles worried that there would be few prisoners left to exchange because "all the Militia &ca. get their parole & the inhabitants of the Town their property." Constrained only by their promise, the militiamen would be prime subjects for rebel recruiters should Washington send another army southward. Hessian officer Johann Ewald believed that Clinton's decision would "cost the English dear, because I am convinced that most of these people will have guns in their hands within a short time." Lieutenant Colonel Alexander Innes simply referred to the terms as "the *cursed* capitulation of Charles Town." To these men, the rebellion had to be crushed, not conciliated.[13]

Another such hardliner was the twenty-six-year-old lieutenant colonel Banastre Tarleton. Probably the ablest, and certainly the most dashing, cavalry commander of the war, Tarleton was already known for his fearlessness and ferocity in battle, but it was in the South that he gained a reputation for brutality. The seeds of that reputation were planted at the end of May, when Tarleton and the green-jacketed troops of the loyalist British Legion caught up with the last remaining American force in the Carolinas at a place in the border region between the two states known as the Waxhaws. The Crown force had advanced more than a hundred miles in just over two days to intercept these Virginia Continentals. Confident in his superior numbers, the American commander,

Colonel Abraham Buford, refused Tarleton's summons to surrender under the terms offered Charleston's garrison. What happened afterward remains clouded in controversy. Sources on both sides agree that upon Buford's refusal, Tarleton's mounted troopers advanced swiftly on the line of 350 American infantrymen. The Virginians withheld their fire until it was too late; the dragoons were soon among them. Some of Buford's men fled, while others begged for their lives. As one of the American officers rode forward with a white flag of surrender, Tarleton was thrown from his horse. Years following the battle, Tarleton claimed that his men believed that "they had lost their commanding officer, which stimulated the soldiers to a vindictive asperity not easily restrained." One of Buford's officers, Colonel H. Boyer, remembered events differently. In his account, American musketry dismounted Tarleton during the surrender negotiations. Furious, the British colonel ordered his men to continue the assault. As Boyer phrased it, "the rage of the British soldiers, excited by the continued fire of the Americans while a negotiation was offered by the flag, impelled them to acts of vengeance that knew no limits." Whatever the cause, the results were the same. In Tarleton's words, "slaughter was commenced," resulting in 113 Americans being killed outright and a further 150 wounded.[14]

To the British, Buford's defeat was a "complete success"; to the Americans, it was a "massacre." Rumors that Tarleton's men had cut down the Virginians after they had surrendered soon began to circulate. North Carolina councilman Thomas Person notified congressional delegate Thomas Burke that "'tis Said [the British Legion] killed at least 200 men in a most Cruel & Inhumane Manner, after piling their Arms" in surrender. It was not long before American newspapers picked up the story. The *American Journal* claimed that "instead of meeting with that reception which the feelings of humanity dictates, or that clemency which our conquered foes have ever received at our hands, no quarter was given" to Buford's surrendering soldiers. The *Massachusetts Spy* accused Tarleton of "the most inhuman acts of cruelty that were ever heard of, viz. in the massacre of the gallant, amiable Col. Buford and 170 of his corps." Although British accounts did not use the term "massacre," Tarleton's official report of the action, which was widely published, seemed to confirm the revolutionaries' version of events. In it he claimed that his men "attacked [the Virginians] and cut them to Pieces." The American reading public knew exactly how to interpret Tarleton's words; the British had not reformed their barbarous ways, and their promises of conciliation and generous treatment were not to be trusted. Appalled by the violence, sixteen-year-old Eliza Wilkinson of Charleston decried British "cruelties and oppressions," believing that her countrymen would be roused by "the spirit of resentment" to oppose the occupiers. She could not have been more prophetic. Throughout the backcountry settlements, militia companies began to organize. General Clinton, safely ensconced in Charleston, was blissfully unaware of the Carolinians' rising antipathy for the British occupation.[15]

Believing that he had pacified South Carolina, Clinton decided to return to New York, though not before making a decision that would fundamentally alter the course and character of the war in the South. On June 3, 1780, he issued a proclamation invalidating article four of the treaty of capitulation of Charleston, which had paroled the militia to their homes. From thenceforth all who had surrendered under the terms of the treaty were "freed and exempted from all such Paroles." With their paroles removed, the men were "restored to all the Rights and Duties belonging to Citizens and Inhabitants" of Great Britain. Acting on spurious intelligence of the strength of loyalist support in the Carolinas, Clinton abrogated the militiamen's paroles in the belief that they would rally to the royal standard and provide the nucleus of a new royal militia that would maintain the peace he had won at Charleston. To further encourage the militiamen to do their duty, Clinton added a not-so-thinly veiled threat to his proclamation. All South Carolinians "who shall afterwards neglect to return to his Allegiance and to his Majesty's Government, will be considered as Enemies and Rebels to the same, and treated accordingly." By 1780, South Carolinians were well aware of how the British treated rebels. Although it had not been his intent, Clinton had drawn a line in the sand; the opportunity for passive neutrality had passed. Cornwallis realized at once the error of his commander's actions and feared that the proclamation would excite neutrals into armed opposition against the Crown. Nonetheless, it also freed the earl to take a more aggressive stance against those who opposed British rule in the South. Soon after issuing his proclamation, Clinton returned to New York, leaving Cornwallis in command of the southern theater. The earl promptly informed his inspector of militia, Major Patrick Ferguson, of his intentions to pursue a "plan of imprisoning those who have rendered themselves obnoxious by their cruelty and persecution of our friends [the loyalists]." The time for conciliation was over.[16]

Predictably, South Carolinians were indignant. Clinton had promised them peace and neutrality, but by reneging on his word, he now forced them back into the conflict. John Weldon is typical of a South Carolina militiaman who had seen enough of war and just wanted to go home, having been "so much injured" in earlier campaigns to be rendered "unfit for service." Nevertheless, when Clinton besieged Charleston, he had rushed to defend the beleaguered capital but had arrived too late; the city had fallen. Arrested but "dismissed on parole and permitted to return home," he had no intention of violating his promise by taking up arms. But after the June 3 proclamation, loyalist troops gave Weldon a choice: "he must deliver himself up [for loyalist militia service] or join the Enemy." For a man who had fought and bled for the revolutionary cause, the choice was simple. Weldon "broke his parole ... and marched to and joined" a band of revolutionary militia under the command of Brigadier General Thomas Sumter. Enraged by Clinton's duplicity and Tarleton's brutality, Carolinians like Weldon wasted no time before attacking Crown forces: first at Ramsour's Mill (North Carolina) on June 20 and then at Williamson's Plantation (South Carolina) on July 12. In both actions the revolutionaries inflicted devastating defeats on the embryonic loyalist militia. Cornwallis feared that these reverses would "much encourage the enemy." If he did not act soon, the entire countryside would erupt in open rebellion.[17]

Lord Cornwallis was no brute, but he was determined. Like both Howe and Clinton, he once had been sympathetic to the colonists' complaints, even voting against the Stamp Act in the House of Lords. Yet once war began, the earl felt compelled by a strict sense of duty, and more than a modicum of ambition, to carry on the conflict in earnest. During the New York Campaign, he had pursued revolutionary forces with a sense of doggedness and alacrity unparalleled by any of Britain's senior officers in America. His superiors in London hoped Cornwallis would bring that same determination to the South. With France and Spain threatening the Caribbean colonies and even the home islands, Britain needed a decisive victory over the Americans. In the earl's opinion, Clinton's compassion and generosity had failed to quell the rebellion; the time had come to "punish severely" the king's enemies. Once in independent command of Crown forces in the South, Cornwallis's first step was to "seize all violent and persecuting rebels and send them directly on parole" to the remote Sea Islands of South Carolina, where they could do little harm to the royal cause. Dozens of Charlestonians thus were dragged from their homes and forced into exile. Those who were "very notorious for acts of cruelty" were sent under guard to the provost's prison in Charleston. To further deter insurrection, Cornwallis made it known that in the future any rebel who broke his parole would "instantly be hanged without any form of trial."[18]

The general's orders were music to the ears of a hardliner like Tarleton. From his point of view, "the insurgents, having taken certificates and paroles, don't deserve lenity," and "none shall they experience." In a statement that has forever cloaked the British officer in infamy, Tarleton boasted, "I shall give these disturbers of the peace no quarter"; if some loyal subjects or neutrals perished in the process, so be it. As he informed Cornwallis, he would "discriminate with severity." Colonel Francis Marion, a revolutionary militia commander who was no stranger to violence, was horrified that "Colonel Tarleton...spares neither Whig nor Tory." But for Tarleton, the path to victory was clear: "Nothing will serve these people but fire and sword." For southerners, revolutionaries and neutrals alike, such tactics had the opposite effect: "Tarleton's Quarter" became a rallying cry for resistance.[19]

The specter of slave revolt compounded rumors of British butchery in the minds of white southerners. Under Clinton's 1779 Philipsburg Proclamation, all slaves belonging to rebel masters could claim freedom within British lines. As with Governor Dunmore's earlier promise of freedom, this declaration was not evidence of Britain's commitment to emancipation. Instead, Clinton intended to weaken slave owners' loyalty to the revolutionary cause by threatening their livelihood; any additional manpower for Crown forces was a bonus. Upward of five thousand South Carolina slaves accepted the offer, many choosing to join loyalist corps such as the regiment of Black Dragoons. Much like his revocation of the militiamen's paroles, Clinton's plan backfired. Armed black men in red uniforms threatened the social and racial hierarchies of the South, infuriating whites from across the political and social spectrum. Tepid loyalists, who might have chanced the field, now stayed home, while fervent whigs rushed to arms to preserve their way of life.[20]

Ignoring both the lackluster loyalist turnout and the growing hatred of the Carolinians, Cornwallis pressed his advance northward. The British juggernaut was briefly stalled in August by an American force under Major General Gates, "the Hero of Saratoga." The two armies literally collided in darkness on the morning of the sixteenth near Camden, South Carolina. The resulting battle was a disastrous defeat for Gates, who fled the field in ignominy. Tarleton, whose dragoons played a critical role in cutting off the Americans' retreat, remembered that "rout and slaughter ensued in every quarter." Over seven hundred American soldiers fell into Crown hands that day. A British soldier with Cornwallis claimed that the prisoners were "treated with civility" and forwarded to "Charleston under guard," but once there, they posed a significant problem for the British commandant of the city, Lieutenant Colonel Nisbet Balfour.[21]

Before Cornwallis had launched his invasion of the South Carolina back-country, the earl had charged Balfour with overseeing the administration of the American prisoners in the city. The general had been confident that the captives would soon be released through a general cartel of exchange, or at the very least provisioned by the American commissary, Captain George Turner. Regrettably for the prisoners, by August, Congress still had not acquiesced to an exchange of Charleston's captive garrison for the Convention Army, and the oft-promised supplies had not been forthcoming. Overwhelmed with enemy prisoners and unable to provide them with the provisions, quarters, and medicines they sorely needed, Balfour despaired to Cornwallis that he found "the *prisoners* by no means an *easy load*." With "sickness and mortality" spreading among the garrison, he had little choice but to confine the Americans on board prison ships, ordering six transport ships converted for this purpose. Once occupied, the vessels soon became cesspools of filth and disease. A militiaman captured at Camden reported that "small pocks" was present on board the ersatz hulks, taking the lives of "a Number of brave men." Without resupply from either London or Philadelphia, Balfour could do little to ease the misery. Clearly pained by their plight, he lamented that "the rebell prisoners die faster than ever they used to desert."[22]

As had been the case during the New York Campaign, revolutionary propagandists laid blame for the prisoners' suffering not on Congress for its unwillingness to exchange the men or its inability to provide for them but upon the British commander. A South Carolinian writing for the *Pennsylvania Packet* urged his fellow statesmen "to take vengeance" on the "perfidious foe . . . Cornwallis" for the "cruelties committed throughout your once flourishing state." Another correspondent, this time purporting to be an escapee from "a most cruel captivity, in Charlestown, South Carolina," enumerated "the many cruelties and enormities that have been, and are now put in practice on our suffering brethren in South Carolina." Referencing the archetypical Roman tyrant, he branded Cornwallis "the British NERO" and accused the general of the "direct violation of the most solemn articles of capitulation." In closing, he warned all Americans to "never expect lenity, nor even common humanity, at their [the British] hands." By this period in the war, revolutionaries everywhere had little cause to doubt his accusations or question his reasoning. Summarizing the temper of backcountry South Carolinians, an aide to General Gates claimed,

"They breathe nothing but revenge, for the unheard-of cruelties committed upon our distressed people." Clinton's plan to pacify the South had failed. Southern loyalists, and their British protectors, would soon know the wrath of American vengeance.[23]

Abuse in the Backcountry

Having routed Gates and the American Southern Army at Camden, Cornwallis concluded that the best way of securing his gains in South Carolina was to invade North Carolina, where he hoped to overawe the people with the celerity and ferocity of his advance. He believed that with both Carolinas in British hands, the rebels would surely see that further resistance was futile. Before marching northward, the earl informed Clinton in New York of his intention "to hang up all those militia men" who had deserted to the enemy. No mere threat, Cornwallis admitted that he personally ordered "several militia men to be executed." Many of his more zealous subordinates jumped at the opportunity to punish recalcitrant rebels as well. Lieutenant Colonel John Harris Cruger, a New York loyalist, delighted in "sending out parties of horse to pick up the traiterous rebels . . . , who will be roughly handled, some very probably suspended [hanged]" for their crimes. Another loyalist officer noted that "twenty seven of them [American prisoners] were hanged at Augusta, & twenty seven brought to Ninety Six [in South Carolina] to share the same fate." North Carolinians rightly feared that such punishments would be in store for them should they oppose the British invader.[24]

In contrast to his general's uncompromising approach, Major Ferguson still believed that restraint, not retaliation, was the best anodyne for the disease of rebellion infecting the southern countryside. Tasked with the dual responsibility of subduing rebel partisan groups and drumming up recruits for his own militia, Ferguson took a small contingent of uniformed loyalists into the backcountry borderlands in the hopes of convincing "the deluded inhabitants of the revolted American provinces" of the king's mercy. Hardly the gaggle of bloodthirsty bandits often depicted, Ferguson's forces were under strict orders "to offer no injury to the persons or propertys of those men that have been on the rebel side" in the past. He warned his soldiers that "those who by plunder and outrage disgrace the name of loyalists" would "be punished even to death." Rather than rampaging through the backcountry, Ferguson advanced cautiously and with moderation. The restrained conduct of his men shocked civilian onlookers expecting little less than "Tarleton's Quarter" from the armed loyalists. One of Ferguson's officers, Surgeon Uzal Johnson, recorded meeting "one Poor Woman [who] expressed great surprise at seeing our Men so mild." Having heard "of the Cruelty of the English," the woman asked Uzal "if there was not Heathens in our Army that eat Children" because "she had been told there was." Notwithstanding the restraint shown by the loyalist column, most backcountry settlers still believed that Ferguson's mission was nefarious; the stories of British atrocities were just too credible. To them, the major and his loyalist minions had to be stopped before they could "lay their country waste with fire and sword."[25]

In early October revolutionary militias, acting independently of either state or congressional orders and thus unbound by rules and regulations, caught up with the loyalist column at Kings Mountain in South Carolina. It was bloody, desperate work. Within an hour, Ferguson was dead and the loyalists' line of retreat cut off. The survivors tried to surrender, but their pleas for quarter had little purchase with the enraged "backwater men." Militiaman Charles Bowen admitted in his pension application that he "shot the first man who hoisted the [white] flag among the enemy." His comrade Joseph Hughes claimed: "We killed near a hundred of them [loyalists] after the surrender. . . . [We] could hardly be restrained from killing the whole of them." The militia had gone into the battle with the countersign "Buford" and the intention to avenge the "massacre" at the Waxhaws. In his journal Lieutenant Alexander Chesney noted that he feared that the militia "would not give quarter" to his loyalist soldiers, and he was not surprised that "the Americans resumed firing" well after the initial surrender. He reported that "a dreadful havoc took place until the flag was sent out a second time when the work of destruction ceased." Believing their ordeal at an end, Chesney and his fellow loyalists threw down their arms, thankful to be alive.[26]

With the battle finally over, the American commanders found themselves in possession of some seven hundred loyalist prisoners but without a plan or protocol for what to do with them. Only a fraction of the captives were uniformed regulars, the remainder being Carolina loyalists. Were these men prisoners of war, and thus eligible for exchange, or were they state prisoners who should be tried for treason? No one in the American camp seemed to know the answer. Their deliberations were interrupted by reports that Tarleton and a British relief column were on the way. The militia commanders reasoned that their best hope of avoiding the British pursuers, and of divesting themselves of their prisoners, was to link up with the remainder of Gates's army in North Carolina; perhaps the general would know what to do with them.[27]

The exhausted prisoners marched over twenty miles a day, impeded by abuse from their militia guards and poor provisions. Chesney recorded that the Americans were continually "cutting and striking us by the road in a savage manner" to prod their advance. Several captives must have perished under this ill treatment; Colonel William Campbell issued an order on October 11 requesting "the officers of all ranks in the army to endeavor to restrain the disorderly manner of slaughtering and disturbing the prisoners." Those who survived attack by the guards nevertheless suffered from lack of sustenance. If the American militia had food to spare, they did not share it with their prisoners, who "were worn out with fatigue and fasting . . . , having no bread or meat for two days." It was not until the column reached Gilbertown, North Carolina, on the thirteenth that the prisoners finally received "an ear of corn" and some old clothing in remuneration for what the militiamen had stolen from them after the battle. Unfortunately for the Crown troops, these tokens of American "liberality" merely masked their captors' real intentions.[28]

To their horror, the prisoners awoke on the morning of October 14 to learn that their commanders would stand trial for their lives. Grumblings among the militiamen for harsher measures had escalated overnight into demands for a drumhead tribunal to try the principal loyalist officers. As one militiaman remembered, he and his comrades hoped to make an example of men who had "committed cool and deliberate murder and other enormities alike atrocious." Acquiescing to the demands of their troops, the American officers organized a kangaroo court under the pretense of a North Carolina law authorizing two magistrates to convene a trial. Surgeon Johnson, who witnessed the proceedings, claimed that the prisoners were tried "for treason" against the state. A contemporaneous account from an unknown loyalist prisoner describes what happened next. "After a short hearing, thirty gentlemen, some of the most respectable characters in that country, had sentences of death passed on them; and at six o'clock of the same day they began to execute" the men. The condemned prisoners, who included socially prominent loyalists such as Colonel Ambrose Mills of Green River, were hanged three at a time in front of the other captives, who "were compelled to attend at the execution of their brave but unfortunate men." Johnson recorded that the men "died like Romans saying they died for their King & his Laws." After the execution of the first nine prisoners, the grisly affair came to an abrupt halt. In his postwar narrative, Colonel Isaac Shelby claimed that he "interfered, and proposed to stop it." In a contemporary account, Lieutenant Chesney maintained that the Americans only suspended the executions because they received news of the impending arrival of Tarleton's British Legion.[29]

Whatever the cause for discontinuing the hangings, the motive that animated the militiamen to begin them in the first place is clear—revenge. Shelby insisted that the "cruel and unjustifiable acts" of the British "required retaliatory measures." In a similar vein, Colonel William Hill, who was with Gates's army at the time, justified the execution of the prisoners because the militiamen had been "provoked to this by the severity of the British who had lately hanged a great number of americans [sic]." Despite its legal varnish, this was not a case of proportional retaliation; the executions were not carried out in response to any particular act of British or loyalist aggression, nor was their purpose to dissuade the enemy from committing future atrocities. The prisoners perished to sate the bloodlust of their captors. Far from appalled by the militia's rash actions, Governor John Rutledge of South Carolina rejoiced that the militia had executed "8 or 10 of the most noted horse Thieves & Tories" in the Carolinas. The tidewater planter and politician agreed wholeheartedly with his backwoods constituents: Tory traitors deserved nothing less than the hangman's noose.[30]

Having witnessed the murder of nine of their fellows and fearing that a similar fate was in store for them, many of the Kings Mountain prisoners resolved to escape. As the column trudged northward, flight became a viable option when more and more of the American militiamen, fed up with poor rations and monotonous marching, deserted. When their remaining guards were not looking, numerous prisoners slipped away. Others were not so lucky. Surgeon Johnson made note of "three Prisoners endeavouring to make their escape, one got shot through the Body"; the wounded man was hanged the next morning. Despite the threat of summary capital punishment, prisoners continued to decamp at a significant rate. Chesney, who received a death sentence for refusing to train the American militia, managed to flee when the column approached Salem (modern Winston-Salem, North Carolina).[31]

Those not agile enough to escape risked falling victim to their captors' fury. According to loyalist lieutenants William Stevenson and John Taylor, the prisoners were "so wearied that many of them were obliged to give out on the road." Unable or unwilling to spare a guard while they recovered, the Americans murdered the exhausted men. When Surgeon Johnson tried to tend to the wounded stragglers, one of the militia commanders, Colonel Benjamin Cleveland, stood in his way, calling the surgeon "a Damnd Villain" who "deserved the Gallows." For the act of aiding the injured men, Cleveland struck him "over the Head with his Sword, and levil'd" the doctor. Repeating the stroke, the colonel "cut his hand with his sword." When Johnson demanded to know his crime, all Cleveland could say was that he was "a Damn'd Traitor to [his] Country." The North Carolina colonel, who would be known to posterity as "the Terror of the Tories," was determined to see all of the prisoners tried and executed for betraying a country they had never claimed. Believing their lives endangered because the Americans "seem'd determined to murder" them, Stevenson and Taylor eventually succeeded in making their escape. Johnson was not far behind, disguising his identity because he knew that many back-country southerners "would not stick at murdering me if they found out I belonged to the British."[32]

The survivors who failed to escape faced a grim choice: abandon their principles and enlist in the American forces or face civil prosecution for treason. Although General Washington was vehemently opposed to enlisting British or loyalist prisoners into the Continental Army, local recruiters were in dire need of trained men who could withstand the discipline and rigors of campaigning. For many prisoners, the choice was simple: they enlisted rather than face the hangman or a slow death in an American prison. In early November Johnson recorded that "most of them [the Kings Mountain prisoners] enlisted in the Continental Service rather than suffer Death by inches Starving with cold & hunger." Aware of the likely outcome of a treason trial, the surgeon could not blame his comrades for their desperate acts of self-preservation. Once the column reached Salisbury, North Carolina, Colonel Martin Armstrong reported that "One hundred & Eighty Eight" prisoners were "taken out of my Hands by the Civil power, & bound over to ye law." William Gist was one loyalist who refused to join the revolutionary effort. In his postwar claim for compensation from the Crown, Gist related his ordeal. Tried for his life, he was "handcuffed and marched two hundred miles," being passed from jail to jail, "with little or nothing to Eat" for two months until he finally managed to escape. When Cornwallis liberated the Salisbury jail in the winter of 1781, the general was appalled. The remaining Kings Mountain men were "almost starved to death." The Americans had retained only a few in custody: nearly three hundred of them had escaped, some had "enlisted in to the Continental Service," and others had paid the ultimate price for their fidelity to the British Crown.[33]

Both Continental and state authorities were furious that the militia had allowed so many prisoners to abscond or enlist. General Gates, who had hoped to exchange the captives for the Americans held at Charleston, reprimanded Armstrong. "These prisoners ought to have been carefully kept confined, to be tried by the Laws of the State, to which they belong . . . or exchanged for our Militia Prisoners of War." Embarrassed, the colonel assured him that had he not enlisted the men, "the officers from The other Side of the Mountain" would have "Kill[ed] every one of Them." Armstrong had done what he thought best under the circumstances. The North Carolina Board of War was unimpressed. Its members demanded to know why he had issued such "Indulgences" to loyalist "Villains" while American prisoners suffered in Charleston under constant threat of being sent to "the West Indies, out of our power, there to rot and die in Gaols." Armstrong would not be allowed to make that mistake again; the North Carolina Legislature suspended him indefinitely. As the colonel learned all too well, enemy prisoners were the state's property, and the governments of the southern states were determined to exact retribution for British atrocities. If Cornwallis denied American soldiers quarter, abused American prisoners on prison ships, and executed American civilians for supposed violations of their paroles, then British and loyalist prisoners would suffer for his cruelty.[34]

When he received news of the treatment of the Kings Mountain prisoners, Cornwallis was apoplectic. He immediately dashed off a letter of protest to Continental brigadier general William Smallwood. In his remonstrance the earl raged against "the cruelty exercised on the prisoners taken under major Ferguson," treatment he found "shocking to humanity." To the British general, the execution of Colonel Mills, "who was always a fair and open enemy" to the American cause, and his eight fellow prisoners was "an act of the most savage barbarity." The loyalist press in New York agreed. Intent on exciting loyalist indignation, the *Royal Gazette* printed a letter from one of Cornwallis's officers describing how the American militia had committed abuses "too shocking for humanity to enumerate" by treating the prisoners "worse than savages, in a most cruel manner." With loyalist resentment running high, Cornwallis informed Smallwood that if he did not use his "authority to stop this bloody scene," the earl would permit the "loyalists to retaliate on the unfortunate persons now in [his] power."[35]

Rather than engage in a cycle of retaliation, Cornwallis proposed a partial exchange to resolve the matter. He was willing to "exchange any of the North or South Carolina militia who may be prisoners with us for those who were taken on Kings Mountain." The Crown commander had earlier hoped to establish a general cartel of exchange, but he was now willing to accept a far more limited swap to preserve the morale of southern loyalists and rid himself of the burden of provisioning and confining captured Americans whose expenses Congress seemed unlikely to recompense. Unfortunately, Smallwood had no prisoners to exchange; the militia had killed some and had permitted the remainder to enlist or escape. Even if he had still possessed the Kings Mountain prisoners, Congress had not yet acquiesced to General Gates's request to engage in exchange negotiations with Cornwallis. Speaking for many revolutionary southerners, Governor Rutledge feared that "many, if not all of 'em [Kings Mountain prisoners] will return to the Enemy" without redeeming a single American captive.[36]

Both sides agreed that an exchange remained a viable option. Replacing Gates as the Continental commander in the southern theater, Major General Nathanael Greene came south in the fall of 1780 armed with a secret weapon: congressional permission to arrange a large-scale exchange of prisoners. The new president of the Continental Congress, Samuel Huntington, informed the Rhode Islander, a former Quaker who had distinguished himself as one of Washington's most able lieutenants, that he was "expressly authorized to negotiate from Time to Time an Exchange of Prisoners with the Commanding Officer of the British Army in that Department." To Greene's frustration, this authorization was circumscribed by the delegates' continued refusal to exchange the Convention Army. As subjects of congressional retaliation, Burgoyne's defeated soldiers were worth more in custody than Lincoln's army ever would be if freed. Thus, if Greene wanted to redeem the Charleston prisoners, he would have to capture a British army of his own.[37]

This was a tall order given the meager force of Continental regulars Washington had been able to spare for the Southern Department, but the Rhode Islander had a plan to recoup the captive Continentals. Rather than sideline the numerous militia and partisan commanders in the South as Gates had done, Greene would aggressively employ them to interdict British supply and communication lines and intimidate the local loyalists, picking up prisoners along the way. He was pleased by the work of Colonel Marion and his fellow partisans, informing Marion that "we must endeavour to keep up a Partizan War." Anticipating a flood of enemy captives, Greene ordered Captain Joseph Marbury to establish a depot in Salisbury, North Carolina, "for the safe Custody of the Prisoners of War." The camp, enclosed by an eighteen-foot stockade, would boast a secure jail for recalcitrant prisoners, a "Scaffold" that would allow the guards to "Watch or fire upon the Prisoners," and "Hutts [sic] within the Pickets for them [the prisoners] to cook and sleep in." While innovative, Greene's plan was overly ambitious. Salisbury's civilian leaders had little interest in spending their finite resources on building a prison for a congressionally appointed general. Additionally, local craftsmen refused to work for nearly worthless Continental dollars. Marbury regretted that he did not have the tools or the "fatigue Men to use them" to build the prison anyway, his soldiers being "naked and sickly." The prison proved to be a pipe dream.[38]

As it turned out, Greene would have little need for a prison depot because few American militiamen had any intention of taking prisoners in the first place. With Ferguson and his loyalist minions defeated and dispersed, militiamen like John Clemmons "wished to take vengeance on them who had cruelly used him." Sometimes with authorization from their respective states but often acting on their own recognizance, such troops plundered, tortured, and murdered loyalists throughout the Carolinas at will. After having served at Kings Mountain, John Waddill enlisted in Colonel Elijah Clarke's militia company for the purpose of suppressing loyalists. During the winter of 1780–81, he and his comrades "killed several Tories in the course of this expedition, and destroyed their property." Explaining his conduct, Waddill argued that his fellow militiamen, "who had been driven from their homes and whose families and relations had been murdered by the Tories and their property destroyed, were so much exasperated, that they could not be restrained from retaliation." Similarly enraged, George Parks, a militiaman who served under Colonel Cleveland, recalled surprising a party of loyalists and capturing seven of them. Instead of turning them over to Continental troops or to civilian authorities for trial, Parks's "party of Minute Men hung two of them" before "whipping the rest nearly to death." In this case, the militiamen were not acting out proportional retaliation for a specific loyalist misdeed but were engaging in what became known in the South as "Lynch's law."[39]

Purportedly named for Virginia militia colonel Charles Lynch, who along with Cleveland had ordered the execution of a loyalist in the summer of 1780 without any other due process than "the joint consent of near three hundred men," the "lynching" of loyalists became all too quotidian until the end of the war. Nathaniel Smith admitted that while employed in "keeping down Tories," he "administered Lynch's law" to his captives. Men who appeared "suspicious"

to Smith and his colleagues were summarily executed by hanging. The North
Carolina Senate officially approved the "lynching" of loyalists on July 27, 1781,
when it passed a bill "to indemnify all such persons as have put to death any
of the subjects of this State, being known & notorious Enemies & Opponents
of the Government thereof." Provided the victim could be identified as a loyalist, the "lyncher" had nothing to fear from the state's revolutionary government.
Predictably, this license to kill terrified both ardent and lukewarm Crown
supporters alike. Lieutenant Colonel Balfour warned Cornwallis from Charleston that the Americans had "adopted the System of murdering every militia
officer of ours as well as every man (although unarmed) who is known to be a
loyalist. *The terror this mode of conduct has struck* you will easily *suppose.*"[40]

Southern militias were not alone in their practice of terrorizing, torturing,
and executing loyalists; northern revolutionaries committed similar acts of
vengeance. Wherever British forces could project enough power to support
loyalist resistance, revolutionary militias and crowds responded with terror
and violence. General Clinton received numerous petitions from northern
loyalists and British prisoners who had suffered in American hands. The case
of Henry Dyer, "a Loyal Refugee from Orange County in the Province of New
York," is uncomfortably typical. Dyer pleaded with Clinton in July 1780 to
arrange for his release from American captivity, which he had endured for over
a year. During this imprisonment, he was "hanged up by the Rebels three
different times to extort Confession or gratify their cruelty." When not being
tortured, he languished for "a long Time in Irons." Unlike Dyer, who escaped
with his life, a Mr. Lantman of Catskill, New York, paid the ultimate price for
his "attachment to the British constitution" when three Albany men broke into
his jail cell to "cooly [sic], deliberately and cruelly" murder him. The culprits
encouraged their fellow townspeople to "view the dismal spectacle" of Lantman's lifeless body hanging from the jail's rafters. Regrettably for loyalists like
Dyer and Lantman, Continental authorities could do little to prevent such
abuses. In January 1781 a Continental officer in New York reported that "a set
of Lawless Ruffians[,] who under the Sanction of being Friends to their Country
disgrace the Name, by Conduct which the most savage Barbarians would
condemn," were engaged in "beating, burning, [and] hanging" Crown supporters and neutral civilians. Because their actions were sanctioned by the
laws of New York, "no Redress can be obtained [f]or the Inhabitants for the
most part are excluded from the Privileges of civil Law." General Heath admitted to Washington that he could do nothing to protect the loyalists because

"if any Officer interferes, he subjects himself to a civil prosecution." The states had criminalized loyalism, making any suspected royalist a suitable target for persecution.[41]

Revengeful violence was not the exclusive purview of revolutionary militias and committees; Continental units were also complicit in the murder and mistreatment of enemy prisoners. In December 1780 Colonel William Washington, the second cousin of the American commanding general, led his 3rd Continental Light Dragoons against Georgia loyalists under the command of Colonel Thomas Waters near Hammond's Store, South Carolina. Seeing the approach of enemy cavalry, the loyalists broke formation and ran for their lives. They were no match for Washington's horsemen, who soon caught up with the fleeing men. Within minutes, 150 loyalists lay dead, dying, or maimed on the field without a single American casualty. Continental captain John Davidson explained the carnage: "Washingtons men had in remembrance some of Mr. Tarltons former Acts and Acted accordingly." The following day Washington's dragoons hanged a loyalist prisoner they accused of aiding hostile Native Americans. Colonel Henry Lee's legion was equally ruthless in its treatment of loyalists. When Lee's Continentals stumbled upon a party of 300–400 loyalist militiamen commanded by Dr. John Pyle in February 1781, they "rushed on the Tories like lightening and cut away." Instantly, the field was transformed into a charnel house. As Lee later admitted: "The conflict was quickly decided and bloody on one side only. Ninety of the royalists were killed and most of the survivors wounded." Again, the Americans suffered no casualties. Justifying the actions of his troops, who cut down unarmed men begging for their lives, Lee claimed that "our safety was not compatible with that of the supplicants" crying out for quarter.[42]

Southern loyalists responded to revolutionary retribution with acts of violence every bit as cruel and devastating as those of their opponents. Militia commanders David Fanning and Thomas Brown were notorious for their persecution of American prisoners. In his postwar narrative Fanning confessed to turning over a captured commissary of prisoners to "some of my men, who he had treated ill when prisoners; and they immediately hung him." At other times Fanning took personal responsibility for ordering the death of his prisoners. Having captured two American militiamen he believed were implicated in the death of one of his officers, Fanning "hung them by way of retaliation, both on the limb of the same tree." Perhaps the most hated loyalist leader of the war, Brown was reportedly responsible for hanging thirteen of his prisoners from a staircase "so that he might have the satisfaction of seeing the victims of his vengeance expire." Greene accused him of having hanged "about thirty persons" at Augusta. The general was horrified that he could not control the seemingly endless violence of this backcountry civil war, in which "the Whigs and Tories persecute each other, with little less than savage fury."[43]

Having experienced the violence of the war in the North firsthand, Greene, much like Clinton, had hoped that the situation would be different in the South. As he informed Cornwallis in December 1780, the Rhode Islander wished "to soften the rigors of war as much as possible." The earl, however, was still furious that the "men taken at King's Mountain were treated with an inhumanity scarcely credible." The British general was determined to enact "severe retaliation for those unhappy men who were so rudely and unjustly put to death at Gilbert Town." For his part, Greene was equally irate that Cornwallis had arrested and deported thirty-eight of "the Inhabitants of Charles-town to St Augustine contrary to the articles of capitulation." The group included some of the most prominent civilians in Charleston, not least of whom was Edward Rutledge, a signer of the Declaration of Independence. In Cornwallis's opinion, Rutledge and his compatriots were "the Ringleaders of Rebellion in this Province," and as such they had to be removed before they could "encourage the disaffected" to take up arms in opposition to the restoration of Crown authority. Following the execution of the nine Kings Mountain prisoners, British commander in Charleston, Lieutenant Colonel Balfour, sent another twenty-two "of the violent and principal men, that were upon parole" to prison in Florida. Although Cornwallis assured Greene that "no man abhors Acts of Cruelty more than myself," the loyalists' "suffering" induced him "to retaliate on their inhuman Oppressors." In the future he would "observe the same Rule of Conduct, which you do in the treatment of the Officers & Soldiers of the Army, the Militia and the Inhabitants of the Country." If Greene really wanted to soften the rigors of war, then he could prove it by reining in the state militias and protecting the loyalists from violence.[44]

Regrettably for those taken on both sides, Greene was not the final arbiter of prisoner treatment in the southern theater. The state militias and partisan groups came and went as they pleased, rarely following his advice, much less his orders. Moreover, the revolutionary governments of the Carolinas and Virginia still considered loyalists to be traitors against their country who deserved prosecution not protection. Soon after taking command of the department, Greene instructed a subordinate that enemy captives should be held for exchange as prisoners of war, not tried "for high treason"; but he had little means of enforcing his orders beyond his immediate command. Compounding the problem, in early January 1781 President Huntington informed him that Congress had determined that "Retaliation is become necessary" for the "cruel & unwarrantable Treatment" of prisoners at Charleston and New York. The delegates expected Greene to treat British and loyalist prisoners every bit as severely as Cornwallis, Balfour, and Tarleton treated American captives. Greene despaired. There seemed to be little hope of ending the pernicious cycle of retaliation.[45]

The prisoners' luck appeared to change when Greene received word that Continental brigadier general Daniel Morgan had routed Tarleton's legion at the Battle of Cowpens on January 17, capturing over five hundred of the enemy. Determined to preserve the prisoners for exchange, Morgan restrained his men, overruling the demands of his militia to give the British "Tarleton's Quarter." According to an American account published in the *Pennsylvania Packet*, Tarleton's soldiers did not expect generous treatment from their captors. "The Highlanders of the 71st British regiment, famous for their butcheries upon those whom the fortune of war had heretofore put within their power, plucked the feathers from their caps, and presenting them on their knees, cryed, 'dear, good Americans, have mercy upon us!'" Understandably proud of his men, Morgan boasted, "Altho the Progress of this Corps was marked with Burnings and Devastations & altho' they have waged the most cruel Warfare, not a man was killed wounded or even insulted after he surrendered." While he was not entirely correct—at least one British soldier had been executed in retaliation for the wounding of an American prisoner—Greene was delighted. Not only had Morgan bested Tarleton but he had also captured enough enemy soldiers to recoup most of the long-suffering Continental prisoners in Charleston.[46]

Keen to regain the veteran troops Tarleton had squandered at Cowpens, Cornwallis quickly contacted Greene with a proposal for a partial exchange that would relieve the "many inconveniences and hardships" endured by prisoners on both sides. In case the American general had forgotten the plight of the Charleston captives, the earl reminded him that "the close manner in which we are obliged to confine the prisoners in Charlestown to prevent their escape must prove fatal to many of them when the warm weather commences." If the impending deaths from disease aboard British prison ships were not motivation enough to accede to an exchange, Cornwallis threatened "to send them in the course of next month to His Majesty's islands in the West Indies," where they would be "permitted to serve in the British regiments employed there." In short, Greene could either exchange the men or never see them again. Not one to be bullied, Greene informed his counterpart that he would never agree "to make an exchange but upon just and equal terms." Congress had deputized him with the authority to conduct an equitable exchange of prisoners, but it had also given him the power "to exercise the law of retaliation." While he could not ship British prisoners to the West Indies, he could send them to Virginia to be indefinitely confined aboard prison ships. In the meantime, Greene ordered the Cowpens prisoners marched northward to Virginia, Maryland, and eventually Pennsylvania.[47]

Despite their threats, both commanders earnestly desired an equitable exchange, but many in the American camp were determined to delay it as long as possible. Cornwallis's army was dwindling due to disease, exhaustion, and capture, and Clinton was in no position to reinforce him. Furthermore, after Ferguson's defeat, fewer and fewer loyalists had come forward to join his forces. To allow him to regain Tarleton's crack troops struck many in Congress as strategically unsound. North Carolina delegate William Sharpe explained the situation as he saw it: "Was the exchange to take place immediately and the enemy at liberty to arm and send forth their liberated troops, it might be a fatal stroke to the State of North Carolina." Although Sharpe was "opposed in this business of delaying the exchange by some of our neighbouring delegates, who has [sic] a passionate fondness for their friends" in captivity, he was convinced that the "critical situation to the southward" militated against the dictates of "humanity." Frustrated by the continual delays on the issue, "particularly the opposition made to it by the delegates of North Carolina," Cornwallis assured Greene that he did not have "the smallest wish to insist upon unequal conditions." Greene, overriding the North Carolina delegation's objections, appointed commissioners "with full powers to settle the terms of an exchange of prisoners." The negotiations did not go smoothly. Both sides continued to quibble, dissemble, and delay until an accord was finally reached in May 1781.[48]

Under the articles of exchange, the Continental prisoners in Charleston, who by then had been in custody for over a year, were to be exchanged for the British troops captured at Cowpens. There were not many left among the captured garrison: disease, escape, and enlistment in the British Army had taken their toll. British records suggest that only 740 Continentals were released under the cartel in the summer of 1781, a far cry from the nearly 4,000 Continental regulars captured during the 1780–81 campaign. Few of these men, who

were malnourished and disease ridden after an arduous captivity, ever returned
to their regiments. Exchanged British prisoners, on the other hand, immediately
rejoined Cornwallis's army. They could not arrive soon enough for the earl.
After his pyrrhic victory over Greene at Guilford Court House in March, his
command was woefully undermanned.[49]

Unfortunately for Cornwallis and the remaining Cowpens prisoners, the
exchange process broke down in late summer after Greene received word of
the execution of Colonel Isaac Hayne of South Carolina. Having accepted
British "protection" after the fall of Charleston, Hayne had promptly returned
to the cause of independence, taking the field as a militia commander. Com-
mensurate with Cornwallis's earlier resolution to execute Americans who
broke their paroles, Balfour had Hayne hanged, following a perfunctory trial,
on August 4, 1781. Appalled by this action, Greene immediately halted all
further exchanges, informing Cornwallis that he intended "to retaliate for
every violence offered" to American citizens in the future. The earl cautioned
that "retaliation" might "prove fatal to many innocent individuals on both
sides," but Greene would not be dissuaded. The remaining Cowpens prisoners
would spend the rest of the war "Prisoners with the rebells." Exasperated and
out of troops, Cornwallis chose to march north to link up with British forces
operating in Virginia. Perhaps if Virginia could be subdued, he reasoned,
American resistance in the Carolinas would finally falter.[50]

The violent civil war in the Carolina backcountry would continue without
the presence of Cornwallis. For two more bloody years, loyalists and revolutionaries persecuted one another without stop, each side seemingly keen to
exceed the other in cruelty. Although he believed that "the Idea of exterminating the Tories is not less barbarous than impolitick," Greene was unable to
restrain his predominantly militia forces from "murder[ing] the defenceless
people just on private [pique]." According to one of his officers, William Pierce,
"scarce a day passes but some poor deluded tory is put to death at his front
door." Viewing "such scenes of desolation, bloodshed and deliberate murder,"
Pierce regretted that, "by copying the manners of the British," his countrymen
had "become perfectly savage." Brutality did not belong to the revolutionaries
alone; the British were equally incapable of curtailing their supporters' violent
excesses. One American officer described the war's pattern: "The British
destroyed the Whigs, and the Whigs retaliated on the Tories, thus none escaped
the devastation." As had been the case in New York and Philadelphia after the
British occupations of those cities, the cycle of retribution escalated precipitously

in the Carolinas. Fiery rhetoric reinforced and amplified the gory reality in the minds of southerners on both sides, and they relentlessly retaliated for real and imagined enemy atrocities. One of Greene's officers aptly summarized the mood in both camps: "Our countrymen breathe nothing but revenge." Loyalists and revolutionaries alike agreed that peace alone could end the bloodletting.[51]

The Yorktown Prisoners

In the summer of 1781, while Greene's partisans chased the remaining Crown forces in South Carolina from their backcountry posts, George Washington had an opportunity, for the first time in his long military career, to conduct a conventional European-style campaign. The commander of France's expeditionary force in America, General Rochambeau, informed him in June that a French fleet was en route to American waters. Delighted by the prospect of enjoying naval superiority over the British, Washington suggested that the combined Franco-American force demonstrate against occupied New York. Rochambeau, who knew that, even with the addition of his French troops, the allied forces were still outnumbered by Clinton's garrison, suggested that they use their assets where they could be most effective: the Virginia coast. Cornwallis had fortified positions at Yorktown and Gloucester Point on either side of the York River, there to establish a naval base and await orders and reinforcements from Clinton. Instead of additional troops transported courtesy of the Royal Navy, to the earl's horror, it was a French fleet he spotted off the Virginia Capes in September, soon followed by the arrival of Washington and Rochambeau's combined force of nearly nineteen thousand men over land. Cornwallis was trapped. The British troops endured eight days of incessant bombardment before the Crown commander sent his American counterpart word that he wished "to settle terms for the surrender of the posts of York and Gloucester." Washington, animated by "an ardent desire to spare the further effusion of blood," acquiesced. Lord Cornwallis's American campaigns were over.[52]

With his opponent's position surrounded and subject to cannonade by land and sea, Washington could have demanded Cornwallis's unconditional surrender; instead, the American general promised him that "the same honors will be granted to the surrendering army as were granted to the garrison of Charlestown." The troops would be prisoners of war, but they could expect "the benevolent treatment of prisoners which is invariably observed by the

Americans." Aware of the ordeal of the Convention Army, this last promise must have been cold comfort to the besieged Britons. Nonetheless, Washington's terms were nothing to balk at: "the officers shall be indulged in retaining their side arms and the officers and soldiers may preserve their baggage and effects." More important for the common soldiers, they were to be "supplied with the same rations of provisions as are allotted to the soldiers in the service of America," the cost of which was to be reimbursed by the British treasury. As soon as convenient, the enlisted men would march to internment "in Virginia, Maryland or Pennsylvania," while the bulk of the officers were "permitted to go on parole" to England or New York; Cornwallis himself could sail for New York, there to be paroled to England, as soon as convenient. Only a handful of staff officers, as well as one junior officer for each fifty soldiers, were required "to reside near their respective regiments, to visit them frequently and be witness of their treatment." Although the garrison was not granted the full honors of war—they could not surrender with their flags flying—Washington did allow the British dragoons to parade "with their swords drawn, trumpets sounding," out of respect for their hard-fought defense of Gloucester. These terms were as generous as Cornwallis could hope for under the circumstances. One of his Hessian soldiers, Stephan Popp, recorded the feelings of his comrades: "We were all glad and happy that this siege had finally come to an end and that it had turned out to be such a reasonable truce."[53]

At four o'clock in the afternoon on October 19, 1781, roughly seven thousand British and Hessian troops filed out of their entrenchments to surrender. Flanked on either side of the road by French and American soldiers, Cornwallis's army marched to an open field outside the siege lines and laid down their arms in defeat. No taunts or shouts of joy could be heard from the ranks of the victorious allies, a "universal silence and order prevailed." While the soldiers surrendered their weapons, Brigadier Charles O'Hara, standing in for Cornwallis—who was "pretending indisposition," according to Continental army surgeon James Thacher—offered the earl's sword to his fellow European officer, Lieutenant General Rochambeau. In deference to his allies, Rochambeau motioned to Washington, who in turn instructed O'Hara to give the sword to Major General Benjamin Lincoln, who had been exchanged for the Convention Army's Major General Phillips in November 1780. By allowing Lincoln to accept the sword, Washington symbolically wiped away the shame of his surrender at Charleston. The conquered had become the conqueror.[54]

Figure 8. The Taking of Yorktown Virginia, October 19, 1781, Surrender and Parade (detail) (Rochambeau receiving the surrender of the British troops), by Louis-Nicolas Van Blarenberghe, 1785. Courtesy Châteaux de Versailles et de Trianon, France. © RMN Grand Palais/Art Resource, NY.

Although they held their American captors beneath contempt, Cornwallis's troops took comfort from the presence of the French army and the strict accordance to European custom during the surrender ritual. Captain Ewald observed that "after the troops were surrendered into captivity, every officer was greeted by the French generals and officers with the greatest courtesy.... One scarcely knew whether he was among his friends or foes." Similarly, British captain Samuel Graham remembered that he received "much courtesy from the French" officers, who offered him generous loans as well as hospitality. In the evening after the surrender, the French officers lavishly entertained their British and German counterparts, excluding their American allies. Ewald thought "that the French officers preferred the company of the English, Ansbach, and Hessian officers to that of their own allies," who were clearly bothered by the camaraderie among the Europeans.[55]

The Americans were in no mood to fraternize with their erstwhile foes, and Washington knew it. That past July, one of his officers had informed him that the militiamen from the southern states were "a People who having Experienced no inconsiderable portion of British Barbarism, are become keen for revenge and appear properly determined." Ewald seconded this assessment. As he phrased it, "the American officer, like his soldier, hates his foes more than we do." The root of the animosity was clear. The British had "practiced the most abominable enormities" that "spread terror and desolation throughout the Southern states," according to Dr. Thacher. The French priest abbé Claude Robin feared for the British prisoners: they "had to bear a great deal from the Americans, who seemed resolved to take ample vengeance for the robberies and murders that had been perpetrated in their habitations." Robin's concerns were well-founded. An American militia colonel who had been a prisoner encouraged his comrades to vent their anger on the captives. "Boys, retaliate," he commanded. "These are the very men that plundered our men, and used them so badly." To ease tensions, Washington prudently sequestered the captured troops, preventing any widespread abuse, but the prisoners knew all too well that the Americans yearned to "steal or plunder or otherwise abuse us as is their usual practice." The European-style siege and surrender ceremony belied the fact that this was no longer a limited conflict constrained by the laws of war; it was a war of vengeance.[56]

When news of the victory at Yorktown reached Congress, the members' exuberance was quickly subsumed by concern over the generous terms Washington had granted Cornwallis. Elias Boudinot, a man who had seen British atrocities firsthand while serving as commissary general of prisoners, feared the terms were "rather too favourable." Although the articles of capitulation were no more generous than those "allowed to our People at Charles Town," Washington had failed to account for the fact that the British had violated those terms repeatedly. Many Americans believed that the time was ripe to exact retribution. As one outraged citizen argued in his petition to Congress, "Providence has thrown into our hands a numerous army" that should be used to revenge the mistreatment of American prisoners at "the expence, if it be necessary, of the[ir] lives." He pressed the delegates to embrace "retaliated confinement as a measure just in its principles." With popular enthusiasm for revenge on the rise, Washington worried that violating the capitulation and punishing defenseless prisoners would "be to the eternal disgrace of the Nation." But the decision was not his to make. "Congress have [retaliation] under consideration," he told one of his generals, "and we must await their determinations." While Washington waited, Boudinot, the new president of Congress, gathered a committee to investigate "the motives which led to the several Articles of the Capitulation."[57]

Conspicuously absent from Boudinot's committee, the delegates from South Carolina, whose state had suffered the most at the hands of Cornwallis's troops, were particularly incensed. In a letter to Aedanus Burke, Arthur Middleton fumed, "It is d[amne]d hard that rascals should be parol'd" when they "deserve[d] hanging." Middleton urged Burke to "remember the Sufferings of our fellow men" and embrace "Retaliation." For him, that "alone is the only magic rod which converts cruelty into mercy and effects wonders." Unwilling to publicly question the wisdom of Washington's decision so soon after a resounding victory, Boudinot's committee resolved to convey "the thanks of the United States in Congress assembled" to both him and General Rochambeau "for the wisdom and prudence manifested in the capitulation." Privately, some members continued to "think no treatment could have been too severe for the [Yorktown] Garrison." In the opinion of South Carolina delegate John Mathews, Cornwallis deserved to have his "neck stretched, as some small sacrifice to the manes of the numbers whose necks he has stretched."[58]

The revolutionary press agreed with the irate congressmen. One whig writer questioned why the "inhuman Earl Cornwallis" and his men should be allowed "to riot upon the fat of the land . . . , let loose upon parole to corrupt and intimidate our citizens," when had he been victorious, Cornwallis would have held American prisoners "upon half an allowance of stinking pork and musty bread in barns and churches . . . , kicked and cursed by every ensign in the British army." Even before his capture, newspapers across the continent had launched a concerted attack on Cornwallis's character and reputation. The *Pennsylvania Packet* named him "the British Cerberus," a reference to the three-headed hound that guards the gates of the underworld in Greek mythology. His "bloody-mindedness" had induced the general to commit crimes so "heinous, that old Beelzebub himself would blush." The author anticipated with glee "the moment when terrible vengeance from heaven may come hurling down upon" the earl. A columnist for the *Independent Chronicle* thought that all Americans should be "astonished at the generous terms granted to Cornwallis and his army" in light of "the innumerable acts of barbarity, with which the Britons have stained themselves and the nation in the American war." In the opinion of the *Freeman's Journal*, Washington had done nothing less than grant "mild terms *to Satan's firstborn son.*" Allowing Cornwallis to return to England on parole while American prisoners daily died in British prison hulks and jails was a "virtue too sublime" under the circumstances. One budding poet captured his countrymen's quest for revenge in a pithy verse: "For Hayne, for Hayne! No death but thine atones; For thee, Cornwallis, how the gallows groans!" To wrathful revolutionaries everywhere, the capitulation at Yorktown looked like the ideal moment to enact "ample retaliation."[59]

Despite the generosity of the articles of capitulation, retaliation was exactly what the British prisoners feared, and many seized the first opportunity to escape their would-be tormentors. Having already escaped from the Convention Army, Sergeant Roger Lamb knew well the rigors of an American prison camp before his recapture at Yorktown. Rather than starve in American custody, Lamb "determined to attempt [his] escape to New York." Fortunately for the British sergeant, confusion reigned in the aftermath of the siege, creating an ideal opportunity to run. One American officer colorfully described this "Scene of Confusion" in the days following the surrender: "British officers, and French Sailors, Soldiers, Marines, fatiguemen, boatmen, British Merchants, American Speculators, Jews & Infidels.—Negroes, British Misses, Soldiers trolls with a song etc. So be-mixed, be-Hurried, be-knave'd, be-frighted & be-Devil'd, that nothing Short of the Pen or the Pencil of Hogarth, could Possibly do them Justice to Delineate or Describe." Capitalizing on his captors' disorganization, Lamb managed to "elude the French and American sentinels" and make good his escape—for the time being.[60]

The less daring prisoners prepared themselves to march into American captivity. The articles of capitulation stipulated that the men be confined in the interior parts of Virginia, Maryland, or Pennsylvania, but the last state was already burdened with the prisoners of the Convention Army. Lancaster alone had over fourteen hundred prisoners, "exclusive of women & children," to feed and house. Pleading with the Executive Council of Pennsylvania to remove the captives, a group of "burgesses and inhabitants" of the town claimed that the county was "exceedingly drained of Provisions for some years past." Furthermore, "a most contagious Disorder [had] raged for some time" that had "proved fatal to very many" of them. In short, Pennsylvania simply could not take any more prisoners of war. Cognizant of this problem, Washington gave orders for the Yorktown captives to be divided into two sections: half would go to Winchester, Virginia, and the remainder to Fort Frederick, Maryland. For the moment, Congress voted to forgo retaliation, but it also neglected to forward any supplies for the starving prisoners. Washington had made promises that the congressional coffers simply could not keep.[61]

In the absence of any assistance from Congress, the prisoners' care and supervision fell by necessity to Virginia. Setting off for their new place of confinement on the morning of October 21, the prisoners were escorted by members of the Virginia militia, who were none too thrilled about their assignment. The task of feeding the men was equally vexing to the state's governor, Thomas Nelson. To solve the problem, he empowered militia general Robert Lawson to impress supplies, as a military necessity, from the local inhabitants when the need arose. Apparently Lawson's definition of "necessity" differed from that of the prisoners. Private Johann Conrad Döhla, of the Von Seybothen Regiment of Ansbach-Bayreuth troops, complained of having "very little food to divide and eat." The rations he did receive were insufficient for men expected to march all day and camp in the open, exposed to the elements. Those with hard currency could supplement their diets by patronizing the merchants and sutlers who flocked to the column to sell their goods, but most had to subsist on "Indian bread," which Döhla found "very unfamiliar." Thankfully, the Virginia militia guards, who "were all from the upper parts of the state, called backwoodsmen," turned a blind eye to the prisoners' creative procurement of provisions from the tidewater plantations along their line of march. Captain Graham remembered that the guards "did not scruple also to let us make free with a turnip field." Discipline was lax, and thus desertion rampant.[62]

For men already exhausted by a taxing summer campaign and an arduous siege, the trek into the Virginia backcountry was grueling. Their earlier trials had not prepared them for the "miserable marching" on a diet of "poor provisions." Hessian prisoner Popp reported covering "18 to 20" miles a day, often in the rain. Compounding their predicament, the weather turned colder as the men approached the Shenandoah River in early November. Fording the river in their only dry suit of clothing, the soldiers thought they "would freeze to death" when they emerged, dripping and shivering, on the opposite bank. In Döhla's opinion, constant marching in cold, wet clothes "caused all sorts of sickness" among the prisoners. Exhaustion and hunger slowed the pace of the column's progress, and the sick and injured began to lag behind. Frustrated, the guards fired on a party of British stragglers, "which resulted in one English prisoner being killed and three men wounded."[63]

As if their problems were not enough, the prisoners had to withstand constant harassment from angry onlookers. Hessian private Berthold Koch reported that "during the entire march, no matter where we went, men, women, and children . . . , young and old, picked up stones and threw them at us as we marched along." In his opinion, the Virginians sought vengeance against "the rascals, who killed [their] husbands, [and] fathers!" Koch and his comrades experienced the consequences of the war's democratization firsthand as ordinary Americans, unfettered by European-style military discipline and the laws of war, vented their frustrations on them. This was not the war Washington had wanted to fight. Instead of the generosity he had urged, the British prisoners received only cruelty from their captors. In the opinion of the loyalist newspaper the *Royal Gazette*, revolutionary Americans after Yorktown were "a high spirited and vengeful populace, elated with victory, and reeking with revenge."[64]

To the prisoners' dismay and indignation, when the first contingent reached Winchester on November 5, they discovered their quarters in complete disarray. Popp and his comrades "were amazed when we saw" the "old tumbledown barracks." Lieutenant Johann Prechtel from Ansbach-Bayreuth was shocked that the buildings "were truly very poorly put together" and "not half adequate for quartering the troops." Döhla described the structures as "numerous wretched huts built of wood and clay, most of which have no roofs or poor roofs, no cots, [and] only poor fireplaces." Snow, rain, and biting wind coursed through the barracks' halls. Each room was crowded with between "twenty or thirty men" who "did not have room enough to stand." The prisoners, "locked in like dogs," had little choice but to make do with quarters that Döhla called "worse than the pig stalls and doghouses are in Germany."[65]

Despite orders from Governor Nelson, the barracks at Winchester had not been adequately repaired or prepared for the prisoners. The local commissary of prisoners, Colonel Joseph Holmes, reported in late October that the site could hold only eight hundred men. Furthermore, he could not persuade the town's craftsmen to build any other structures because the government had still not paid them for building the initial barracks the previous year. If the prisoners wanted shelter, they would have to build it themselves, Holmes regretfully concluded. Resigned, the prisoners tried to repair their quarters as best they could, but tools and materials were in short supply. No one in town would so much as spare a hammer to help them build huts. Under the circumstances, Commissary Holmes had no alternative but to order more than a thousand prisoners to make camp in the open without tents. It was not long before snow blanketed the ground, covering the men as they slept. British private John Robert Shaw recalled that at Winchester, "we suffered much: our houses had no covering to shelter us from the inclemency of the weather; and we were exposed to cold, hunger and want of clothing; and all manner of ill treatment, insult and abuse."[66]

The paucity of provisions in Winchester was even more dispiriting to the prisoners than their shoddy quarters. Because local farmers refused to trade their produce for promises of future remuneration, Commissary Holmes had not been able to establish a sufficient store of food at the barracks. The demoralized and downtrodden men pleaded with their guards for foodstuffs that simply did not exist. Rations "were meted out to us very sparingly and of poor quality," Döhla griped. "We received absolutely no bread except for an occasional uncooked Indian bread." Merchants in town were more than pleased to accept the prisoners' hard currency for goods at drastically inflated prices, but all shunned Continental paper money; those without solid coin went hungry. Such treatment was clearly a violation of the surrender terms, but few Americans felt any compunction about the captives' distressed situation. The Yorktown prisoners were not only a burdensome intrusion for the inhabitants of the Virginia backcountry but also the living embodiment of British depravity and cruelty, the very men who had burned and pillaged their way across the South. They would receive no aid from their new neighbors. Instead of the full rations and commodious quarters they were promised in the surrender agreement, Popp and his fellow prisoners endured "hunger and cold . . . in abundance."[67]

The prisoners' hunger pangs stemmed not just from the avarice and anger of the locals but also from a fundamental disagreement between Congress and the government of Virginia. Years of printing unbacked currency had resulted in extensive inflation, and despite significant loans from France and other sympathetic European powers, Congress was broke. Completely incapable of providing for the prisoners' needs, the delegates looked to the state government to take responsibility. Having already supplied the convention troops for years, Virginia's governor and Board of War were in no mood to be cooperative. The commissioner of the board, William Davies, was determined to protect the state's financial future. He told Commissary Holmes, "it is the particular duty of Major Forsyth the continental commissary of provisions to make the necessary purchases and procure the proper supplies for the prisoners at Winchester." He further declared that he would "always be much averse to adopt any step that will have a tendency to throw the burthun of supplying these men on Virginia." In a letter to Quartermaster General Timothy Pickering, Virginia major Richard Claiborne was even more explicit: the "government [of Virginia] decline[s] advancing any thing farther for the Continent." The prisoners could expect little help from state authorities.[68]

Virginia's intransigence meant that the prisoners had to survive on next to nothing. Men sold anything they had, including the coats off their backs, to local farmers in exchange for food. They had little option. As Döhla described on December 7, "the issue of rations is much behind schedule and we already were twenty days behind in our issue of flour, which was a bad situation." Exposure and malnutrition weakened the prisoners' immune systems, and predictably disease flourished. Lieutenant Prechtel noted the presence "of consumption in the barracks," which claimed the life of one of his grenadiers. Döhla reported that "the wife of musketeer [Georg] Meichel" and "Private [Johann Georg] Korn had also perished." Commissary Holmes knew that something had to be done or few of the prisoners would be left to see the spring.[69]

Frustrated by the apparent lack of preparation on the part of the American commissaries and by the townspeople's indifference to their soldiers' misery, British officers began to take matters into their own hands. Captain Graham, the senior officer at the barracks, fired off a barrage of letters to anyone he thought might help his men. One of these arrived at the nearby home of Daniel

Morgan, the American victor of the Battle of Cowpens. Although the general had resigned his commission, Graham hoped that he would use his influence with Washington and Congress to relieve "the distresses of the Soldiers." In the meantime, the captain appealed to Holmes for permission to quarter his men in one of the town's five churches. Given the rapidly accumulating snow, the commissary saw no reason to deny this request. "Accordingly, 500 men were brought in [to the church], and the huts thus emptied were distributed among the other prisoners." For the first time since they had left their entrenchments at Yorktown, the men all had shelter, dilapidated and cramped though it was.[70]

When Morgan learned of Graham's intentions, he was furious at the officer's temerity. To quarter Cornwallis's soldiers in a house of God was sacrilegious and disrespectful to the memories of those Americans who had perished at their hands. In a stern letter of reproach, he told the captain that "Col. Holmes had no Right to bring them to town, thay were ordered to the Barrack[s], and thare thay ought to have continued." Citing his own experience in British captivity during the Canadian campaign, Morgan claimed, "I have been a prisoner as well as thay, and was kept in close goale five month and twelve days; six and thirty officers and there servts in one room, so that when we lay down upon our straw we covered the whole floore." Considering the British treatment of American prisoners, the general thought Graham's men had "nothing to grumble at." Morgan, confident that his actions would meet with Washington's "approbation," ordered all of the prisoners back to the barracks. All Graham could do was continue his letter-writing campaign, which to his dismay "had but little effect." According to one American officer, by Christmas 1781, "the prisoners at Winchester [were] in a calamitous situation."[71]

Initially, Maryland seemed far more receptive to the second contingent of Yorktown prisoners than Virginia had been to the first. Unlike that state's government, which had shirked its responsibility to the captives, the State Council of Maryland appointed merchant George Murdock as a commissary, with instructions to "forward a sufficient Quantity of Supplies" for "at least 2000" men. The council was less forthcoming with instructions for where to house the prisoners. In his orders to the new Commissary General of Prisoners Abraham Skinner, Washington had suggested that the men be confined at Fort Frederick, a Seven Years' War–era stone fortification in western Maryland that had been used to confine members of the Convention Army. The site, however, was in ruins. Skinner apprised the general that "the barracks at Fort Frederick was insufficient for the reception of the prisoners—indeed they are almost totally destroyed and cannot be repaired." In his opinion as head commissary, the best option was to confine the men in the stone barracks within the town of Frederick itself. In order to prepare the buildings for habitation, Skinner ordered a stockade erected around the perimeter and a supply of "beef & flour for about Six Weeks" put into storage. With the captives on their way, the council soon realized that the barracks alone would be "insufficient to hold the Prisoners," authorizing Colonel Philip Thomas to appropriate "the Poor's House, Logged Gaol and every other empty House proper for Barracks." If these buildings were still not sufficient to comfortably house the men, Thomas had permission to "take Possession of any such Buildings which you may deem necessary."[72]

Thomas's and Murdock's orders were far more detailed than those Holmes had received in Winchester, but the two men were incapable of fully executing the council's commands. The townspeople, who had lived among British prisoners since December 1777, were overwhelmed by the additional captives. The convention troops had already stripped the area of cattle and grain and had damaged most of the public buildings in Frederick. According to one resident, the neighborhood was "continually plundered, owing as it is thought in great measure to the prisoners & Guards being so badly supplied with provisions." Compounding the problem, the town had provided numerous soldiers to serve in Greene's Southern Army, many of whom had fallen in action against Cornwallis's troops. Thus the spirit of resentment ran high in Frederick. Sergeant Lamb, who had been recaptured after his escape following the siege and brought to the Maryland town, recalled being "used in the most cruel manner" by his guards, who were constantly "rejoicing in my distress." Explaining the "reason of the bad usage" he received, Lamb claimed that "this town had suffered much by the deaths of several young men, who had been killed during the war," which was the "source of general inveteracy to all British prisoners." As one townsman put it, "I hope the time [is] not far of[f] that we shall return" British abuses "measure for measure." Murdock and Thomas could count on little assistance from the local inhabitants, who yearned for revenge and restitution.[73]

Just as at Winchester, when the first Yorktown prisoners arrived at Frederick on November 4, they were appalled by their accommodations and provisions. According to Lamb, "our place of confinement was a most deplorable situation. Forty or fifty British soldiers crowded together in a small room." The men "huddled" together for warmth "as the winter was remarkably cold." The contingent's commander, Captain Eyre Coote, was deeply concerned for his men's health. He informed his superiors in New York that "when the whole arrive, our numbers here will amount to near Two Thousand men, & very sickly." The prisoners "suffer[ed] extremely for want of Blankets." Worse yet, Coote feared that his troops would not be "supplyed with Provisions in the Winter, as there is no magazine here," the men upon arrival having already gone "two or three days without meat." Officials in Maryland had done their best to acquire provisions, but there were simply none to be had. Commissary Thomas Price had purchased cattle from neighboring Virginia, but the sellers, looking "to rid that State of the Trouble of maintaining them through the Winter," had sent him a herd that was "intirely unfit for Slaughter." At a loss for what to do, the Maryland council was forced to admit that there were "many Difficulties and Impediments in providing for the British Prisoners. . . . [W]e are totally unprepared for their Reception."[74]

Frigid and starving, the prisoners soon became restive. When American guards ordered one group to cut wood for their fires, the men refused. Unwilling to brook revolt, the Americans leveled their bayonets and charged at them. The guard's commander, Captain Montjoy Bayley, explained to Coote that his troops had "been under the disagreeable necessity of making use of Violents [sic] to keep the prisoners in order." Coote did not see it that way. As he protested to Commissary General Skinner, "there has been three soldiers wounded by the Militia with Bayonets, and I am induced to believe those men did not deserve that Treatment." Predictably, this protest availed him nothing. Maryland's commissary of prisoners, Colonel Moses Rawlings, informed him that not only would the guards not be prosecuted but the prisoners should expect equally harsh treatment in the future. Rawlings was resolute in his determination "to punish [the prisoners] Agreeable to Offences." American troops could and would use force when necessary. Nevertheless, the colonel knew that violence alone would not solve his problems. The prisoners' situation was unsustainable. If fresh provisions did not arrive soon, he would have a full-scale riot on his hands.[75]

While the prisoners struggled to survive the increasingly deplorable conditions of their confinement, the governments of Virginia and Maryland took steps to rid themselves of the captives. In mid-December 1781 the State Council of Maryland sent word to the Continental superintendent of finance, Robert Morris, "that from the exhausted Situation of this State, it is not within the Compass of our Abilities to subsist the Prisoners quartered upon us, without your Assistance." If Congress could not produce £20,000 in hard currency, the captives would have to be moved. The Virginia House of Delegates was even more determined to see their allotted prisoners leave, resolving "that provisions ought not to be impressed for the support of the British prisoners after the first day of January [1782]." Without impressments, the captives could not possibly be fed even at a bare subsistence level. The Virginians further resolved to inform Congress "of the inability of this country in the present exhausted state of its treasury to furnish" the prisoners at all; the sooner they departed, the better.[76]

Just as had been the case with the Convention Army, congressional authorities settled on relocation. Morris, acting on behalf of Congress, responded to Virginia's ultimatum by proposing to transport the men "from Winchester to Frederick [Maryland]." The delegates followed up on Morris's suggestion by resolving to send half of the Yorktown prisoners to Frederick and half to Lancaster and York in Pennsylvania, where they would be confined alongside the Saratoga prisoners. Once settled in these locations, the office of the secretary at war, which had been established by Congress in February 1781, would take responsibility for their maintenance. In order to placate the Maryland government, Secretary at War Benjamin Lincoln promised that only the German prisoners, who as rented soldiers had no vested interest in Crown victory and from experience proved less of a security risk than their British comrades, would be quartered in that state. Congress still hoped that lenient treatment and lax confinement would induce many Hessians to desert and join the revolutionary cause. The same could not be said for the British prisoners. "Convinced that a strict hand will be necessary over the British," Lincoln ordered them to be "closely confined under Continental Guards" at Lancaster. The move was slated to take place in January 1782, as soon as adequate wagons and guards could be assembled. This was hardly the "benevolent treatment of Prisoners" that Washington had promised Cornwallis.[77]

The prospect of a second winter march so soon after their arrival in Winchester greatly distressed the prisoners. Commissary Holmes had finally succeeded in securing shelter for the remaining men, and he regretted "the hardship & difficulty" they would "encounter on the March" due to the "extreme coldness of the season." They were "almost as naked as the hour they were born, & not an ounce of animal food" was to be had for them. Without adequate provisions and clothing, how could they be expected to survive another winter march? As he confessed to Colonel James Wood, "it seems to shock the feelings of humanity to drive out of a warm habitation a poor creature stark naked in such a season." Holmes's appeal on humanitarian grounds had little traction with Virginia's governor, who could not wait to see the prisoners depart. Consequently, on January 27, 1782, the Winchester contingent marched out amid the worst snowstorm they had yet encountered. Lieutenant Prechtel reported that during the march, "three English private soldiers froze to death" because they had "to camp in the woods on the snow." Popp left this vivid account of the agonizing march to Frederick: "The first day we made a march of 12 miles, and then camped out in the open snow. We did make large fires, but still could not keep warm, because of the great cold. The snow was up to our knees where we had to remain over night. The sharp wind continued all night without letup, so that we believed we would all freeze. Besides, we were poorly clothed. . . . [M]any had sold their uniforms and everything else out of poverty, just to stave off hunger. . . . [M]any had wrapped their feet in plain rags. But they had to march along too, so it wasn't long before their feet were exposed and were completely frozen."[78]

The British prisoners, despised by the militia guards who had been habituated to think of all Britons as barbarians, had to contend with constant abuse as well as nature's trials during the march. According to Private Shaw, "the cruelty of this new guard exceeded anything we had yet seen; their conduct was indeed shameful and altogether incompatible with the profession of either soldiers or christians [sic]; they drove us like so many bullocks to the slaughter." He claimed that the captain of the guard "broke his broad sword by cutting and slashing the prisoners, who were too much weekend [sic] by hunger and former ill treatment to keep up in the march." Another officer, whom Shaw derided for his lowly birth, stabbed one of the prisoners in the back. Far from behaving like gentlemen of sensibility and humanity, the Americans acted in a manner that "was a disgrace" even for men more suited to a "chimney corner" than to a military command. Shaw and his comrades' only consolation was the hope that Pennsylvania would bring better rations, superior quarters, and speedy release "from such cruel bondage."[79]

Arrived at their new prison camps in early February 1782, both the German and British captives were profoundly distressed to discover that the conditions of their confinement were not much improved. Popp observed that "as far as our quarters were concerned they were all much in ruins." He and thirty-nine of his fellows were "too thickly quartered" in the barracks and "always bumping [one] another." Private Koch's entire company shared one room in a

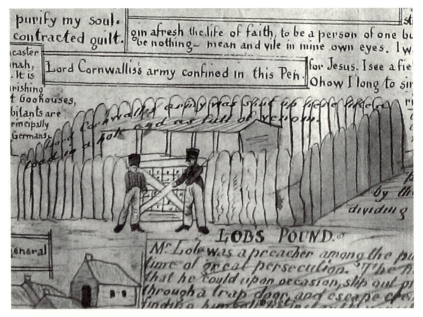

Figure 9. Page from a scrapbook compiled by Roger Lamb, circa 1800. Courtesy National Army Museum, London, UK. Acc. 2010-11-16.

"poorhouse" that "was so small that no one could lie down." All were covered with "vermin" that were "so numerous we could hardly bear it." Döhla remembered that "frequent epidemics occurred, and bugs and lice in great numbers appeared in our tattered clothing." Things were much the same at Lancaster and York, where "the soldiers of lord Cornwallis's army were closely confined in their pen," according to Sergeant Lamb. Captain Graham described the barracks at Lancaster as "surrounded by a high stockade, and strictly guarded." Years after the war, Lamb sketched a depiction of his "Pen," emphasizing the makeshift and cramped character of the enclosure. While the German prisoners in Lancaster were eventually allowed to hire their labor to local farmers and thus escape the crowded barracks, the British were closely confined and forbidden to leave the stockade for any purpose. In a note scribbled on the drawing, Lamb summarized the seething resentment of his fellow prisoners: "Lord Cornwallis' army was shut up here like a toad in a hole and as full of venom." Their sole remaining hope for release was that Congress would agree to exchange them for the American captives in New York. In this, too, they would be disappointed.[80]

Soon after he received word of the capitulation terms at Yorktown, General Clinton reached out to Washington "to treat for the Exchange" of Cornwallis and his army. Although the two commanders had never before been able to reach an agreement on a general cartel, Clinton was confident that the time was ripe for a large-scale exchange. Many of the American senior officers captured at Charleston remained bound by parole, and Washington harbored deep concern for "the extreme sufferings of" American sailors dying daily aboard the *Jersey* prison hulk at New York. Clinton was particularly anxious to exchange Cornwallis, both to prevent the earl from being recalled from his parole at the capricious whim of Congress and to forestall any claim that the British commander in chief was inattentive to his case because of personal enmity. Cornwallis had informed Clinton that Washington was willing to exchange him for the former president of the Continental Congress (and principal author of the nullification of the Convention of Saratoga) Henry Laurens. En route to France to serve in a diplomatic capacity, Laurens had been captured at sea in September 1780. Instead of treating the diplomat as a prisoner of war, British authorities had locked the South Carolinian in the Tower of London on charges of treason. Exchanging Laurens for Cornwallis, though technically unorthodox since the American did not hold military rank, was not without precedent. Clinton was happy to acquiesce to the swap, but he was also willing to exchange Cornwallis by composition—that is, to trade several American officers of lesser rank for the British general—a commonplace practice in European warfare. Washington responded with assurances of his intention to appoint commissioners who were "fully authorized to treat [for] the Exchange of Lord Cornwallis and the Honble Mr Laurens," but he could give no "assurance His Lordship should be exchanged for Mr Laurens" because the matter rested with Congress—which, as it turns out, had other plans.[81]

Just as they had opposed the generous Yorktown terms, so too did the South Carolina congressional delegates object to exchanging Cornwallis on any terms whatsoever. In a series of notes he made in preparation for a speech before Congress, Arthur Middleton enumerated the many disadvantages he saw to liberating the British general. Some of his reasons had to do with Cornwallis's military acumen and Middleton's concern that he would return to America determined "to retrieve lost Honor." But the South Carolinian's principal objection centered on the manner in which the general had waged the war in the South. To him, the earl was "a Barbarian. An Infringer [of] Capitulations, sacred." Releasing Cornwallis would deny the people of South Carolina their longed-for vengeance. Middleton knew his constituents—their anger and their thirst for revenge—and he knew that it would "affect the people [of the] South to see a Beast let Loose." In his estimation, Cornwallis's "non-exchange [was the] only mode of retaliating for his misdeeds and corrects the mild but impolitic Capitulation of York Town."[82]

Middleton was not alone in his determination to prevent the earl's release. On February 18, 1782, Congress passed a secret resolution "prohibiting the exchange of Lieut General Lord Cornwallis." Washington was puzzled by this decision, knowing that the British would never agree to a cartel that specifically excluded the earl. In a letter of protest to the new president, John Hanson, Washington confessed feeling "so exceedingly embarrassed by the operation of the Secret Resolve." To detain Cornwallis when he could so easily be exchanged would seem like "a conduct so apparently strange" to American prisoners, who expected imminent release. Moreover, the British could claim a "breac[h] of faith" on the part of Congress and thus justifiably renege on their obligation to provide reimbursement for the prisoners' provisions. The Continental commander in chief believed that the resolution would "operate against the public interest" in the long run.[83]

Confident of failure, Washington nonetheless proceeded with negotiations. He instructed Commissary Skinner that when meeting with the British commissary, he would have "to wave [sic] the exchange of Lord Cornwallis" for the time being "in as delicate a manner as possible." Predictably, Skinner's efforts were of little avail. He apologized to Washington that British commissary Joshua Loring "refuse[d] to Exchange the whole of our Officers without reserving a certain Number of them, equal to the Value of His Lordship." If a straightforward swap for Laurens was impossible, surely Congress would trade one disgraced general, now comfortably on parole in England, for several long-confined American junior officers, Loring reasoned; forgoing the exchange was simply not in America's best interest militarily. Persuaded by this logic, Washington pleaded with Congress to reverse its decision on Cornwallis. As he later explained to John Laurens, whose father still occupied a cell in the Tower of London, "*I am sorry to inform you,* that upon my arrival at Philadelphia, and for a long time after I had been there, I experienced the greatest *disinclination in Congress to the exchange of Lord Cornwallis; upon any terms.*" Mindful of his subordinate position to the civilian authority but deeply concerned for both his own reputation and that of the infant country he served, not to mention the welfare of his officers in British hands, Washington continued to press for an exchange that included the earl.[84]

For Congress, preventing Cornwallis's exchange was a symbolic gesture of retaliation for his conduct of the war in the South. Unsurprisingly, southern delegates were particularly keen to block the exchange of a man they viewed as "remarkably cruel and barbarous." Because Cornwallis was "an Officer whose foot steps have been stained by the blood of innocent Citizens," North Carolina delegate Hugh Williamson believed that Congress was under no obligation to agree to his release. Summarizing their position, Middleton argued that the general "ought not to be exchanged by composition at this time, not from any apprehensions of his influence or superior abilities; but because they look upon him not in the light of a British general, but a barbarian" who had "infringed every rule of war established among civilized nations."[85]

After several extended debates, Congress eventually consented to the exchange, though not before tying Cornwallis's release to several prerequisites to which the British were unlikely to agree. Washington could exchange the earl by composition only if the British first released Henry Laurens on parole and then reimbursed Congress for the expenses incurred by feeding the Saratoga prisoners since October 1777. The delegates were well aware that Parliament would never agree to pay the more than £200,000 they demanded. When Washington's commissioners, Gouverneur Morris and Major General Henry Knox, met with their British counterparts at Elizabethtown, New Jersey, in late March 1782, they did so with their hands tied. Negotiations continued for weeks but came to naught. Ultimately, the men of Cornwallis's army would never be exchanged.[86]

While the commissioners fruitlessly negotiated at Elizabethtown, a "regrettable incident," known to historians as "the Asgill Affair," roused the indignation of many revolutionary Americans to a fever pitch. On April 12 a party of armed loyalists under the command of Captain Richard Lippincott executed American captain Joshua Huddy near Sandy Hook, New Jersey. Acting under directions from the newly formed Board of Associated Loyalists in New York, Lippincott hanged Huddy as an act of retaliation for the execution of loyalist Philip White in late March. Reportedly, Lippincott's men affixed a sign to the captain before hanging him that read, "Up goes Huddy for Philip White." To loyalists, Lippincott's actions were nothing more than proportional retaliation.

To the irate inhabitants of Monmouth County, Huddy's death was a "horrid and almost unparalleled murder." Pointing to a congressional resolve promising to "take such exemplary vengeance" on the enemy in order to arrest "their present career of barbarity," Monmouth residents demanded that Washington "bring a British officer of the same rank to a similar end." If the general did not act, they would take matters into their own hands. The *Freeman's Journal* declared that "the people of Monmouth were determined to retaliate"; they even had an officer in mind.[87]

Outraged though he was by the hanging, Washington had no desire to execute an innocent British officer at a time when peace negotiations were on the horizon. He begged Clinton to surrender Lippincott to American authorities for trial, though he must have realized that the British general could not turn over the captain without repudiating the Board of Associated Loyalists and infuriating the king's friends. Clinton promised Washington that he would order "a strict inquiry to be made" and bring any perpetrators "to immediate trial," but the Virginian knew this promise would never placate those who demanded retribution. Fanning the fire of vengeance, newspapers across the country demanded retaliatory justice for Huddy. For many, his death came to personify British cruelty and perfidy. British prisoner Captain Graham remembered that "in all the papers we observed many inflammatory paragraphs calling upon General Washington and Congress to retaliate for cruelties exercised upon the Americans." Washington could not ignore the people's demands; he had little choice but to act decisively.[88]

After conferring with his officers, Washington determined that "a British officer of equal Rank, must atone for the Death of the unfortunate Huddy." On May 3 he instructed Colonel Moses Hazen that, because "the Enemy, persisting in that barbarous line of Conduct they have pursued during the course of this war, have lately most inhumanly Executed Capt. Joshua Huddy," he had no choice but to order Hazen to pick a British captain by lot "from among the Prisoners at any of the Posts either in Pennsylvania or Maryland" for the "disagreeable necessity" of retaliation. As fate would have it, the subject of revolutionary retribution would be one of the prisoners captured at Yorktown: an aristocratic, affluent, and well-connected nineteen-year-old captain named Charles Asgill.[89]

When Washington received word of the selection, he immediately regretted it. The general had already executed one popular young British aristocrat, Major John André, as a spy, and he certainly did not relish sending another to his grave. Moreover, as a prisoner under the capitulation of Yorktown, Captain Asgill was supposed to be exempt from any act of retaliation, the fourteenth article of the treaty stating that the terms could not be "infringed on pretence of reprisals." In a letter to Secretary at War Lincoln, Washington admitted that "Colo. Hazen's sending an officer under the capitulation of York Town for the purpose of retaliation, has distressed me exceedingly." He had requested specifically that Hazen exempt both the Yorktown and Convention Army prisoners, but the colonel had not been able to locate a suitable alternative. Washington was in a quandary. Executing Asgill would violate the treaty of capitulation and break his word to Cornwallis. On the other hand, "if some person is not sacrificed to the Manes of poor Huddy," he thought that "the whole business will have the appearance of a farce." Congress had made it abundantly clear that it approved of retaliation, his own officers had advised him to be swift and decisive, and the people demanded blood. Former congressman Robert Livingston of New York summarized the situation: "It is a melancholy reflection that the innocent must suffer for the guilty; but it is to be hoped this will prove mercy in the end, as it may bring the most savage nation in the world to reflect that their crimes will in the end fall upon their own heads." Unpleasant though it was, Washington was determined: Asgill would hang.[90]

The British, for their part, had no intention of allowing Asgill to be sacrificed without a fight. Major James Gordon, the captain's immediate superior at Lancaster, petitioned Congress, Washington, and Lincoln, demanding the young man's release on the grounds that his death would be a violation of the articles of capitulation. Aware that the revolutionaries had violated such agreements in the past, Gordon went one step further, appealing to the French ambassador in Philadelphia to intercede on Asgill's behalf. The major hoped that the diplomat could get a letter to General Rochambeau or Rear Admiral François, comte de Grasse who, as gentlemen and European officers, would undoubtedly be repulsed by the actions of their allies. Gordon's pleas worked; news of Asgill's fate soon circulated on the other side of the Atlantic. When the young man's mother heard of her son's sentence, she implored the French foreign minister, comte de Vergennes, to use his "high influence in behalf of innocence, in the cause of justice, of humanity." Vergennes, "as a man of sensibility" who had fully imbibed the norms of Europe's culture of war, was deeply moved by her words. Acting with the blessing of his sovereign, the foreign minister beseeched Washington "to deliver Mr. Asgill from the fate which threatens him." Killing the innocent was not justice, Vergennes argued. Instead, in his opinion, the general should exercise "clemency" in order to put an end to the cycle of violence. The French minister's letter was deferentially worded, but it was not a request. He reminded Washington that Asgill would never have been captured had it not been for the French troops and ships at Yorktown. Vergennes was confident that the general would do the right thing.[91]

Although he remained steadfast in his belief that "retaliation was apparently necessary," Washington, who had never been comfortable with the prospect of executing Asgill, looked to Congress for a final decision. Forwarding Vergennes's letter to his civilian superiors, the Virginian confessed his conviction that the affair was "a great national concern, upon which an individual ought not to decide." Much to Washington's irritation, Congress delayed. Explaining the "dilatoriness" of a response, New York delegate James Duane informed the general that the committee charged with the matter was overwhelmed with "complaints respecting the Execution of Col. Haynes, and the Infringement of the Cartell [sic]." The delegates had to consider Asgill's fate in light of the "uncommon Degree of Resentment and even Rage" felt by their constituents. Duane himself thought the execution "not Justifiable," but he knew that many Americans felt "the Impulse of Just Indignation at the enormous Cruelties of the Enemy" and wished "for Victims . . . [for] our Murdered Friends." In the end, Duane won out. Out of deference to their French allies and to the peace negotiations then in process, the delegates resolved on November 7, 1782, to release Asgill and to forgo retaliation for the time being.[92]

Unappeased, southern delegates sought to tie Asgill's liberation to a formal declaration of retaliatory warfare. They proposed a resolution that would authorize Washington and Greene "to cause suitable retaliation to be forthwith made on British officers without waiting for the directions from Congress on the subject." The proposal was apparently "espoused by many; with great warmth in particular by the Delegates of N.C. & S.C.," but in the end, it was deemed impolitic and unnecessary given the military situation. The British had ceased offensive operations in the South and were preparing to abandon Charleston. Proclaiming a unilateral policy of vengeance would only infuriate America's allies and complicate the peace settlement. Instead, Congress directed Washington to inform Asgill that he was free to return to England on his parole.[93]

French intervention saved Captain Asgill's life, but the remaining Yorktown prisoners were not so fortunate. The young officer's release did not temper the revolutionaries' enthusiasm for retribution or congressional decisions to decline the prisoners' exchange for political purposes. But neither could Congress afford to hold the men without British reimbursement for their expenses. Once it became clear that Clinton's replacement as commander in chief, General Sir Guy Carleton, would not pay for the prisoners' upkeep, Congress resolved to sell the Germans into indentured servitude and to reduce the British soldiers' rations. In early May 1782 Robert Morris convened a meeting of senior revolutionaries, including Secretary at War Lincoln and General Knox, to determine what to do with the Yorktown prisoners. After some debate, all present agreed that "the Hessian and other foreign Prisoners should be Sold, the British close confined and put to short allowance." Congress officially approved this plan in early June. To the enraged American populace, these retaliatory measures were entirely justified. As one Pennsylvania farmer admonished his countrymen that summer, "Say not that the capitulations can save any of them from being retaliated upon" because Americans were "justified, before God and man, in inflicting a dreadful punishment upon . . . those whom the chance of war hath put in our power."[94]

With congressional authorization, American recruiters soon entered the Hessian barracks, eager to fill their quotas of men from among the well-disciplined Germans. Telling the prisoners that the government could no longer afford to house or feed them, the Americans gave them the choice of either enlisting in the Continental Army for a term of three years or paying a fine of eighty Spanish dollars, an enormous sum for men who had not received their pay in months. If a soldier could not pay and refused to enlist, he could indenture himself to local farmers or craftsmen who would remunerate Congress for the use of their labor. One Hessian sergeant claimed that "the prisoners were mistreated in order to make them enlist." Another group of Hessians informed their commander in New York that they were in "extreme despair" because the Americans had sent them a "barbarous proposition" to either pay up or indenture themselves. The congressional resolve, which effectively transformed "free soldiers" into slaves, "completely stunned" the Germans. To them, it seemed as if the Americans were determined to treat them "not like prisoners of war to a Christian Nation, but like wretches fallen into the hands of Barbarians." According to Secretary Lincoln, few among them accepted the offer to enlist; most preferred indentured servitude to the betrayal of their commanders and comrades.[95]

While no doubt draconian, at least the Germans had a choice; the British prisoners were rounded up and closely confined in jails, dungeons, and camps throughout Pennsylvania. On July 11, 1782, Congress ordered the secretary at war to "have all the British prisoners of war closely confined, and to stop all issues of provision to the women and children who are with them." The soldiers' rations were also reduced again. Predictably, the jails soon became scenes of agony, anguish, and despair. The Hessian adjutant general, Major Carl Leopold Baurmeister, claimed that "instead of twenty men per room, thirty men were packed together, which makes the condition of these people even worse. Eight hundred and eighty-two English prisoners in Philadelphia endured their misery within even narrower confines." In October a group of British prisoners begged General Knox to "consider our Masaurable Satuation." The men had "No Cloaths But is all moste Nacat for want [of] Cloathing and the coald weather is Coming on and we have No Releaf Heare." Knox could do nothing to help them without disobeying Congress. Pitying the deplorable confinement of the "wretched creatures," Baurmeister decried the Americans' "unreasonably revengeful" policy as "contrary . . . to the law of nations." As an aristocratic European officer, the major could not comprehend what Congress and the American people knew all too well: Vattel and his laws had no place in a war of vengeance. For seven years, the revolutionaries had endured innumerable British violations of the laws of nations, and they were no longer afraid to return the favor.[96]

The Yorktown prisoners' nineteen-month ordeal finally came to an end when they received word in early May 1783 that the United States had ratified the preliminary articles of peace with Great Britain. Despite some opposition to ratification on the grounds that the prisoners should be held as security for British compliance, on April 15 Congress authorized Washington to "inform the Commander in Chief of the British forces in America that the U.S. are ready to liberate . . . all prisoners of war." The expense of holding the captives outweighed any political advantage that would be gained by further detaining them. When news of their impending release reached the men in Frederick, they were exuberant, throwing a raucous party in their barracks to celebrate their liberation and to honor their king. Their toasts of "Hyroh [sic] for the King George! God save the King George!" elicited the ire of their American guards. The commander "sent in a large patrol and ordered it to beat [the prisoners] and arrest them." Four prisoners were fatally wounded in the altercation.[97]

The death of their comrades could not dampen the remaining prisoners' enthusiasm. Private Döhla was elated by "the joyful news and long-wished-for and passionately awaited order, to begin our departure march." On May 13 he and the German prisoners "marched out of the barracks at Frederick, having spent a year and three and one-half months here, wretchedly, very often hungry and thirsty." Stephan Popp was just happy that he and his friends "had lived to see the day of our release." Many of his fellows had not.[98]

Although gaps in the archival record preclude any definitive accounting of the surviving Yorktown captives, Secretary Lincoln estimated that there were approximately 6,000 enemy prisoners, including women, children, and the Saratoga Convention troops, remaining in American hands at war's end. He neglected to note how many had perished on his watch, but surviving sources paint a grim picture. Of the 89 members of Döhla's Von Quesnoy Company of Ansbach-Bayreuth troops captured at Yorktown, 73 were liberated that spring. Only 5 of Döhla's comrades were listed as deserters (5.6 percent), while 11 prisoners in the company died during captivity (12.4 percent). From the Hessian Von Bose Regiment's returns, of the 365 common soldiers who surrendered at Yorktown, 104 men deserted (28 percent), while 33 (9 percent) perished in American custody. The Hessian mortality rate, while low when compared to the startling mortality of American sailors on board British prison ships in New York Harbor (upward of 60 percent), was much higher than that of either the American seamen confined in landlocked English prisons (5 percent) or civilian prisoners in the late eighteenth-century Netherlands (4 percent). Yet compared to their British counterparts, the Hessians were relatively healthy. For much of their captivity, these prisoners enjoyed the freedom to move about the countryside, procure extra provisions, and even work for wages. These privileges, which Congress granted in the hopes of inducing them to abandon their British employers, shielded many from the deprivation and disease of the camps.[99]

Cornwallis's British troops were not so fortunate. From a sampling of the muster rolls of the 43rd Regiment of Foot, 14 of the 36 men of Captain Cameron's company died during their imprisonment after Yorktown (38.8 percent). The soldiers of Major Ferguson's company were even more unhealthy. Of the 54 enlisted men, noncommissioned officers, and musicians in his company, 25 perished while in captivity (46.3 percent). Captain Thorne's company had a mortality rate of 29.4 percent, while Lieutenant Colonel Marsh's company suffered 41.4 percent losses. The statistics for the 80th Regiment of Foot are similar. Of the 48 privates in Captain Arbuthnot's company, 15 died in American captivity (31.3 percent). Captain Cumine's company of the same regiment lost

15 of their 47 men during the same period (31.9 percent). The soldiers of Major Gordon's company were comparatively healthy: only 10 of their 47 succumbed while in American hands (21.3 percent). If the experiences of these two regiments are indicative of those of their comrades in other corps, the overall mortality rate for British Yorktown prisoners was 34 percent—one out of every three men captured did not survive their imprisonment. To put these numbers in perspective, the mortality rate of Union prisoners of war at the notorious Confederate prison at Andersonville, Georgia, during the American Civil War was 28 percent. By the standards of eighteenth-century European warfare, these statistics were truly "shocking to humanity."[100]

* * *

The war in the South was violent, extremely so, but it was not an anomaly. When General Clinton sailed toward Charleston in the winter of 1780, he hoped to escape the cycle of violence that had characterized the war in the North. Largely untouched by conflict, the South seemed the ideal location to practice a new policy: magnanimity. Yet his hopes were dashed, in part by his own misjudgment of the extent of southern loyalism, in part by his officers' commitment to putting down the rebellion by force. Instead of pacification, Clinton inadvertently inaugurated a war of vengeance. For three years after the fall of Charleston, southern revolutionaries and loyalists persecuted each other with relentless fury. Quarter was often denied, and when irregular forces did take prisoners, the captives were victimized, tortured, and at times murdered. In short, "Lynch's law" replaced the law of nations.

The arrival of French troops in 1781 changed the nature of the war in the South, but only temporarily. For a brief period, French officers protected their British counterparts and ensured that the lenient terms of the capitulation at Yorktown were observed. But France's war was elsewhere—in the Caribbean, in the Mediterranean, and in India. Soon after Yorktown, Rochambeau's army departed America. With French troops removed, Congress saw no reason to deny its constituents' demands for retribution: it held the Yorktown prisoners without exchange for the remainder of the war, either closely confined in deplorable conditions or sold into indentured servitude. The delegates in Philadelphia knew that the American people would never have approved their release. For many, the Yorktown prisoners, along with their comrades in the Convention Army, were the living embodiment of British brutality.

Eight years of bloody war had infected Americans, revolutionaries and loyalists alike, with the virulent contagion of vengeance, for which peace alone was the remedy. Peace, however, could not erase the memory of revolutionary warfare. With the war won and independence secured, the new republic's elite would attempt to conceal the conflict's violence in patriotic rhetoric and myth making, but for those who experienced and endured it, that violence could not be so quickly forgotten.

Conclusion

The Memory of War

Between sermons on his circuit through central Pennsylvania in March 1848, Reverend William Raber noticed something unusual. His interest piqued, the minister asked some locals about the "large number of graves" he saw near the town of York. They informed him that "a number of English soldiers were kept as prisoners in the time of the Revolutionary War." Disease had entered the camp, claiming the lives of "large numbers" of captives, whose headstones now stood testament to the plight of the Revolution's prisoners. Although it had been at least six decades since the men had perished, Raber was overcome with sympathy for their suffering. "Poor fellows, they came to fight for King George! The king of terrors slew them, and now their bodies are moldering in American soil." The long-buried prisoners, likely men captured at Yorktown, elicited no ire from the clergyman, no feelings of righteous retribution. Instead, they were a pitiful curiosity. Their fate fit uncomfortably with his image of the war that had birthed his nation.[1]

Educated nineteenth-century Americans like Raber inherited a narrative of the Revolution scrubbed of its violence and vengeance. Because they gloried in independence but decried the "excess of democracy" required to achieve it, elite revolutionaries—the men and women who wrote the histories Raber read and painted the pictures he viewed—had erased the radical transformation of the war's conduct from their depictions. By celebrating wartime heroism and downplaying its destruction, they had crafted a collective memory of the conflict that belied its brutal realities. This process began soon after the fighting stopped. In December 1783 the *South-Carolina Gazette*, an imprint that only recently had indicted the British for the "inhumane, cruel, savage, and barbarous usage" of American prisoners, now printed an order from the Court of General Sessions of the Peace urging South Carolinians to forgo "vengeance for past injuries" in favor of forgiveness. "The bitter hardships of the war," the court advised, "ought, like the past dangers of the sea, to be forgotten." Putting the war's violence behind them proved attractive to a population wearied by eight years of civil warfare. No longer occupying their cities and imprisoning their citizens, the British, once reviled as "barbarians," began to appear benign. Trade with their former tormentors soon resumed, and Americans once again read British books, wore British woolens, and drank British tea. In the now peaceful United States, even former loyalists could be forgiven. Defeated and dispossessed, the loyalists looked like objects of pity, not retribution. Each state soon passed laws pardoning those they had once so vigorously persecuted. The memory of British and loyalist atrocities, as well as American acts of retribution and revenge, began to fade.[2]

Nevertheless, elite revolutionaries remained uneasy about the war and their role in its violence. When they embraced force as the only means to redress their grievances, men like George Washington, John Adams, and Alexander Hamilton assumed that they could control its practice. They were mistaken. To borrow J. Franklin Jameson's metaphor, vengeance, once incited, became a flood that spread forth across the continent. Unable to stem its tide during the war, the founding leadership worked tirelessly to manage violence in the new republic. Meeting in secret in Philadelphia in the summer of 1787, these elite nationalists framed a new form of government intended to curtail the influence of ordinary citizens. The Constitution of the United States granted the national legislature the sole right "to declare war, grant letters of marque and reprisal," and "make rules for the government and regulation of the land and naval forces." Lest the individual state legislators assume that these rules applied only to the national armed forces, the Constitution further enunciated Congress's prerogative "to provide for organizing, arming, and disciplining, the militia." No believers in perpetual peace, the framers were determined that the next war would be different. In the future, the power to exact retribution on America's enemies would reside exclusively with the national authority.[3]

Even those founders skeptical of expanding the power of the national government sought ways to restrain the violence of war. In September 1784 Jefferson sketched a series of rules for the future conduct of war, and especially the treatment of prisoners, in his draft of a model "treaty of Amity and Commerce" between the United States and the kingdom of Denmark. Far more than a straightforward trade agreement, Jefferson's treaty was nothing short of a repudiation of the way Americans had won independence. Article 24 of the document—the longest and most detailed article in the draft—forbade either nation from confining prisoners "in dungeons, prisonships [*sic*], nor prisons" in times of war between the two powers. Once captured, enlisted men were not to "be put into irons, nor bound, nor otherwise restrained in the use of the[ir] limbs," and the officers were to be released "on their paroles within convenient districts and have comfortable quarters." Both sides would furnish their prisoners with the same "ration[s] as they allow to a common souldier in their own service," the cost of which would be reimbursed equitably at the cessation of hostilities. Most importantly, both nations would "sacredly" uphold the treaty and under no pretense violate its articles. Bad behavior by one side did not justify retaliation by the other. This was a significant departure from Vattel's treatise *The Law of Nations*, which authorized proportional retaliation in cases of gross violation. Unlike the mid-eighteenth-century Swiss jurist, Jefferson made no allowance for reprisal, no matter the provocation.[4]

While serving as governor of Virginia during the war, Jefferson had seen firsthand how easily proportional retaliation could devolve into a violent cycle of vengeance. He personally had ordered British officers to be chained and locked in dank, overcrowded prisons; he had sent loyalist civilians and British enlisted men to their deaths aboard disease-infested prison ships; and he had refused to supply the prisoners of the Convention Army with anything resembling rations equal to those received by American soldiers. Jefferson had fought a war of vengeance, he knew its horrors, and he never wanted his countrymen, or their opponents, to endure it again. Inexplicably, Article 24 was not included in the final treaty with Denmark, but it was reintroduced and ratified in the 1785 treaty between the United States and the kingdom of Prussia. Defending the article to Prussian envoy Baron Friedrich Wilhelm von Thulemeier, Jefferson and his fellow commissioners, Benjamin Franklin and Adams, asked: "Why should not this Law of Nations go on improving?" In their opinion, though still necessary for adjudicating national disputes, war could be further moderated "by softening and diminishing" its "calamities."[5]

Though the treaty was popular, for many in the new republic, lessening the severity of future wars was not enough; the war of the Revolution itself had to be reimagined. In the late 1780s and early 1790s, believing the brutality of retaliatory warfare behind them, elite Americans crafted a narrative of their revolution as a glorious conflict between virtuous republican Americans and wrongheaded, though civilized and refined, British regulars. The king's officers were no longer portrayed as barbarians beyond the pale of civilization but instead as the innocent tools of a tyrannical ministry. In this reimagination,

Figure 10. *The Capture of the Hessians at Trenton*, by John Trumbull, 1786–1828. Courtesy Yale University Art Gallery.

the war was limited, restrained, and moderate, its violence safely enacted under the watchful eye of gentlemanly officers on both sides who shared a common code of honor. Working out of a London studio, the painter John Trumbull, the son of Connecticut's wartime governor and himself a former prisoner of the British, crafted a series of dynamic historical paintings portraying the nobility and humanity of American forces and the civility and refinement of the enemy. Illustrating the Hessian surrender at Trenton in 1776, Trumbull placed a mounted Washington center stage, empathetically reaching out to comfort the mortally wounded Hessian colonel Johann Rall, who is gently supported by one of the general's aides. Compassion, not anger or vindictiveness, characterizes the countenance of every American soldier present. Trumbull, in his autobiography, claimed that he "composed the picture, for the express purpose of giving a lesson to all living and future soldiers in the service of their country, to show mercy and kindness to a fallen enemy,—their enemy no longer when wounded and in their power." The viewer cannot escape his message: revolutionary Americans had treated their honorable, though misguided, captives with humanity.[6]

Trumbull's humanitarian vision of the war comes through even more forcefully in his most violent illustration of the conflict, *The Death of General Warren at the Battle of Bunker's Hill*. Depicting the climax of that engagement, the painter shows a wounded Joseph Warren threatened by a British grenadier's bayonet. Rather than allowing the American officer to be impaled, in Trumbull's rendering of the scene, Major John Small restrains the soldier, grasping his weapon before it can harm the dying man. Despite little evidence that Small had done anything in Warren's favor, Trumbull wanted to honor the British officer, whom he described in his catalog as a man "equally distinguished by acts of humanity and kindness to his enemies, as by bravery and fidelity to the cause he served." He knew well that a depiction of Warren's actual death—his face shattered by a British ball and his body riddled with bayonet wounds— would have done little to reconcile American viewers to their erstwhile foes. For Trumbull and many of his contemporaries in the upper echelons of early republican society, British officers were not barbarians capable of butchering virtuous foes like Warren, they were gentlemen of humanity and sensibility who curtailed the violent instincts of the common soldiery. None of Trumbull's works contain the least inkling of the violent war of vengeance that gripped the continent after 1776.[7]

Figure 11. *The Death of General Warren at the Battle of Bunker's Hill, 17 June, 1775*, by John Trumbull, 1815–31. Photograph © Museum of Fine Arts, Boston.

In a similar vein, the early historian of the Revolution David Ramsay, who also had been a British prisoner, portrayed the war as a gentlemanly contest and lavished encomiums on formerly odious enemies. He praised Lieutenant General Burgoyne for the restrained conduct of his army on its march toward Albany in 1777. Ramsay went to great pains to describe the British commander's determination to "repress [the] barbarity" of his Native American allies. While the revolutionary press had felt no compunction at demonizing Burgoyne after the death of Jane McCrea, Ramsay excused the general of any "premeditated barbarity." "The cruelties of the Indians," not any failure on Burgoyne's part, were the cause of her unfortunate death. In Ramsay's racialized narrative, Indians, who continued to threaten the young republic, remained "savages," while their British allies had become "civilized." Impressed by Burgoyne's conduct, he was "at a loss whether to admire most, the magnanimity of the victorious [Horatio Gates], or the fortitude of the vanquished general." Although he did not deny the war's violence—he had experienced too much of it himself for that—the historian all but absolved the Revolution's European opponents of blame for its escalation.[8]

For Ramsay, "the calamities of the American war" could be directly traced to the Revolution's democratizing influence on American society. In order to raise recruits for their forces, he argued, American propagandists had painted the British as barbarians who instigated their loyalist and Native allies to ever-greater acts of atrocity. The propaganda had succeeded. Tales of terrorism "impressed on the minds of the inhabitants a general conviction, that a vigorous determined opposition was the only alternative for the preservation of their property, their children and their wives." Thus mobilized and acting "under the specious veil of patriotism," the "common people" vented their anger on their loyalist neighbors and British prisoners. Narrating a cycle of retaliation common to civil wars, "which produce the greatest quantity of human woes," Ramsay described how local revolutionary committees punished loyalist prisoners for treason against a country they never claimed. Once released, embittered loyalists "carried with them a keen remembrance of the vengeance of committees, and when opportunity presented, were tempted to retaliate." In this manner "one instance of severity begat another, and they continued to encrease [sic] in a proportion that doubled the evils of common war."[9]

By relying on ordinary Americans to fight the war, which soon devolved into civil strife, revolutionary leaders had failed, Ramsay suggested, to uphold

European customs of hierarchical but limited warfare. He despaired, "Humanity would shudder at a particular recital of the calamities which the whigs inflicted on the tories, and the tories on the whigs." From his perspective, the mistreatment of prisoners during the war was a lamentable consequence of independence, but it did not mar the glorious cause. Portraying the revolutionary conflict largely as a conventional and restrained war between the Continental Army and its Crown opponents, Ramsay banished the stories of civil war and prisoner abuse to the obscurity of an appendix at the end of his second volume. There the tales of mistreatment, retaliation, and revenge would be comfortably forgotten until the next generation of Americans faced the prospect of war with their old enemy the British.[10]

In the first decade of the nineteenth century, with Europe engulfed by war, some Americans sought to revive the memory of the Revolution's prisoners for partisan purposes. In the imaginations of those who sought closer ties to revolutionary and imperial France, usually identifying themselves as Democratic-Republicans, the British were once again "savages" and "barbarians." In 1807 the *National Aegis*, a staunchly Republican paper, reminded its readers that the British government had "murdered our fellow citizens at Lexington . . . , carried on a seven years war to reduce this country to unconditional submission . . . , [and] added to the necessary calamities of honorable warfare, the horrors and barbarity of the tomahawk and scalping knife." Most importantly, the author wanted every Republican to recall that it was the British who had "incarcerated upwards of twenty thousand of our seamen and soldiers, in the prisons and prison ships at New-York." The Republican *New-Hampshire Gazette* was even more explicit in its denunciation of Crown mistreatment of captured Americans. The British, according to the *Gazette*, were responsible for "the poisoning of thousands of *farmers* in the Jersey prison ships [*sic*] at New York." For the *Public Advertiser*, "the unhappy victims of British barbarity" deserved to be remembered. Although their deaths had been slow, "those who perished in thousands on board [the] Jersey prison ships" had been "murdered" by the British nonetheless. Nowhere in these denunciations of the mistreatment of American prisoners can be found mention of the thousands of British, German, and loyalist prisoners who expired on American prison ships or in American jails and camps. The popular cry for retaliation and Congress's acquiescence to it were effaced from the history of the Revolution in the nineteenth century, coloring even to this day our popular and scholarly conceptions of that conflict.[11]

* * *

Both Trumbull's image of courtly combat and the Republicans' picture of deliberate British brutality obscure the real war that secured American independence. When colonial Americans took up arms to defend their English liberties, they did not envision or desire a revolutionary conflict. In their vision of "civilized" warfare, violence was restricted to the field of battle, and captive enemy soldiers could expect generous treatment according to their rank and social station. It was not long, however, before the revolutionaries discovered that the realities of their struggle bore little resemblance to their idealized images. Atrocity rhetoric compounded real accounts of British mistreatment of American captives in the press, inciting an enraged populace to wage an ever-more-violent war for retribution. Seen as rebels and traitors by their former friends and neighbors after independence, loyalists received the brunt of revolutionary fury. But the quest for revenge did not end with the subjugation of the loyalists. For years, Congress detained large numbers of British and German prisoners for the purpose of retaliation, despite being politically constrained from raising the necessary funds to provide for their needs. The results were predictably gruesome. Although the total number of enemy prisoners who perished in American custody eludes us, the captives' suffering did not escape the notice of the founding generation. Winning independence had been messy, violent, and horrifying. It had to be forgotten.

While the founding elite were content to shroud the conflict in a haze of patriotic lore, enemy prisoners, and the revolutionary Americans who captured, guarded, tortured, and at times killed them, could not so easily escape the war's violence. Men like William Gipson, a North Carolina militiaman, were not ashamed of the role they had played. Motivated not by republican rhetoric but by British brutality and perhaps, more importantly, heavily embroidered atrocity stories, he and his fellow soldiers had wreaked havoc on their Crown opponents in the name of revenge. In his 1832 pension application, Gipson admonished his readers not to judge him too harshly for the torture of loyalist prisoners. Had they seen "the unrelenting cruelties of the Tories," they too would have felt "no little satisfaction" at having achieved vengeance. Gipson's revolution did not look like a Trumbull painting, but his was the revolution that enemy prisoners remembered. Loyalist pension applications read like a laundry list of persecution, imprisonment, sorrow, and suffering. Similarly, deprivation, hunger, exposure, and cruelty permeate virtually every extant memoir of British and German prisoners of war. British private John Shaw could not have summarized his fellow captives' experience better: "The treatment of prisoners in general during the American war was harsh, severe, and in many instances, inhuman." These men had survived the war's revolutionary transformation, and they could not forget its horrors. If we seek to understand the nation born of that war, in all its complexities and contradictions, its tragedies as well as its triumphs, then neither should we.[12]

Abbreviations

AA	Peter Force, comp. *American Archives: A Collection of Authentick Records, State Papers, Debates, and Letters and Other Notices of Publick Affairs . . .* 4th ser., 6 vols.; 5th ser., 3 vols. Washington, DC, 1837–53.
AAS	American Antiquarian Society, Worcester, MA.
AO	Audit Office.
CL-UM	Clements Library, University of Michigan, Ann Arbor.
CO	Colonial Office.
Cornwallis Papers	Ian Saberton, ed. *The Cornwallis Papers: The Campaigns of 1780 and 1781 in the Southern Theatre of the American Revolutionary War.* 6 vols. East Sussex, UK: Naval and Military Press, 2010.
CSRNC	*The Colonial and State Records of North Carolina.* 30 vols. Raleigh, 1886–1905. Online at Documenting the American South, University Library, University of North Carolina at Chapel Hill, 2007, http://docsouth.unc.edu/csr.
CVSP	William Pitt Palmer, Sherwin McRae, and Raleigh Edward Colston, eds. *Calendar of Virginia State Papers and Other Manuscripts . . .* 11 vols. Richmond: R. F. Walker, 1875.
DLAR	David Library of the American Revolution, Washington's Crossing, PA.
Founders Online	*Founders Online,* NARA, http://founders.archives.gov.
Greene Papers	Nathanael Greene. *The Papers of General Nathanael Greene.* Ed. Roger N. Parks et al. 13 vols. to date. Chapel Hill: University of North Carolina Press, 1976–.
HSP	Historical Society of Pennsylvania, Philadelphia.

JCC	Worthington C. Ford et al., eds. *Journals of the Continental Congress, 1774–1789.* 34 vols. Washington, DC, 1904–37.
JPC	*Journal of the New York Provincial Congress, Provincial Convention, Committee of Safety and Council of Safety of the State of New York.* 2 vols. Albany: Thurlow Weed, 1842.
LC	Library of Congress, Washington, DC.
LDC	Paul H. Smith et al., eds. *Letters of Delegates to Congress, 1774–1789.* 25 vols. Washington, DC: Library of Congress, 1976–2000.
LMCC	Edmund Cody Burnett, ed. *Letters of Members of the Continental Congress.* 8 vols. Washington, DC: Carnegie Institution of Washington, 1921–36.
LSC	Library of the Society of the Cincinnati, Washington, DC.
MHS	Massachusetts Historical Society, Boston.
NARA	National Archives and Records Administration, Washington, DC.
NYPL	New York Public Library.
PCC	Papers of the Continental Congress, Record Group 360, M247, NARA.
PFPC	Peter Force Papers and Collection, Manuscript Division, LC.
PHL	Henry Laurens. *The Papers of Henry Laurens.* Ed. David R. Chestnutt, C. James Taylor, Peggy J. Clark, and David Fischer. 16 vols. Columbia: University of South Carolina Press, 1968–2002.
PRCC	Charles J. Hoadly et al., eds. *The Public Records of the Colony of Connecticut.* 15 vols. Hartford: Case, Lockwood & Brainard, 1850–90.
PRM	Robert Morris. *The Papers of Robert Morris, 1781–1784.* Ed. James E. Ferguson. 9 vols. to date. Pittsburgh: University of Pittsburgh Press, 1973–.
TNA	The National Archives of the United Kingdom, Kew.
WO	War Office.

Notes

Introduction

1. "Draft of a Declaration on the British Treatment of Ethan Allen, [2 January 1776]," *Founders Online*.

2. Ibid.; *JCC*, 4:21.

3. Jefferson to William Phillips, July 22, 1779, *Founders Online*; Jefferson to John Jay, June 19, 1779, ibid.; Jefferson to George Mathews, October 8, 1779, ibid.

4. For the best analysis of the escalation of violence in both riot and war in colonial America, see Wayne E. Lee, *Crowds and Soldiers in Revolutionary North Carolina: The Culture of Violence in Riot and War* (Gainesville: University Press of Florida, 2001). On the escalation of violence more broadly, see Charles Tilly, *The Politics of Collective Violence* (Cambridge: Cambridge University Press, 2003).

5. Fred Anderson and Andrew R. L. Cayton, *The Dominion of War: Empire and Liberty in North America* (New York: Viking, 2005), 162–63. I agree with John Morgan Dederer's account that stresses the colonists' inexperience with European-style warfare in 1775. Dederer, *War in America to 1775: Before Yankee Doodle* (New York: New York University Press, 1990), 22. Guy Chet argues that colonial Americans never abandoned European practices of warfare and increasingly relied on the British military for security against French and Native American adversaries over the course of the eighteenth century. Chet, *Conquering the American Wilderness: The Triumph of European Warfare in the Colonial Northeast* (Amherst: University of Massachusetts Press, 2003). For studies that argue for the militancy of early America, especially in reference to conflict with Native Americans, see John Ferling, *A Wilderness of Miseries: War and Warriors in Early America* (Westport, CT: Greenwood, 1980); and John Grenier, *The First Way of War: American War Making on the Frontier* (Cambridge: Cambridge University Press, 2005). For the conception of European colonization as an armed "invasion," see Francis Jennings, *Invasion of America: Indians, Colonialism, and the Cant of Conquest* (New York: W. W. Norton, 1975); Ian K. Steele, *Warpaths: Invasions of North America* (Oxford: Oxford University Press, 1994); John Ferling, *Struggle for a Continent: The Wars of Early America* (Arlington Heights, IL: Harlan Davidson, 1993); and Wayne E. Lee, *Barbarians and Brothers: Anglo-American Warfare, 1500–1865* (Oxford: Oxford University Press, 2011), 122–24.

6. Throughout this study, I define violence broadly. It is not only the physical infliction of injury but also the use of force for coercion. I agree with Andrew Cayton's definition of violence as "a form of power that negates liberty and denies another person's humanity by abandoning persuasion for force, consent for coercion." Cayton, "'The Constant Snare of the Fear of Man': Authority and Violence in the Eighteenth-Century British Atlantic," in *Between Sovereignty and*

Anarchy: The Politics of Violence in the American Revolutionary Era, ed. Patrick Griffin, Robert G. Ingram, Peter S. Onuf, and Brian Schoen (Charlottesville: University of Virginia Press, 2015), 21. For recent scholarship on violence and the American Revolution, see Holger Hoock, *Scars of Independence: America's Violent Birth* (New York: Crown, 2017); and Alan Taylor, *American Revolutions: A Continental History, 1750–1804* (New York: W. W. Norton, 2016).

7. Edwin Burrows, *Forgotten Patriots: The Untold Story of American Prisoners During the Revolutionary War* (New York: Basic Books, 2008), xi, 197–201, 316–17nn7–12. Howard H. Peckham argued for a significantly lower number. In his "conservative guess," 18,152 Americans were imprisoned, of whom 8,500 perished. Peckham, ed., *The Toll of Independence: Engagements & Battle Casualties of the American Revolution* (Chicago: University of Chicago Press, 1974), 132. Although they disagreed on overall numbers, Peckham and Burrows did not significantly diverge regarding the overall death rate of American prisoners. For Peckham, 47 percent of American captives died in British custody, while Burrows believed the number closer to 60 percent. Based on their calculations, it seems safe to assume that the prisoners' death rate was around 50 percent. On the British Army's response to prior rebellions, see Geoffrey Plank, *Rebellion and Savagery: The Jacobite Rising of 1745 and the British Empire* (Philadelphia: University of Pennsylvania Press, 2006). On the violence of the British Army's suppression of the American "rebellion," see Stephen Conway, "'The Great Mischief Complain'd Of': Reflections on the Misconduct of British Soldiers in the Revolutionary War," *William and Mary Quarterly* 47, no. 3 (1990): 370–90. Robert Parkinson has persuasively argued that revolutionary leaders played on popular fears of hostile Native Americans and insurrectionary African slaves to promote support for the "common cause." Parkinson, *The Common Cause: Creating Race and Nation in the American Revolution* (Chapel Hill: University of North Carolina Press, 2016).

8. Parkinson, *Common Cause*; Hoock, *Scars of Independence*; John Shy, *A People Numerous and Armed: Reflections on the Military Struggle for American Independence* (Oxford: Oxford University Press, 1976), 183–92; Robert M. Calhoon, "Civil, Revolutionary, or Partisan: The Loyalists and the Nature of the War for Independence," in *Tory Insurgents: The Loyalist Perception and Other Essays,* ed. Calhoon et al. (Columbia: University of South Carolina Press, 2010), 204–16; T. Cole Jones, "'The rage of tory-hunting': Loyalist Prisoners, Civil War, and the Violence of American Independence," *Journal of Military History* 81, no. 3 (July 2017): 719–46. See also Robert Calhoon, *The Loyalists in Revolutionary America, 1760–1781* (New York: Harcourt Brace Jovanovich, 1973). For studies of the American treatment of captured African Americans, see Benjamin Quarles, *The Negro in the American Revolution* (Chapel Hill: University of North Carolina Press, 1961); and Alan Gilbert, *Black Patriots and Loyalists: Fighting for Emancipation in the War for Independence* (Chicago: University of Chicago Press, 2012). For the Native American experience of the war and their brutal treatment in American hands, see Colin Calloway, *The American Revolution in Indian Country: Crisis and Diversity in Native American Communities* (Cambridge: Cambridge University Press, 1995); and Max M. Mintz, *Seeds of Empire: The American Revolutionary Conquest of the Iroquois* (New York: New York University Press, 2001). In denying Native American warriors the protections of prisoner-of-war status, the revolutionaries continued the practice of the British Army and Anglo-American Provincial forces during the Seven Years' War and prior imperial conflicts. See Ian K. Steele, *Setting All the Captives Free: Capture, Adjustment, and Recollection in Allegheny Country* (Montreal: McGill-Queen's University Press, 2013), 73–74. For accounts that stress the violence of the war in the borderlands around British-occupied New York City, see Sung Bok Kim, "Impact of Class Relations and Warfare in the American Revolution: The New York

Experience," *Journal of American History* 69, no. 2 (1982): 326–46 and "The Limits of Politicization in the American Revolution: The Experience of Westchester County, New York," *Journal of American History* 80, no. 3 (1993): 868–89; Harry M. Ward, *Between the Lines: Banditti of the American Revolution* (Westport, CT: Praeger, 2002); and Mark V. Kwasny, *Washington's Partisan War, 1775–1783* (Kent, OH: Kent State University Press, 1996). For the best work on loyalists and the war in the South, see Jim Piecuch, *Three Peoples, One King: Loyalists, Indians, and Slaves in the Revolutionary South, 1775–1782* (Columbia: University of South Carolina Press, 2008). See also John S. Pancake, *This Destructive War: The British Campaign in the Carolinas, 1780–1782* (Tuscaloosa: University of Alabama Press, 1985). Kathleen DuVal's recent study of the war in the Gulf Coast region successfully reorients the conflict's traditional geographic boundaries. DuVal, *Independence Lost: Lives on the Edge of the American Revolution* (New York: Random House, 2015).

9. On political legitimacy during the Revolution, see Jerrilyn Greene Marston, *King and Congress: The Transfer of Political Legitimacy, 1774–1776* (Princeton, NJ: Princeton University Press, 1987). On the relationship between violence and the state, see Norbert Elias, *The Civilizing Process*, trans. Edmund Jephcott (Cambridge, MA: Blackwell, 1994); Julius R. Ruff, *Violence in Early Modern Europe, 1500–1800* (Cambridge: Cambridge University Press, 2001); and Steven Pinker, *The Better Angels of Our Nature: Why Violence Has Declined* (New York: Viking, 2011). For the relationship between republican political thought and standing armies, see J. G. A. Pocock, *The Machiavellian Moment: Florentine Political Thought and the Atlantic Republic Tradition* (Princeton, NJ: Princeton University Press, 1975); and Lois G. Schwoerer, *"No Standing Armies!": The Antiarmy Ideology in Seventeenth-Century England* (Baltimore: Johns Hopkins University Press, 1974). For more on the Continental Congress's difficulty provisioning its military forces, see E. Wayne Carp, *To Starve the Army at Pleasure: Continental Army Administration and American Political Culture, 1775–1783* (Chapel Hill: University of North Carolina Press, 1984); and Jack N. Rakove, *The Beginnings of National Politics: An Interpretive History of the Continental Congress* (New York: Alfred A. Knopf, 1979). On the importance of localism during the war, see Michael A. McDonnell, *The Politics of War: Race, Class, and Conflict in Revolutionary Virginia* (Chapel Hill: University of North Carolina Press, 2007); and Gregory T. Knouff, *The Soldiers' Revolution: Pennsylvanians in Arms and the Forging of Early American Identity* (University Park: Pennsylvania State University Press, 2004).

10. Gordon Wood, *The Radicalism of the American Revolution* (New York: Vintage Books, 1991), 3; Timothy Tackett, *The Coming of the Terror in the French Revolution* (Cambridge, MA: Harvard University Press, 2015), 355. On the "consensus interpretation" of the American Revolution, see Alfred F. Young and Gregory H. Nobles, *Whose American Revolution Was It? Historians Interpret the Founding* (New York: New York University Press, 2011), 47–59. Arno Mayer pursued a similar line of argument to Tackett. Mayer, *The Furies: Violence and Terror in the French and Russian Revolutions* (Princeton, NJ: Princeton University Press, 2000), 26–27. For a comparative history of the American and French revolutions that emphasizes their similarities, see R. R. Palmer, *The Age of the Democratic Revolution: A Political History of Europe and America, 1760–1800* (Princeton, NJ: Princeton University Press, 2014). The flood of recent scholarship on the "founding fathers" has done more to glorify the war than to illuminate its horrors. See, for instance, Joseph Ellis, *Founding Brothers: The Revolutionary Generation* (New York: Alfred A. Knopf, 2000); John Ferling, *Setting the World Ablaze: Washington, Adams, Jefferson, and the American Revolution* (Oxford: Oxford University Press, 2000); and Stephen Brumwell, *George Washington: Gentleman Warrior* (New York: Quercus, 2012).

11. For examples of the "Neo-Progressive" school of American Revolutionary historiography, see Gary Nash, *The Unknown American Revolution: The Unruly Birth of Democracy and the Struggle to Create America* (New York: Viking, 2005); Jesse Lemisch, *Jack Tar vs. John Bull: The Role of New York's Seamen in Precipitating the Revolution* (New York: Garland, 1997); Ray Raphael, *A People's History of the American Revolution: How Common People Shaped the Fight for Independence* (New York: New Press, 2001); T. H. Breen, *American Insurgents, American Patriots: The Revolution of the People* (New York: Hill and Wang, 2010); Alfred F. Young, *Liberty Tree: Ordinary People and the American Revolution* (New York: New York University Press, 2006); and Woody Holton, *Forced Founders: Indians, Debtors, Slaves, and the Making of the American Revolution in Virginia* (Chapel Hill: University of North Carolina Press, 1999). For a fresh take on the relationship between ordinary white men and elite revolutionaries during the conflict, see Barbara Clark Smith, *The Freedoms We Lost: Consent and Resistance in Revolutionary America* (New York: New Press, 2010). For an overview of the field, see Young and Nobles, *Whose American Revolution Was It?*

12. Shy, *People Numerous and Armed*, 161. For military histories of the war, see Robert Middlekauff, *The Glorious Cause: The American Revolution, 1763–1789* (Oxford: Oxford University Press, 2005); Don Higginbotham, *The War of American Independence: Military Attitudes, Policies, and Practice, 1763–1789* (New York: Macmillan, 1971); and Christopher Ward, *The War of the Revolution*, ed. John Richard Alden, 2 vols. (New York: Macmillan, 1952). For an excellent, though geographically limited, study of the interplay of atrocity and restraint during the war in North Carolina, see Lee, *Crowds and Soldiers*. Recent work that has explored Anglo-American conflicts with Native Americans has further obfuscated just how widespread the violence of the revolutionary era really was by overemphasizing the violence of the frontier war in contrast to the "regular" war. See Peter Silver, *Our Savage Neighbors: How Indian War Transformed Early America* (New York: W. W. Norton, 2008); Grenier, *First Way of War*; and Patrick Griffin, *American Leviathan: Empire, Nation, and Revolutionary Frontier* (New York: Hill and Wang, 2007).

13. Taylor, *American Revolutions*; McDonnell, *Politics of War*; Patrick Griffin, *America's Revolution* (Oxford: Oxford University Press, 2013); Hoock, *Scars of Independence*; Griffin, Ingram, Onuf, and Schoen, *Between Sovereignty and Anarchy*; Allan Kulikoff, "Revolutionary Violence and the Origins of American Democracy," *Journal of the Historical Society* 2, no. 2 (Spring 2002): 232; Shy, *People Numerous and Armed*, 119.

14. Piers Mackesy, *The War for America, 1775–1783* (Lincoln: University of Nebraska Press, 1964), 4; Much like Mackesy, S. P. MacKenzie has argued that "the War of Independence at the level of the main armies was, in many respects, the last war of the *ancien régime* rather than the first war of the era of revolutions." MacKenzie, *Revolutionary Armies in the Modern Era: A Revisionist Approach* (London: Routledge, 1997), 27. Prisoners of war do not figure prominently in either Charles Royster, *A Revolutionary People at War: The Continental Army and American Character, 1775–1783* (Chapel Hill: University of North Carolina Press, 1979) or James Kirby Martin and Mark Edward Lender, *A Respectable Army: The Military Origins of the Republic* (Wheeling, IL: Harlan Davidson, 2006). For the British treatment of American prisoners, see Burrows, *Forgotten Patriots*. Robert P. Watson has recently rearticulated Burrows's thesis. Watson, *The Ghost Ship of Brooklyn: An Untold Story of the American Revolution* (New York: Da Capo, 2017). See also Larry G. Bowman, *Captive Americans: Prisoners During the American Revolution* (Athens: Ohio University Press, 1976); William R. Lindsey, *The Treatment of American Prisoners of War During the Revolution*, Emporia State Research Studies, vol. 22, no. 1 (Emporia: School of Graduate and Professional Studies of the Kansas State Teachers College, 1973); Charles Henry Metzger, *The Prisoner in the*

American Revolution (Chicago: Loyola University Press, 1971), 5–32; Richard H. Amerman, "Treatment of American Prisoners During the Revolution," *Proceedings of the New Jersey Historical Society* 78 (1960): 257–75; Eugene L. Armbruster, *The Wallabout Prison Ships, 1776–1783* (New York, 1920); Danske Dandridge, *American Prisoners of the Revolution* (Charlottesville, VA: Michie, 1911); Alice M. Earle, *Martyrs of the Prison-Ships of the Revolution* (Philadelphia, 1895); and George Taylor, *Martyrs to the Revolution in the British Prison-Ships in Wallabout Bay* (New York, 1855). For accounts of American treatment of enemy prisoners that stress American "humanity" in contrast to British "barbarity," see Gerald Haffner, "The Treatment of Prisoners of War by the Americans During the War of Independence" (Ph.D. diss., Indiana University, 1952); Daniel Krebs, *A Generous and Merciful Enemy: Life for German Prisoners of War During the American Revolution* (Norman: University of Oklahoma Press, 2013); Kenneth Miller, *Dangerous Guests: Enemy Captives and Revolutionary Communities During the War for Independence* (Ithaca, NY: Cornell University Press, 2014); Judith L. Van Buskirk, *Generous Enemies: Patriots and Loyalists in Revolutionary New York* (Philadelphia: University of Pennsylvania Press, 2002); Martha W. Dixon, "Divided Authority: The American Management of Prisoners in the Revolutionary War" (Ph.D. diss., University of Utah, 1977); Paul J. Springer, *America's Captives: Treatment of POWs from the Revolutionary War to the War on Terror* (Lawrence: University Press of Kansas, 2010); and Robert C. Doyle, *The Enemy in Our Hands: America's Treatment of Enemy Prisoners of War from the Revolution to the War on Terror* (Lexington: University Press of Kentucky, 2010). For a concise overview of the "American Way of War" debate, see Wayne Lee, "Early American Ways of War: A New Reconnaissance, 1600–1815," *Historical Journal* 44 (March 2001): 259–89. Despite an otherwise balanced account of the Revolution's violence, Holger Hoock's recent study is exemplary of this trend. On the issue of prisoner treatment, he concludes, "At the moment of her violent birth, the United States led with the power of moral example." Americans had learned "the value of appealing and adhering to humanitarian standards." Hoock, *Scars of Independence*, 398, 399.

15. Evan Thomas, "Founders Chic: Live from Philadelphia," *Newsweek*, July 9, 2001, 48; Boudinot to James Wilson and Christian Forster, July 5, 1777, *"Their Distress is almost intolerable": The Elias Boudinot Letterbook, 1777–1778*, ed. Joseph Lee Boyle (Westminster, MD: Heritage Books, 2002), 14; David Hackett Fischer, *Washington's Crossing* (Oxford: Oxford University Press, 2004), 375. For newspaper editorials and scholarly works that have attempted to contrast alleged U.S. violations of the laws of war during the "war on terror" with the revolutionaries' supposed adherence to them, see Thomas L. Friedman, "George W. to George W.," *New York Times*, March 24, 2005; Brian O'Malley, "Lessons on Iraq from a Founding Father," *Washington Post*, March 1, 2008; Jane Mayer, *The Dark Side: The Inside Story of How the War on Terror Turned into a War on American Ideals* (New York: Doubleday, 2008); Philippe Sands, *Torture Team: Rumsfeld's Memo and the Betrayal of American Values* (New York: Palgrave, 2008); and Louis Fisher, *American Military Tribunals and Presidential Power: American Revolution to the War on Terrorism* (Lawrence: University Press of Kansas, 2005). For the most balanced account of this issue, see John Fabian Witt, *Lincoln's Code: The Laws of War in American History* (New York: Free Press, 2012).

16. Woody Holton, *Unruly Americans and the Origins of the Constitution* (New York: Hill and Wang, 2007); Terry Bouton, *Taming Democracy: "The People," the Founders, and the Troubled Ending of the American Revolution* (New York: Oxford University Press, 2007). For the new American republic's commitment to European legal conventions, see Eliga H. Gould, *Among the Powers of the Earth: The American Revolution and the Making of a New World Empire* (Cambridge, MA: Harvard University Press, 2012). On the Federalists' military policies, see Richard H. Kohn, *Eagle*

and Sword: The Federalists and the Creation of the Military Establishment in America, 1783–1802
(New York: Free Press, 1975); and William B. Skelton, *An American Profession of Arms: The Army Officer Corps, 1784–1861* (Lawrence: University Press of Kansas, 1993).

17. For accounts of how early Americans remembered the Revolution, see Sarah J. Purcell, *Sealed with Blood: War, Sacrifice, and Memory in Revolutionary America* (Philadelphia: University of Pennsylvania Press, 2002); and Michael A. McDonnell, Clare Corbould, Frances M. Clarke, and W. Fitzhugh Brundage, eds., *Remembering the Revolution: Memory, History, and Nation Making from Independence to the Civil War* (Amherst: University of Massachusetts Press, 2013). On the importance of the memory of the Revolution to the construction of American nationalism in the early republic, see David Waldstreicher, *In the Midst of Perpetual Fetes: The Making of American Nationalism, 1776–1820* (Chapel Hill: University of North Carolina Press, 1997); Simon Newman, *Parades and the Politics of the Street: Festive Culture in the Early American Republic* (Philadelphia: University of Pennsylvania Press, 1997); and Len Travers, *Celebrating the Fourth: Independence Day and the Rites of Nationalism in the Early Republic* (Amherst: University of Massachusetts Press, 1997). On the relationship between violence and American national identity, see Carroll Smith-Rosenberg, *This Violent Empire: The Birth of an American National Identity* (Chapel Hill: University of North Carolina Press, 2010). On the connections between violence, democracy, and civil war, see James T. Kloppenberg, *Towards Democracy: The Struggle for Self-Rule in European and American Thought* (Oxford: Oxford University Press, 2016).

Chapter 1

1. Washington to Gage, August 11, 1775, *Founders Online*; "A Journal Kept by John Leach during His Confinement by the British, in Boston Gaol, in 1775," *New England Historical and Genealogical Register* 19 (1865): 259, 260.

2. Gage to Washington, August 13, 1775, *Founders Online*; Wayne E. Lee, *Crowds and Soldiers in Revolutionary North Carolina: The Culture of Violence in Riot and War* (Gainesville: University Press of Florida, 2001), 99. Both Washington and Gage had been present when British general Edward Braddock's army was defeated by a much smaller French, Ottawa, and Potawatomi force at the Battle of the Monongahela on July 9, 1755. See David Preston, *Braddock's Defeat: The Battle of the Monongahela and the Road to Revolution* (Oxford: Oxford University Press, 2015).

3. On the rise of standing armies and the aristocratic officer corps in Europe, see Samuel P. Huntington, *The Soldier and the State: The Theory and Politics of Civil-Military Relations* (Cambridge, MA: Harvard University Press, 1957), chap. 2. See also Michael Howard, *War in European History* (Oxford: Oxford University Press, 2009), chap. 4.

4. Peter H. Wilson, "Prisoners in Early Modern European Warfare," in *Prisoners of War*, ed. Sibylle Scheipers (Oxford: Oxford University Press, 2010), 49, 51–52; Norbert Elias, *The Civilizing Process*, trans. Edmund Jephcott (Cambridge, MA: Blackwell, 1994), 163; David Bell, *The First Total War: Napoleon's Europe and the Birth of Warfare as We Know It* (New York: Mariner Books, 2007), 45. Take, for instance, the siege of Magdeburg by imperial troops in 1631: the city was destroyed, and over 20,000 people were killed. Wilson, "Prisoners in Early Modern European Warfare," 45.

5. Recent scholarship has nuanced our understanding of eighteenth-century European warfare as "restrained," but the stark contrast to the wars of the previous century remains largely

intact. Erica Charters, Eve Rosenhaft, and Hannah Smith, eds., *Civilians and War in Europe, 1618–1815* (Liverpool: Liverpool University Press, 2014), 3–10. Barbara Donagan has argued that "military honour" and the restraint of violence already went hand in hand during the English Civil Wars of the mid-seventeenth century. Donagan, "The Web of Honour: Soldiers, Christians, and Gentlemen in the English Civil War," *Historical Journal* 44, no. 2 (2001): 365–89. See also Donagan, *War in England, 1642–1649* (New York: Oxford University Press, 2008). For an account that stresses atrocity and largely unbridled violence during these conflicts, see Charles Carlton, *Going to the Wars: The Experience of the British Civil Wars, 1638–1651* (London: Routledge, 1992).

    6. Geoffrey Parker, *The Military Revolution: Military Innovation and the Rise of the West, 1500–1800* (Cambridge: Cambridge University Press, 1996); James Q. Whitman, *The Verdict of Battle: The Law of Victory and the Making of Modern War* (Cambridge, MA: Harvard University Press, 2012), 133–71. For the best summary of this ongoing "military revolution" debate, see Clifford J. Rogers, ed., *The Military Revolution Debate: Readings in the Military Transformation of Early Modern Europe* (Boulder, CO: Westview, 1995).

    7. Robert C. Stacey, "The Age of Chivalry," in *The Laws of War: Constraints on Warfare in the Western World*, ed. Michael Howard, George J. Andreopoulous, and Mark. R. Shulman (New Haven, CT: Yale University Press, 1994), 30; Erica Charters, "The Administration of War and French Prisoners of War in Britain, 1756–1763," in *Civilians and War in Europe*, ed. Charters, Rosenhaft, and Smith, 92; Wilson, "Prisoners in Early Modern European Warfare," 53, 52.

    8. Wilson, "Prisoners in Early Modern European Warfare," 50–52; Paul J. Springer, *America's Captives: Treatment of POWs from the Revolutionary War to the War on Terror* (Lawrence: University Press of Kansas, 2010), 10; Caroline Cox, *A Proper Sense of Honor: Service and Sacrifice in George Washington's Army* (Chapel Hill: University of North Carolina Press, 2004), 204; Stephen C. Neff, *War and the Law of Nations: A General History* (Cambridge: Cambridge University Press, 2005), 88. For information on the cartel system during the Seven Years' War, see Erica Charters, "The Administration of War and French Prisoners of War in Britain, 1756–1763," in *Civilians and War in Europe*, ed. Charters, Rosenhaft, and Smith, 87–99; and Reginald Savory, "The Convention of Écluse, 1759–1762: The Treatment of the Sick and Wounded, Prisoners of War, and Deserters of the British and French Armies During the Seven Years War," *Journal of the Society for Army Historical Research* 42, no. 170 (1964): 68–72.

    9. Armstrong Starkey, *War in the Age of Enlightenment, 1700–1799* (Westport, CT: Greenwood, 2003), chap. 3; Markus Meumann, "Civilians, the French Army, and Military Justice During the Reign of Louis XIV, circa 1640–1715," in *Civilians and War in Europe*, ed. Charters, Rosenhaft, and Smith,100–117; Bell, *First Total War*, 50. James Whitman has downplayed the importance of aristocratic culture as a factor limiting wartime violence in the eighteenth century. Whitman, *Verdict of Battle*, 141–42, 160. On the importance of disciplining soldiers' bodies in the eighteenth century, see Michel Foucault, *Discipline and Punish: The Birth of the Prison* (New York: Vintage Books, 1995), 135–84.

    10. On the relationship between honor and violence in Europe, see Petrus Cornelis Spierenburg, *Men and Violence: Gender, Honor, and Rituals in Modern Europe and America* (Columbus: Ohio State University Press, 1998). See also Bertram Wyatt-Brown, *Southern Honor: Ethics and Behavior in the Old South* (Oxford: Oxford University Press, 1982). On honor and dueling culture in early America, see Joanne B. Freeman, *Affairs of Honor: National Politics in the New Republic* (New Haven, CT: Yale University Press, 2001).

11. Bell, *First Total War*, 34; Michael Howard, "Temperamenta Belli: Can War Be Controlled?" in *Restraints on War: Studies in the Limitation of Armed Conflict*, ed. Michael Howard (Oxford: Oxford University Press, 1979), 5; Nicole Eustace, *Passion Is the Gale: Emotion, Power, and the Coming of the American Revolution* (Chapel Hill: University of North Carolina Press, 2008), 153–60. For German sociologist Norbert Elias's account of the transformation of the European aristocracy from the warrior elite of the medieval period to the courtier elite of the eighteenth century, see *Civilizing Process*, esp. 387–97. See also Elias, *The Court Society* (New York: Pantheon Books, 1983); and Elias, *The History of Manners* (New York: Pantheon Books, 1982).

12. Elias, *Civilizing Process*, 161–72; Wayne E. Lee, *Barbarians and Brothers: Anglo-American Warfare, 1500–1865* (New York: Oxford University Press, 2011), 3. As Emer de Vattel phrased it, "If, sometimes, in the heat of action, the soldier refuses to give quarter, it is always contrary to the inclination of the officers, who eagerly interpose to save the lives of such enemies as have laid down their arms." Vattel, *The Law of Nations; or, Principles of the Law of Nature Applied to the Conduct and Affairs of Nations and Sovereigns*, bk. 3, http://www.constitution.org/vattel/vattel_03 .htm (accessed June 15, 2018).

13. Cox, *Proper Sense of Honor*, 206; Renaud Morieux, "French Prisoners of War, Conflicts of Honour, and Social Inversions in England, 1744–1783," *Historical Journal* 56, no. 1 (2013): 55–88.

14. Geoffrey Best, *Humanity in Warfare* (New York: Columbia University Press, 1980), 61; Starkey, *War in the Age of Enlightenment*, 95; Cox, *Proper Sense of Honor*, 206.

15. Geoffrey Parker, "Early Modern Europe," in *Laws of War*, ed. Howard, Andreopoulous, and Shulman, 55; Best, *Humanity in Warfare*, 60.

16. For a thorough examination of the relationship between war and the Enlightenment, see Starkey, *War in the Age of Enlightenment*. Geoffrey Best has famously argued that the eighteenth century experienced an "Enlightenment consensus" that sought to humanize the practices of war. Best, *Humanity in Warfare*, 25–36. But Geoffrey Parker has convincingly suggested that the principal factors that constrained the practice of war in the eighteenth century existed before 1700. See Parker, "Early Modern Europe," 40–58. For a strong caution against overemphasizing the effects of Enlightenment thought on the practice of war, see Bell, *First Total War*, 51, 52–83.

17. Michael Howard, "Constraints on Warfare," in *Laws of War*, ed. Howard, Andreopoulous, and Shulman, 3. According to Eliga H. Gould, Vattel "enjoyed near canonical status in Britain and the colonies." Gould, "Zones of Law, Zones of Violence: The Legal Geography of the British Atlantic, circa 1772," *William and Mary Quarterly*, 3rd ser., 60, no. 3 (July 2003): 477.

18. Vattel, *Law of Nations*, bk. 3. Vattel drew on a Christian framework for the justification of war developed by Saint Augustine and Thomas Aquinas that allowed the prosecution of war to recover belongings, to provide for future safety, or to defend oneself from injury. Starkey, *War in the Age of Enlightenment*, 17.

19. Vattel, *Law of Nations*, bk. 3. On the rise of "humanitarianism" and the culture of "sensibility" in eighteenth-century Europe and the Americas, see G. J. Barker-Benfield, *The Culture of Sensibility: Sex and Society in Eighteenth-Century Britain* (Chicago: University of Chicago Press, 1992); Sarah Knott, *Sensibility and the American Revolution* (Chapel Hill: University of North Carolina Press, 2009); Karen Halttunen, "Humanitarianism and the Pornography of Pain in Anglo-American Culture," *American Historical Review* 100, no. 2 (April 1995): 303–34; Lynn Hunt, *Inventing Human Rights: A History* (New York: W. W. Norton, 2007); Justin Roberts, *Slavery and the Enlightenment in the British Atlantic, 1750–1807* (Cambridge: Cambridge University Press, 2013); Amanda B. Moniz, *From Empire to Humanity: The American Revolution and the Origins of*

Humanitarianism (Oxford: Oxford University Press, 2016); and Steven Pinker, *The Better Angels of Our Nature: Why Violence Has Declined* (New York: Penguin, 2011), 129–87. On the politics of sensibility and politeness in early America, see Steven C. Bullock, *Tea Sets and Tyranny: The Politics of Politeness in Early America* (Philadelphia: University of Pennsylvania Press, 2017).

20. Vattel, *Law of Nations*, bk. 3; Samuel Johnson, "The Introduction to the Proceedings of the Committee Appointed to Manage the Contributions, Begun at London, December 18, 1758, for Clothing French Prisoners of War," in *The Works of Samuel Johnson, L.L.D.*, ed. Arthur Murphy, 12 vols. (Boston: Hastings, Etheridge, and Bliss, 1809), 2:420; Charters, "Administration of War and French Prisoners of War in Britain," 96–97.

21. Vattel, *Law of Nations*, bk. 3; Best, *Humanity in Warfare*, 54–55. Vattel's work built on Hugo Grotius's treatise *On the Law of War and Peace*. Wayne Lee has argued, "In many ways, Grotius, Vattel, and other early modern jurists merely codified customs created in previous centuries, but this process of codification created a kind of feedback loop in which custom and written premise (or 'law') reinforced each other." Lee, *Barbarians and Brothers*, 189. According to Ira Gruber's study of the reading preferences of British officers during the American Revolution, Grotius's *On the Law of War and Peace* "was clearly among the books on war that [these] officers considered an authority." Gruber, *Books and the British Army in the Age of the American Revolution* (Chapel Hill: University of North Carolina Press, 2010), 180.

22. Bell, *First Total War*, chap. 1; Best, *Humanity in Warfare*, chap. 1; Parker, "Early Modern Europe," 56–57; Harold E. Selesky, "Colonial America," in *Laws of War*, ed. Howard, Andreopoulos, and Shulman, 59–85. For an account of how European norms of legitimate violence in warfare devolved during the 1675 conflict in Massachusetts known to the colonists as King Philip's War, see Jill Lepore, *The Name of War: King Philip's War and the Origins of American Identity* (New York: Vintage Books, 1998).

23. Vattel, *Law of Nations*, bk. 3.

24. For more on the Jacobite challenge to the Protestant succession in Britain, see Tim Harris, *Revolution: The Great Crisis of the British Monarchy, 1685–1720* (London: Allen Lane, 2006); Bruce Lenman, *The Jacobite Risings in Britain, 1689–1746* (London: Eyre Methuen, 1980); and Linda Colley, *Britons: Forging the Nation, 1707–1837* (New Haven, CT: Yale University Press, 2009).

25. W. A. Speck, *The Butcher: The Duke of Cumberland and the Suppression of the '45* (Cardiff, UK: Welsh Academic Press, 1995), 148–49, 164. For a general account of the suppression of the 1745 Jacobite Rebellion, see Jeremy Black, *Culloden and the '45* (Stroud, UK: Sutton, 1990). For an analysis of how the British government dealt with Jacobite prisoners during the earlier 1715 rebellion, see Margaret Sankey, *Jacobite Prisoners of the 1715 Rebellion: Preventing and Punishing Insurrection in Early Hanoverian Britain* (Aldershot, UK: Ashgate, 2005).

26. Starkey, *War in the Age of Enlightenment*, 149; Edwin Burrows, *Forgotten Patriots: The Untold Story of American Prisoners During the Revolutionary War* (New York: Basic Books, 2008), chap. 2.

27. For the best account of the issue of "rebellion" and the conduct of the British Army during the 1745 uprising, see Geoffrey Plank, *Rebellion and Savagery: The Jacobite Rising of 1745 and the British Empire* (Philadelphia: University of Pennsylvania Press, 2006).

28. Lee, *Barbarians and Brothers*, 1; Guibert quoted in Starkey, *War in the Age of Enlightenment*, 56.

29. Stephen Conway, "The British Army, 'Military Europe,' and the American War of Independence," *William and Mary Quarterly*, 3rd ser., 67, no. 1 (January 2010): 99; Washington to Gage,

August 19, 1775, *Founders Online*. I agree with Conway that the British Army shared the values and customs of a broader "military Europe."

30. Francis Jennings, *Invasion of America: Indians, Colonialism, and the Cant of Conquest* (New York: W. W. Norton, 1975); Ian K. Steele, *Warpaths: Invasions of North America* (Oxford: Oxford University Press, 1994); John Ferling, *Struggle for a Continent: The Wars of Early America* (Arlington Heights, IL: Harlan Davidson, 1993) and *A Wilderness of Miseries: War and Warriors in Early America* (Westport, CT: Greenwood, 1980); John Grenier, *The First Way of War: American War Making on the Frontier* (Cambridge: Cambridge University Press, 2005), 21–22; Lee, *Barbarians and Brothers*, 121–41.

31. Steele, *Warpaths*, chap. 3. Christian Crouch charts a similar divergence between metropolitan and colonial warfare in New France. Crouch, *Nobility Lost: French and Canadian Martial Cultures, Indians, and the End of New France* (Ithaca, NY: Cornell University Press, 2014).

32. John Morgan Dederer, *War in America to 1775: Before Yankee Doodle* (New York: New York University Press, 1990), 184; Cox, *Proper Sense of Honor*, 7. On the influence of radical whig and classical republican political thought on early modern England's defense policy and the institution of the militia, see Bernard Bailyn, *The Ideological Origins of the American Revolution* (Cambridge, MA: Harvard University Press, 1967); J. G. A. Pocock, *The Machiavellian Moment: Florentine Political Thought and the Atlantic Republican Tradition* (Princeton, NJ: Princeton University Press, 1975); and Lois G. Schwoerer, *"No Standing Armies!": The Antiarmy Ideology in Seventeenth-Century England* (Baltimore: Johns Hopkins University Press, 1974).

33. Dederer, *War in America*, 119, 187.

34. Ibid., 122; Grenier, *First Way of War*, 29–52; Adam J. Hirsch, "The Collision of Military Cultures in Seventeenth-Century New England," *Journal of American History* 74, no. 4 (March 1988): 1187–1212. On the Iroquoian practice of "mourning-war," see Daniel K. Richter, "War and Culture: The Iroquois Experience," *William and Mary Quarterly*, 3rd ser., 40, no. 4 (October 1983): 528–59.

35. Lee, *Crowds and Soldiers*, 117 and *Barbarians and Brothers*, 166. For English colonists' prior experience with extirpative war, see Ferling, *Wilderness of Miseries*; and Grenier, *First Way of War*. For the effects, or lack thereof, of Native American cultures of war on warfare in early America, see Guy Chet, *Conquering the American Wilderness: The Triumph of European Warfare in the Colonial Northeast* (Amherst: University of Massachusetts Press, 2003); Grenier, *First Way of War*; and Armstrong Starkey, *European and Native American Warfare, 1675–1815* (Norman: University of Oklahoma Press, 1998). For an examination of English colonists' unwillingness to grant Native American warriors the customary protections of European warfare, see Selesky, "Colonial America," 60–62; and Ian K. Steele, "Surrendering Rites: Prisoners on Colonial North American Frontiers," in *Hanoverian Britain and Empire: Essays in Memory of Philip Lawson*, ed. Stephen Taylor, Richard Connors, and Clyve Jones (Suffolk, UK: Boydell, Woodbridge, 1998), 137–57. For the role of print in the dehumanization of Native peoples, see Peter Silver, *Our Savage Neighbors: How Indian War Transformed Early America* (New York: W. W. Norton, 2008).

36. Harold E. Selesky, *War and Society in Colonial Connecticut* (New Haven, CT: Yale University Press, 1990), x. On the origins of the name, see Fred Anderson, *Crucible of War: The Seven Years' War and the Fate of Empire in British North America, 1754–1766* (New York: Knopf, 2000), 747n1.

37. Huntington, *Soldier and the State*, 22–27. For eighteenth-century British officers' taste in French military books, see Gruber, *Books and the British Army*. Although not widely represented, at least one of the forty-two officers Gruber studied owned a copy of Vattel's *The Law of Nations*.

A copy of Hugo Grotius's *On the Law of War and Peace* was owned by 19 percent of Gruber's sample. Anderson's *Essay on the Art of War* was one of the "books preferred" by British officers. Gruber, *Books and the British Army*, 141, 180, 227. On the British Army during the Seven Years' War, see Stephen Brumwell, *Redcoats: The British Soldier and War in the Americas, 1755–1763* (Cambridge: Cambridge University Press, 2002), esp. 162–90.

38. James Anderson, *Essay on the Art of War: In which the General Principles of All the Operations of War in the Field are Fully Explained: The Whole Collected from the Opinions of the Best Authors* (London: A. Miller, 1761), 206–7, 518, 576.

39. Fred Anderson, *A People's Army: Massachusetts Soldiers and Society in the Seven Years' War* (Chapel Hill: University of North Carolina Press, 1984), 113, 117; Geoffrey Plank, "A Medieval Response to a Wilderness Need: Anglicizing Warfare in Colonial America," in *Anglicizing America: Empire, Revolution, Republic*, ed. Ignacio Gallup-Diaz, Andrew Shankman, and David J. Silverman (Philadelphia: University of Pennsylvania Press, 2015); Fred Anderson and Andrew R. L. Cayton, *The Dominion of War: Empire and Liberty in North America* (New York: Viking, 2005), 162–63; Washington to Robert Orme, March 15, 1755, *Founders Online*; Washington to Maj. Andrew Lewis, May 21, 1758, ibid.; Johann Ewald, *Belehrungen iiber den Krieg*, quoted in Sandra L. Powers, "Studying the Art of War: Military Books Known to American Officers and Their French Counterparts During the Second Half of the Eighteenth Century," *Journal of Military History* 70, no. 3 (July 2006): 791. See also Oliver L. Spaulding Jr., "The Military Studies of George Washington," *American Historical Review* 29, no. 4 (July 1924): 675–80. The Library of Congress has compiled a list of all known military manuals that George Washington owned. See Virginia Steele Wood, "George Washington's Military Manuals," http://www.loc.gov/rr/genealogy/bib_guid/Washington MilitaryManuals.pdf (accessed September 3, 2012). For the best overview of the military campaigns of the Seven Years' War, see Anderson, *Crucible of War*.

40. Steele, "Prisoners on Colonial North American Frontiers," 154; Lord Barrington to the Mayor of Bath, April 18, 1757, WO 4/54/3, TNA. British and colonial American forces rarely took Native warriors prisoner. When they did, the unfortunate captives were usually sold into slavery. Likewise, French colonists captured alongside Native warriors, especially if wearing Indian dress, could expect little mercy. Brumwell, *Redcoats*, 182–83. On the enslavement of Indians in early America, see Margaret Ellen Newell, *Brethren by Nature: New England Indians, Colonists, and the Origins of American Slavery* (Ithaca, NY: Cornell University Press, 2015); and Alan Gallay, ed., *Indian Slavery in Colonial America* (Lincoln: University of Nebraska Press, 2010).

41. Brumwell, *Redcoats*, 184; *New-Hampshire Gazette* (Portsmouth), August 26, 1757; Ian K. Steele, *Betrayals: Fort William Henry and the Massacre* (New York: Oxford University Press, 1990), 149; Crouch, *Nobility Lost*, 92–94.

42. Steele, *Betrayals*, 131; Anderson, *Crucible of War*, 198–99; Crouch, *Nobility Lost*, 86–91; Jeffery Amherst to M. de la Pause, quoted in Anderson, *Crucible of War*, 408.

43. Kevin Kenny, *Peaceable Kingdom Lost: The Paxton Boys and the Destruction of William Penn's Holy Experiment* (New York: Oxford University Press, 2009), 1; Patrick Griffin, *American Leviathan: Empire, Nation, and Revolutionary Frontier* (New York: Hill and Wang, 2007), 46–49; Edward Shippen quoted in Silver, *Our Savage Neighbors*, 179.

44. *New-York Mercury*, September 18, 1758; *Boston Evening-Post*, March 1, 1756; Anderson and Cayton, *Dominion of War*, 105–6, 127–29.

45. Anderson and Cayton, *Dominion of War*, 157. Legal historian John Fabian Witt has called Washington "the living embodiment of the Enlightenment way of war." Witt, *Lincoln's Code: The*

Laws of War in American History (New York: Free Press, 2012), 19. Ira Gruber eloquently summarized the revolutionary leadership's prevailing understanding of war: "George Washington and other American commanders had come to understand warfare through British eyes." Gruber, *Books and the British Army*, 51. David Hackett Fischer has observed that "New England produced a remarkable generation of self-taught military commanders who trained themselves by systematic study." Fischer, *Paul Revere's Ride* (Oxford: Oxford University Press, 1994), 247.

46. Josiah Smith Letter Book, 1771–84, Collection 03018, Southern Historical Collection, Wilson Special Collections Library, University of North Carolina, Chapel Hill. Harold Selesky has observed a similar development in colonial Connecticut. Selesky, *War and Society*, 67. For an analysis of the raising of provincial regulars in Massachusetts, see Anderson, *People's Army*. For the best narrative account of the Battles of Lexington and Concord, see Fischer, *Paul Revere's Ride*.

47. Josiah Smith to James Poyas, May 18, 1775, Josiah Smith Letter Book; *Massachusetts Spy* (Worcester), May 3, 1775; Israel Putnam to the Committee of New-London and Lyme, *Norwich (CT) Packet*, April 22, 1775; *New-Hampshire Gazette* (Portsmouth), April 21, 1775; Josiah Smith to George Appleby, June 16, 1775, Josiah Smith Letter Book. On April 26, 1775, the Provincial Assembly of Massachusetts published a resolve condemning the actions of the British troops at Lexington and Concord as "ravages" that "would disgrace the annals of the most uncivilized nations." *The Remembrancer, or Impartial Repository of Public Events*, 17 vols. (London: J. Almon, 1775), 1:3.

48. Gage to Barrington, April 22, 1775, *The Correspondence of General Gage*, ed. Clarence E. Carter, 2 vols. (New Haven, CT: Yale University Press, 1931–33), 2:673–74; Gage to Barrington, May 13, 1775, ibid., 2:678; *Connecticut Courant* (Hartford), May 8, 1775. During the retreat from Concord, Lieutenant Colonel Smith lost command and control of his column. He and his officers did little to restrain their men. See Robert Middlekauff, *The Glorious Cause: The American Revolution, 1763–1789* (Oxford: Oxford University Press, 2005), 278–79.

49. "Letter from Wethersfield, in Connecticut, to a Gentleman in New-York," April 23, 1775, *AA*, 4th ser., 2:362; "Narrative of Loyalist John Peters, Lieutenant-Colonel of the Queen's Loyal Rangers in Canada, written in letter to a friend in London, Pimlico [Eng.], June 5, 1786," *Daily Globe* (Toronto), July 16, 1877; Thomas Jefferson to Williams Small, May 7, 1775, *Founders Online*. For examples of popular attacks upon loyalists in the aftermath of the fighting at Lexington and Concord, see Memorial of Isaac Bell, AO 13/76/5–6; and Robert Cook, AO 13/21/120–21, TNA.

50. "Deposition of Lieutenant Edward Thornton Gould. Medford, Massachusetts," April 25, 1775, *Remembrancer*, 1:38; "Extract from an intercepted letter of the Soldiery in Boston," May 2, 1775, *AA*, 4th ser., 2:441.

51. Samuel Adams Drake, *History of Middlesex County, Massachusetts, Containing Carefully Prepared Histories of Every City and Town in the County*, 2 vols. (Boston: Estes and Lauriat, 1880), 1:302.

52. John Hancock to the Massachusetts Committee of Safety, April 24, 1775, *AA*, 4th ser., 2:384; Resolutions of the Massachusetts Committee of Safety, April 26, 1775, ibid., 746; Expenses incurred by prisoners in the Worcester Jail, folder 3, box 1, U.S. Revolution Collection, AAS. When Boyce refused to pay for the prisoner's transportation, the committeemen ordered the prisoner returned to their custody. The Committee of Safety of Massachusetts to Mr. Vose, May 2, 1775, *AA*, 4th ser., 2:474; "Account of the commencement of hostilities between Great Britain and America, in the Province of Massachusetts-Bay, by the Reverend Mr. William Gordon, of Roxbury, in a Letter to a Gentleman in England," ibid., 625.

53. Proceedings of the Massachusetts Provincial Council, April 30, 1775, *AA*, 4th ser., 2:776; Israel Putnam to the Committee of New-London and Lyme, *Norwich (CT) Packet*, April 22, 1775; *Memoirs of Major-General William Heath by Himself*, ed. William Abbatt (New York, 1901), 10; *Remembrancer*, 1:41.

54. Frederick Mackenzie, *Diary of Frederick Mackenzie: Giving a Daily Narrative of His Military Service as an Officer of the Regiment of Royal Welch Fusiliers During the Years 1775–1781 in Massachusetts, Rhode Island, and New York*, 2 vols. (Cambridge, MA: Harvard University Press, 1930), 1:42; Gage to Barrington, May 13, 1775, in *Correspondence of General Gage*, ed. Carter, 2:678; "Report of Committee on liberating Prisoners taken by Gen. Gage, the 19th of April, (Note) Resolve on the same subject," Watertown, MA, May 3, 1775, *AA*, 4th ser., 2:784.

55. *Remembrancer*, 1:42; Fischer, *Paul Revere's Ride*, 265. Thomas Pownall assisted Almon in compiling the documents in *The Remembrancer*.

56. Drake, *History of Middlesex County*, 1:134; *Norwich (CT) Packet*, June 15, 1775. This same article from the *Packet* appears in numerous publications, including the *Connecticut Gazette*, the *Pennsylvania Evening Post*, and the *New-York Gazette*. The exchange took place on an equal basis, without regard to military rank, social standing, or race. The nine British prisoners included three officers and six enlisted men, while the Americans were all civilians. The Britons were Major Dunbar, Lieutenant Hamilton, Lieutenant Potter, John Hilton, Alexander Campbell, John Tyne, Samuel Marcy, Thomas Parry, and Thomas Sharp. They were exchanged for Americans John Peck, James Hews, James Brewer, Daniel Preston, Samuel Frost, Seth Russell, Joseph Bell, Elijah Seaver, and Caeser Augustus, "a negro servant of Mr. Tileston, of Dorchester."

57. Colley, *Britons*, 137–45; *Morning Chronicle and London Advertiser*, June 2, 1775; *General Evening Post* (London), May 30–June 1, 1775. See also *St. James's Chronicle or the British Evening Post* (London), June 3–6, 1775. For a sense of the extent of this disbelief that the Americans would fire on British troops, see "Observations on the Skirmish near Boston with a state of Facts," *General Evening Post* (London), May 30–June 1, 1775. For discussions of British popular response to the American Revolution, see Eliga H. Gould, *The Persistence of Empire: British Political Culture in the Age of the American Revolution* (Chapel Hill: University of North Carolina Press, 2000), chap. 5.

58. Gage's proclamation, *Connecticut Gazette* (New London), June 23, 1775; John Morton to Thomas Powell, June 8, 1775, in *LMCC*, 1:114; "Journal Kept by John Leach," 257; Journal of Peter Edes, in *Peter Edes: Pioneer Printer in Maine, A Biography*, ed. Samuel Lane Boardman (Bangor, ME, 1901), 100. For more on John Leach, see "John Leach," *Ex Libris* 1, no. 1 (July 1896): 20–27.

59. Journal of Peter Edes, in *Peter Edes*, ed. Boardman, 99, 102; "Journal Kept by John Leach," 258; Joseph Reed to Maj. Christopher French, September 3, 1775, enclosed in French to Washington, September 3, 1775, n. 1, *Founders Online*.

60. Washington to Gage, August 19, 1775, *Founders Online*; ibid., n. 1.

Chapter 2

1. Ethan Allen, *A Narrative of Colonel Ethan Allen's Captivity Written by Himself* (Burlington, VT: Chauncey Goodrich, 1846), 29, 30, 32, 33; Ethan Allen to Richard Prescott, September 25, 1775, Transcripts of the Ethan Allen Papers, ser. 7E, reel 1, PFPC. In reconstructing the narrative of the Canadian campaign, I found the following works particularly useful: Robert McConnell Hatch, *Thrust for Canada: The American Attempt on Quebec in 1775–1776* (Boston: Houghton

Mifflin, 1979); Michael P. Gabriel, *Major General Richard Montgomery: The Making of an American Hero* (Madison, NJ: Fairleigh Dickinson University Press, 2002); Hal T. Shelton, *General Richard Montgomery and the American Revolution* (New York: New York University Press, 1994); James Kirby Martin, *Benedict Arnold, Revolutionary Hero: An American Warrior Reconsidered* (New York: New York University Press, 1997); Michael A. Bellesiles, *Revolutionary Outlaws: Ethan Allen and the Struggle for Independence on the Early American Frontier* (Charlottesville: University Press of Virginia, 1995); Paul David Nelson, *General Sir Guy Carleton, Lord Dorchester: Soldier-Statesman of Early British Canada* (Madison, NJ: Fairleigh Dickinson University Press, 2000); Kevin Phillips, *1775: A Good Year for Revolution* (New York: Viking, 2012); and Mark R. Anderson, *The Battle for the Fourteenth Colony: America's War of Liberation in Canada, 1774–1776* (Lebanon, NH: University Press of New England, 2013).

2. Alexander Spotswood to George Washington, April 30, 1775, *Founders Online*; Philip Schuyler to John Hancock, January 23, 1776, *AA*, 4th ser., 4:818. On the revolutionary elite's insistence that the conduct of the war reflect the virtue of the American cause, see Charles Royster, *A Revolutionary People at War: The Continental Army and American Character, 1775–1783* (Chapel Hill: University of North Carolina Press, 1979); and Eliga H. Gould, *Among the Powers of the Earth: The American Revolution and the Making of a New World Empire* (Cambridge, MA: Harvard University Press, 2012). For the importance Congress placed on performing its sovereignty and legitimacy, see Benjamin H. Irvin, *Clothed in Robes of Sovereignty: The Continental Congress and the People Out of Doors* (Oxford: Oxford University Press, 2011).

3. Willard Sterne Randall, *Ethan Allen: His Life and Times* (New York: W. W. Norton, 2011), 339–43, 348.

4. For an excellent brief overview of the colonial wars, see John Ferling, *Struggle for a Continent: The Wars of Early America* (Arlington Heights, IL: Harlan Davidson, 1993).

5. Hatch, *Thrust for Canada*, 29–42.

6. Gabriel, *Major General Richard Montgomery*, 88–89; Hatch, *Thrust for Canada*, 48.

7. Hatch, *Thrust for Canada*, chap. 5.

8. "Articles Proposed by Major Stopford for the Surrender of Chambly," *AA*, 4th ser., 3:1133; Hatch, *Thrust for Canada*, chap. 5.

9. "Major Brown's Answer," *AA*, 4th ser., 3:1133; Shelton, *General Richard Montgomery*, 109–10. The colors of the 7th Foot were presented to Congress on November 3, 1775. Samuel Adams to Elbridge Gerry, November 4, 1775, *AA*, 4th ser., 3:1248.

10. Montgomery to Schuyler, October 20, 23, 1775, reel 19, Philip Schuyler Papers, 1705–1864, MssCol 2701, NYPL.

11. Montgomery to Schuyler, October 23, 1775, reel 19, Schuyler Papers; Schuyler to John Hancock, October 21, 1775, *AA*, 4th ser., 3:1130; Margaret Sankey, *Jacobite Prisoners of the 1715 Rebellion: Preventing and Punishing Insurrection in Early Hanoverian Britain* (Aldershot, UK: Ashgate, 2005), 104.

12. Gabriel, *Major General Richard Montgomery*, 123; Nelson, *General Sir Guy Carleton*, 69–70; Allen, *Narrative*, 33.

13. Montgomery to Schuyler, September 28, 1775, reel 19, Schuyler Papers.

14. Montgomery to Maj. John Brown, October 6, 1775, *AA*, 4th ser., 3:1098; Montgomery to Schuyler, October 20, 1775, reel 19, Schuyler Papers.

15. Montgomery to Carleton, October 22, 1775, *AA*, 4th ser., 3:1138–39; Shelton, *General Richard Montgomery*, 30; Gabriel, *Major General Richard Montgomery*, 123.

16. Montgomery to Stopford, October 20, 1775, *AA*, 4th ser., 3:1134; Montgomery to Carleton, October 22, 1775, ibid., 1138–39; Carleton to Dartmouth, October 28, 1775, quoted in Victor Coffin, *The Province of Quebec and the Early American Revolution* (Madison: University of Wisconsin Press, 1896), 370.

17. Hatch, *Thrust for Canada*, 91–92.

18. John Childs, "Surrender and the Laws of War in Western Europe, c. 1660–1783," in *How Fighting Ends: A History of Surrender*, ed. Holger Afflerbach and Hew Strachan (Oxford: Oxford University Press, 2012), 162; "Articles of Capitulation Proposed by Major Charles Preston," St. John's, November 2, 1775, *AA*, 4th ser., 3:1394; Montgomery to Preston, November 1, 1775, ibid., 1393.

19. "Articles of Capitulation Proposed by Major Charles Preston"; Montgomery to Schuyler, November 3, 1775, *AA*, 4th ser., 3:1392.

20. Schuyler to Trumbull, November 10, 1775, *AA*, 4th ser., 3:1426; Schuyler to John Hulbert, November 1, 1775, PCC, item 68, p. 55; Schuyler to Trumbull, October 27, 1775, *AA*, 4th ser., 3:1207.

21. Carleton to Dartmouth, October 28, 1775, quoted in Coffin, *Province of Quebec*, 370. Gerald Haffner, and more recently Edwin Burrows, have argued that Allen was sent to England to stand trial for treason. Haffner, "The Treatment of Prisoners of War by the Americans During the War of Independence" (Ph.D. diss., Indiana University, 1952), 64; Burrows, *Forgotten Patriots: The Untold Story of American Prisoners During the Revolutionary War* (New York: Basic Books, 2008), 39. In his letter to Lord Dartmouth, Cramahé made it clear that the reason was expediency rather than justice. Cramahé to Dartmouth, November 9, 1775, Calendar of the State Papers of Canada, in Douglas Brymner, *Report on the Canadian Archives for 1890* (Ottawa: Brown Chamberlin, 1891), 66.

22. Allen, *Narrative*, 37, 38.

23. Burrows, *Forgotten Patriots*, 30; Montgomery to Janet Montgomery, November 24, 1775, Janet Montgomery Papers, Edward Livingston Collection, Mudd Manuscript Library, Princeton University; Montgomery to Schuyler, November 24, 1775, *AA*, 4th ser., 3:1694.

24. James Clinton, John Nicholson, and Lewis Dubois to Montgomery, November 23, 1775, *AA*, 4th ser., 3:1695; Montgomery to Schuyler, November 24, 1775, ibid.; Schuyler to John Hancock, December 8, 1775, ibid., 4:219; Shelton, *General Richard Montgomery*, 121.

25. Gabriel, *Major General Richard Montgomery*, 139–40; Montgomery to Schuyler, November 13, 1775, reel 19, Schuyler Papers.

26. *Boston-Gazette*, November 6, 1775; *New-York Gazette*, November 6, 1775; Gabriel, *Major General Richard Montgomery*, 108. See also Sarah J. Purcell, *Sealed with Blood: War, Sacrifice, and Memory in Revolutionary America* (Philadelphia: University of Pennsylvania Press, 2002), 24–25. For the articles of capitulation for Fort Chambly, see *Connecticut Journal* (New Haven), November 15, 1775. For the articles of capitulation for Saint John's, see *Pennsylvania Gazette* (Philadelphia), November 15, 1775. For the same for Montreal, see *New-York Gazette*, December 4, 1775.

27. "Address of the principal Inhabitants on Lake Champlain to Benedict Arnold," July 3, 1775, *AA*, 4th ser., 2:1088; Hancock to Montgomery, November 30, 1775, ibid., 3:1718. On Montgomery's reputation, see Royster, *Revolutionary People at War*, 122. On the relationship between courage and benevolence in the "culture of sensibility" in early America, see Andrew Burstein, *Sentimental Democracy: The Evolution of America's Romantic Self-Image* (New York: Hill and Wang, 1999), 68. Henry Knox praised Schuyler for being "sensible and polite" and behaving with "vast

propriety to the British officers who, by the course of war, have fallen into our hands." Henry Knox to Lucy Knox, January 5, 1776, folder 8, box 2, U.S. Revolution Collection, AAS.

28. Schuyler to Trumbull, November 10, 1775, *AA*, 4th ser., 3:1426; Resolution of the Connecticut Assembly, October 11, 1775, *PRCC*, 15:145, 146. See also Trumbull to Hancock, November 11, 1775, *AA*, 4th ser., 3:1529. For French prisoners being sent to Albany in 1755, see William Cockcroft to Sir William Johnson, September 20, 1755, *The Papers of Sir William Johnson*, ed. Alexander C. Flick, 14 vols. (Albany: State University of New York Press, 1921–65), 2:63; and Sir William Johnson to Spencer Phips, October 10, 1755, ibid., 163. For information on French prisoners in Connecticut during the war, see Connecticut Archives, Colonial War Records, 1675–1775, ser. 1, 6:139, 8:242, 8:243, 9:133, Connecticut State Library, Hartford. On the experience of British prisoners in Hartford, see Herbert H. White, "British Prisoners of War in Hartford During the Revolution," in *Papers of the New Haven Colony Historical Society*, vol. 8 (New Haven, CT, 1914), 255–76.

29. Ezekiel Williams to Elias Boudinot, September 13, 1777, box 1, Elias Boudinot Papers, 1773–1812, MMC-0721, LC.

30. Maj. Gen. David Wooster to Capt. David Dimon, July 10, 1775, in *Letters and Documents of Ezekiel Williams of Wethersfield, Connecticut*, ed. John C. Parsons (Hartford, CT: Acorn Club, 1976), 43; Trumbull to the Committee Appointed to Take Care of Prisoners, July 22, 1775, in ibid., 44.

31. Albany Committee Minutes, October 23, 1775, *Minutes of the Albany Committee of Correspondence, 1775–1778*, ed. James Sullivan (Albany: New York Division of Archives and History, 1923), 276; "The Cases of Neill McFall and William Elphinston, New York Provincial Congress," October 20, 1775, *AA*, 4th ser., 3:1299.

32. Albany Committee Minutes, August 24, 1775, in *Minutes of the Albany Committee*, ed. Sullivan, 212.

33. Proceedings of the Connecticut Committee of Safety, November 23, 1775, *AA*, 4th ser., 3:1638.

34. *Connecticut Courant* (Hartford), October 16, 1775. For the discussion of a potential cartel for prisoner exchange, and the severance of communication between both officers, see Howe to Washington, August 22, 1775, *Founders Online*; and Washington to Howe, August 23, 1775, ibid. Washington broke his silence to remonstrate against the treatment of Ethan Allen. Washington to Howe, December 18, 1775, ibid.

35. Thomas Seymour to Washington, September 18, 1775, *Founders Online*; Washington to French, September 26, 1775, ibid. French was captured in Philadelphia, not in Canada, but he and an ensign from the 47th Regiment were transferred to Hartford to be confined alongside the Canadian prisoners. Samuel Hazard, ed., *Colonial Records of Pennsylvania, 1683–1800*, 16 vols. (Philadelphia, 1852–53), 10:302–6.

36. French to Washington, September 18, 1775, *Founders Online*. For the best discussion of the social, legal, and cultural place of the small sword in seventeenth- and eighteenth-century England, see J. D. Aylward, *The Small-Sword in England: Its History, Its Forms, Its Makers, and Its Masters* (London: Hutchinson's Scientific & Technical Publications, 1945).

37. Washington to French, September 26, 1775, *Founders Online*; Washington to the Hartford Committee of Safety, September 26, 1775, ibid.

38. Washington to French, October 25, 1775, *Founders Online*; Sheldon S. Cohen, ed., "The Connecticut Captivity of Major Christopher French," *Connecticut Historical Society Bulletin* 55, nos. 3–4 (1990): 127.

39. "Questions for the Committee, 18 October, 1775," *Founders Online*; Minutes of the Conference, October 18–24, 1775, ibid. The committee comprised Deputy Governor Griswold and Nathaniel Wales of Connecticut; Deputy Governor Cooke of Rhode Island; Thomas Lynch, Benjamin Franklin, and Benjamin Harrison, all from the Continental Congress; and James Bowdoin, Colonel James Otis, William Sever, and Walter Spooner from the Committee of the Council of Massachusetts Bay.

40. Washington to Hancock, November 8, 1775, *Founders Online*; Schuyler to Hancock, November 27, 1775, *AA*, 4th ser., 3:1681.

41. Washington to Hancock, November 8, 1775, *Founders Online*.

42. *JCC*, 3:358, 404. For the best account of the detention of British and Hessian prisoners of war in Lancaster, see Kenneth Miller, *Dangerous Guests: Enemy Captives and Revolutionary Communities During the War for Independence* (Ithaca, NY: Cornell University Press, 2014). On Carlisle, see Judith Ridner, *A Town In-Between: Carlisle, Pennsylvania, and the Early Mid-Atlantic Interior* (Philadelphia: University of Pennsylvania Press, 2010).

43. Committee of Safety of Lancaster to Messrs. Lynch, Lewis, and Allen, a subcommittee of the Continental Congress, December 9, 1775, Charles Swift Riché Hildeburn Collection, 1760–77, AM 6093, HSP; Hancock to William Livingston, November 17, 1775, PCC, item 12a, 1:19; Return of Prisoners at Lancaster, Hildeburn Collection; John W. Jordan, "Bethlehem During the Revolution: Extracts from the Diaries in the Moravian Archives at Bethlehem, Pennsylvania," *Pennsylvania Magazine of History and Biography* 12, no. 4 (January 1889): 388. See also Daniel Krebs, *A Generous and Merciful Enemy: Life for German Prisoners During the American Revolution* (Norman: University of Oklahoma Press, 2013), 126–28.

44. Minutes of the Lancaster County Committee of Safety, December 9, 1775, ser. 8D:96, item 86, reel 48, PFPC; Reading Committee of Safety to the Pennsylvania Delegation to the Continental Congress, February 4, 1776, PCC, item 69, 1:91; Committee of Safety of Lancaster to Messrs. Lynch, Lewis, and Allen, a subcommittee of the Continental Congress, December 9, 1775, Hildeburn Collection.

45. Minutes of the Lancaster County Committee of Safety, December 9, 1775, ser. 8D:96, item 86, reel 48, PFPC; Reading Committee of Safety to the Pennsylvania Delegation to the Continental Congress, February 4, 1776, PCC, item 69, 1:91.

46. Committee of Safety of Lancaster to Messrs. Lynch, Lewis, and Allen, a subcommittee of the Continental Congress, December 9, 1775, Hildeburn Collection.

47. "Notes from the Bethlehem Diary," January 30, 1776, Hildeburn Collection; Committee of Safety of Lancaster to Messrs. Lynch, Lewis, and Allen, a subcommittee of the Continental Congress, December 9, 1775, ibid.; "Return of Clothing, Necessaries, &c., that was lost, belonging to the Prisoners of His Majesty's Seventh Regiment of Royal Fusiliers," January 24, 1776, *AA*, 4th ser., 4:817; Lancaster Committee of Safety to the Continental Congress, January 10, 1776, Hildeburn Collection.

48. *JCC*, 3:399. For the best account of David Franks's involvement with the provisioning of prisoners of war, see Mark Abbot Stern, *David Franks: Colonial Merchant* (University Park: Pennsylvania State University Press, 2010), chap. 2. See also Krebs, *Generous and Merciful Enemy*, 128–29.

49. Washington to Hancock, February 9, 1776, *Founders Online*; Washington to Hancock, February 14, 1776, ibid.

50. Germain to Howe, February 1, 1776, *AA*, 4th ser., 4:902; Stern, *David Franks*, 117.

51. John Hancock to the Lancaster Committee of Safety, January 18, 1776, *AA*, 4th ser., 4:761; Holly A. Mayer, *Belonging to the Army: Camp Followers and Community During the American Revolution* (Columbia: University of South Carolina Press, 1996), 8–9; Lancaster Committee of Safety to the Continental Congress, January 10, 1776, Hildeburn Collection; Stern, *David Franks*, 117.

52. Lancaster Committee of Safety to the Continental Congress, January 10, 1776, Hildeburn Collection.

53. Officers of the 7th, 26th, and Royal Highland Emigrant Regiments to John Hancock, January 20, 1776, *AA*, 4th ser., 4:801; Hancock to the Lancaster Committee of Safety, January 18, 1776, ibid., 761.

54. Lancaster Committee of Safety to John Hancock, December 21, 1775, PCC, item 69, 1:45; Resolve of Congress, December 16, 1775, *JCC*, 3:434.

55. Royster, *Revolutionary People at War*, chap. 1; Col. Arthur Sinclair to Hancock, January 27, 1776, *AA*, 4th ser., 4:867; Lancaster Committee of Safety to Hancock, January 25, 1776, ibid., 801. British enlisted prisoners proved useful in the training of American soldiers. John Andrews, "a prisoner of war, taken at St. John's," petitioned the Provincial Congress of New York for his release from confinement in the Morristown Jail on account of his having "disciplined two battalions of Provincial troops." *AA*, 5th ser., 2:830.

56. Articles proposed by Major Stopford for the capitulation of Chambly, *AA*, 4th ser., 3:1133; Peter H. Wilson, "Prisoners in Early Modern European Warfare," in *Prisoners of War*, ed. Sibylle Scheipers (Oxford: Oxford University Press, 2010); David Bell, *The First Total War: Napoleon's Europe and the Birth of Warfare as We Know It* (New York: Mariner Books, 2007), 45.

57. Hancock to the Lancaster Committee, January 18, 1776, *AA*, 4th ser., 4:761; Congress's response to the Complaints and Demands of the British Officers, prisoners at Lancaster, ibid., 801.

58. Congressional Regulations for the Subsistence of the Officers, January 12, 1776, *AA*, 4th ser., 4:1640; Officers of the 7th, 26th, and Royal Highland Emigrant Regiments to John Hancock, January 20, 1776, ibid., 801.

59. Lancaster Committee of Safety to Hancock, April 11, 1776, *AA*, 4th ser., 5:848; Officers of the 7th, 26th, and Royal Highland Emigrant Regiments to Hancock, January 20, 1776, ibid., 4:801. See also Laura Becker, "Prisoners of War in the American Revolution: A Community Perspective," *Military Affairs* 46, no. 4 (December 1982): 168–73.

60. Cohen, "The Connecticut Captivity of Major Christopher French," 138, 142.

61. Jasper Yeates to the Pennsylvania Committee of Safety, March 29, 1776, Hildeburn Collection; Lancaster Committee of Safety to Hancock, January 3, 1776, PCC, item 69, 1:55; Miller, *Dangerous Guests*, 70; Resolve of Congress, February 28, 1776, *AA*, 4th ser., 4:1689.

62. Petition from the Inhabitants of the Town of Reading, March 6, 1776, *AA*, 4th ser., 5:675; Pennsylvania Committee of Safety to Hancock, February 20, 1776, PCC, item 69, 1:95.

63. John Shuttleworth to John Spencer, November 23, 1775, in Anna Maria Wilhelmina Stirling, *Annals of a Yorkshire House from the Papers of a Macaroni and his Kindred*, 2 vols. (London: John Lane, 1911), 2:17; John Shuttleworth to Walter Stanhope, Spring 1777, ibid., 19; John André quoted in Robert M. Hatch, *Major John André: A Gallant in Spy's Clothing* (New York: Houghton Mifflin, 1986), 67; British Prisoners of War at Carlisle to the Committee of Inspection and Observation of Cumberland County, August 1, 1776, box 1, Boudinot Papers, LC. For accounts of Allen's

mistreatment, see *Connecticut Gazette* (New London), December 1, 1775; *Pennsylvania Evening Post* (Philadelphia), December 2, 1775; and *Pennsylvania Ledger* (Philadelphia), December 2, 1775.

64. Narrative of Capt. W. Home of the Royal Fusiliers, Carleton Papers, reel 3, no. 339, DLAR, microfilm.

65. Franklin to Anthony Todd, March 29, 1776, *Founders Online*; Trumbull to Schuyler, March 21, 1776, *AA*, 4th ser., 5:454; Washington to Howe, December 18, 1775, *Founders Online*.

66. Washington to Howe, December 18, 1775, *Founders Online*.

67. *JCC*, 4:21; *Pennsylvania Evening Post* (Philadelphia), January 4, 1776. The resolutions were also printed over the next month in the *Pennsylvania Ledger* (Philadelphia), *Dunlap's Maryland Gazette* (Baltimore), *Maryland Journal* (Baltimore), *Pennsylvania Gazette* (Philadelphia), *New-England Chronicle* (Cambridge, MA), *Newport (RI) Mercury*, and *Virginia Gazette* (Williamsburg).

68. Allen, *Narrative*, 44, 43.

69. "Petition to the Honorable Continental Congress," *Connecticut Gazette* (New London), April 19, 1776; *New-England Chronicle* (Cambridge, MA), March 28, 1776.

70. *LMCC*, 1:326, 333; *JCC*, 4:101; *Philadelphia Evening Post*, February 1, 1776. See also Hancock to Washington, January 29, 1776, *Founders Online*.

71. *JCC*, 4:107; *LMCC*, 1:337, 440; Amos Wilkinson to Hancock, February 7, 1776, PCC, item 58, p. 209.

72. Deposition of Thomas Walker, April 24, 1776, *AA*, 4th ser., 4:1176; "Remarks on the difference in the treatment of Colonel Allen, Mr. Walker, and General Prescott," April 26, 1776, *AA*, 4th ser., 4:1178; Lancaster Committee to the Berks County Committee, May 9, 1776, Hildeburn Collection.

73. *Connecticut Gazette* (New London), April 19, 1776; *JCC*, 4:361–62n4, 370–73.

74. The original draft of the congressional resolution reads, "as nearly conformable as the Circumstances of this Country will admit of, to the Custom of England and France." May 16, 1776, *JCC*, 4:361, 370–73. For the best account of Anglo-American republican political culture's influence on Congress's difficulty funding the war effort, see E. Wayne Carp, *To Starve the Army at Pleasure: Continental Army Administration and American Political Culture, 1775–1783* (Chapel Hill: University of North Carolina Press, 1984).

75. Hatch, *Thrust for Canada*, chap. 6; Martin, *Benedict Arnold*, chap. 7.

76. Benedict Arnold to Lt. Gov. Hector Cramahé, November 15, 1775, *AA*, 4th ser., 3:1685. For further discussion of this incident, see Hatch, *Thrust for Canada*, 116.

77. "The Journal of Captain Thomas Ainslie," in *Blockade of Quebec in 1775–1776*, ed. Fred C. Wurtele (Quebec: Library and Historical Society of Quebec, 1905), 30, 32, 36, 42; John Joseph Henry, *An Accurate and Interesting Account of the Hardships and Sufferings of that Band of Heroes, Who Traversed the Wilderness in the Campaign Against Quebec in 1775* (Lancaster, PA: William Greer, 1812), 121, 127, 133; Arnold to General Wooster, January 2, 1776, *AA*, 4th ser., 4:666; Hancock to Washington, January 20, 1776, *Founders Online*.

78. Henry, *Accurate and Interesting Account*, 125; Hatch, *Thrust for Canada*, 169; "Journal of Captain Thomas Ainslie," 34.

79. "Journal of Captain Thomas Ainslie," 63; Henry, *Accurate and Interesting Account*, 163–64; Nelson, *General Sir Guy Carleton*, 82. Surprisingly, John Henry did not blame Carleton for the treatment he received. He believed "that the virtuous and beneficent Carleton, taking into view

his perilous predicament, did every thing for us, which an honest man and a good Christian could." Henry, *Accurate and Interesting Account*, 166.

80. Henry, *Accurate and Interesting Account*, 169, 170; Joseph A. Waddell, ed., "Diary of a Prisoner of War at Quebec," *Virginia Magazine of History and Biography* 9, no. 2 (October 1901): 147.

81. Hatch, *Thrust for Canada*, 194–96; Arnold to Washington, May 8, 1776, *Founders Online*. General Schuyler reported to Washington, "the Caghnawagas are friendly, but refuse to take up arms in our Favor." Schuyler to Washington, May 26, 1776, *Founders Online*.

82. "The Journal of Zephaniah Shepardson," quoted in Hatch, *Thrust for Canada*, 197; Arnold to Washington, May 8, 1776, *Founders Online*.

83. Andrew Parke, *An Authentic Narrative of Facts Relating to the Exchange of Prisoners Taken at the Cedars* (London, 1777), 23; Waddell, "Diary of a Prisoner of War at Quebec," 146; Charles Carroll, *The Journal of Charles Carroll of Carrolton During his Visit to Canada in 1776 as one of the Commissioners from Congress*, ed. Brantz Mayer (Baltimore: Maryland Historical Society, 1845), 99. For more detailed narratives of the events of the Battle of the Cedars, see Hatch, *Thrust for Canada*, chap. 10; and Douglas R. Cubbison, *The American Northern Theater Army in 1776: The Ruin and Reconstruction of the Continental Force* (Jefferson, NC: McFarland, 2010), 94–96.

84. Parke, *Authentic Narrative*, 25, 26.

85. "Extract of a Letter from Major Henry Sherburne to a Gentleman in Providence, Rhode Island," June 18, 1776, *AA*, 4th ser., 6:598; Hospice-Anthelme Verreau, *Invasion du Canada: Collection de Mémoires Recueillis et Annotés par M. l'Abbé Verreau* (Montreal: E. Senécal, 1873), 278–79. Sources vary on the number of men killed during this action. Sherburne recalled "twenty-eight men killed in action, wounded, killed in cold blood, and carried off by the savages." *AA*, 4th ser., 6:598. Lieutenant Parke maintained that only "5 or 6" Americans were killed. Parke, *Authentic Narrative*, 27.

86. "Extract of a Letter from Major Henry Sherburne to a Gentleman in Providence, Rhode Island"; Parke, *Authentic Narrative*, 28–29. For the best discussion of the Iroquoian practice of "mourning war," see Daniel K. Richter, "War and Culture: The Iroquois Experience," *William and Mary Quarterly*, 3rd ser., 40, no. 4 (October 1983): 528–59.

87. Shepardson quoted in Hatch, *Thrust for Canada*, 201; Parke, *Authentic Narrative*, 32.

88. Arnold to the Commissioners in Canada, May 27, 1776, *AA*, 4th ser., 6:595; Parke, *Authentic Narrative*, 36.

89. Articles of Agreement between George Forster, Capt. Commanding the King's Troops and Brig-Gen Benedict Arnold, the Cedars, May 27, 1776, Carleton Papers, reel 2a, no. 192; Hatch, *Thrust for Canada*, 205. The four hostages were Captains Theodore Bliss, Ebenezer Sullivan, John Stevens, and Ebenezer Green, all from Bedel's command.

90. Arnold to the Commissioners in Canada, May 27, 1776, *AA*, 4th ser., 6:595; Arnold to De Haas, May 27, 1776, "Orderly Book of the 1st Pennsylvania Battalion of Foot, November 26 to April 6, 1776, J. P. de Haas commanding," Mss L1988.190.337 [Bound], LSC.

91. Forster to De Haas, May 29, 1776, "Orderly Book of the 1st Pennsylvania"; Parke, *Authentic Narrative*, 37; Shepardson quoted in Hatch, *Thrust for Canada*, 205; De Haas to Samuel Chase, June 12, 1776, "Orderly Book of the 1st Pennsylvania."

92. Arnold to the Commissioners in Canada, May 27, 1776, *AA*, 4th ser., 6:595; Washington to Arnold, September 14, 1775, *Founders Online*; Orders from Arnold to De Haas, May 29, 1776, "Orderly Book of the 1st Pennsylvania"; Arnold to De Haas, May 31, 1776, ibid. For the American

response to the British use of Native American "proxies" during the Canadian campaign, see Robert Parkinson, *The Common Cause: Creating Race and Nation in the American Revolution* (Chapel Hill: University of North Carolina Press, 2016), 235–41. See also Martin, *Benedict Arnold*, 216–17.

93. Parke, *Authentic Narrative*, 3.

94. Hatch, *Thrust for Canada*, 206; Nelson, *General Sir Guy Carleton*, 87; Carroll, *Journal*, 81.

95. Henry, *Accurate and Interesting Account*, 167–68, 171; Carleton to Germain, August 10, 1776, CO 42/35, TNA.

96. Arnold to Congress, June 2, 1776, *AA*, 5th ser., 1:165; Parkinson, *Common Cause*, 235–40.

97. *JCC*, 5:535–36, 538, 539. Not everyone agreed that the British had violated the terms of the cartel. Captain Sullivan, one of Carleton's American hostages, believed that Congress "had a wrong Representation on the Matter." He was horrified that his government would allow "the breach of a Treaty which even the Savages have ever held sacred." The British eventually released all four hostages. Hatch, *Thrust for Canada*, 208. While Congress never approved the cartel, Pennsylvania authorities had exchanged most of the prisoners captured in Canada by November 1776. Krebs, *Generous and Merciful Enemy*, 138.

98. David Armitage, *The Declaration of Independence: A Global History* (Cambridge, MA: Harvard University Press, 2007), 169; Parkinson, *Common Cause*, 251–55.

99. Armitage, *Declaration of Independence*, 169; *JCC*, 5:539. For more on the Declaration of Independence and the laws of war, see Parkinson, *Common Cause*, 242–63.

100. "A Watchman to the People of Pennsylvania," Philadelphia, June 13, 1776, *AA*, 4th ser., 6:835.

101. Resolve of Congress, April 3, 1776, *AA*, 4th ser., 5:1443.

Chapter 3

1. Diary of John Adams, March 4, 1776, *Founders Online*; John Adams to Abigail Adams, March 14, 1777, ibid.; Abigail Adams to John Adams, May 18, 1777, ibid.

2. Boudinot to James Wilson and Christian Forster, July 5, 1777, *"Their Distress is almost intolerable": The Elias Boudinot Letterbook, 1777–1778*, ed. Joseph Lee Boyle (Westminster, MD: Heritage Books, 2002), 14. On the importance of restraint in early American warfare, see Wayne E. Lee, *Crowds and Soldiers in Revolutionary North Carolina: The Culture of Violence in Riot and War* (Gainesville: University Press of Florida, 2001). For accounts of the New York Campaign that emphasize restraint rather than escalating violence, see David Hackett Fischer, *Washington's Crossing* (Oxford: Oxford University Press, 2004); and Judith L. Van Buskirk, *Generous Enemies: Patriots and Loyalists in Revolutionary New York* (Philadelphia: University of Pennsylvania Press, 2002), 73–105.

3. David Armitage, *The Declaration of Independence: A Global History* (Cambridge, MA: Harvard University Press, 2007), 169; Fischer, *Washington's Crossing*, 111–13; Colonel von Heeringen quoted in Edward Jackson Lowell, *The Hessians and the Other German Auxiliaries of Great Britain in the Revolutionary War* (New York: Harper and Brothers, 1884), 66. On American fear of "foreign mercenaries," see Robert Parkinson, *The Common Cause: Creating Race and Nation in the American Revolution* (Chapel Hill: University of North Carolina Press, 2016), 214–23.

4. Frederick Mackenzie, *Diary of Frederick Mackenzie: Giving a Daily Narrative of His Military Service as an Officer of the Regiment of Royal Welch Fusiliers During the Years 1775–1781 in Massachusetts, Rhode Island, and New York*, 2 vols. (Cambridge, MA: Harvard University Press, 1930), 1:109; *Independent Chronicle and the Universal Advertiser* (Boston), December 5, 1776.

5. Samuel J. Atlee, "Journal of the Transactions of the 26th of August 1776 upon Long Island," American Papers, vol. 2, no. 36, George Bancroft Collection, 1606–1887, MssCol 195, Manuscripts and Archives Division, NYPL, transcription, p. 717; Colonel von Heeringen quoted in Lowell, *Hessians*, 65, 68; Extract of a letter from an officer in General Frazer's Battalion, September 3, 1776, AA, 5th ser., 1:1259; Nathanael Greene to Washington, November 11, 1776, ibid., 3:638. On the British efforts to recruit Hessian auxiliaries and the soldiers' experience in America, see Charles W. Ingrao, *The Hessian Mercenary State: Ideas, Institutions, and Reform Under Frederick II, 1760–1785* (Cambridge: Cambridge University Press, 1987; repr., 2003), 135–64.

6. Ron Chernow, *Washington: A Life* (New York: Penguin, 2010), 262. Rodney Atwood places the number at 2,818. Atwood, *The Hessians: Mercenaries from Hessen-Kassel in the American Revolution* (Cambridge: Cambridge University Press, 1980), 78; Diary of Chaplain Philipp Waldeck, trans. Bruce Burgoyne, Hessian Papers, no. 28, box 2, Bancroft Collection, NYPL, transcription; Stephen Kemble, *The Kemble Papers*, 2 vols. (New York: New-York Historical Society, 1983–85), 1:100.

7. Mackenzie, *Diary*, 1:39, 111.

8. Diary of William Slade, Appendix B in *American Prisoners of the Revolution*, by Danske Dandridge (Charlottesville, VA: Michie, 1911), 495 (available online at Archive.org, https://archive .org/details/cu31924093960825); Atlee, "Journal of the Transactions of the 26th of August 1776 upon Long Island," 717.

9. Diary of William Slade, in Dandridge, *American Prisoners*, 495; "Avadavat of Samuel Young and William Houston," December 15, 1776, PCC, item 53, p. 25; Mackenzie, *Diary*, 1:111–12.

10. Van Buskirk, *Generous Enemies*, 21–22; Howe to Lord George Germain, New York, December 3, 1776, *The Parliamentary Register; or, History of the Proceedings and Debates of the House of Commons*, 17 vols. (London: J. Almon, 1775–80), 11:364. Howe suggested to Washington that he would "send Mr. Joshua Loring, my Commissary, to Elizabethtown, as a proper place for the exchange of prisoners." Howe to Washington, September 21, 1776, AA, 5th ser., 2:437. On the fire in New York City, see Benjamin L. Carp, "The Night the Yankees Burned Broadway: The New York City Fire of 1776," *Early American Studies* 4, no. 2 (2006): 471–511.

11. Sheldon S. Cohen, *Yankee Sailors in British Gaols: Prisoners of War at Forton and Mill, 1777–1783* (Cranbury, NJ: Associated University Presses, 1995), 18–22; Edwin Burrows, *Forgotten Patriots: The Untold Story of American Prisoners During the Revolutionary War* (New York: Basic Books, 2008), 9–10. For British administration of enemy prisoners during the Seven Years' War, see Erica Charters, *Disease, War, and the Imperial State: The Welfare of the British Armed Forces During the Seven Years' War* (Chicago: University of Chicago Press, 2014), 172–90. For Howe's orders not to formally acknowledge the United States as a sovereign power, see Germain to Howe, February 1, 1776, AA, 4th ser., 4:902. Contemporary loyalist historian Thomas Jones considered the position of commissary general of prisoners to be a sinecure. Jones, *History of New York During the Revolutionary War*, ed. E. F. De Lancey, 2 vols. (New York: New-York Historical Society, 1879), 1:1351.

12. Washington to Howe, July 30, 1776, *Founders Online*; Howe to Washington, August 1, 1776, ibid.

13. Mackenzie, *Diary*, 1:39; Ira D. Gruber, *The Howe Brothers and the American Revolution* (Chapel Hill: University of North Carolina Press, 1972), 135; Extract of a letter from an officer in General Frazer's Battalion, September 3, 1776, *AA*, 5th ser., 1:1259.

14. Howe to Washington, July 16, 1776, *Founders Online*; Elbridge Gerry to Samuel and John Adams, July 21, 1776, ibid.

15. Howe to Washington, September 21, 1776, *Founders Online*; Howe to Washington, August 1, 1776, ibid.; Howe to Washington, February 2, 1776, ibid. McDonald had been breveted a brigadier by North Carolina's royal governor, Josiah Martin, but he was only a commissioned major in the regular army and thus could not be equitably exchanged for a general in the Continental forces. For the best account of Admiral Lord Richard Howe and General William Howe's involvement in the British peace commission of 1776, see Gruber, *Howe Brothers*, 72–78.

16. *Virginia Gazette* (Williamsburg), September 20, 1776; Sheldon S. Cohen, ed., "The Connecticut Captivity of Major Christopher French," *Connecticut Historical Society Bulletin* 55, nos. 3–4 (1990): 183; Barrington to Howe, November 12, 1776, Carleton Papers, reel 3, no. 325, DLAR, microfilm. For an example of the change in newspaper coverage, see *Massachusetts Spy* (Worcester), November 27, 1776.

17. Congress established its supremacy in all matters relating to the exchange of prisoners of war captured by Continental forces in May 1776 but clarified the role of the army's commander in chief in these exchanges on July 22. *JCC*, 4:362, 5:599. John Hancock informed Washington that he was empowered to negotiate the exchange of prisoners on July 24. Hancock to Washington, July 24, 1776, *Founders Online*. Continental privateers captured two British transports ships, the *George* and the *Annabella*, in Boston Harbor on June 16, 1776, carrying two companies of the 2nd Battalion, 71st Highland Regiment of Foot, commanded by Lieutenant Colonel Archibald Campbell. Major General Artemas Ward estimated their number at 210 officers and men. Ward to Washington, June 16–17, 1776, ibid.; Board of War to the Maryland Convention, August 6, 1776, Philadelphia, *LMCC*, 2:39–40.

18. Washington to Hancock, September 25, 1776, *Founders Online*; Washington to Howe, September 23, 1776, ibid.

19. Howe to Washington, November 8, 1776, *Founders Online*.

20. Washington to Howe, November 9, 1776, *Founders Online*; Washington to Hancock, March 1, 1777, ibid.

21. At this stage in the conflict, state-organized exchanges were widespread. Other states besides those listed were almost certainly conducting independent swaps at this time as well. For a discussion of state-based exchanges, see Martha W. Dixon, "Divided Authority: The American Management of Prisoners in the Revolutionary War" (Ph.D. diss., University of Utah, 1977), 250–51. On July 22, 1776, Congress resolved "that each state hath a right to make any exchange they think proper for prisoners taken from them or by them." For examples of state exchanges, see John Russell Bartlett, ed., *Records of the Colony of Rhode Island and Providence Plantations*, 10 vols. (Providence, RI: A. C. Green and Brothers, 1856), 8:72–73; and *AA*, 5th ser., 3:1207, 1209.

22. Washington to Trumbull, September 26, 1776, *Founders Online*; Trumbull to Washington, October 2, 1776, ibid.; Washington to Trumbull, October 8, 1776, ibid. See also Washington to the New Hampshire Council, September 29, 1776, *Documents and Records Relating to New Hampshire, 1623–1800*, ed. Nathaniel Bouton et al., 40 vols. (Concord, NH: Edward A. Jenks, 1874), 8:367–68. On October 14, 1776, Congress postponed a vote on a resolution that would have included all of the British prisoners, regardless of their skilled status, in the proposed

exchange. *JCC*, 6:870. For the best account of the delegates' lack of knowledge of military affairs, see Kenneth Schaffel, "The American Board of War, 1776–1781" (Ph.D. diss., City University of New York, 1983), chap. 1.

23. Mackenzie, *Diary*, 1:104; Cols. Samuel Miles and Samuel Atlee to Washington, n.d. [likely written on November 12, 1776], enclosed within Washington to Hancock, November 19, 1776, n. 1, *Founders Online*; Charles Lee to Howe, November 26, 1776, box 2, Schoff Revolutionary War Collection, CL-UM. Unlike General Gage, who had refused to acknowledge any rank that did not derive from a king's commission, Howe, likely animated by a desire for reconciliation, ordered Joshua Loring to treat the men according to their American military rank and social station. Pennsylvania officer Daniel Broadhead heard that the captured officers in New York were "well treated." Daniel Broadhead to unknown, September 5, 1776, *Pennsylvania Archives: Selected and Arranged from Original Documents in the Office of the Secretary of the Commonwealth*, ed. Samuel Hazard, ser. 1, 12 vols. (Philadelphia: Joseph Severns, 1853), 5:23. See also Burrows, *Forgotten Patriots*, 16; and Caroline Cox, *A Proper Sense of Honor: Service and Sacrifice in George Washington's Army* (Chapel Hill: University of North Carolina Press, 2004), 218–19.

24. Greene to Washington, November 11, 1776, *Founders Online*; Diary of William Slade, in Dandridge, *American Prisoners*, 495; Howe to Washington, February 5, 1778, *Founders Online*.

25. Stephen Brumwell, *Redcoats: The British Soldier and War in the Americas, 1755–1763* (Cambridge: Cambridge University Press, 2002), 151–53; Burrows, *Forgotten Patriots*, 19. See also Michael N. McConnell, *Army & Empire: British Soldiers on the American Frontier, 1758–1775* (Lincoln: University of Nebraska Press, 2004), chap. 6. Danske Dandridge claimed that British provost marshal Captain William Cunningham was responsible for starving the prisoners to death. Dandridge, *American Prisoners*, 2. Edwin Burrows argued, "Although the British did not deliberately kill American prisoners in New York, they might as well have done." Burrows, *Forgotten Patriots*, xi. Robert Watson has recently suggested that "the British command intended the *Jersey* [prison ship] to be a weapon of terror." Watson, *The Ghost Ship of Brooklyn: An Untold Story of the American Revolution* (New York: Da Capo, 2017), 9. Colonels Atlee and Miles informed Washington that the prisoners "have no means of adding Vegitables or any other nourishing article for want of Cash." Washington to Hancock, November 19–21, 1776, n. 6, *Founders Online*.

26. Mackenzie, *Diary*, 1:103; Washington to Hancock, November 19, 1776, *Founders Online*.

27. Washington to Hancock, November 19–21, 1776, *Founders Online*; Joseph Webb to unknown, December 28, [1776?], Mss 81.1.654, LSC; *JCC*, 3:375. See also Mark Abbot Stern, *David Franks: Colonial Merchant* (University Park: Pennsylvania State University Press, 2010), 117. On Washington's inability to provide his own soldiers with food and funds, see Washington to Hancock, November 23, 1776, *Founders Online*. See also Washington to Atlee, November 25, 1776, ibid.

28. Colonels Magaw, Miles, and Atlee to Howe, December 8, 1776, Carleton Papers, reel 3, no. 341; Capt. Robert Mackenzie to Colonels Magaw, Atlee, West, and Burd, November 25, 1776, ibid., no. 331.

29. Richard Peters to Washington, November 19, 1776, *Founders Online*; Rowland Chambers to Gov. William Livingston, October 14, 1776, PCC, item 68, p. 321. Colefox and Williams were native New Englanders who had been captured and impressed into British service before falling into American hands. *JCC*, 6:919. On the difficulties of forwarding the British prisoners for exchange, see *Archives of Maryland*, 99 vols. (Baltimore: Maryland Historical Society, 1883–2000),

12:456, 486–87; and Gerald Haffner, "The Treatment of Prisoners of War by the Americans During the War of Independence" (Ph.D. diss., Indiana University, 1952), 296.

30. Diary of William Slade, in Dandridge, *American Prisoners*, 498, 500–501; Burrows, *Forgotten Patriots*, 64, 197–201, 316–17nn7–12. Slade, along with most of the surviving Fort Washington prisoners, was released on January 25, 1777. On British officers celebrating Christmas, see John Peebles, *John Peebles' American War: The Diary of a Scottish Grenadier*, ed. Ira D. Gruber (Mechanicsburg, PA: Stackpole Books, 1998), 10n40.

31. Burrows, *Forgotten Patriots*, 199, 201; James Little Pension Application, W8256, Revolutionary War Pension Applications, Record Group 15, NARA; David Sproat to Thomas Bradford, September 10, 1780, Bradford Family Papers, 1620–1906, Collection 1676, Naval Prisoners, box 13, folder 12, HSP; Hartley to Washington, February 12, 1777, *Founders Online*. For more on the *Jersey*, see Burrows, *Forgotten Patriots*, 163–81. For more on maritime prisoners of war, see T. Cole Jones, "'The dreadful effects of British cruilty': The Treatment of British Maritime Prisoners and the Radicalization of the Revolutionary War at Sea," *Journal of the Early Republic* 36, no. 3 (Fall 2016): 435–65.

32. Cohen, *Yankee Sailors in British Gaols*, 18–22; Burrows, *Forgotten Patriots*, 277n15.

33. Timothy Parker to Trumbull, December 9, 1776, Trumbull Papers, vol. 5, pt. 2, no. 278a, Connecticut State Library, Hartford; *Pennsylvania Evening Post* (Philadelphia), January 9, 1777. The article was picked up by newspapers in numerous other states. See, for example, *Connecticut Gazette* (New London), January 17, 1777; *Boston Gazette*, January 27, 1777; *Freeman's Journal* (Portsmouth, NH), January 28, 1777; and *Essex Journal* (Newburyport, MA), January 30, 1777. See also Burrows, *Forgotten Patriots*, 283n8. On the revolutionary leadership's efforts to "propagate" stories of prisoner abuse, see Parkinson, *Common Cause*, 401–2.

34. Miles to Boudinot, July 24, 1777, box 1, Elias Boudinot Papers, MMC-0721, LC; Miles to Joseph Reed, September 1, 1776, Samuel Miles Papers, B M589, American Philosophical Society, Philadelphia; Miles to unknown Pennsylvanian, April 6, 1777, ibid. Miles did not fully absolve the British of blame, noting that they could and should have done more to ease the suffering of the American enlisted prisoners. An examination of an unknown American prisoner, dated June 20, 1777, confirms the colonel's indictment of Congress. PCC, item 78, 2:215. Commissary Boudinot apprised Congress of the prisoners' resentment in a letter to Richard Peters on June 20, 1777, ibid., 211.

35. *Pennsylvania Packet* (Lancaster), March 4, 1777. For another example, see *Freeman's Journal* (Portsmouth, NH), January 21, 1777. See also Parkinson, *Common Cause*.

36. On the historically contingent concept of civil war, see David Armitage, *Civil Wars: A History in Ideas* (New York: Alfred A. Knopf, 2017), 3–27. On the distinction between civil war within the British Empire and "America's first civil war," see Holger Hoock, *Scars of Independence: America's Violent Birth* (New York: Crown, 2017), 13–14, 23–51. For a discussion of how "internal wars" differ from civil or revolutionary wars, see Robert M. Calhoon et al., eds., *The Loyalist Perception and Other Essays* (Columbia: University of South Carolina Press, 1989), 155–56. For the theory of "internal wars," see Harry Eckstein, "On the Etiology of Internal Wars," *History and Theory* 4 (1954–55): 133–63. Historians now estimate that as much as 19 percent of the white American population remained loyal to the Crown during the war. See Paul H. Smith, "The American Loyalists: Notes on Their Origination and Numerical Strength," *William and Mary Quarterly*, 3rd ser., 25 (1968): 258–77. On the violence of crowd actions, see T. H. Breen, *American Insurgents, American Patriots: The Revolution of the People* (New York: Hill and Wang, 2010), 43, 48, 186, 207–12;

and Alan Taylor, *American Revolutions: A Continental History, 1750–1804* (New York: W. W. Norton, 2016), 216–19.

37. Kevin Phillips, *1775: A Good Year for Revolution* (New York: Viking, 2012), 160–63; Mark V. Kwasny, *Washington's Partisan War, 1775–1783* (Kent, OH: Kent State University Press, 1996), 21; Piers Mackesy, *The War for America, 1775–1783* (Lincoln: University of Nebraska Press, 1964), 36; JCC, 4:19, 20; John Lovell to Maj. Thomas Moncrieffe, August 7, [1778?], Sir Henry Clinton Papers, vol. 229, fol. 15, CL-UM. See also Memorial on behalf of John Lovell, AO 13/24/325–28, TNA; Lorenzo Sabine, *Biographical Sketches of Loyalists of the American Revolution*, 2 vols. (Boston: Little, Brown, 1864), 2:30; and Breen, *American Insurgents*, 183.

38. Jason Sharples, "The Flames of Insurrection: Fearing Slave Conspiracy in Early America" (Ph.D. diss., Princeton University, 2010), 312–20; Michael A. McDonnell, *The Politics of War: Race, Class, and Conflict in Revolutionary Virginia* (Chapel Hill: University of North Carolina Press, 2007), 148, 162; William Woodford to Edmund Pendleton, December 5, 1776, *Revolutionary Virginia: The Road to Independence*, ed. Robert L. Scribner and Brent Tarter, 7 vols. (Charlottesville: University Press of Virginia), 5:57; Woodford to the President of the Convention at Williamsburg, December 12, 1775, ibid., 117. On Dunmore's alleged violations of "the practices of war among civilized nations," see ibid., 436. See also ibid., 127, 286–87, 432. For Woodford's "instructions," see ibid., 4:270–71. For examples of loyalists who were captured at the Battle of Great Bridge, briefly imprisoned, and then released, see Memorial of John Begg, AO 13/27/309–11; and Memorial of John Patient, AO 13/32/241–49, TNA.

39. Journal of an unidentified North Carolina Scottish highlander captured at the Battle of Moore's Creek Bridge, February 1776, Clinton Papers, vol. 14, fol. 10; Journals of the Provincial Congress, *CSRNC*, 10:486, 503, 544, 22:985; Claude Halstead Van Tyne, *The Loyalists in the American Revolution* (New York: Macmillan, 1902), 218. In his memorial to Sir Henry Clinton, Captain Angus Campbell claimed that he was exchanged in August 1778. Clinton Papers, vol. 209, fol. 5.

40. JCC, 3:280; Diary of William Judd, August 10, 1775–July 11, 1776, Mss L2010G28.3 M, LSC; Memorial of Rev. Jonathan Odell, AO 13/19/253–58, TNA. See also Henry J. Young, "Treason and Its Punishment in Revolutionary Pennsylvania," *Pennsylvania Magazine of History and Biography* 90, no. 3 (July 1966): 288.

41. "Narrative of Loyalist John Peters, Lieutenant-Colonel of the Queen's Loyal Rangers in Canada, written in letter to a friend in London, Pimlico [Eng.], June 5, 1786," *Daily Globe* (Toronto), July 16, 1877; Edward Countryman, *A People in Revolution: The American Revolution and Political Society in New York, 1760–1790* (Baltimore: Johns Hopkins University Press, 1981), 121–22; Philip Ranlet, *New York Loyalists*, 2nd ed. (Lanham, MD: University Press of America, 2002), 142–43. On "disaffection" and the revolutionaries' escalating intolerance of it after independence, see Aaron Sullivan, "Uncommon Cause: The Challenges of Disaffection in Revolutionary Pennsylvania," in *The American Revolution Reborn*, ed. Patrick Spero and Michael Zuckerman (Philadelphia: University of Pennsylvania Press, 2016), 48–67.

42. Mackesy, *War for America*, 43–45. The British had planned to raise regiments of "provincial" regulars in the past, but with their main force bottled up in Boston, they had been unable to tap the loyalists' military potential. See General Howe's Orders, November 17, 1775, *Kemble Papers*, 1:252–53. See also Paul H. Smith, *Loyalists and Redcoats: A Study in British Revolutionary Policy* (Chapel Hill: University of North Carolina Press, 1964), chaps. 1–2; and John Shy, *A People*

Numerous and Armed: Reflections on the Military Struggle for American Independence (Oxford: Oxford University Press, 1976), 184–85.

43. *AA*, 4th ser., 6:455, 1163–65; Ensign Peter Clayes to Washington, May 12, 1776, *Founders Online*; *JPC*, 1:491, 497, 500; Arrest Warrant from a Secret Committee of the New York Provincial Congress, June 21, 1776, *Founders Online*; Jonathan Trumbull to Ezekiel Williams, August 1, 1776, in *Letters and Documents of Ezekiel Williams of Wethersfield, Connecticut*, ed. John C. Parsons (Hartford, CT: Acorn Club, 1976), 45; General Orders, New York, June 27, 1776, *Founders Online*. For discussions of this alleged conspiracy, see Brian F. Carso, *"Whom Can We Trust Now?": The Meaning of Treason in the United States from the Revolution Through the Civil War* (Oxford: Lexington Books, 2006), 57–59; and Bradley Chapin, *The American Law of Treason: Revolutionary and Early National Origins* (Seattle: University of Washington Press, 1964), 35–38.

44. *JCC*, 5:475; Joseph Hawley to Elbridge Gerry, July 17, 1776, in James T. Austin, *The Life of Elbridge Gerry, with Contemporary Letters*, 2 vols. (Boston, 1828–29), 1:206–8. See also Carso, *"Whom Can We Trust Now?,"* 60; and Don Higginbotham, *The War of American Independence: Military Attitudes, Policies, and Practice, 1763–1789* (New York: Macmillan, 1971), 270–72. For examples of individual states' treason laws, see James Tyndale Mitchell, ed., *The Statutes at Large of Pennsylvania from 1682 to 1801*, 18 vols. (Philadelphia: Wm. Stanley Ray, 1903), 9:18–19, 45–47; Peter Wilson, comp., *Acts of the Council and General Assembly of the State of New Jersey* (Trenton, 1784), 4–5; Alexander Contee Hanson, ed., *Laws of Maryland: Made since M,DCC,LXIII, [1763]* (Annapolis, MD: Frederick Green, 1787), chap. 20, pp. 171–75; Charles J. Hoadly, ed., *The Public Records of the State of Connecticut*, vol. 1 (Hartford: Case, Lockwood, and Brainard, 1894), 4; *JPC*, 1:527; and James Iredell, ed., *Laws of the State of North Carolina* (Edenton, 1799), 284–86.

45. James Shepard, "The Tories of Connecticut," *Connecticut Quarterly* 4, no. 1 (January, February, March 1898): 140; Cohen, "The Connecticut Captivity of Major Christopher French," 150; Richard Harvey Phelps, *Newgate of Connecticut: Its Origins and Early History* (Hartford, CT: American Publishing, 1876), 34; Samuel Peters, *The Rev. Samuel Peters' LL.D. General History of Connecticut*, ed. Samuel Jarvis McCormick (New York: D. Appleton, 1877), 143; *New-York Journal*, January 25, 1776; "Account allowed by the Committee of Safety for the town of Simsbury, 1776," Ms 101958, Connecticut Historical Society, Connecticut Digital Archives Collections, http://collections.ctdigitalarchive.org/islandora/object/40002%3A103415#page/1/mode/2up; *New-York Mirror*, March 13, 1824. For examples of loyalists who suffered and survived confinement at Newgate, see Elisha Beckwith, AO 13/26/37–38, TNA; Thomas Gilbert, AO 13/24/198–300, ibid.; and Justus Sherwood, AO 13/15/360–61, ibid. See also the account of the confinement at Newgate of Ebenezer Hathaway and Thomas Smith, loyalists who escaped in 1781, *Royal Gazette* (New York), June 9, 1781. For another contemporaneous description of the prison, see Roger Newberry to Governor Trumbull, October 25, 1781, PCC, item 149, 1:327–28.

46. Mitchell, *Statutes at Large of Pennsylvania*, 9:18; Joseph Stansbury to the Council of Safety, December 10, 1776, Pennsylvania State Government Papers, reel 36, no. 167, DLAR. Those guilty of misprision of treason were to forfeit one-third of their property. Mitchell, *Statutes at Large of Pennsylvania*, 9:19.

47. *JPC*, 1:527, 638; Washington to Livingston, July 6, 1776, *Founders Online*. For the best study of the loyalism on Staten Island and the efforts to suppress it, see Phillip Papas, *That Ever Loyal Island: Staten Island and the American Revolution* (New York: New York University Press, 2007).

48. Intelligence to William Tryon from New York, April 17, 1776, Clinton Papers, vol. 15; Oliver De Lancey to Col. Edmund Fanning, September 5, 1776, transcribed by Todd W. Braisted, On-Line Institute for Advanced Loyalist Studies (last updated December 15, 1999), http://www .royalprovincial.com/military/rhist/delancey/dellet2.htm; Calhoon et al., *Loyalist Perception*, 151. For recent studies of loyalism in New York, see Ruma Chopra, *Unnatural Rebellion: Loyalists in New York City During the Revolution* (Charlottesville: University Press of Virginia, 2011); and Van Buskirk, *Generous Enemies*.

49. John Graves Simcoe, *Simcoe's Military Journal: A History of the Operations of a Partisan Corps, Called the Queen's Rangers* ... (New York: Bartlett and Welford, 1844), 35–36, 38, 63; *Diary of Samuel Richards, Captain of the Connecticut Line* (Philadelphia, 1909), 77; *Connecticut Gazette* (New London), March 14, 1777. For the best study of conflicts that occurred "between the lines" around New York, see Harry M. Ward, *Between the Lines: Banditti of the American Revolution* (Westport, CT: Praeger, 2002), chap. 2. On the importance of "war stories," see Parkinson, *Common Cause*.

50. Washington to David Forman, November 24, 1776, *Founders Online*; George Clinton, *Public Papers of George Clinton*, ed. Hugh Hastings, 10 vols. (Albany: James B. Lyon, 1900), 1:456; George Clinton to William Heath, January 1, 1777, William Heath Papers, ser. 7E:20, reel 14, item 57.2, PFPC; Leonard Gansevoort to Jonathan Trumbull, April 11, 1777, PCC, item 67, 2:54. See also John Bayly to President Wharton, June 27, 1777, Lancaster County Manuscripts, Coll. 352, HSP; and Parkinson, *Common Cause*, 199–200. For the best history of the loyalist insurrection in New Jersey, see David J. Fowler, "Loyalty Is Now Bleeding in New Jersey: Motivations and Mentalities of the Disaffected," in *The Other Loyalists: Ordinary People, Royalism, and the Revolution in the Middle Colonies, 1763–1787*, ed. Joseph S. Tiedemann, Eugene R. Fingerhut, and Robert W. Venables (Albany: State University of New York Press, 2009), 51–55. For loyalist uprisings in Delaware and Maryland, see Wayne Bodle, "'The Ghost of Clow': Loyalist Insurgency in the Delmarva Peninsula," ibid., 19–44. For the situation in Westchester County, see Sung Bok Kim, "The Limits of Politicization in the American Revolution: The Experience of Westchester County, New York," *Journal of American History* 80, no. 3 (1993): 868–89.

51. Proclamation of Gov. William Livingston, February 5, 1777, folder 25, box 2, U.S. Revolution Collection, AAS; Diary of Margaret Morris, December 13, 1776–January 12, 1777, transcribed in George Morgan Hills, *History of the Church in Burlington, New Jersey* (Trenton, NJ: William S. Sharp, 1876), 321; Memorial of Archibald Kennedy, Clinton Papers, vol. 228, fol. 45. See also Memorial of Robert Morris, AO 13/24/362–65, TNA.

52. Kirkwood Orderly Book, May 29, June 11, 1777, ser. 7E:23, reel 16, item 67.1, PFPC; Peter Dubois to Sir Henry Clinton, December 3, 1777, Clinton Papers, vol. 27, fol. 52. See also *Documents Relating to the Revolutionary History of the State of New Jersey*, 2nd ser., 5 vols. (Trenton, NJ: John L. Murphy, 1901–17), 2:7–8, 12–13.

53. *Norwich (CT) Packet*, February 3, 1777; Autobiography of Moses Dunbar, in Epaphroditus Peck, "Loyal to the Crown: Discussion of Alleged Inhuman Treatment of Moses Dunbar, Tory, by the Civil Authorities," *Connecticut Magazine* 7, no. 2 (1904): 299; *Connecticut Journal* (New Haven), March 26, 1777. For a thoroughly researched recent study that tracks the parallel lives of Moses Dunbar and Nathan Hale, see Virginia Anderson, *The Martyr and the Traitor: Nathan Hale, Moses Dunbar, and the American Revolution* (Oxford: Oxford University Press, 2017).

54. *Royal American Gazette* (New York), March 6, 1777; Richard W. Stockton to Thomas Peters, ca. 1777, Mss L1998E444, LSC; "Letter from sundry prisoners in Carlisle goal, recd. 25

Octr. [1777]," PCC, item 78, 18:117–18; Memorial of Asher Dunham, AO 13/21/154–55, TNA; Memorial of Will Frish, AO 13/24/289–91, ibid. See also AO 13/24/400–401, ibid.

55. Clinton, *Public Papers*, 2:339; *JPC*, 1:908, 937, 1050; Jones, *History of New York*, 1:220, 710. Numerous Quakers who refused to take oaths of allegiance to the state of New York were also confined at Fleet Prison. See A. Day Bradly, "Friends in the Fleet Prison at Esopus," *Quaker History* 55, no. 2 (Autumn 1966): 114–17. See also Burrows, *Forgotten Patriots*, 190.

56. Resolution of the Convention of New York, May 4, 1777, PCC, item 67, 2:55; Resolution of the Convention of New York, May 5, 1777, ibid., 57; *Freeman's Journal* (Portsmouth, NH), May 31, 1777.

57. James Campbell to William Smallwood, February 28, 1777, Letter 9, William Smallwood Papers, Mss L1999LA3 (nos. 1–46) M, LSC; Sarah Shepherd to William Shepherd, April 12, 1777, Pennsylvania State Government Papers, reel 36, no. 383; *New-York Gazette*, November 18, 1776.

58. "Journal of Capt. William Beatty, 1776–1781," *Maryland Historical Magazine* 3, no. 2 (June 1908): 108; Washington to Preudhomme de Borre, August 3, 1777, *Founders Online*.

59. Gage to Washington, August 13, 1775, *Founders Online*; Emer de Vattel, *The Law of Nations; or, Principles of the Law of Nature Applied to the Conduct and Affairs of Nations and Sovereigns*, bk. 3, http://www.constitution.org/vattel/vattel_03.htm (accessed August 5, 2008), 3. It appears that the wave of official executions of loyalists for treason waned after 1777. The more secure the revolutionaries were in their military and political position, the less likely they were to punish loyalists with death. Nonetheless, both formal and informal trials persisted, and loyalists continued to face execution at the hands of the revolutionaries throughout the war. See, for example, *Pennsylvania Packet* (Lancaster), August 5, 1777; *Connecticut Courant* (Hartford), June 23, 1778; Dr. Samuel Adams to Sally Preston Adams, July 20, 1778, no. 28, Sol Feinstone Collection, DLAR; Deputy Commissary of Prisoners John Adam to Elias Boudinot, August 12, 1777, vol. 1, (PHi) 68, Elias Boudinot Papers, HSP; and Marquis de Lafayette to Governor Lee, April 17, 1781, *Archives of Maryland*, 47:196.

60. Fischer, *Washington's Crossing*, 155, 419. See, for instance, Higginbotham, *War of American Independence*, 165–71. Having examined both American returns and British and Hessian accounts, Daniel Krebs has suggested that 848 Hessian enlisted men were captured at Trenton. Krebs, *A Generous and Merciful Enemy: Life for German Prisoners of War During the American Revolution* (Norman: University of Oklahoma Press, 2013), 78.

61. *Independent Chronicle* (Boston), January 16, 1777; John Lovell to Maj. Thomas Moncrieffe, August 7, [1778?], Clinton Papers, vol. 229, fol. 15; "Fragment of a letter about the Battle of Trenton sent to Lord Auckland," reel 1, fol. 165, Auckland Papers, DLAR; Daniel Krebs, "Approaching the Enemy: German Captives in the American War of Independence, 1776–1783" (Ph.D. diss., Emory University, 2007), 169–82; Parkinson, *Common Cause*, 310–11.

62. Christopher Marshall, *Extracts from the Diary of Christopher Marshall: Kept in Philadelphia and Lancaster During the American Revolution, 1774–1781*, ed. William Duane (Albany, NY: J. Munsell, 1877), 110; Executive Committee to Hancock, December 30, 1776, *AA*, 5th ser., 3:1483; Sara Fisher, "'Diary of Trifling Occurrences': Philadelphia, 1776–1778," *Pennsylvania Magazine of History and Biography* 82, no. 4 (October 1958): 419; "Diary of Hessian Lieutenant Jakob Piel from 1776 to 1783," January 9, 1777, trans. Bruce Burgoyne, no. 28, Hessian Papers, Bancroft Collection.

63. Extract of a Letter from an English officer, December 3, 1776, New York, *AA*, 5th ser., 3:1059; "Diary of Hessian Lieutenant Jakob Piel," December 31, 1776, Hessian Papers, Bancroft

Collection; Diary of Johannes Reuber, 1776–83, trans. Bruce Burgoyne, no. 32, Hessian Papers, Bancroft Collection.

64. Washington to the Pennsylvania Council of Safety, December 29, 1776, *Founders Online*; Testimony of Christian Guiler, enclosed within Brig. Gen. Hugh Mercer to Washington, October 16, 1776, n. 1, ibid.

65. Resolves of Congress, August 14, 1776, *JCC*, 5:654–55; Washington to the Board of War, November 15, 1776, *Founders Online*; Executive Committee to Hancock, December 30, 1776, *AA*, 5th ser., 3:1483. As the Pennsylvania Council of Safety phrased it: "It is our interest to improve the present opportunity to make them our friends, and sow the seeds of dissension between them and the British troops. The Germans, by treating them as brethren and friends, may do the most essential service to our cause." Council of Safety, Philadelphia, December 31, 1776, ibid., 1511. Piel was impressed by Washington. He thought the American general's "expression when he spoke inspired love and respect." "Diary of Hessian Lieutenant Jakob Piel," December 28, 1776, Hessian Papers, Bancroft Collection.

66. Address of the Council of Safety of Pennsylvania to the Public, December 31, 1776, *Pennsylvania Archives*, 5:146; Reuber Diary, Hessian Papers, Bancroft Collection. For the role of the press in the transformation in American public opinion about the Hessians, see Parkinson, *Common Cause*, 310–15.

67. Clement Biddle to the Philadelphia Council of Safety, December 28, 1776, in Washington to the Pennsylvania Council of Safety, December 29, 1776, n. 1, *Founders Online*; Minutes of the Lancaster Committee of Safety, January 3, 1777, Lancaster County Committee of Safety Records, ser. 7E:23, reel 16, item 68, PFPC; Reuber Diary, Hessian Papers, Bancroft Collection.

68. Reuber Diary, Hessian Papers, Bancroft Collection; Krebs, "Approaching the Enemy," 238–40; Samuel M. Sener, *The Lancaster Barracks: Where the British and Hessian Prisoners Were Detained During the Revolution* (Harrisburg, PA: Harrisburg Publishing, 1896); Douglas R. Cubbison, "Eight Pence a Day: The Pay of the Private British Soldier During the War for American Independence," *Liberty Tree Newsletter* 9 (July/August 2007). Christopher Ludwick, a revolutionary of German descent, also suggested that "the permission to breathe in the open fragrancy of American air would be to them [the Hessians] a renewed instance of American public benevolence and lay them under further Obligation to a generous and merciful Enemy." William Ward Condit, "Christopher Ludwick, the Patriotic Gingerbread Baker," *Pennsylvania Magazine of History and Biography* 81 (1957): 377. A "stiver" was a "small coin (originally silver) of the Low Countries; applied to the nickel piece of 5 cents of the Netherlands (one-twentieth of a florin or gulden, or about a penny English)." *Oxford English Dictionary* (Oxford: Oxford University Press, 2013). Noncommissioned officers were apparently paid even more. Sergeant Kappes received fifteen shillings for six days of work. "An Account of Wages due to Hessian Labourers Working at the Public buildings in Lancaster, August 16, 1777," Mss 88.190.228, LSC.

69. General Orders, February 6, 1777, Charles Swift Riché Hildeburn Collection, 1760–77, AM 6093, HSP.

70. Levy Andrew Levy to Patrick Rice, April 25, 1777, MacAllister Mss, HSP; Kenneth Miller, *Dangerous Guests: Enemy Captives and Revolutionary Communities During the War for Independence* (Ithaca, NY: Cornell University Press, 2014), 108; "Petition of Two Corporals and Twenty-Five Privates belonging to the 16th, or Queen's Regiment of Light Dragoons, to the Philadelphia Committee of Safety," January 22, 1777, Pennsylvania State Government Papers, reel 36, no. 348; British prisoners to the Lancaster Committee of Safety, May 3, 1777, ser. 9, box 9:20, reel 103, PFPC.

71. Acknowledgment of William Henry, February 15, 1777, Pennsylvania State Government Papers, reel 36, no. 410; George Fenwick Jones, "The Black Hessians: Negros Recruited by the Hessians in South Carolina and Other Colonies," *South Carolina Historical Magazine* 83, no. 4 (October 1982): 296–97; Lowell, *Hessians*, 106; Benjamin Quarles, *The Negro in the American Revolution* (Chapel Hill: University of North Carolina Press, 1961), 147.

72. William W. Hening, ed., *The Statutes at Large; Being a Collection of All the Laws of Virginia from the First Session of the Legislature in the Year 1619*, 13 vols. (New York: R. & W. & G. Bartow, 1819–23), 9:106; Petition of Moss Armistead, June 12, 1784, no. 3611, folder 10, box 65, Legislative Petitions of the General Assembly, 1776–1865, Library of Virginia, Richmond; Sylvia R. Frey, "Slavery and Freedom: Virginia Blacks in the American Revolution," *Journal of Southern History* 49, no. 3 (August 1983): 384; Alexander Hamilton to Col. Elias Dayton, July 7, 1777, *Founders Online*. See also Quarles, *Negro in the American Revolution*, 107, 155.

73. Lancaster County Committee of Safety, June 5, 1777, ser. 8D:96, reel 48, item 86, PFPC; *Pennsylvania Archives*, 5:376; Reuber Diary, Hessian Papers, Bancroft Collection; Miller, *Dangerous Guests*, 109.

74. Richard Peters to Elias Boudinot, April 29, 1777, War Office, Philadelphia, box 1, Boudinot Papers, LC; Washington to Boudinot, April 1, 1777, *Founders Online*; Boudinot to the Governors and Executive Bodies of the Thirteen States, April 17, 1777, "*Their Distress is almost intolerable,*" ed. Boyle, 1; Elias Boudinot, *Journal or Historical Recollections of American Events During the Revolutionary War* (Philadelphia: Frederick Bourquin, 1894), 9. See also Burrows, *Forgotten Patriots*, 84–85; and George Adams Boyd, *Elias Boudinot: Patriot and Statesman, 1740–1821* (Princeton, NJ: Princeton University Press, 1952), 33–35.

75. Elias Boudinot to Richard Peters, June 16, 1777, "*Their Distress is almost intolerable,*" ed. Boyle, 8–9; Report of the Board of War, June 20, 1777, PCC, item 147, 1:231; Krebs, "Approaching the Enemy," 266; Dixon, "Divided Authority," 98–100; Haffner, "Treatment of Prisoners of War," 178–80.

76. Boudinot to Washington, June 26, 1777, box 1, Boudinot Papers, LC; Dixon, "Divided Authority," 96; Secret Committee of the Continental Congress to Washington, May 2, 1777, *Founders Online*; Burrows, *Forgotten Patriots*, 86; Boudinot, *Journal or Historical Recollections*, 10. Lewis Pintard complained that the flour Boudinot sent "will not furnish one half of them." Pintard to Boudinot, September 20, 1777, vol. 1, (PHi) 68, Elias Boudinot Papers, HSP.

77. Washington to Brig. Gen. Alexander McDougall, December 28, 1776, *Founders Online*; Washington to Howe, December 17, 1776, ibid.; Washington to Trumbull, December 21, 1776, *Parliamentary Register*, 11:368; Howe to Lord George Germain, December 18, 1776, ibid.; Washington to Trumbull, December 21, 1776, *Founders Online*.

78. Fischer, *Washington's Crossing*, 146–59. See also John Richard Alden, *General Charles Lee: Traitor or Patriot?* (Baton Rouge: Louisiana State University Press, 1951).

79. Washington to John Augustine Washington, March 31, 1776, *Founders Online*; Abigail Adams to John Adams, July 16, 1775, ibid.; Hancock to Washington, December 23, 1776, ibid.; Fischer, *Washington's Crossing*, 147–49.

80. Capt. John Bowater to the Earl of Denbigh, June 5–11, 1777, in *The Lost War: Letters from British Officers During the American Revolution*, ed. Marion Balderston and David Syrett (New York: Horizon, 1975), 130–31; "Ode on the Success of his Majesty's Arms," *General Advertiser and Morning Intelligencer* (London), December 12, 1777.

81. Burrows, *Forgotten Patriots*, 71–72; Jones, *History of New York*, 1:173.

82. *New-England Chronicle* (Cambridge, MA), January 2, 1777; *Freeman's Journal* (Portsmouth, NH), February 11, 1777; JCC, 7:16.

83. Burrows, *Forgotten Patriots*, 63–65, 79; Washington to the Continental Congress Executive Committee, January 12, 1777, *Founders Online*; Trumbull to Washington, February 24, 1777, ibid. A British return lists 1,701 Americans released during the preceding year. "A General Return of Prisoners," Philadelphia, January 10, 1778, vol. 1, Boudinot Papers, HSP. Howe claimed to have released "Two Thousand Two hundred Privates of the Enemy, his prisoners." Paper from Lt. Col. William Walcott, April 2, 1777, *Founders Online*.

84. JCC, 7:135; "Diary of Hessian Lieutenant Jakob Piel," March 1777, Hessian Papers, Bancroft Collection; Lt. Col. Archibald Campbell to Howe, February 14, 1777, James Murray Robins Papers, Ms. N-801, MHS.

85. Lt. Col. Archibald Campbell to Howe, February 14, 1777, Robins Papers, MHS; Campbell to Mrs. Inman, May 14, 1777, ibid.; Burrows, *Forgotten Patriots*, 71.

86. Washington to Hancock, January 12, 1777, *Founders Online*; Washington to Hancock, March 1, 1777, ibid.; Greene to Adams, March 3, 1777, ibid.; JCC, 7:179; Hancock to Washington, March 17, 1777, *Founders Online*. See also Washington to Morris, March 2, 1777, ibid.

87. JCC, 7:197; William Walcott to Howe, March 11, 1777, Carleton Papers, reel 3, no. 435; "Minutes of the Meeting between Lieut. Colos. Harrison and Walcott," March 10, 1777, Brunswick, NJ, ibid., no. 436; Dixon, "Divided Authority," 255–59.

88. Germain to Howe, September 3, 1777, Carleton Papers, reel 3, no. 661; Alexander Stuart to James Stuart, March 20, 1777, folder 27, box 2, U.S. Revolution Collection, AAS.

89. *Connecticut Journal* (New Haven), January 30, 1777; Diary of John Adams, March 4, 1776, *Founders Online*; John Adams to Abigail Adams, August 19, 1777, ibid.

90. Washington to Adm. Lord Richard Howe, January 13, 1777, *Founders Online*.

Chapter 4

1. James Wilkinson, *Memoirs of My Own Times*, 2 vols. (Philadelphia: Abraham Small, 1816), 1:321; John Ferling, *Almost a Miracle: The American Victory in the War of Independence* (New York: Oxford University Press, 2007), 232. See also Max von Eelking, *Memoirs, and Letters and Journals, of Major General Riedesel, During His Residence in America*, ed. and trans. William L. Stone, 2 vols. (Albany, NY: J. Munsell, 1868), 1:190.

2. Articles of Convention, in George W. Knepper, "The Convention Army, 1777–1783" (Ph.D. diss., University of Michigan, 1954), 271–72. On the culture of surrender in early modern Europe, see John Childs, "Surrender and the Laws of War in Western Europe, c. 1650–1783," in *How Fighting Ends: A History of Surrender*, ed. Holger Afflerbach and Hew Strachan (Oxford: Oxford University Press, 2012).

3. Thomas Anburey, *Travels Through the Interior Parts of America*, 2 vols. (London: William Lane, 1789), 2:2–4.

4. William Digby, *The British Invasion from the North: Digby's Journal of the Campaigns of Generals Carleton and Burgoyne from Canada, 1776–1777*, ed. James P. Baxter (New York: Da Capo, 1970), 320. The number of troops who surrendered at Saratoga remains disputed. The British provided two conflicting returns, one suggesting that 6,350 officers and men capitulated, while the other gives the total as 5,871. In Gates's official return to Congress, he claimed that

5,863 officers and men surrendered, of whom 2,522 were British, 2,444 were German, and 897 were Canadian. Under the articles of the Saratoga Convention, Burgoyne's Canadian auxiliaries were allowed to return home and thus were not part of the Convention Army. It seems that neither Gates's return nor the second British return accounted for the sick and wounded prisoners. The most accurate return appears to be the one completed by Deputy Adjutant General Robert Kingston of Burgoyne's staff, which puts the total number of surrendered officers and men at 6,350. Of these, 2,442 were healthy British officers and enlisted men, 2,198 were healthy Germans, and 1,100 were Canadians; in addition, there were 12 staff officers and 598 sick and wounded. Subtracting the Canadians, the total number of men encompassed by the convention was 5,250. If we divide the number of staff officers and sick evenly, that would add an additional 305 men to both the British and German contingents. By this calculation, the total number of British soldiers was 2,747; the total number of Germans was 2,503. I believe this return is the most accurate and have used it for the purposes of my calculations throughout this study. Knepper, "Convention Army," 12–13, 273–74. Regrettably, we do not know how many camp followers and children accompanied the army into captivity. At war's end, roughly 800 men, or 15 percent of those who surrendered under the terms of the convention, remained with the army. Anburey, *Travels*, 2:438.

5. Although the Convention Army remains the best-studied contingent of Crown prisoners during the war, its story has not been properly contextualized within the larger history of prisoner-of-war treatment during the conflict. For earlier works on the convention troops, see Richard Sampson, *Escape in America: The British Convention Prisoners, 1777–1783* (Wiltshire, UK: Picton, 1995); Martha W. Dixon, "Divided Authority: The American Management of Prisoners in the Revolutionary War" (Ph.D. diss., University of Utah, 1977), 201–43; William M. Dabney, *After Saratoga: The Story of the Convention Army* (Albuquerque: University of New Mexico Press, 1954); Knepper, "Convention Army"; and Charles R. Lindsey, "The Treatment of Burgoyne's Troops Under the Convention of Saratoga," *Political Science Quarterly* 22 (1907): 441–59.

6. Henry Laurens to Robert Howe, October 25, 1777, *Correspondence of Henry Laurens*, ed. Frank Moore (New York: Zenger Club, 1861), 58; Wilkinson, *Memoirs*, 1:323–32; *Massachusetts Spy* (Worcester), October 23, 1777; Kirkwood Orderly Book, ser. 7E:23, item 67.1, reel 16, PFPC; JCC, 9:854–55, 861–62.

7. "The Journal of Ralph Cross of Newburyport," in *Historical Magazine: And Notes and Queries Concerning the Antiquities, History, and Biography of America*, 2nd ser., vol. 7 (Morrisania, NY: Henry B. Dawson, 1870), 10; Lloyd Brown and Howard Peckham, eds., *Revolutionary War Journals of Henry Dearborn, 1775–1783* (Berwyn Heights, MD: Heritage Books, 2007), 111.

8. Wilkinson, *Memoirs*, 1:332; Dabney, *After Saratoga*, 15–16.

9. Sampson, *Escape in America*, 43–44. Upon receiving confirmation of the convention articles, John Rutledge of South Carolina declared, "I dislike the terms of the Convention much." John Rutledge to Henry Laurens, November 7, 1777, *PHL*, 12:36. See also Committee for Foreign Affairs to the American Commissioners, October 31, 1777, *Founders Online*.

10. Samuel Cooper to John Adams, October 22, 1777, *Founders Online*; Gates to Burgoyne, September 2, 1777, *Pennsylvania Evening Post* (Philadelphia), September 19, 1777; Laurens quoted in David Duncan Wallace, *The Life of Henry Laurens: With a Sketch of the Life of Lieutenant-Colonel John Laurens* (New York: G. P. Putnam's Sons, 1915), 247; Lafayette to Henry Laurens, February 19, 1778, quoted in James Kirby Martin, *Benedict Arnold, Revolutionary Hero: An American Warrior Reconsidered* (New York: New York University Press, 1997), 406.

11. George Washington to Richard Henry Lee, October 28, 1777, *Founders Online*; Samuel Blackley Webb, *Correspondence and Journals of Samuel Blachley Webb*, ed. Worthington C. Ford, 3 vols. (New York: Wickersham, 1893), 1:232.

12. Rev. Samuel Cooper to Benjamin Franklin, October 25, 1777, *Founders Online*; Edward Stevens to Alexander Hamilton, December 23, 1777, ibid.; "General Burgoyne's Proclamation, issued at Fort Ticonderoga," July 2, 1777, *Pennsylvania Evening Post* (Philadelphia), August 21, 1777; Wilkinson, *Memoirs*, 1:200; S. Sydney Bradford, ed., "Lord Francis Napier's Journal of the Burgoyne Campaign," *Maryland Historical Magazine* 57 (1962): 306–8; James Lunt, *John Burgoyne of Saratoga* (New York: Harcourt Brace Jovanovich, 1975), 176; Henry Laurens to the Marquis de Lafayette, October 23, 1777, *PHL*, 11:581.

13. Max Mintz, *The Generals of Saratoga: John Burgoyne & Horatio Gates* (New Haven, CT: Yale University Press, 1990), 182; *Connecticut Courant* (Hartford), September 8, 1777; *Pennsylvania Evening Post* (Philadelphia), September 4, 1777; Council of Safety of New York at Marble Town to John Hancock, November 5, 1777, PCC, item 67, 2:87.

14. Knepper, "Convention Army," 10; Digby, *British Invasion from the North*, 320; Johann F. Specht, *The Specht Journal: A Military Journal of the Burgoyne Campaign*, trans. Helga Doblin, ed. Mary C. Lynn (New York: Greenwood, 1995), 102–3; J. F. Wasmus, *An Eyewitness Account of the American Revolution, and New England Life: The Journal of J. F. Wasmus, German Company Surgeon, 1776–1783*, trans. Helga Doblin, ed. Marcy C. Lynn (New York: Greenwood, 1990), 83; Mercy Otis Warren, *History of the Rise, Progress and Termination of the American Revolution*, 3 vols. (Boston: Manning and Loring, 1805), 2:41. See also Daniel Krebs, "Ritual Performance: Surrender During the American War of Independence," in *How Fighting Ends*, ed. Afflerbach and Strachan, 169–83.

15. Earl J. Coates and James L. Kochan, *Don Troiani's Soldiers in America, 1754–1865* (Mechanicsburg, PA: Stackpole Books, 1998), 35; Specht, *Journal*, 103; William Leete Stone, trans., *Letters of Brunswick and Hessian Officers During the American Revolution* (Albany, NY: Joel Munsell's Sons, 1891), 146; Journal of Alpheus Woods, Mss Octavo Vols. W, AAS; Anburey, *Travels*, 2:38–39. Twelve members of the Convention Army perished on the march to Boston. Sampson, *Escape in America*, 49.

16. Baroness von Riedesel, *Baroness von Riedesel and the American Revolution: Journal and Correspondence of a Tour of Duty, 1776–1783*, trans. Marvin L. Brown (Chapel Hill: University of North Carolina Press, 1965), 64, 65; Eelking, *Memoirs, and Letters and Journals, of Major General Riedesel*, 1:214–16.

17. Heath to Washington, August 30, 1777, box 1, Elias Boudinot Papers, MCC 721, LC; Heath to Washington, October 25, 1777, *Founders Online*; Winthrop to Warren, November 11, 1777, Elizabeth F. Ellet, *The Women of the American Revolution*, 3 vols. (New York: Baker and Scribner, 1848–50), 1:98; Jeremiah Powell to Hancock, October 25, 1777, PCC, item 65, 1:269.

18. Heath to Washington, October 25, 1777, *Founders Online*. The government of Massachusetts, known as the Massachusetts Assembly or General Court, was composed of the council and the house of representatives. Without a governor, the council served as the executive of the state.

19. Samuel F. Batchelder, *Bits of Cambridge History* (Cambridge, MA: Harvard University Press, 1930), 9–10; Knepper, "Convention Army," 271–72; "Resolve for making provision for the Troops under Gen. Burgoyne, and assigning them certain limits," October 25, 1777, *Resolves of the General Assembly of the State of Massachusetts Bay*, 4th sitting (Boston: John Gill, 1777), 39, 40.

20. Winthrop to Warren, November 11, 1777, Ellet, *Women of the American Revolution*, 1:97.

21. Ibid.; Winthrop to Warren, February 4, 1778, *Warren-Adams Letters: Being Chiefly a Correspondence Among John Adams, Samuel Adams, and James Warren, 1743–1814,* 2 vols. (Boston: Massachusetts Historical Society, 1917–25), 2:4–5; Roger Lamb, *A British Soldier's Story: Roger Lamb's Narrative of the American Revolution,* ed. Don N. Hagist (Baraboo, WI: Ballindalloch, 2004), 56.

22. Sampson, *Escape in America,* 56; Helga B. Doblin and Mary C. Lynn, trans., "A Brunswick Grenadier with Burgoyne: The Journal of Johann Bense, 1776–1783," *New York History* 66, no. 4 (October 1985): 420–44, 436; Lamb, *British Soldier's Story,* 55; Depy. Adj. Genl. J. Keith to the Massachusetts Council, November 22, 1777, William Heath Papers, MHS, 7:131.

23. Anburey, *Travels,* 2:59; Stone, *Letters of Brunswick and Hessian Officers,* 153, 154; Col. William Raymond Lee to Heath, November 1, 1777, Thomas Amory Lee, *Colonel William Raymond Lee of the Revolution* (Boston: Essex Institute, 1917), 15.

24. Knepper, "Convention Army," 39–40, 271; Joseph Trumbull to Heath, November 7, 1777, Heath Papers, MHS, 7:44; Anburey, *Travels,* 2:60. For examples of the general's pleas for assistance, see Heath to the President of the Massachusetts Council, November 1, 1777, Heath Papers, MHS, 7:23; Heath to Gov. Jonathan Trumbull, November 2, 1777, ibid., 20; and Heath to Pres. Henry Laurens, November 19, 1777, ibid., 109. See also Heath to Washington, November 23, 1777, *Founders Online.*

25. Burgoyne to Heath, November 10, 1777, *The Parliamentary Register; or, History of the Proceedings and Debates of the House of Commons,* 17 vols. (London: J. Almon, 1775–80), vol. 12, Appendix to the Canada Papers, iv.

26. Heath to Laurens, November 27, 1777, Heath Papers, MHS, 7:155; Emer de Vattel, *The Law of Nations; or, Principles of the Law of Nature Applied to the Conduct and Affairs of Nations and Sovereigns,* bk. 3, http://www.constitution.org/vattel/vattel_03.htm (accessed August 5, 2008); Heath to Burgoyne, November 23, 1777, Heath Papers, MHS, 7:137.

27. Heath to the Council of Massachusetts, December 12, 1777, Heath Papers, MHS, 7:265; Heath to Washington, November 23, 1777, *Founders Online.*

28. Knepper, "Convention Army," 53, 197; Heath to Laurens, January 5, 1778, Heath Papers, MHS, 8:36.

29. William Heath, *Memoirs of Major General William Heath … by Himself* (Boston: I. Thomas and E. T. Andrews, 1798), 145; Burgoyne to Gates, November 14, 1777, PCC, item 57, p. 34; Gates to Laurens, December 3, 1777, *PHL,* 12:126–28.

30. *JCC,* 9:949; Knepper, "Convention Army," 62; Laurens to Heath, December 23, 1777, *LMCC,* 2:596; *JCC,* 9:950.

31. Riedesel, *Baroness von Riedesel,* 72–73; Knepper, "Convention Army," 67.

32. Gates to Laurens, December 3, 1777, *PHL,* 12:126–28; *JCC,* 9:1059.

33. List of British Infractions of the Saratoga Convention, PCC, item 57, p. 339; *JCC,* 9:1061, 1063. See also Anburey, *Travels,* 2:55.

34. Richard Henry Lee to Washington, November 20, 1777, *Founders Online; JCC,* 9:1064.

35. Knepper, "Convention Army," 68.

36. *The Works of John Witherspoon, D.D. …,* 9 vols. (Edinburgh: Ogle and Aikman, J. Pillans, J. Ritchie, J. Turnbull, 1805), 9:108–16.

37. Laurens to Washington, January 5, 1778, *LMCC,* 3:13; Laurens to Heath, January 8, 1778, ibid., 18. William Ellery of Rhode Island, Eliphalet Dyer of Connecticut, Abraham Clark of New Jersey, and John Harvie of Virginia voted against the resolution. Francis Dana of Massachusetts

abstained. *JCC*, 10:30–35. Congress was in no hurry to see the Saratoga Convention ratified, according to Laurens, "having upon further consideration judged it impolitic & unnecessary to inform the Court of Great Britain authentickly of the suspension of Genl Burgoyne's embarkation until such information [news of the suspension] shall proceed from him [Burgoyne]." Laurens to Washington, January 19, 1778, *Founders Online*.

38. Howe to Burgoyne, November 16, 1777, Sir Henry Clinton Papers, vol. 27, fol. 2, CL-UM. See also Jane Clark, "The Convention Troops and the Perfidy of Sir William Howe," *American Historical Review* 37 (1932): 721–23.

39. John Laurens to Isaac Motte, January 26, 1778, *LMCC*, 3:52; John Thaxter to Abigail Adams, March 21, 1778, Mss 88.190.291, LSC; Daniel Roberdeau to John Adams, January 21, 1778, *Founders Online*.

40. *New-Jersey Gazette* (Burlington), February 25, 1778. This article was widely reprinted. For information on Livingston's pseudonyms, see William Livingston, *The Papers of William Livingston*, ed. Carl E. Prince, Dennis P. Ryan, Pamela B. Schafler, and Donald W. White, 5 vols. (Trenton: New Jersey Historical Commission, 1979), 2:3–6.

41. Hamilton to George Clinton, March 12, 1778, *The Papers of Alexander Hamilton*, ed. Harold C. Syrett and Jacob E. Cooke, 26 vols. (New York: Columbia University Press, 1961), 1:440; John Laurens to Henry Laurens, January 23, 1778, *The Army Correspondence of Colonel John Laurens in the Years 1777–8*, ed. William Gilmore Simms (New York, 1868), 110; Wilkinson to Gates, January 15, 1778, in Wilkinson, *Memoirs*, 1:379.

42. Washington to Laurens, January 9, 1778, *Founders Online*.

43. Washington to Howe, January 20, 1778, *Founders Online*; Heath to Laurens, January 8, 1778, Heath Papers, MHS, 8:54.

44. Ray Pettengill, trans., *Letters from America, 1776–1779: Being Letters of Brunswick, Hessian, and Waldeck Officers with the British Armies During the American Revolution* (Boston: Houghton Mifflin, 1924), 131; Heath, *Memoirs*, 149; General Report of the Garrison at Cambridge, January 7, 1778, Heath Papers, MHS, 8:45.

45. Israel Putnam to Jonathan Trumbull, January 6, 1778, Trumbull Papers, vol. 8, no. 34a, Connecticut State Library, Hartford; John Beatty to James McHenry, October 15, 1778, folder 17, box 1, Beatty Family Collection, AM 15176, Princeton University Special Collections, Princeton, NJ; Jonathan Rice to Lieutenant Colonel Pollard, August 21, 1778, Heath Papers, MHS, 11:115. For examples of the intense newspaper coverage of British abuses of American prisoners, see *Norwich (CT) Packet*, January 20, 1777; *Continental Journal* (Boston), February 13, 1777, January 22, 1778; *Boston Gazette*, June 16, 1777; and *Independent Ledger* (Boston), November 2, 1777.

46. Ezekiel Williams to Elias Boudinot, February 25, 1778, vol. 1, (PHi) 68, Elias Boudinot Papers, HSP; Joshua Mersereau to Elias Boudinot, November 4, 1777, Elias Boudinot (1740–1821) Collection, MS 2958.1071.1, New-York Historical Society; Charles J. Hoadly, ed., *The Public Records of the State of Connecticut*, vol. 1 (Hartford: Case, Lockwood, and Brainard, 1894), 418, 580.

47. Journal of the Massachusetts Council, Boston, April 23, 1777, *Naval Documents of the American Revolution*, ed. William Bell Clark, William James Morgan, William S. Dudley, and Michael J. Crawford, 11 vols. (Washington, DC: Government Printing Office, 1996), 8:406; Thomas Hughes, *A Journal by Thos. Hughes . . .* (Cambridge: Cambridge University Press, 1947), 21, 23; *Parliamentary Register*, vol. 12, app., ix–x. Regarding the Brunswick prisoners aboard the prison ship, see Wasmus, *Eyewitness Account*, 80; and Robert Webler, "Records of Massachusetts Bay

Concerning Brunswick Army Prisoners from the Battle of Bennington," *Hessians: Journal of the Johannes Schwalm Historical Association* 8 (2005): 51–57.

48. Burgoyne to Heath, January 9, 1778, Heath Papers, MHS, 8:64.

49. Heath to Burgoyne, January 10, 1778, Heath Papers, MHS, 8:71; Sampson, *Escape in America*, 95.

50. Sampson, *Escape in America*, 95; Knepper, "Convention Army," 84–85.

51. Heath to Burgoyne, February 4, 1778, Heath Papers, MHS, 8:216; Heath to Laurens, February 7, 1778, ibid., 237; Washington to Heath, January 22, 1778, ibid., 150; Sampson, *Escape in America*, 96–97.

52. Heath to Henry Laurens, November 27, 1777, *PHL*, 12:98; Anburey, *Travels*, 53; Maj. Patrick Campbell to Duncan Campbell of Glenure, March 14, 1778, Papers of the Campbell Family of Barcaldine, GD 170/1176, National Archives of Scotland; John Adams to Francis Dana, December 25, 1778, *Founders Online*. See also *The Parliamentary History of England, from the Earliest Period to the Year 1803*, 36 vols. (London, 1806–20), 19:1277–1402, 20:1–94.

53. Lamb, *British Soldier's Story*, 56; Mersereau to Elias Boudinot, April 29, 1778, American Revolutionary War Manuscripts Collection, Boston Public Library; Heath to Laurens, March 10, 1778, Heath Papers, MHS, 8:413. Mersereau believed that the Germans were far less likely to desert to the enemy than were the British.

54. Heath to Laurens, March 10, 1778, Heath Papers, MHS, 8:413; Laurens to Heath, December 27, 1777, *PHL*, 12:214–18; *JCC*, 9:1037; Knepper, "Convention Army," 88–90, 95.

55. Frederick Mackenzie, *Diary of Frederick Mackenzie: Giving a Daily Narrative of His Military Service as an Officer of the Regiment of Royal Welch Fusiliers During the Years 1775–1781 in Massachusetts, Rhode Island, and New York*, 2 vols. (Cambridge, MA: Harvard University Press, 1930), 1:235; *JCC*, 10:44–45; Howe to Washington, December 21, 1777, *Founders Online*; Knepper, "Convention Army," 116–17.

56. Phillips to Clinton, quoted in Sampson, *Escape in America*, 88; Phillips to Heath, May 18, 1778, Heath Papers, MHS, 9:424; Heath to Phillips, May 19, 1778, ibid.

57. Phillips to Heath, June 17, 1778, Heath Papers, MHS, 10:97; Heath to Phillips, June 18, 1778, ibid., 98; Heath to Laurens, June 19, 1778, ibid., 112; Phillips to Heath, June 19, 1778, ibid., 101.

58. Minutes of the Evidence brought against the prisoners, May 18, 1778, Heath Papers, MHS, 9:441; Minutes of the Court of Inquiry held at Cambridge, May 18, 1778, ibid., 404.

59. Sampson, *Escape in America*, 102; Daniel Krebs, *A Generous and Merciful Enemy: Life for German Prisoners of War During the American Revolution* (Norman: University of Oklahoma Press, 2013), 187; James Warren to Samuel Adams, June 28, 1778, *Warren-Adams Letters*, 2:28.

60. John Mercier to Thomas Bradford, April 24, 1778, folder 4, box 21, Bradford Family Papers, HSP; *JCC*, 9:1036–37, 1069; Trumbull to Henry Laurens, January 13, 1778, PCC, item 66, 1:359. For Washington and Howe's discussion of a general cartel, see, for instance, Washington to Howe, November 14–15, 1777, *Founders Online*; Howe to Washington, February 5, 1778, ibid.; Washington to Howe, February 10, 1778, ibid.; and Howe to Washington, February 14, 1778, ibid.

61. Washington to Laurens, March 7–8, 1778, *Founders Online*; Edwin Burrows, *Forgotten Patriots: The Untold Story of American Prisoners During the Revolutionary War* (New York: Basic Books, 2008), 127; Washington to Laurens, April 4, 1778, *Founders Online*. See also Betsy Knight, "Prisoner Exchange and Parole in the American Revolution," *William and Mary Quarterly*, 3rd ser., 48, no. 2 (April 1991): 202–6. Thirty-four privates and three surgeons were also exchanged.

62. JCC, 10:184–85; Knepper, "Convention Army," 177–21.

63. Isaac Tuckerman to Col. Jonathan Chase, September 5, 1778, Massachusetts Council Papers, 1778–79, Massachusetts Archives Collection (Felt Collection), 169:155, Massachusetts State Archives, Boston.

64. Mersereau to Boudinot, August 26, 1778, Letters and Other Materials Received as Commissary General of Prisoners, 1775–90, ser. 5, Bound Volumes, Stimson Collection of Elias Boudinot, C0228, Manuscripts Division, Dept. of Rare Books and Special Collections, Princeton University Library; G. Speakman to Heath, October 16, 1778, Heath Papers, MHS, 12:20; Anburey, Travels, 2:214, 236. See also Jeremiah Powell to Henry Laurens, April 28, 1778, PHL, 13:216–7.

65. JCC, 12:901–2; William Eden to Sir Henry Clinton, November 7, 1778, Clinton Papers, vol. 45, fol. 22; Clinton to Germain, October 25, 1778, quoted in Knepper, "Convention Army," 129; Jonathan Clarke to Clinton, n.d. [ca. October 25, 1778], Clinton Papers, vol. 44, fol. 14; Phillips to Richard Prescott, October or November 1778, ibid., fol. 44.

66. JCC, 12:1016; Knepper, "Convention Army," 137; Sampson, Escape in America, 105–6.

67. Heath to Washington, November 12, 1778, Founders Online; Knepper, "Convention Army," 139. See also Heath to Washington, October 25, 1778, Heath Papers, MHS, 7:1; and Heath to Washington, October 26, 1778, ibid., 12:96. For conflicting accounts of the distance from Cambridge to Charlottesville, see Pettengill, Letters from America, 146; J. A. Houlding and G. Kenneth Yates, "Corporal Fox's Memoir of Service, 1766–1783: Quebec, Saratoga, and the Convention Army," Journal of the Society of Army Historical Research 68, no. 275 (Autumn 1990): 162; and Riedesel, Baroness von Riedesel, 80. Andrew O'Shaughnessy has estimated that the main force traveled 641 miles from Cambridge, Massachusetts, to Charlottesville, Virginia. O'Shaughnessy, The Men Who Lost America: British Leadership, the American Revolution, and the Fate of Empire (New Haven, CT: Yale University Press, 2013), 159.

68. Anburey, Travels, 2:250, 257; Lamb, British Soldier's Story, 61; Knepper, "Convention Army," 139; Heath to Laurens, October 29, 1778, Heath Papers, MHS, 12:111; Pettengill, Letters from America, 146.

69. Houlding and Yates, "Corporal Fox's Memoir of Service," 162; Lamb, British Soldier's Story, 61–62. On the eve of the prisoners' departure in late October 1778, Heath informed the Council of Massachusetts, "The British are 2,263, including officers, the German 1,882." "The Heath Papers," Collections of the Massachusetts Historical Society, ser. 7, vol. 4 (Boston: Massachusetts Historical Society, 1904), 279. According to a British return compiled in August 1779 (Clinton Papers, CL-UM) examined by George Knepper, 1,035 British and 333 German enlisted men were lost during their confinement in Massachusetts. If this return is accurate, that would mean that 1,712 British and 2,170 Germans marched for Virginia. These numbers do not accord with either Heath's very precise accounting or a British return done in November 1778 that stipulates the number of British and German conventioners as 2,340 and 1,949, respectively. The British 1778 return would have included the convention prisoners left behind at Rutland, thus the discrepancy with Heath's accounting. By comparing the 1778 British return and Heath's numbers, it appears that 77 British and 67 Germans were left behind at Rutland, presumably too sick to make the march south. Using the total of 5,250 officers and men who surrendered under the Convention of Saratoga according to the Kingston return (2,747 British troops and 2,503 Germans), we can calculate the number of prisoners who died or deserted during their year in Massachusetts. Taking into account those men left behind, 407 British soldiers (15 percent) and

554 Germans (22 percent) died or deserted that year. CO 5/171, TNA; Knepper, "Convention Army," 197, 274.

70. Theodorick Bland to George Washington, December 19, 1778, *Founders Online*; Diary of Alexander King, Henry A. Sykes Collection, 1687–1789, Mss 83254, Connecticut Historical Society, Hartford, bk. 6, p. 13; Riedesel, *Baroness von Riedesel*, 79, 80; Houlding and Yates, "Corporal Fox's Memoir of Service," 163; Jefferson to Gov. Patrick Henry, March 27, 1779, *Founders Online*.

71. Philander D. Chase, "'Years of Hardships and Revelations': The Convention Army at the Albemarle Barracks, 1779–1781," *Magazine of Albemarle History* 41 (1983): 16–18; *JCC*, 13:39; Anburey, *Travels*, 2:317; Doblin and Lynn, "Brunswick Grenadier," 436, 439; Houlding and Yates, "Corporal Fox's Memoir of Service," 163.

72. *JCC*, 12:1020–21; Anburey, *Travels*, 2:318, 364; Chase, "'Years of Hardships,'" 24; Bland to Phillips, December 5, 1778, *The Bland Papers . . .* , ed. Charles Campbell, 2 vols. (Petersburg, VA: Edmund and Julian C. Ruffin, 1840), 1:110.

73. William Finnie to Congress, February 5, 1779, PCC, item 78, 9:221–23; Jefferson to Patrick Henry, March 27, 1779, *Founders Online*; *JCC*, 13:216–17. For a full recitation of Jefferson's argument, see Knepper, "Convention Army," 157–58.

74. Anburey, *Travels*, 2:361, 363, 364, 384, 436; Riedesel, *Baroness von Riedesel*, 82, 83; Knepper, "Convention Army," 183; Houlding and Yates, "Corporal Fox's Memoir of Service," 163.

75. Houlding and Yates, "Corporal Fox's Memoir of Service," 163; British return of August 1779, CO 5/170, TNA, in Knepper, "Convention Army," 274; Riedesel, *Baroness von Riedesel*, 84.

76. Heath to Gates, November 18, 1778, Heath Papers, MHS, 12:190; Mersereau to Heath, April 9, 1779, ibid., 286; Mersereau to Heath, May 28, June 2, 1779, Rutland, MA, ibid., 13:27, 46; Mersereau to Heath, April 18, 1779, ibid., 12:316; Gates to Heath, May 4, 1779, ibid., 373.

77. Knepper, "Convention Army," 179–81; Phillips to Washington, January 6, 1779, *Founders Online*; Washington to Phillips, December 25, 1778, ibid.

78. Thomas McKean to Congress, November 19, 1778, PCC, item 159, p. 292; Germain to Clinton, June 25, 1779, Clinton Papers, vol. 61, fol. 40; *JCC*, 14:679; Knepper, "Convention Army," 213–14, 226–28.

79. James Hamilton to Congress, March 6, 1780, PCC, item 57, p. 433; Anthony Wayne to Col. Walter Stewart, June 7, 1779, Walter Stewart Papers, New-York Historical Society. See also Robert Parkinson, *The Common Cause: Creating Race and Nation in the American Revolution* (Chapel Hill: University of North Carolina Press, 2016), chap. 7.

80. John Hill to James Hamilton, May 12, 1780, British and Hessian Revolutionary War Collection, New-York Historical Society; Anburey, *Travels*, 2:349–50, 370, 374, 422.

81. Anburey, *Travels*, 2:436; Francis Tate to Deputy Commissary General of Purchases Robert Forsyth, [March 1780], James Wood Papers, Acc. 28960, Library of Virginia, Richmond; Wood to Jefferson, June 8, 1780, *Founders Online*; James Hamilton to Washington, August 24, 1780, Gratz Collection, HSP; Wood to the Assembly of Virginia, [July 1780], Wood Papers.

82. *JCC*, 18:842–43; Sampson, *Escape in America*, 144–45.

83. Anburey, *Travels*, 2:466; Brunswick and Hesse Hanau Officers to Clinton, [1780], Clinton Papers, vol. 136, fol. 11; Leonard Morse to Sir Benjamin Thompson, February 5, 1781, ibid., vol. 145, fol. 29.

84. Hamilton to Clinton, December 17, 1780, Clinton Papers, vol. 134, fol. 13; Knepper, "Convention Army," 209–10; Rawlings to Lee, December 5, 1780, *Archives of Maryland*, 99 vols. (Baltimore: Maryland Historical Society, 1883–2000), 45:199.

85. Rawlings to Lee, December 5, 1780, *Archives of Maryland*, 45:199; James Wood to Lee, December 15, 1780, ibid., 203; Council of Maryland to Trustees for the Poor of Frederick County, January 8, 1781, ibid., 267; Hamilton to Lee, January 30, 1781, ibid., 47:41–42; Council of Maryland to Hamilton, February 8, 1781, ibid., 45:306; Jefferson to Samuel Huntington, January 15, 1781, *Founders Online*.

86. *JCC*, 19:229–30, 299–302. For more on the congressional debate over relocation, see ibid., 259, 263; and Sampson, *Escape in America*, 165. On March 25, 1781, Lieutenant Colonel Jonathan Hill of the 9th Regiment compiled a return of the British prisoners at Frederick Town. At that time there were 610 men and 209 officers, noncommissioned officers, musicians, and supernumeraries present. *Archives of Maryland*, 47:147.

87. Sampson, *Escape in America*, 166; Knepper, "Convention Army," 249; Deposition of James Kidd, May 20, 1781, Clinton Papers, vol. 156, fol. 6; Anburey, *Travels*, 2:509.

88. William Atlee to President Reed, June 13, 1781, *Pennsylvania Archives: Selected and Arranged from Original Documents in the Office of the Secretary of the Commonwealth*, ed. Samuel Hazard, ser. 1, 12 vols. (Philadelphia: Joseph Severns, 1853), 9:203–5; Sampson, *Escape in America*, 170; Deposition of Hugh Torence, April 16, 1781, Clinton Papers, vol. 152, fol. 34; Col. Adam Hubley to President Reed, July 13, 1781, *Pennsylvania Archives*, 9:279; Houlding and Yates, "Corporal Fox's Memoir of Service," 165.

89. William Irvine to Joseph Reed, August 9, 1781, *Pennsylvania Archives*, 9:346; Houlding and Yates, "Corporal Fox's Memoir of Service," 166; Horace W. Sellers, ed., "Letter of Surgeon's Mate Benjamin Shield to Brigadier-General James Hamilton, 1781," *Pennsylvania Magazine of History and Biography* 19, no. 1 (1895): 116–18; Deposition of Richard Bradshaw and William Simmons, August 13, 1781, Clinton Papers, vol. 170, fol. 14.

90. Doblin and Lynn, "Brunswick Grenadier," 442; Krebs, *Generous and Merciful Enemy*, 196.

91. President Reed to Col. William Scott, [July 1781], *Pennsylvania Archives*, 9:302; Board of War to President Reed, July 17, 1781, ibid., 290; Reed to Scott, [August 1781], ibid., 350; Krebs, *Generous and Merciful Enemy*, 196.

92. Knight, "Prisoner Exchange and Parole," 209–10; Sampson, *Escape in America*, 143; Germain to Phillips, quoted in ibid. For an example of a petition to Congress to demand retaliation, see petition of Andrew Hodge, John Nixon, Samuel Meredith, and seventy-six other inhabitants of Philadelphia to the Continental Congress, July 14, 1779, PCC, item 42, 6:218. For constituent frustrations with "the slow and forbearing disposition of Congress" on the subject of "revenge," see Marine Committee to Benjamin Franklin, [after July 19, 1779], *Founders Online*. Congress's embrace of retaliation gave Stephen Ward of New York "no small degree of Consolation." Stephen Ward to John Jay, December 6, 1778, PCC, item 78, 23:104.

93. Henry J. Retzer, "The Hessian POWs in Reading Revisited," *Historical Review of Berks County* 66, no. 4 (Fall 2001): 159; Doblin and Lynn, "Brunswick Grenadier," 443; Johann Ewald, *Diary of the American War: A Hessian Journal*, trans. and ed. Joseph P. Tustin (New Haven, CT: Yale University Press, 1979), 349; Houlding and Yates, "Corporal Fox's Memoir of Service," 166. For the identities of the British prisoners known to have escaped or attempted escape, see Sampson, *Escape in America*, app. 5. Like most convention officers, Anburey was exchanged in September 1781. The enlisted soldiers who served under him remained in American hands until April 1783. Anburey, *Travels*, 2:528.

94. *New-England Chronicle* (Cambridge, MA), June 25, 1778.

Chapter 5

1. Sir Henry Clinton, *The American Rebellion: Sir Henry Clinton's Narrative of His Campaigns, 1775–1782* ..., ed. William B. Willcox (New Haven, CT: Yale University Press, 1954), 171; John Peebles, *John Peebles' American War: The Diary of a Scottish Grenadier*, ed. Ira D. Gruber (Mechanicsburg, PA: Stackpole Books, 1998), 335; Andrew O'Shaughnessy, *The Men Who Lost America: British Leadership, the American Revolution, and the Fate of Empire* (New Haven, CT: Yale University Press, 2013), 231.

2. *Original Papers Relating to the Siege of Charleston, 1780* (Walker, Evans & Cogswell, 1898), 47, 50; Carl P. Borick, *Relieve Us of This Burthen: American Prisoners of War in the Revolutionary South, 1780–1782* (Columbia: University of South Carolina Press, 2012), 3–4. See also Carl P. Borick, *A Gallant Defense: The Siege of Charleston, 1780* (Columbia: University of South Carolina Press, 2003).

3. Franklin B. Hough, *The Siege of Charleston* ... (Albany, NY: J. Munsell, 1867), 99, 105, 171; Laurens to the S.C. Delegates in Congress, May 23, 1780, *PHL*, 15:298.

4. Clinton to Germain, May 13, 1780, in Banastre Tarleton, *A History of the Campaigns of 1780 and 1781, in the Southern Provinces of North America* ... (Dublin, 1787), 44; Clinton to Patrick Ferguson, May 22, 1780, Sir Henry Clinton Papers, vol. 100, fol. 15, CL-UM; Hough, *Siege of Charleston*, 25; Clinton, *American Rebellion*, 171; Lord Germain to Gen. James Robertson, July 5, 1780, *Documents of the American Revolution, 1770–1783*, ed. K. G. Davies, 21 vols. (Dublin: Irish University Press, 1978), 18:115. See also John Shy, *A People Numerous and Armed: Reflections on the Military Struggle for American Independence* (Oxford: Oxford University Press, 1976), 212–13.

5. North Carolina Board of War to Col. John Lutrell, October 17, 1780, *CSRNC*, 14:427; Pension Application of Moses Hall, W10105, transcribed by Will Graves, Southern Campaigns Revolutionary War Pension Statements & Rosters, http://revwarapps.org/w10105.pdf (last updated January 23, 2019). See also Holger Hoock, *Scars of Independence: America's Violent Birth* (New York: Crown, 2017), 320–21.

6. Viewing the southern campaigns as distinctive rather than as a culmination of an ongoing process of violent escalation, these works have downplayed both the violence of the war in the North and the violence enacted by the regular forces of Great Britain and the United States during the campaigns in the South. See, for instance, John S. Pancake, *This Destructive War: The British Campaign in the Carolinas, 1780–1782* (Tuscaloosa: University of Alabama Press, 1985); W. Robert Higgins, ed., *The Revolutionary War in the South: Power, Conflict, and Leadership* (Durham, NC: Duke University Press, 1979); Robert S. Lambert, *South Carolina Loyalists in the American Revolution* (Columbia: University of South Carolina Press, 1987); Dan L. Morrill, *Southern Campaigns of the American Revolution* (Baltimore: Nautical & Aviation Publishing, 1993); Walter Edgar, *Partisans and Redcoats: The Southern Conflict That Turned the Tide of the American Revolution* (New York: Perennial, 2001); John Grenier, *The First Way of War: American War Making on the Frontier* (Cambridge: Cambridge University Press, 2005), chap. 5; James Webb, *Born Fighting: How the Scots-Irish Shaped America* (New York: Broadway Books, 2004); John Richard Alden, *The South in the Revolution, 1763–1789* (Baton Rouge: Louisiana State University Press, 1957); John Buchanan, *The Road to Guilford Courthouse: The American Revolution in the Carolinas* (New York: John Wiley and Sons, 1997); James Swisher, *The Revolutionary War in the Southern Backcountry* (Gretna, LA: Pelican, 2008); Ronald Hoffman, Thad W. Tate, and Peter J. Albert, eds., *An Uncivil War: The*

Southern Backcountry During the American Revolution (Charlottesville: University Press of Virginia, 1985); and Wayne E. Lee, *Crowds and Soldiers in Revolutionary North Carolina: The Culture of Violence in Riot and War* (Gainesville: University Press of Florida, 2001).

7. *Boston Evening-Post*, July 27, 1782.

8. Peebles, *John Peebles' American War*, 372. See also Johann Ewald, *Diary of the American War: A Hessian Journal*, trans. and ed. Joseph P. Tustin (New Haven, CT: Yale University Press, 1979), 238; William Moultrie, *Memoirs of the American Revolution . . .*, 2 vols. (New York: David Longworth, 1802), 2:108; and Borick, *Gallant Defense*, 220–21.

9. O'Shaughnessy, *Men Who Lost America*, 223–28; Borick, *Relieve Us*, 4, 7; Fayssoux to Dr. David Ramsay, March 26, 1785, in Moultrie, *Memoirs*, 2:398.

10. Hough, *Siege of Charleston*, 130; Moultrie, *Memoirs*, 2:109, 209, 210; Clinton to Germain, June 4, 1780, in *Documents of the American Revolution*, ed. Davies, 18:102.

11. Clinton to Cornwallis, May 20, 1780, *Cornwallis Papers*, 1:49; O'Shaughnessy, *Men Who Lost America*, 231; Clinton to Cornwallis, May 29, 1780, *Cornwallis Papers*, 1:54.

12. James Simpson to Clinton, May 15, 1780, Alan S. Brown, "James Simpson's Reports on the Carolina Loyalists, 1779–1780," *Journal of Southern History* 21, no. 4 (November 1955): 519; Uzal Johnson, *Captured at Kings Mountain: The Journal of Uzal Johnson*, ed. Wade S. Kolb III and Robert M. Weir (Columbia: University of South Carolina Press, 2011), 19; Clinton to Maj. Patrick Ferguson, May 22, 1780, Clinton Papers, vol. 100, fol. 15. See also Cornwallis to Tarleton, April 25, 1780, *Cornwallis Papers*, 1:25, 105.

13. Peebles, *John Peebles' American War*, 373; Ewald, *Diary*, 242; Innes to Cornwallis, June 8, 1780, *Cornwallis Papers*, 1:111.

14. Tarleton, *Campaigns of 1780 and 1781*, 31, 32; Alexander Garden, *Anecdotes of the American Revolution . . .* (Charleston, SC: A. E. Miller, 1828), 138; Anthony J. Scotti, *Brutal Virtue: The Myth and Reality of Banastre Tarleton* (Westminster, MD: Heritage Books, 2007), 173–78. See also Edgar, *Partisans and Redcoats*, 56–57; and J. Tracy Power, "'The Virtue of Humanity Was Totally Forgot': Buford's Massacre, May 29, 1780," *South Carolina Historical Magazine* 93, no. 1 (January 1992): 5–14.

15. Tarleton, *Campaigns of 1780 and 1781*, 32; *Massachusetts Spy* (Worcester), September 14, 1780; Thomas Person to Thomas Burke, June 21, 1780, *CSRNC*, 14:858; *American Journal* (Providence, RI), August 16, 1780; Eliza Wilkinson, *Letters of Eliza Wilkinson During the Invasion and Possession of Charlestown, S.C. by the British in the Revolutionary War*, ed. Caroline Gilman (New York: Samuel Colman, 1839), 89; Edgar, *Partisans and Redcoats*, 66. For Tarleton's after-action report, see *Royal Gazette* (New York), June 17, 1780; and *New-York Gazette*, June 19, 1780. On the effects of revolutionary propaganda on militia mobilization, see George Turnbull to Cornwallis, June 15, 1780, *Cornwallis Papers*, 1:139.

16. Hough, *Siege of Charleston*, 183; Cornwallis to Balfour, June 13, 1780, *Cornwallis Papers*, 1:88; Cornwallis to Ferguson, June 16, 1780, ibid., 109; Jim Piecuch, *Three Peoples, One King: Loyalists, Indians, and Slaves in the Revolutionary South, 1775–1782* (Columbia: University of South Carolina Press, 2008), 182–83; Borick, *Relieve Us*, 86–87.

17. John Weldon Pension Application, S32053, Revolutionary War Pension Applications, Record Group 15, NARA; Cornwallis to Clinton, July 15, 1780, *Cornwallis Papers*, 1:170. For accounts similar to Weldon's, see James Dickson Pension, R2942, NARA; Philip Gruber Pension, S21778, ibid.; and Arthur Parr Pension, S16219, ibid.

18. O'Shaughnessy, *Men Who Lost America*, 250–52; Cornwallis to Clinton, August 29, 1780, *Cornwallis Papers*, 2:41; Cornwallis to Maj. James Wemyss, July 15, 1780, ibid., 1:310. The islands were James, John's, Edisto, Saint Helena, and Port Royal. Ibid., 123.

19. Tarleton to Cornwallis, August 5, 1780, *Cornwallis Papers*, 1:365; Marion to Gates, November 9, 1780, PCC, item 154, 2:334; Tarleton to Lt. Col. George Turnbull, November 5, 1780, *Cornwallis Papers*, 3:334. For works that have explained (or even excused) American atrocities by referencing "Tarleton's Quarter," see Christopher Ward, *The War of the Revolution*, ed. John Richard Alden, 2 vols. (New York: Macmillan, 1952), 2:742; Cynthia A. Kierner, *Southern Women in the Revolution, 1776–1800: Personal and Political Narratives* (Columbia: University of South Carolina Press, 1998), 17; and Edgar, *Partisans and Redcoats*, xvi, xvii, 71. For a highly persuasive exception to this trend, see Piecuch, *Three Peoples, One King*.

20. Hoock, *Scars of Independence*, 305–7; Piecuch, *Three Peoples, One King*, 317. See also Alan Gilbert, *Black Patriots and Loyalists: Fighting for Emancipation in the War for Independence* (Chicago: University of Chicago Press, 2012).

21. O'Shaughnessy, *Men Who Lost America*, 257–58; Tarleton, *Campaigns of 1780 and 1781*, 111; Borick, *Relieve Us*, 12; John Robert Shaw, *John Robert Shaw: An Autobiography of Thirty Years, 1777–1807*, ed. Oressa M. Teagarden and Jeanne L. Crabtree (Athens: Ohio University Press, 1992), 33.

22. Borick, *Relieve Us*, 14, 15–19; Balfour to Cornwallis, October 22, 1780, *Cornwallis Papers*, 2:130; Petition of William Scott, quoted in Borick, *Relieve Us*, 17; Balfour to Rawdon, October 26, 1780, *Cornwallis Papers*, 2:133. Washington agreed with Congress, believing that "if motives of policy are ever to prevail over those of humanity, they seem to apply at present against a general exchange." Washington to Samuel Huntington, July 10, 1780, *Founders Online*.

23. *Pennsylvania Packet* (Philadelphia), August 21, 1781; *New-Hampshire Gazette* (Portsmouth), September 3, 1781; "Extract of a letter from an officer of the state of Georgia and aide to Major General Gates," December 26, 1780, *Connecticut Journal* (New Haven), January 25, 1781.

24. Edgar, *Partisans and Redcoats*, 113; Cornwallis to Clinton, August 29, 1780, *Cornwallis Papers*, 2:41; Cruger to Nisbet Balfour, September 19, 1780, ibid., 103; Johnson, *Captured at Kings Mountain*, 29.

25. Ferguson's Declaration, September 9, 1780, *Cornwallis Papers*, 2:150; Ferguson's instructions to loyalists, n.d. [September 1780], ibid., 151–52; Johnson, *Captured at Kings Mountain*, 28; Lyman C. Draper, *King's Mountain and Its Heroes: History of the Battle of King's Mountain . . .* (Cincinnati: Peter G. Thomson, 1881), 169.

26. Pension Application of Charles Bowen, in Robert M. Dunkerly, ed., *The Battle of King's Mountain: Eyewitness Accounts* (Charleston, SC: History Press, 2012), 18; Pension Application of Joseph Hughes, ibid., 52; Alexander Chesney, *The Journal of Captain Alexander Chesney: A South Carolina Loyalist in the Revolution and After*, ed. E. Alfred Jones (Columbus: Ohio State University, 1921), 18. See also "Captain Abraham DePeyster's Report to Cornwallis," October 11, 1780, in Dunkerly, *Battle of King's Mountain*, 134. On the militiamen's intention to revenge the Waxhaws, see "Colonel Isaac Shelby's Pamphlet to the Public, 1823," ibid., 77.

27. Edgar, *Partisans and Redcoats*, 119; Chesney, *Journal*, 18; *Royal Gazette* (New York), February 24, 1781.

28. Chesney, *Journal*, 18–19; "John Spelts's Account," in Dunkerly, *Battle of King's Mountain*, 84; *Royal Gazette* (New York), February 24, 1781; "William Campbell's General Orders," October 11,

1780, in Dunkerly, *Battle of King's Mountain*, 28; "Diary of Lieut. Anthony Allaire, of Ferguson's Corps," in Draper, *King's Mountain and Its Heroes*, 510, 511.

29. "Ensign Robert Campbell's Account," in Dunkerly, *Battle of King's Mountain*, 22; Johnson, *Captured at Kings Mountain*, 32; "Description of the Treatment of British Prisoners of War," December 27, 1780, *Scots Magazine*, January 1781, *CSRNC*, 15:183; "Colonel Isaac Shelby's Account, 1815," in Dunkerly, *Battle of King's Mountain*, 74; Chesney, *Journal*, 18.

30. "Colonel Isaac Shelby's Account, 1815," in Dunkerly, *Battle of King's Mountain*, 74; "Colonel William Hill's Account," in ibid., 52; Rutledge to the Delegates of the State of South Carolina in Congress, November 20, 1780, Joseph W. Barnwell, ed., "Letters of John Rutledge," *South Carolina Historical and Genealogical Magazine* 17, no. 4 (October 1916): 143–44. For an account that stresses the restraint of the militia in the aftermath of the battle, see Lee, *Crowds and Soldiers*, 186–91. See also Lambert, *South Carolina Loyalists*, 138–46; and Edgar, *Partisans and Redcoats*, 116–21.

31. Johnson, *Captured at Kings Mountain*, 33; Chesney, *Journal*, 19.

32. Statement of Lts. William Stevenson and John Taylor, November 30, 1780, *Cornwallis Papers*, 3:459; Johnson, *Captured at Kings Mountain*, 34, 43.

33. Johnson, *Captured at Kings Mountain*, 35; Armstrong to Gates, November 7, 1780, *CSRNC*, 14:728–29; Claim of William Gist, AO 13/129, TNA; Cornwallis to Greene, February 4, 1781, *Cornwallis Papers*, 4:74n3.

34. Gates to the Board of War at Hillsborough in reference to Col. Martin Armstrong, November 16, 1780, PCC, item 154, 2:331; Armstrong to Gates, November 19, 1780, *CSRNC*, 14:745–46; North Carolina Board of War to Martin Armstrong, November 14, 1780, ibid., 463–64; Resolve of the North Carolina Legislature, February 3, 1781, ibid., 17:668.

35. Cornwallis to Smallwood, November 10, 1780, *Cornwallis Papers*, 3:401; *Royal Gazette* (New York), February 28, 1781.

36. Cornwallis to Smallwood, November 10, 1780, *Cornwallis Papers*, 3:401; Gates to Jefferson, November 1, 1780, *Founders Online*; Rutledge to the Delegates of the State of South Carolina in Congress, November 20, 1780, Barnwell, "Letters of John Rutledge," 143.

37. Huntington to Greene, October 31, 1780, *Greene Papers*, 6:451; Washington to Greene, November 8, 1780, ibid., 469.

38. Greene to Marion, December 4, 1780, *Greene Papers*, 6:519; Greene to Marbury, December 4, 1780, ibid., 521; Marbury to Greene, December 17, 1780, ibid., 594. See also Col. Abraham Buford to Greene, January 4, 1781, ibid., 7:49. For more on Greene and his opinions on partisan warfare, see John Buchanan, "'We must endeavor to keep up a Partizan War,'" in *General Nathanael Greene and the American Revolution in the South*, ed. Gregory D. Massey and Jim Piecuch (Columbia: University of South Carolina Press, 2012), 119–46.

39. Pension Application of John Clemmons, S8215, transcribed by Will Graves, Southern Campaigns Revolutionary War Pension Statements & Rosters, http://revwarapps.org/s8215.pdf (last updated January 23, 2019); Pension Application of John Waddill, R10977, transcribed by Will Graves, ibid., http://revwarapps.org/r10977.pdf (last updated January 23, 2019); Pension Application of George Parks (Parkes), W27457, transcribed by Will Graves, ibid., http://revwarapps.org/w27457.pdf (last updated January 23, 2019).

40. Col. William Campbell to Col. Arthur Campbell, July 25, 1780, *Frontier Retreat on the Upper Ohio: 1779–1781*, ed. Louise Phellps Kellogg (Madison: Wisconsin Historical Society, 1917), 240; Ashraf H. A. Rushdy, *American Lynching* (New Haven, CT: Yale University Press, 2012), 23–24; Pension Application of Nathaniel Smith, R9817, transcribed by C. Leon Harris, Southern

Campaigns Revolutionary War Pension Statements & Rosters, http://revwarapps.org/r9817.pdf (last updated January 23, 2019); Minutes of the North Carolina Senate, June 29, 1781, *CSRNC*, 17:827; Balfour to Cornwallis, April 26, 1781, *Cornwallis Papers*, 4:177.

41. Sung Bok Kim, "The Limits of Politicization in the American Revolution: The Experience of Westchester County, New York," *Journal of American History* 80, no. 3 (1993): 885–89; Memorial of Henry Dyer to Sir Henry Clinton, July 14, 1780, Clinton Papers, vol. 111, fol. 41; *Royal Gazette* (New York), July 25, 1781. "Mr. Lantman" was likely Jacob Lantman, who was apprehended as "a dangerous and disaffected Person" on April 21, 1781. Victor Hugo Paltsits, ed., *Minutes of the Commissioners for Detecting and Defeating Conspiracies in the State of New York: Albany County Sessions, 1778–1781*, 3 vols. (Albany: J. B. Lyon, State Printers, 1909–10), 2:686; Lt. Col. William Hull to Washington, January 6, 1781, enclosed within Heath to Washington, January 8, 1781, *Founders Online*. For other cases like Dyer's, see George Beckwith to Capt. John André, September 27, 1779, Clinton Papers, vol. 69, fol. 19; and Jacob Schieffelin to Sir Henry Clinton, July 14, 1780, ibid., vol. 111, fol. 40.

42. Capt. John Davidson to Mordecai Gist, January 10, 1781, Mordecai Gist Papers, MS 390, Maryland Historical Society, Baltimore; William Seymour, "A Journal of the Southern Expedition, 1780–1783," in *Papers of the Delaware Historical Society*, vol. 15 (Wilmington: Historical Society of Delaware, 1896), 12–13; William A. Graham, *General Joseph Graham and His Papers on North Carolina Revolutionary History* (Raleigh, NC: Edwards and Broughton, 1904), 319; Robert E. Lee, ed., *The Revolutionary War Memoirs of General Henry Lee* (Boston: Da Capo, 1998), 258. See also Piecuch, *Three Peoples, One King*, 239.

43. *The Narrative of Colonel David Fanning . . .* (New York: Joseph Sabin, 1865), 52, 46; Edward J. Cashin, *The King's Ranger: Thomas Brown and the American Revolution on the Southern Frontier* (Athens: University of Georgia Press, 1989), 118–19; "A List of Persons executed by the Enemy," enclosed with Greene to Cornwallis, December 17, 1780, *Cornwallis Papers*, 3:407; Greene to Alexander Hamilton, January 10, 1781, *Greene Papers*, 7:88. See also Pancake, *This Destructive War*, 84.

44. Greene to Cornwallis, December 17, 1780, *Greene Papers*, 6:592; Cornwallis to Gates, December 1, 1780, *Cornwallis Papers*, 3:405 (Cornwallis was unaware at this time that Greene had assumed command from Gates); Greene to Cornwallis, December 17, 1780, *Greene Papers*, 6:592; Cornwallis to Germain, September 19, 1780, *CSRNC*, 15:282; Balfour to Cornwallis, November 15, 1780, *Cornwallis Papers*, 3:76; Cornwallis to Greene, December 27, 1780, *Greene Papers*, 7:6. See also Borick, *Relieve Us*, 94.

45. Greene to Col. John Marshel, December 25, 1780, *Greene Papers*, 6:612; Samuel Huntington to Greene, January 9, 1781, ibid., 7:86; *JCC*, 19:28.

46. Don Higginbotham, *Daniel Morgan: Revolutionary Rifleman* (Chapel Hill: University of North Carolina Press, 1961), 140; *Pennsylvania Packet* (Philadelphia), February 17, 1781; Morgan to Greene, January 19, 1781, *Greene Papers*, 7:153. On the execution of one of the Cowpens prisoners, see James Simons to William Washington, November 3, 1803, enclosed within Pension Application of Lawrence Everhart, S25068, transcribed by C. Leon Harris, Southern Campaigns Revolutionary War Pension Statements & Rosters, http://revwarapps.org/s25068.pdf (last updated January 23, 2019). Cornwallis claimed that other British prisoners had been abused. See Cornwallis to Greene, March 4, 1781, *Cornwallis Papers*, 4:76. For the best scholarly account of the Battle of Cowpens, see Lawrence E. Babits, *A Devil of a Whipping: The Battle of Cowpens* (Chapel Hill: University of North Carolina Press, 2000).

47. Cornwallis to Greene, February 4, 1781, *Cornwallis Papers*, 4:75; Greene to Jefferson, January 24, 1781, *CVSP*, 1:458. On the Cowpens prisoners' peregrinations, see Samuel Huntington to Thomas Jefferson, March 4, 1781, *Founders Online*; and Thomas Sim Lee to Jefferson, March 17, 1781, ibid. The prisoners arrived in Lancaster, Pennsylvania, in early March 1781. *Freeman's Journal* (Portsmouth, NH), April 25, 1781.

48. Walpole to Rev. William Mason, June 14, 1781, *The Letters of Horace Walpole, Earl of Orford*, ed. Peter Cunningham, 9 vols. (London: Henry G. Bohn, 1861), 8:53; Sharpe to Gen. William Lee Davidson, November 9, 1780, *Cornwallis Papers*, 4:91; Greene to Cornwallis, March 8, 1781, ibid., 77.

49. Balfour to Cornwallis, June 22, 1781, *Cornwallis Papers*, 5:284; Borick, *Relieve Us*, 79; Service Record of Capt. Robertson Duncanson, 71st Regiment of Foot, June 4, 1784, box 2, Schoff Revolutionary War Collection, CL-UM. See also Balfour to Cornwallis, June 22, 1781, *Cornwallis Papers*, 5:283.

50. *Royal South-Carolina Gazette* (Charleston), May 17, 1781; Greene to Cornwallis, August 26, 1781, *Cornwallis Papers*, 6:78; Borick, *Relieve Us*, 104–5; Cornwallis to Greene, September 15, 1781, *Cornwallis Papers*, 6:82; Muster Rolls of Captain Darby's Company of Light Infantry, 7th Regiment of Foot, WO 12/2475, TNA. See also Deposition of John Marks, June 9, 1781, Clinton Papers, vol. 158, fol. 31; and John D. Grainger, *The Battle of Yorktown, 1781: A Reassessment* (Woodbridge, UK: Boydell and Brewer, 2005), 31–32.

51. Greene to Andrew Pickens, June 5, 1781, *Greene Papers*, 8:350; William Pierce to St. George Tucker, July 20, 1781, Charles Washington Coleman Jr., ed., "Southern Campaign of General Greene, 1781–1782," *Magazine of American History* 7 (December 1881): 434; Journal of Lt. Enos Reeves, April 16, 1782, box 1, Enos Reeves Papers, Special Collections, Duke University, Durham, NC; "Extract of a letter from General Greene's camp," August 25, 1781, *New-Jersey Gazette* (Trenton), September 26, 1781. For further examples of violence directed toward British and loyalist prisoners of war after Cornwallis's decision to depart for Virginia, see Wade to Greene, April 4, 1781, *Greene Papers*, 8:53; and Emmet to Greene, April 9, 1781, ibid., 8:74. For loyalist retaliation, see ibid., 74n3. For an example of a senior American officer's justification of prisoner abuse as retribution for the "barbarous massacres" committed by the British, see Andrew Pickens to Greene, April 8, 1781, *Greene Papers*, 8:70–72. See also Pickens to Greene, June 7, 1781, ibid., 359. For official British retaliation, see "Balfour to the prisoners aboard the Torbay prison ship in Charlestown Harbor," *Worcester (MA) Gazette*, July 26, 1781.

52. Edward G. Lengel, *General George Washington: A Military Life* (New York: Random House, 2005), 335–44; Morrill, *Southern Campaigns*, 171–84; Grainger, *Battle of Yorktown*, 93–149; Cornwallis to Washington, October 17, 1781, *Cornwallis Papers*, 6:112; Washington to Cornwallis, October 17, 1781, ibid., 113.

53. Washington to Cornwallis, October 18, 1781, *Cornwallis Papers*, 6:114; Articles of Capitulation, October 19, 1781, ibid., 119; Stephan Popp, *A Hessian Soldier in the American Revolution: The Diary of Stephan Popp*, trans. Reinhart J. Pope (Private printing, 1953), 25. These generous terms did not apply to former slaves captured with Cornwallis's army. They were re-enslaved. "A Negro Man named BILL" who was "taken at the capture of Cornwallis" appears to have escaped his master by "endeavor[ing] to get into New-York." *Connecticut Courant*, February 18, 1783.

54. James Thacher, *Military Journal of the American Revolution . . .* (Hartford, CT: Hurlbut, Williams, 1862), 289, 290; Ewald, *Diary*, 339. There is some dispute about the total number of prisoners surrendered at Yorktown. Thomas Durie, the deputy commissary of prisoners with

Washington's army, submitted his "General Return of Officers and Privates Taken Prisoner" on October 19. He claimed that there were 7,171 captives, not including the naval prisoners (who, according to the articles of capitulation, were claimed by the French). Another return by Durie, enclosed in Washington's letter to Congress of October 27, lists 6,935 land prisoners plus the 2,000 seamen turned over to the French. The list also counted 80 "followers of the army." See [George Washington], "[Diary entry: 20 October 1781]," n. 1, *Founders Online*.

55. Ewald, *Diary*, 342; Samuel Graham, *Memoir of General Graham* . . . , ed. James J. Graham (Edinburgh: R. and R. Clark, 1862), 64–65.

56. Marinus Willett to Washington, July 6, 1781, *Founders Online*; Ewald, *Diary*, 342; Thacher, *Military Journal*, 292; Abbé Claude Robin, *New Travels Through North-America* . . . (Philadelphia: Robert Bell, 1783), 65; Journal of Col. Daniel Trabue, in *Colonial Men and Times* . . . , ed. Lillie DuPuy VanCulin Harper (Philadelphia: Innes & Sons, 1916), 115; Johann Conrad Döhla, *A Hessian Diary of the American Revolution*, trans. Bruce E. Burgoyne (Norman: University of Oklahoma Press, 1990), 178.

57. Boudinot to William Livingston, October 24, 1781, *LDC*, 18:163; Jonathan Trumbull to the President of Congress, April 24, 1782, PCC, item 66, 2:225, 226; Washington to Greene, December 15, 1781, *Founders Online*; Tench Tilghman to Washington, October 27, 1781, ibid. In his petition to Congress, Connecticut governor Trumbull summarized the sentiments of several of his constituents, who demanded retaliation for the mistreatment of their friend in a British prison. For their petition to Trumbull, see PCC, item 66, 2:228–29. Edmund Randolph, Elias Boudinot, and Daniel Carroll served on the investigatory committee. See Tench Tilghman to Washington, October 27, 1781, *Founders Online*.

58. Middleton to Burke, n.d. [November 1781], *LDC*, 18:221; *JCC*, 21:1080; Tench Tilghman to Washington, October 27, 1781, *Founders Online*; John Mathews to Greene, October 22, 1781, *LDC*, 18:154.

59. *Newport (RI) Mercury*, December 1, 1781; *Pennsylvania Packet* (Philadelphia), September 6, 1781; *Independent Chronicle* (Boston), November 29, 1781; *Freeman's Journal* (Portsmouth, NH), November 7, 1781. At least one columnist argued that generosity, not vengeance, should characterize the American response to "the barbarous Cornwallis." *Connecticut Gazette* (New London), December 7, 1781.

60. Lamb, *British Soldier's Story*, 93; Journal of Lt. Enos Reeves, November 4, 1781, box 1, Reeves Papers. On the prisoners' fear of retaliation, see *Memoir des Corporal Justus Eggertt vom Bayreuther Regiment, Brandenburg-Ansbach-Bayreuth*, quoted in Daniel Krebs, "Approaching the Enemy: German Captives in the American War of Independence, 1776–1783" (Ph.D. diss., Emory University, 2007), 353.

61. "Petition and Memorial of the burgesses and inhabitants of Lancaster to the President & Supreme Executive Council of the Commonwealth of Pennsylvania," July 14, 1781, ser. 2, box 7, Jasper Yeates Papers, Collection 740, HSP; Washington to Abraham Skinner, October 25, 1781, *Founders Online*; *JCC*, 21:1073–74.

62. Edward M. Riley, ed., "St. George Tucker's Journal of the Siege of Yorktown, 1781," *William and Mary Quarterly*, 3rd ser., 5, no. 3 (July 1948): 394; James Linwood Carpenter, Jr., "The Yorktown Prisoners: A Narrative Account of the Disposition of the British Army Which Capitulated at Yorktown, October 19, 1781" (M.A. thesis, College of William and Mary, 1950), 7; Döhla, *Hessian Diary*, 183; Graham, *Memoir*, 66.

63. Popp, *Hessian Soldier*, 30; Döhla, *Hessian Diary*, 184, 188.

64. Berthold Koch, *The Battle of Guilford Courthouse and the Siege and Surrender at Yorktown*, trans. and ed. Bruce E. Burgoyne (Bowie, MD: Heritage Books, 2002), 23; *Royal Gazette* (New York), March 30, 1782.

65. Popp, *Hessian Soldier*, 31; Bruce E. Burgoyne, trans. and ed., *A Hessian Officer's Diary of the American Revolution: Translated from an Anonymous Ansbach-Bayreuth Diary ... and the Prechtel Diary* (Bowie, MD: Heritage Books, 2008), 230–31; Döhla, *Hessian Diary*, 189.

66. Holmes to Nelson, October 26, 1781, *CVSP*, 2:569–70; Holmes to Col. William Davies, November 6, 1781, *CVSP*, 2:579; Shaw, *John Robert Shaw*, 45.

67. Döhla, *Hessian Diary*, 190; Popp, *Hessian Soldier*, 31.

68. Davies to Holmes, December 17, 1781, Virginia Board of War Letterbook, misc. reel 632, Library of Virginia, Richmond; "Extract from M. Clairborne's letter to Pickering dated at Richmond December 24, 1781," enclosed in Pickering to Washington, January 17, 1782, *Founders Online*. For Congress's distressed financial situation in 1781, see E. Wayne Carp, *To Starve the Army at Pleasure: Continental Army Administration and American Political Culture, 1775–1783* (Chapel Hill: University of North Carolina Press, 1984), chap. 7.

69. Döhla, *Hessian Diary*, 192–93; Burgoyne, *Hessian Officer's Diary*, 233.

70. Graham to Morgan, November 22, 1781, enclosed in Morgan to Washington, November 25, 1781, *Founders Online*; Graham, *Memoir*, 68.

71. Morgan to Graham, November 28, 1781, Graham, *Memoir*, 69; Morgan to Washington, November 25, 1781, *Founders Online*; "Extract from Major Claiborne's letter of December 23, 1781," enclosed in Timothy Pickering to George Washington, January 17, 1782, ibid. Washington thanked Morgan for "the trouble you had taken with the prisoners of War" but gently chided him for overstepping his bounds. Washington to Morgan, December 12, 1781, ibid.

72. Council of Maryland to George Murdock, November 2, 1781, *Archives of Maryland*, 99 vols. (Baltimore: Maryland Historical Society, 1883–2000), 45:659; Washington to Skinner, October 25, 1781, *Founders Online*; Skinner to Washington, November 23, 1781, ibid.; Council of Maryland to Col. Philip Thomas, November 2, 1781, *Archives of Maryland*, 45:659–60.

73. Andrew Krug, "'Such a Banditty You Never See Collected!': Frederick Town and the American Revolution," *Maryland Historical Magazine* 95 (2000): 15; Baker Johnson to Gov. Thomas Lee, February 17, 1780, *Archives of Maryland*, 47:74; Lamb, *British Soldier's Story*, 97–99; Fielder Gannt to Gov. Thomas Lee, February 1, 1780, *Archives of Maryland*, 47:46.

74. Lamb, *British Soldier's Story*, 97; Coote to Adj. Gen. Oliver De Lancey, November 4, 1781, Sir Eyre Coote Papers, CL-UM; Thomas Price to Governor Lee, November 23, 1781, *Archives of Maryland*, 47:555; Council of Maryland to Col. Philip Thomas, November 10, 1781, ibid., 45:665.

75. Captain Bayley to Coote, December 1, 1781, Coote Papers; Coote to Abraham Skinner, December 2, 1781, ibid.; Rawlings to Washington, December 2, 1781, *Founders Online*.

76. Council of Maryland to Robert Morris, December 14, 1781, *Archives of Maryland*, 48:24; Instruction to Virginia Delegates, November 29, 1781, *Founders Online*.

77. Instruction to Virginia Delegates, November 29, 1781, n. 1, *Founders Online*; *JCC*, 21:1164; Benjamin Lincoln to the County Lieutenant of Frederick, VA, December 12, 1781, *CVSP*, 2:653; Washington to Moses Rawlings, December 12, 1781, *Founders Online*; Washington to Cornwallis, October 18, 1781, ibid. For background on the formation of the office of secretary at war, see Lucille E. Horgan, *Forged in War: The Continental Congress and the Origin of Military Supply* (Westport, CT: Greenwood, 2002), 44–48. For more information on Congress's policy of treating German prisoners more generously than British captives, see Daniel Krebs, *A Generous and Merciful Enemy:*

Life for German Prisoners of War During the American Revolution (Norman: University of Oklahoma Press, 2013), 7–8, 143–55.

78. Holmes to Wood, January 24, 1782, "As Others Saw Us," *Tyler's Quarterly Historical and Genealogical Magazine* 3, no. 1 (July 1921): 13; Burgoyne, *Hessian Officer's Diary*, 234–35; Popp, *Hessian Soldier*, 31–32.

79. Shaw, *John Robert Shaw*, 46.

80. Popp, *Hessian Soldier*, 33; Koch, *Battle of Guilford Courthouse and the Siege and Surrender at Yorktown*, 24; Döhla, *Hessian Diary*, 201; Lamb, *British Soldier's Story*, 100–101; Graham, *Memoir*, 73.

81. Clinton to Washington, November 24, 1781, *Founders Online*; Clinton to Washington, January 25, 1781, ibid.; Clinton to Washington, February 11, 1782, ibid.; Washington to Clinton, February 26, 1782, ibid. See also *LDC*, 18:357n1.

82. Arthur Middleton, notes for a speech in Congress, February [23?], 1782, *LDC*, 18:355, 357.

83. Washington to John Hanson, February 20, 1782, *Founders Online*. For the actual resolve that authorized Washington to engage in negotiations for a general cartel of exchange but was not to be "construed to authorize the exchange of Lieutenant General Cornwallis by composition," see *JCC*, 22:776–77.

84. Washington to Skinner, December 5, 1781, *Founders Online*; Skinner to Washington, February 18, 1782, ibid.; Washington to John Laurens, April 22, 1782, ibid.

85. "Motion of Mr. Williamson," PCC, item 19, 3:457; *JCC*, 22:93–94.

86. *JCC*, 22:95; Washington to Henry Knox, March 11, 1782, *Founders Online*. In the end, Lord Cornwallis's exchange was only arranged as part of the preliminary articles of peace in early January 1783. The British released Henry Laurens in March 1782, and Benjamin Franklin, acting independently in France, agreed to absolve the general's parole that June. Yet Congress did not officially agree to negotiate for the earl's exchange as part of the peace negotiations until November 26. *JCC*, 23:754. Even then some delegates, such as Hugh Williamson, John Rutledge, and James Duane, opposed the measure on the grounds that "Cornwallis had rendered himself so execrable by his barbarities." "Notes on Debates, 22 November 1782," *Founders Online*. See also "Franklin: Discharge of Cornwallis from His Parole, 9 June 1782," ibid.; *Correspondence of Charles, First Marquis Cornwallis*, ed. Charles Ross, 3 vols. (London: John Murray, 1859), 1:141–42; and Joseph J. Casino, "Elizabethtown 1782: The Prisoners-of-War Negotiations and the Pawns of War," *New Jersey History* 102, nos. 1–2 (1984): 1–35, esp. 12–18.

87. Carl Leopold Baurmeister, *Revolution in America: Confidential Letters and Journals, 1776–1784, of Adjutant General Major Baurmeister of the Hessian Forces*, ed. and trans. Bernhard A. Uhlendorf (New Brunswick, NJ: Rutgers University Press, 1957), 502; *Independent Chronicle* (Boston), May 9, 1782; John Covenhoven and other inhabitants of the county of Monmouth, New Jersey, to Washington, April 14, 1782, *Founders Online*. Reportedly, Monmouth residents had already detained a "capt. Tilton" for the purpose of retaliation. *Freeman's Journal* (Portsmouth, NH), April 17, 1782. For a recent interpretation of the "Asgill Affair," see Hoock, *Scars of Independence*, 335–57. For the most accurate account, see Shelia L. Skemp, *William Franklin: Son of a Patriot, Servant of a King* (New York: Oxford University Press, 1990), 256–66.

88. Washington to Clinton, April 21, 1782, *Founders Online*; Clinton to Washington, April 25, 1782, ibid.; Graham, *Memoir*, 80. See also *New-Jersey Gazette* (Trenton), April 24, 1782.

89. Washington to John Hanson, April 20, 1782, *Founders Online*; Washington to John Brooks, April 19, 1782, ibid.; Washington to Hazen, May 3, 1782, ibid. See also William M. Fowler, *American*

Crisis: George Washington and the Dangerous Two Years After Yorktown, 1781–1783 (New York: Walker, 2011), 64–65.

90. Article 14 of the Capitulation of Yorktown, *Cornwallis Papers*, 6:121; Washington to Lincoln, June 5, 1782, *Founders Online*; Livingston to Francis Dana, May 29, 1782, *The Revolutionary Diplomatic Correspondence of the United States*, ed. Francis Wharton, 6 vols. (Washington, DC: Government Printing Office, 1889), 5:447.

91. James Gordon to Washington, June 18, 1782, *Founders Online*; Graham, *Memoir*, 90; De Grasse to Benjamin Franklin, August 26, 1782, *Founders Online*; Lady Asgill to Vergennes, July 18, 1782, quoted in Graham, *Memoir*, 102; Vergennes to Washington, July 29, 1782, *Founders Online*; Sarah Knott, "Sensibility and the American War for Independence," *American Historical Review* 109, no. 1 (February 2004): 37.

92. Washington to James Duane, September 20, 1782, *Founders Online*; Washington to John Hanson, August 19, October 25, 1782, ibid.; James Duane to Washington, October 12, 1782, ibid.

93. *JCC*, 23:845–48 (for the actual resolution, see ibid., 719–20); James Madison to Edmund Randolph, November 5, 1782, *Founders Online*; Washington to Asgill, November 13, 1782, ibid.

94. *PRM*, 5:90; *JCC*, 22:321; "Extract of a letter from a farmer in Juniata County to a correspondent in Philadelphia," August 14, 1782, *Pennsylvania Packet* (Philadelphia), August 22, 1782. The editor of the *Pennsylvania Gazette* argued on pragmatic as well as ideological grounds to prevent the exchange of Cornwallis's troops. See *Pennsylvania Gazette* (Philadelphia), September 4, 1782.

95. *JCC*, 22:316–17; *PRM*, 5:557; Krebs, "Approaching the Enemy," 395; Hesse-Hanau sergeant Vaupel, quoted in ibid., 401; Prisoners of the Regiment von Knyphausen to Colonel von Borck, quoted in ibid., 399–400; "Translation of a Letter from Hessian Prisoners of War of the Regt. De Knyphausen in the Gaol at Philadelphia," July 28, 1782, British Headquarters Papers, reel 24, DLAR; Benjamin Lincoln to the President of Congress, September 13, 1782, PCC, item 149, 2:171.

96. *JCC*, 22:382; Baurmeister, *Revolution in America*, 518, 530, 569; Petition of Sgt. Samuel Caswell and six other prisoners to Henry Knox, October 9, 1782, Henry Knox Papers, reel 10, p. 43, MHS.

97. *JCC*, 24:251–52; Martha W. Dixon, "Divided Authority: The American Management of Prisoners in the Revolutionary War" (Ph.D. diss., University of Utah, 1977), 302–5; Döhla, *Hessian Diary*, 221.

98. Döhla, *Hessian Diary*, 221, 222; Popp, *Hessian Soldier*, 33.

99. "Agreement for Liberating British Prisoners, 19 April 1783," *Founders Online*; Krebs, *Generous and Merciful Enemy*, 248, table 8; Krebs, "Approaching the Enemy," 412. For the mortality rates on board British prison ships in New York, see Edwin Burrows, *Forgotten Patriots: The Untold Story of American Prisoners During the Revolutionary War* (New York: Basic Books, 2008), 200. For the mortality rate at British prisons in England, see Paul Gilje, *Liberty on the Waterfront: American Maritime Culture in the Age of Revolution* (Philadelphia: University of Pennsylvania Press, 2004), 119. For the calculations of the yearly mortality rate in Dutch prisons between 1781 and 1800, see Pieter Spierenburg, *The Prison Experience: Disciplinary Institutions and Their Inmates in Early Modern Europe* (New Brunswick, NJ: Rutgers University Press, 1991), 191.

100. Muster rolls of Capt. Duncan Cameron's, Maj. David Ferguson's, Capt. William Thorne's, and Lt. Col. James Marsh's companies of the 43rd Regiment of Foot, June 1781–June 1783, WO 12/5562, TNA; muster rolls of Capt. Alexander Arbuthnot's, Capt. George Cumine's, and Maj.

James Gordon's companies of the 8oth Regiment of Foot, June 1781–June 1783, WO 12/8454, ibid. The official mortality rate for Andersonville Prison was 28.1 percent, but some historians argue that it was higher. For example, Robert Scott Davis estimates that 31.5 percent is more realistic. Davis, *Ghosts and Shadows of Andersonville: Essays on the Secret Social Histories of America's Deadliest Prison* (Macon, GA: Mercer University Press, 2006), 30. Horrific mortality rates were not restricted to the prison camps in the interior of Pennsylvania. Take, for instance, the fate of the nineteen men of the 22nd Regiment of Foot captured at the Battle of Connecticut Farms on June 7, 1780. The soldiers were confined in Philadelphia's "New Goal" until the end of the war. Six of the men died while in American custody, yielding a mortality rate of 31.6 percent. Two additional soldiers perished within eight months of their release, raising the mortality rate to 42.1 percent. In his pension application, survivor Peter McQueen claimed to have suffered from "Bad Health being long a Prisoner," and John Reynolds was discharged for being "sickly and worn out." WO 120/12, TNA. I am indebted to Don Hagist for assistance with these muster rolls and pension applications.

Conclusion

1. "William B. Raber's Journal, 1847–1852," *Chronicle: Journal of the Historical Society of the Central Pennsylvania Conference of the United Methodist Church* 7 (Spring 1996): 12.

2. *South-Carolina Gazette and General Advertiser* (Charleston), May 24, December 16, 1783; Kariann Akemi Yokota, *Unbecoming British: How Revolutionary America Became a Post-Colonial Nation* (Oxford: Oxford University Press, 2011), 13, 62–114; Judith L. Van Buskirk, *Generous Enemies: Patriots and Loyalists in Revolutionary New York* (Philadelphia: University of Pennsylvania Press, 2002), 177, 181, 188–95; Robert M. Calhoon, "The Reintegration of the Loyalists and the Disaffected," in *Tory Insurgents: The Loyalist Perception and Other Essays*, ed. Robert M. Calhoon et al. (Columbia: University of South Carolina Press, 2010); Edwin Burrows, *Forgotten Patriots: The Untold Story of American Prisoners During the Revolutionary War* (New York: Basic Books, 2008), 208–9. See also Rebecca Brannon, *From Revolution to Reunion: The Reintegration of the South Carolina Loyalists* (Columbia: University of South Carolina Press, 2016); and Brett Palfreyman, "Peace Process: The Reintegration of the Loyalists in Post-Revolutionary America" (Ph.D. diss., Binghamton University, 2014). On elite fears of the Revolution unleashing an "excess of democracy," see Terry Bouton, *Taming Democracy: "The People," the Founders, and the Troubled Ending of the American Revolution* (Oxford: Oxford University Press, 2007); and Woody Holton, *Unruly Americans and the Origins of the Constitution* (New York: Hill and Wang, 2007).

3. J. Franklin Jameson, *The American Revolution Considered as a Social Movement* (Princeton, NJ: Princeton University Press, 1926), 9; *The Constitution of the United States, as recommended to Congress the 17th September, 1787* (Portsmouth, [NH]: John Melcher, 1789), 16–17. Although the Constitution made clear the national government's monopoly on war making, the division of power between the legislative and executive branches remained up for debate. See Jack N. Rakove, *Original Meanings: Politics and Ideas in the Making of the Constitution* (New York: Vintage Books, 1996), 263–64; and Charles A. Lofgren, "War-Making Under the Constitution: The Original Understanding," *Yale Law Journal* 81, no. 4 (1972): 672–702. On the "nationalization" of defense during the early republic, see Richard H. Kohn, *Eagle and Sword: The Federalists and the Creation of the Military Establishment in America, 1783–1802* (New York: Free Press, 1975).

4. "IV. Draft of a Model Treaty, 1784," *Founders Online*; Daniel Krebs, *A Generous and Merciful Enemy: Life for German Prisoners of War During the American Revolution* (Norman: University of Oklahoma Press, 2013), 268–70.

5. Krebs, *Generous and Merciful Enemy*, 270–71; "American Commissioners to De Thulemeier, with Observations on Treaty," November 10, 1784, *Founders Online*.

6. John Trumbull, *Autobiography, Reminiscences, and Letters of John Trumbull, from 1756 to 1841* (New York: Wiley and Putnam, 1841), 420. See also Irma B. Jaffe, *John Trumbull: Patriot-Artist of the American Revolution* (New York: New York Graphic Society, 1975).

7. Trumbull quoted in Elisa Tamarkin, *Anglophilia: Deference, Devotion, and Antebellum America* (Chicago: University of Chicago Press, 2008), 134; Sam Forman, *Dr. Joseph Warren: The Boston Tea Party, Bunker Hill, and the Birth of American Liberty* (Gretna, LA: Pelican, 2012), 303–4.

8. David Ramsay, *The History of the American Revolution*, 2 vols. (Trenton, NJ: James J. Wilson, 1811), 2:43, 54, 76.

9. Ibid., 2:55, 359, 364, 365.

10. Ibid., 2:366.

11. *National Aegis* (Worcester, MA), April 8, 1807; *New-Hampshire Gazette* (Portsmouth), March 31, 1807; *Public Advertiser* (New York), May 6, 1807. See also Burrows, *Forgotten Patriots*, 212–16. On how nineteenth-century Americans effaced the violence of the war from their narratives of the Revolution, see Holger Hoock, *Scars of Independence: America's Violent Birth* (New York: Crown, 2017), 389–408.

12. Pension Application of William Gipson, S17437, transcribed by Will Graves, Southern Campaigns Revolutionary War Pension Statements & Rosters, http://revwarapps.org/s17437.pdf (last updated August 29, 2015); John Robert Shaw, *John Robert Shaw: An Autobiography of Thirty Years, 1777–1807*, ed. Oressa M. Teagarden and Jeanne L. Crabtree (Athens: Ohio University Press, 1992), 47.

Index

Abu Ghraib prison, 8

Adams, Abigail, 91, 133, 159

Adams, John, 91, 98, 99, 136, 138, 144, 159, 241

Adlum, John, 94

African Americans: Britain supported by, 2, 5, 110–11, 197; British promises of freedom for, 128, 197; fears of revolt by, 118, 178, 197; Hessian enlistment of, 128; owners concerned to keep, 192; as prisoners of war, 5, 111, 128–29

Ainslie, Thomas, 80

Albany Committee of Correspondence, 59

Alexander, William, 98

Allen, Ethan, 45, 47–48, 50–51, 54–55, 58, 73–76, 80, 98, 132, 133, 170

America: concerns about legitimacy of, 9, 13, 40, 46, 52, 59, 69, 85, 90, 123, 157, 160, 165–66; independence of, 89; internecine struggles in, 4, 5, 10, 11, 91–92, 109, 122–23, 190, 199–213, 246–47; national monopoly on violence in, 4, 6, 11, 186, 241. *See also* colonial America

American Journal (newspaper), 194

American prisoners of war: attitudes toward, 12; in Charleston, 198, 211; deaths of, 4, 105–6, 135, 237, 247, 254n7; diseases experienced by, 87–88, 106, 134–35, 198; food provided for, 79, 84, 87–88, 102–3; Native Americans' treatment of, 82–84; in New York, 94–109; numbers of, 4, 39, 96, 106; officers among, 42–43, 45, 79, 102, 187; plundering of, 95; recruitment of, 80; release of, 134–35; treatment of, 1–3, 10, 12–13, 42–43, 45, 50–51, 54, 79–84, 87–88, 92, 94–96, 98–99, 102–9, 128, 131, 159–62,

177, 191–92, 208–9. *See also* prisoner exchange; prisoner management

Amherst, Jeffery, 32

Anburey, Thomas, 140, 147, 151, 152, 165, 170–76, 178–79, 182, 185, 292n93

Anderson, James, *Essay on the Art of War*, 29–30

André, John, 73, 232

Aquinas, Thomas, 260n18

aristocracy, 15, 17–21

Armstrong, Martin, 203–4

Arnold, Benedict, 47, 54, 57, 78–82, 84–88, 145

Asgill, Charles, 232–34

Asgill Affair, 231–34

Atlee, Samuel, 102, 104

Atlee, William, 182

Augustine, Saint, 21, 260n18

Aylett, William, 174

Balfour, Nisbet, 198, 207, 209–10, 212

Barrington, Lord, 30, 39, 99

Baurmeister, Carl Leopold, 236

bayonets, 94

Beatty, John, 162–63

Bedel, Timothy, 81–82

Bennington, Battle of, 163

Bense, Johann, 151, 174, 183, 185

Biddle, Clement, 126

Black Dragoons, 197

Bland, Theodorick, 175

Blarenberghe, Louis-Nicolas Van, *The Taking of Yorktown Virginia, October 19, 1781, Surrender and Parade* (detail), 215

Board of Associated Loyalists, 231–32

Board of War (Congress), 99, 105, 130–31, 135,
   157, 174, 181, 183, 184
Board of War (North Carolina), 189, 204
Board of War (Virginia), 222
Boston, housing of Convention Army near,
   148–54
Boston Evening-Post (newspaper), 190
Boston Gazette (newspaper), 42
Boudinot, Elias, 9, 92, 108, 130–32, 162–63,
   216–17
Bowen, Charles, 200
Boyer, H., 194
Braddock, Edward, 12, 30, 33
Breen, T. H., 7, 110
Brewer, Elisabeth, 119
Britain: attitudes toward the American
   rebellion, 41; militias in, 27; and rules
   of war, 1–2, 4, 25–26; and Seven Years'
   War, 29–33; suppression of rebellion in,
   23–25
British Army: accused of depredations and
   violating rules of war, 1–2, 36–37, 46,
   82–83, 86, 88–92, 94–95, 108–9, 145–46,
   159, 178, 186, 193–95, 197, 199–200, 216,
   246–48; African American auxiliaries of,
   2, 5, 110–11, 197; colonists' admiration for,
   29–30; inability of, to restrain Native
   Americans, 82–83, 86, 88, 90, 145–46;
   loyalists' appeals to, 96; Native American auxiliaries of, 5, 81–89; prisoner
   management by, 96; provisioning of, 96,
   103. *See also* British prisoners of war
British Legion, 193–94, 202
British prisoners of war: absence of scholarship on, 8; attitudes toward, 10, 71–74;
   dangers posed by, 65, 72, 130; deaths of,
   247; early in Revolutionary War, 37–39;
   employment of, 58, 100, 101; families of,
   67–68; lack of plans for, 38; numbers of, 3,
   39; officers among, 49, 58, 60–61, 69–71,
   76–77, 135–36; plundering of, 56; recruitment of, 69–70, 77, 105; treatment of, 2–3,
   5, 8–10, 43–44, 46, 49–50, 53, 57–78,
   68–69, 73, 92, 127–30, 160, 162–64, 190,
   208, 227, 235–36. *See also* Convention

Army; prisoner exchange; prisoner man-
   agement; Yorktown prisoners
Brooklyn, Battle of, 93–94
Browne, Montfort, 98
Brown, John, 48
Brown, Richard, 167–68
Brown, Thomas, 208–9
Buford, Abraham, 194
Bunker Hill, Battle of, 42, 44
Burgoyne, John, 87–88, 139–74, 177, 186, 190–
   91, 205, 246
Burke, Aedanus, 217
Burke, Thomas, 194
Burrows, Edwin, 103, 106, 254n7, 276n25
Butterfield, Isaac, 82

Camden, Battle of, 197
Campbell, Archibald, 134–36, 170
Campbell, James, 121
Campbell, William, 201
Canada: invasion of, 47–57, 78–90; Native
   Americans in, 81–89; prisoners from invasion of, 57–78
capitulation, terms of, 52–53, 56, 69–70, 82,
   140
Caribbean colonies, 196. *See also* West Indies
Carl, J. H., *Drittes Regiment Garde*, 129
Carleton, Guy, 50–52, 54, 73–74, 78–81,
   87–88, 235
Carroll, John, 82
cartels, for prisoner exchange: American
   offers of, 62–63; American refusal of, 6,
   177, 184; in British conflicts with France
   and Spain, 96; British refusal of, 60, 67,
   97; defined, 16; in early modern Europe,
   16; in Revolutionary War, 59, 84–86; uses
   and value of, 16, 29, 96; violation of, 86, 88,
   273n97
Cayton, Andrew, 253n6
Cedars, 81–89
Chambers, Rowland, 105
Charles I, King, 27
Charles XII, King, 133
Charleston, South Carolina, 187–88, 190–98,
   211, 234

Chase, Jonathan, 170

Chesney, Alexander, 200–202

Chet, Guy, 253n5

Christianity, 20, 37, 57, 65, 74, 81, 120, 227, 235, 260n18

civil war: nature of, 123; revolutionary struggle as, 4, 5, 10, 11, 91–92, 109, 122–23, 199–213, 246–47; in the South, 190

Claiborne, Richard, 222

Clarke, Elijah, 206

Clarke, Jonathan, 171

Clemmons, John, 206

Cleveland, Benjamin, 203, 206

Clinton, George, 118, 160

Clinton, Henry, 113, 119, 167, 171, 172, 177, 180, 183, 184, 187–99, 207, 211, 213, 229, 232, 235, 238

Cohen, Sheldon, 106

Colefox, Robert, 105

colonial America: British army as model for colonial forces, 29–30; French colonial adversaries in, 29–33; militias in, 27–28, 37–38, 42; Native American adversaries in, 28, 33; warfare in, 26–35

commissary of prisoners, 9, 16, 63, 66–67, 78, 87, 92, 96, 99, 101, 130–31, 162, 174, 179, 221, 223

Commission for Sick and Hurt Seamen and the Exchange of Prisoners (Britain), 96

Committee of Safety (Connecticut), 59, 60–62

Committee of Safety (Massachusetts), 38

Committee of Safety (New York), 118

Committee of Safety (Philadelphia), 127–28

Committee of Safety (Virginia), 111

committees/councils of safety, 62, 64–65, 66, 73, 99, 100–101, 110, 112, 170

Concord. See Lexington and Concord, Battles of

Congress. See Continental Congress

Connecticut: housing of prisoners in, 53–54, 57–64; loyalists in, 114–15, 119–20; prisoner exchanges arranged by, 101; treason in, 114–15, 119–20

Connecticut Gazette (newspaper), 75

consensus school of historiography, 7, 255n10

Constitution (1787), 11, 241

consumption, 222

Continental Congress: British mistreatment of American prisoners blamed on, 104–9; on Burgoyne's surrender and his character, 143–44, 155–58; criminalization of loyalists by, 114; currency of, 148, 166, 221–22; financial difficulties of, 222; and independence, 89; oversight of war by, 35, 46; and prisoner exchanges, 62, 97, 99–101, 136–37, 169–70, 177, 184, 190, 198, 205, 211, 229–31, 275n17; prisoner management by, 6, 46, 58, 62–78, 99, 130; and prisoners' treatment, 1, 75–77, 88–89; retaliatory actions of, 140, 142, 154–71, 177, 184, 186, 190, 210, 231, 233–36, 238; states' independence from, 108; and treason, 114; on Yorktown surrender, 216–17

Convention Army: appearance/clothing of, 150, 172–73, 185; attitudes toward, 150–51, 162, 168, 170, 177–78; behavior of, 162, 168, 180; British plot to free, 158–59; congressional resolution on, 154–71; dangers posed by, 149–50, 168; deaths of, 162, 167–68, 176, 182–83, 290n69; diseases experienced by, 140, 151, 163, 168, 176, 182–83; escapes/desertions from, 154, 166, 173, 185, 290n69; factors in treatment of, 142; food provided for, 147, 151, 152, 174–76, 179–84; housing of, 148–54; money and resources for sustaining, 142, 148–49, 151–53, 166–67, 169, 170, 171, 174–75, 177–84; numbers of, 140, 173, 176, 182, 184–85, 284n4, 290n69; officers of, 148–53, 175, 178–80; prospects of exchange for, 142, 158–59, 169–71, 177, 178, 184, 188, 191, 198, 205; regimental colors of, 155–56; relocations/marches of, 147–48, 170–85; symbolic value of, for Continental Congress, 177, 184, 205; tensions with American captors, 161–62, 164, 166–68; terms of surrender for, 140, 146; treatment of, 140, 146–47, 170–71, 173–83; wartime conditions experienced by, 147

Convention of Saratoga, 10, 140, 144, 149, 152, 154, 157–60, 165, 167, 170–72, 181, 186

conventions (agreements for suspension of hostilities), 19, 52, 140

Conway, Stephen, 25–26

Cooper, Samuel, 144–45

Coote, Eyre, 225

Cornwallis, Charles, 2nd Earl, 190, 192, 195–218, 223–24, 226, 228–31, 233, 237, 301n86

Council of Safety (New York), 121, 146

Council of Safety (Pennsylvania), 126

councils of safety. *See* committees/councils of safety

Cowpens, Battle of, 210

Cox, Cornelius, 130

Cramahé, Hector, 54, 79

Cross, Ralph, 144

Cruger, John Harris, 199

Cruise, Walter, 42

Cumberland, William Augustus, Duke of, 24, 41, 146

currency: Continental, 148, 166, 221–22; hard, 171, 219, 221, 226

Dandridge, Danske, 276n25

Davidson, John, 208

Davies, William, 222

Dearborn, Henry, 144

deaths: of American prisoners, 4, 105–6, 135, 237, 247, 254n7; of Convention Army, 162, 167–68, 176, 182–83, 290n69; of loyalist prisoners, 115, 201–2, 247; of Union prisoners in American Civil War, 238; of Yorktown prisoners, 222, 227, 236–38, 302n100

Declaration of Independence, 1, 89, 93, 209

Dederer, John Morgan, 27, 253n5

De Haas, John, 85–87

De Lancey, Oliver, 117

Democratic-Republicans, 247

Denmark, 242–43

Dewees, Thomas, 112

Dieskau, Jean-Armand, baron de, 30

Digby, William, 147

disease: American prisoners' experience of, 87–88, 106, 134–35, 198; Convention Army's experience of, 140, 151, 163, 168, 176, 182–83; prison ships as sites for, 120, 163, 198, 210; Yorktown prisoners' experience of, 220, 222, 240. *See also* consumption; smallpox; typhus

Döhla, Johann Conrad, 219–22, 228, 236–37

Duane, James, 233–34

Dubois, Peter, 119

Dumont, Egbert, 64

Dunbar, Moses, 119–20

Dunmore, John Murray, 4th Earl, 110–11, 178, 197

Dyer, Henry, 207

Edes, Benjamin, 42

Edes, Peter, 42

English Bill of Rights, 115

English Civil Wars, 23

Enlightenment, 20, 26, 260

enslaved Africans. *See* African Americans

Ewald, Johann, 30, 185, 193, 216

Fanning, David, 208

Fayssoux, Peter, 191–92

Ferguson, Patrick, 195, 199–200

Finnie, William, 175

Fischer, David Hackett, 9

Fisher, Sara, 124

Fleet Prison, 120–21

food: for American prisoners, 79, 84, 87–88, 102–3; for Convention Army, 147, 151, 152, 174–76, 179–84; for German prisoners, 126, 147; for loyalist prisoners, 121, 201; for Yorktown prisoners, 219, 221–22, 225

Forbes, John, 33

Forster, George, 82–88

Forsyth, Robert, 179

Fort Chambly, 48–49, 51

Fort Frederick, 180, 223–24

Fort Independence, 149

Fort Saint John's, 48–49, 51–53

Fort Ticonderoga, 45

Fort Washington, 93–95, 118, 144, 146

Fox, George, 174, 176, 182, 185

France: as American ally in war, 190, 191, 196, 213, 216, 233–34, 238; colonization in North America, 28–33, 263n40

Franklin, Benjamin, 73, 301n86

Franks, David, 66–68, 77, 104

Frederick the Great, 70

Freeman's Journal (newspaper), 218

French, Christopher, 60–62, 71, 99, 114

French and Indian War. *See* Seven Years' War

French Revolution, 6–7, 123

Frish, Will, 120

Gage, Thomas, 12–13, 36–37, 39–43, 47, 60, 123, 276n23

Gansevoort, Leonard, 118

Gaspé (ship), 45, 50

Gates, Horatio, 139–56, 160, 164, 176–77, 197, 201, 204, 246

genocide, 24

George II, King, 24

George III, King, 6, 89, 98

Gerald, James Fill, 168

Germain, George, Lord, 63, 96, 137, 177, 184, 188, 191, 192

German prisoners of war: attitudes toward, 125, 150; employment of, 127, 179; escapes/desertions of, 173 237; mortality rates of, 176, 237; numbers of, 123, 173; prospects of exchange for, 158; recruitment of, 125–26, 226, 235; regimental colors of, 155; surrender of, 214; treatment of, 124–27, 130, 135–36, 147, 151–52, 172–73, 176, 179–80, 183–85, 226, 227

Gerry, Elbridge, 98, 114

Gilbert, George, 168

Gipson, William, 248

Gist, William, 203

Glorious Revolution (1688), 23, 27

Glover, John, 154

Gordon, James, 233

Gordon, William, 39

Gould, Edward, 38

Graham, Samuel, 216, 219, 222–23, 228

Grasse, François, comte de, 233

Great Bridge, Battle of, 110

Greene, Nathanael, 102, 113, 136, 190, 205–6, 209–13, 224, 234

Grosvenor (ship), 105

Grotius, Hugo, 20, 261n21

Gruber, Ira, 261n21, 264n45

Guantanamo Bay detention camp, 8

Guibert Jacques de, 25

Hall, Moses, 189

Haller, Henry, 65

Hamilton, Alexander, 10, 26, 145, 160, 241

Hamilton, Henry, 175

Hamilton, James, 180

Hancock, John, 38, 57, 63, 64, 67–70, 80, 99, 100, 124, 133, 136, 148

Hanson, John, 230

Harrison, Henry, 136–37

Hartley, Thomas, 106

Harvard College, 168

Harvie, John, 174

Hawley, Joseph, 114

Hayne, Isaac, 211, 218, 233–34

Hazen, Moses, 232–33

Heath, William, 39, 149–55, 158, 161–62, 164–73, 176–77, 207–8

Henley, David, 161–62, 164–65

Henry, Patrick, 175, 179

Henry, Samuel, 128

Hessians, 123–37; appearance of, 124, 126; attitudes toward, 124–26; fearsome reputation of, 94, 104, 124–25; in war, 93–94. *See also* German prisoners of war

Hickey, Thomas, 113–14

Hill, William, 202

historiography, of American Revolution, 6–8, 11, 246–47

Holmes, Joseph, 221–24, 226–27

Home, W., 73

honor, 15, 17–21, 32–33

honors of war, 18, 32–33, 94, 139–40, 214

Hoock, Holger, 257n14

Hopkins, Esek, 98
Houston, William, 95
Howe, Richard, 1st Earl, 138
Howe, William, 60, 62, 63, 74, 93–109, 117,
    120, 123, 125, 132–37, 158–59, 161, 166, 167,
    169, 171, 187–89, 276n23
Hubley, Adam, 182
Huddy, Joshua, 231–33
Hughes, Joseph, 200
Hughes, Thomas, 163
humanitarianism, 21–22, 26, 29, 33, 244
Huntington, Edward, 115
Huntington, Samuel, 29, 205, 210

Iliff, James, 119
indentured servitude, for German prisoners,
    235
Independent Chronicle (newspaper), 124, 218
indigenous populations, deemed outside
    rules of war, 22–23. See also Native
    Americans
Innes, Alexander, 193
internment sites, map of, x

Jacobite Rebellion (1745–46), 23–25, 41
James II, King, 27
Jameson, J. Franklin, 241
Jay, John, 2
Jefferson, Thomas, 1–4, 5, 37, 89, 93, 173–75,
    179–81, 241–42
Jersey (ship), 4, 106, 107, 229
Johnson, Samuel, 22
Johnson, Uzal, 200–203
Johnson, William, 30, 32
Jones, Ephraim, 39
Jones, Thomas, 121, 134
Judd, William, 112
jus ad bellum, 20
jus in bello, 20

Kemble, Stephen, 94–95
Kennedy, Archibald, 119
King, Alexander, 173
Kings Mountain, Battle of, 200

Knox, Henry, 10, 26, 231, 235, 236
Knyphausen, Wilhelm von, 191
Koch, Berthold, 220, 227–28
Korn, Johann Georg, 222
Kulikoff, Allan, 8

Lamb, Roger, 150, 166, 172, 173, 218, 224, 228
Lantman (loyalist), 207, 297n41
Laurens, Henry, 143, 145, 146, 153–61, 164,
    166, 168, 172, 188, 229–31, 301n86
Laurens, John, 160, 188, 230
Lawson, Robert, 219
Leach, John, 42
Lee, Charles, 102, 132–37, 170
Lee, Henry, 208
Lee, Richard Henry, 145, 157
Lee, Thomas Sim, 180
Lee, Wayne, 12, 13–14, 189, 261n21
Lee, William Raymond, 152
Lemisch, Jesse, 7
Lexington and Concord, Battles of, 35–41, 44
lex talionis, 22, 51, 136, 159. See also propor-
    tional retaliation
Lincoln, Benjamin, 187–88, 190, 214, 226,
    232–33, 235, 237
Lippincott, Richard, 231–32
Livingston, Robert, 233
Livingston, William, 105, 109, 117, 119, 159–60
Loring, Joshua, 96, 131, 134, 230
Lovell, James, 42, 98
Lovell, John, 110, 124
loyalist prisoners: deaths of, 115, 201–2, 247;
    escapes of, 202–3; food provided for, 121,
    201; officers among, 111; recruitment of,
    203; treatment of, 111–12, 114–15, 119–21,
    200–203
loyalists, 109–23; armed resistance of, 110–11,
    117–19; attitudes toward, 5, 10, 37, 92, 110,
    113, 118, 121; in colonial America, 112–13;
    depredations committed by, 118, 122, 189,
    208–9, 231; execution of, 114, 119–23, 189,
    201–2, 206–8, 281n59; prevalence of,
    277n36; recruitment of, 113; rise of, 92; in
    the South, 113, 192–93; suspected plots of,

113–14, 118–19, 121–22; treason imputed to, 5, 113–23, 169, 201, 209; vengeance sought by, 192–93, 199, 231, 246; violence against, 5, 37, 109–10, 206–8, 212, 246
Lynch, Charles, 206
Lynch's law (lynching), 206–7, 238

MacDonald, Donald, 98
Mackenzie, Frederick, 39, 95, 97, 102, 103–4
Magaw, Robert, 94
Marbury, Joseph, 205–6
Marion, Francis, 197, 205
Martin, Josiah, 110, 111
Maryland: housing of prisoners in, 179–81, 223–26; loyalists in, 121, 122
Maryland Council, 180
Massachusetts: early revolutionary fighting in, 36–41; housing of prisoners in, 148–73, 176; prisoner exchanges arranged by, 101
Massachusetts Assembly, 149, 286n18
Massachusetts Council, 134, 135, 152–54, 166, 169, 286n18
Massachusetts Provincial Congress, 39
Massachusetts Spy (newspaper), 36, 143, 194
Mathews, John, 217
Matthews, David, 113–14
McCrea, Jane, 146, 246
Mee, John, 119
Meichel, Georg, 222
mercenaries, 14
Mersereau, Joshua, 163, 166, 170, 176–77
Middleton, Arthur, 217, 229–31
Miles, Samuel, 102, 104, 105, 108–9
military revolution, 15–16, 25
militias: American, in the South, 188, 192–93, 195, 199; in Britain, 27; in colonial America, 27–28, 37–38, 42; depredations committed by, 200–204; of loyalists, 196, 208; parole granted to, 188, 192–93, 195; threats of violence against, 195, 199; vengeance sought by, 200–203, 206
Mills, Ambrose, 201, 204
Moncrief, Thomas, 40
Montcalm, Louis-Joseph, marquis de, 32

Montgomery, Richard, 11, 26, 47–57, 78–80, 101, 133
Montreal, Canada, 47–57, 87
Moore's Creek Bridge, Battle of, 111
Morgan, Daniel, 210, 222–23
Morris, Gouverneur, 231
Morris, Margaret, 119
Morris, Robert, 225, 235
Morton, John, 41–42
Moultrie, William, 191–92
mourning war, 83
Murdock, George, 223–24
musicians, 69, 128

Nash, Gary, 7
National Aegis (newspaper), 247
nationalists, 10–11
Native Americans: as British allies, 81–89; colonists' attacks on, 28, 33; as prisoners of war, 5, 254n8, 263n40; in Seven Years' War, 30, 32; uncontrollability of, 32, 82–83, 86, 88, 90, 145–46, 246; warfare customs of, 13–14, 28, 32, 82–84
Nelson, Thomas, 219, 221
Neo-Progressive historians, 7, 256n11
New-England Chronicle (newspaper), 75
Newgate Prison (Simsbury mines), Connecticut, 114–15, 116, 162
New-Hampshire Gazette (newspaper), 247
New Jersey: loyalists in, 118–19; treason in, 119; war in, 123
New-Jersey Gazette (newspaper), 159
New Jersey Volunteers, 117, 119, 120
Newsweek (magazine), 8
New York: American prisoners in, 94–109, 131–32; housing of prisoners in, 59; loyalists in, 117, 118, 120–21; treason in, 117
New York Campaign, 91–92, 137, 196
New-York Gazette (newspaper), 122
North, Frederick, Lord, 41
North Carolina: loyalists in, 111–12; Revolutionary War in, 199–211

Northern Army, 47–57, 78–90
Norwich Packet (newspaper), 40

Odell, Jonathan, 112
officers: education of, in colonial America,
30; education of, in Europe, 29; as prisoners of war, 14, 16, 18–20, 30, 32, 42–43, 45,
49, 58, 60–61, 69–71, 76–77, 79, 102, 111,
135–36, 148–53, 175, 178–80, 187, 214
O'Hara, Charles, 214

Parke, Andrew, 87
Parker, Jonas, 178
Parker, Timothy, 106, 108
Parks, George, 206
parole, for militias, 192–93
parole (word, promise): American officers'
experience of, 102, 105; breaking of, 196,
212; British officers' experience of, 49, 53,
58–60, 214; captors' violation of norms of,
42; commoner soldiers' ineligibility for,
59; loyalist officers granted, 111–12; for
militias, 195–96; norms of, 14, 18, 61, 77,
120; refusal to accept, 70; refusal to grant,
45, 120, 133–34
Paxton Boys, 33, 35
Peale, Charles Willson, *Colonel George Wash-
ington of the Virginia Regiment*, 34, 35
Peale, James, *Horatio Gates at Saratoga*, 140
Peckham, Howard H., 254n7
Peebles, John, 193
Pennsylvania: housing of prisoners in, 63–78,
181–85, 190, 219, 226–28, 236; loyalists in,
115, 120, 121–22; treason in, 115
Pennsylvania Evening Post (newspaper), 74, 108
Pennsylvania Executive Council, 219
Pennsylvania Packet (newspaper), 198, 218
Person, Thomas, 194
Peters, John, 37, 112
Peters, Richard, 130–31
Peters, Samuel, 114–15
Philipsburg Proclamation, 197
Phillips, William, 167–68, 170–72, 175, 177,
184, 214
Pickering, Timothy, 222
Piel, Jakob, 125–26, 135

Pierce, William, 212
Pierpont, Robert, 163
Pinker, Steven, 21
Pintard, Lewis, 131–32
Popp, Stephan, 214, 220, 222, 227, 237
Powell, Jeremiah, 148
Pownall, Thomas, 40
Prechtel, Johann, 220, 222, 227
Prescott, Richard, 45, 55, 59, 70, 74–76, 98, 170
Preston, Charles, 48–49, 52–54, 59
Price, Thomas, 225
prisoner exchange: in British conflicts with
France and Spain, 30, 32; Continental
Congress and, 62, 97, 99–101, 136–37, 169–
70, 177, 184, 190, 198, 205, 211, 229–31,
275n17; Convention Army as object of,
142, 158–59, 169–71, 177, 178, 184, 188, 191,
198, 205; early in Revolutionary War, 40;
in early modern Europe, 14–15; officers'
incentives for, 20; opposition to, 211; in
Southern war, 204–5, 210–12; state
involvement in, 6, 101; use and value of,
204; Washington and, 6, 60, 97–102, 132,
134–37, 159, 169–70, 177, 229–31, 275n17;
Yorktown prisoners as object of, 228–31.
See also cartels, for prisoner exchange
prisoner management: British Army and, 96;
of British prisoners captured in Canada,
58–78; Continental Congress and, 6, 46,
58, 62–78, 99, 130; costs of, 62; criticisms
of, 59; hardships of, 60–62, 69–71;
humane model of, 46; insufficient provisions for, 6, 58, 64–66; by states/local
authorities, 6, 77–78, 92, 99, 101, 128, 130–
31, 142; Washington and, 63, 67. *See also*
prisoner exchange
prisoners of war: African Americans as, 5, 111,
128–29; in early modern Europe, 14–22;
execution of, 10, 21–22, 23; founders' proposals for, 242; Native Americans as, 5,
263n40; Native Americans' treatment of,
28; negotiations concerning, 48–49; officers as, 14, 16, 18–20, 30, 32; rules on
treatment of, 1–2, 14–22, 29, 30, 33. *See also*
American prisoners of war; British prisoners of war; Convention Army; German

prisoners of war; loyalist prisoners; prisoner exchange; Yorktown prisoners
prison ships: American prisoners confined to, 105–8, 128, 137, 191, 198, 210, 229, 237, 247; British prisoners confined to, 162–64, 168, 177; conditions on, 106, 108, 120, 128, 163, 191, 198, 210, 237; loyalists confined to, 120–21
proportional retaliation: dangers of, 242, 246; *lex talionis* principle, 22, 51, 136, 159; rejection of, 158, 163, 186, 190, 202, 206; role of, in rules of war, 3, 22, 75, 79, 161, 231, 242. *See also* retribution; vengeance
provincial regulars, 30
Prussia, 243
Public Advertiser (newspaper), 247
Putnam, Israel, 36, 39, 40, 113, 162
Pyle, John, 208

Quebec, Canada, 54–55, 78–85
Queen's American Rangers, 117
Quin, Mary, 119

Raber, William, 240
Rall, Johann, 123, 244
Ramsay, David, 246–47
Ramsour's Mill, Battle of, 196
rangers, 28
Raphael, Ray, 7
Rawlings, Moses, 180, 225
rebellion: equated with treason, 23, 24, 55, 80; loyalism viewed as, 118, 121, 123; punishment for, 41–42, 45, 50, 55, 79; Revolutionary War as, 40–42; rules of war abrogated by, 25; violence as response to, 22–24, 41. *See also* revolutionaries
rebels. *See* revolutionaries
reciprocity, in prisoner treatment, 50, 61–62, 66
Reed, James, 38
Reed, Joseph, 42, 182–84
Republicans, 247, 248
resentment, 91
retaliation. *See* proportional retaliation; retribution; vengeance

retribution: American demands for, 3, 6, 9, 10, 46, 73, 75, 92, 137, 142, 146, 186, 204, 217, 232, 234, 238; army's use of, 51; Asgill Affair and, 232–34; congressional policy of seeking, 142, 238; cycles of, 208–9, 212–13; loyalist demands for, 137, 192–93; role of, in Southern culture, 189. *See also* proportional retaliation; vengeance
Reuber, Johannes, 125, 130
revenge. *See* vengeance
revolt. *See* rebellion
revolutionaries, disdain for and mistreatment of, 4, 41–43, 52, 54–55, 67, 79–80, 94–96, 97, 108. *See also* American prisoners of war; rebellion
Revolutionary War: as American civil war, 4, 5, 10, 11, 91–92, 109, 122–23, 190, 199–213, 246–47; British attitudes toward, 41; creation of national narrative of, 240–49; historiography of, 6–8, 11, 246–47; moderate and humanitarian conduct of, 41, 240–49; political aspects of, 8, 11; popular support for, as sole means of sustaining, 4, 61, 190; social aspects of, 7; violence of, 3–5, 7–8, 10–11, 189–239, 240–49
Rhode Island, prisoner exchanges arranged by, 101
Rice, George, 174
Rice, Jonathan, 163
Riedesel, Frederika von, 148, 155–56, 173, 176
Riedesel, Friedrich Adolf von, 148
Roberdeau, Daniel, 159
Robin, Claude, 216
Rochambeau, Jean Baptiste Donatien de Vimeur, comte de, 190, 213, 214, 217, 233, 238
Royal Gazette (newspaper), 204, 220
Royal Highland Emigrants, 80
Royster, Charles, 69
rules of war: Americans' attitudes toward, 1–3, 9, 11; British attitude toward, 1–2, 4, 25–26; constraints on, 22; Declaration of Independence on, 1, 89; European attitude toward, 9, 12; factors in disregard of, 4; historical development of, 14–26; social structure underpinning, 17–18, 21; Washington on, 12–13

Rutledge, Edward, 209
Rutledge, John, 202, 205

Saratoga Convention. *See* Convention of
    Saratoga
Saxe, Maurice de, *Reveries*, 56
Schuyler, Philip, 46, 50–51, 53–58, 63, 69, 70,
    148
Scotland, 23–24
Scott, William, 184
Scottish Highlanders, 93–94
scurvy, 81, 87, 103, 151, 176, 179
Second Continental Congress. *See* Conti-
    nental Congress
Sedgwick, John, 71
sedition. *See* treason
Seven Years' War (1756–63), 3, 16, 22, 27,
    29–33, 35, 106
Seymour, Thomas, 60–61
Sharpe, William, 211
Shaw, John Robert, 221, 227, 249
Shelby, Isaac, 202
Shepardson, Zephaniah, 82, 86
Shepherd, Sarah, 121–22
Sherburne, Henry, 83–84
Shield, Benjamin, 183
Shippen, Edward, 33
Short, John, 115
Shuttleworth, John, 73
Shy, John, 8
siege warfare, 15
Skene, Philip, 60, 98
Skinner, Abraham, 223–25, 230
Skinner, Cortland, 117
Slade, William, 79–80, 102–3, 105–6
slavery. *See* African Americans
Slough, Matthias, 65
Small, John, 244
smallpox, 105, 132, 134, 150, 168, 198
Smallwood, William, 204–5
Smith, Josiah, 35–36
Smith, Nathaniel, 206–7
South: British strategies in, 188–99; loyalists
    in, 113; vengeance and violence in, 10,
    189–239

South Carolina, Revolutionary War in, 192–
    200, 217. *See also* Charleston, South
    Carolina
South-Carolina Gazette (newspaper), 240
Southern Army, 199, 224
Spain, 196
Sproat, David, 106
Stamp Act, 196
Stansbury, Joseph, 115
states: autonomy of, 108; prisoner exchanges
    arranged by, 6, 101; prisoner management
    by, 6, 92, 99, 128, 130–31, 142; treason laws
    of, 114–15, 169
St. Clair, Arthur, 69, 70
Stevens, Edward, 145
Stevenson, William, 202–3
Stockton, Richard, 120
Stopford, Joseph, 48–49, 70
Stuart, Prince Charles Edward, 24
Sullivan, John, 98
Sumter, Thomas, 196
swords, symbolic significance of, 18, 25, 53,
    61–62, 139, 188, 214

Tackett, Timothy, 7
Tarleton, Banastre, 193–94, 196–97, 200, 202,
    208, 210–11
Tarleton's Quarter, 197, 200, 210
Tate, Francis, 179
Taylor, John, 202–3
Terror (France), 6, 123
Thacher, James, 214
Thaxter, John, 159
Thomas, Philip, 224
Thompson, William, 177
Thulemeier, Friedrich Wilhelm von, 243
tories. *See* loyalists
torture, 5, 28, 83, 206, 207, 238, 248
treason: Continental Congress's legislation
    on, 114; Lee's actions viewed as, 133;
    loyalism viewed as, 5, 113–23, 169, 201,
    209; punishment for, 169 (*see also* loyal-
    ists, execution of); rebellion equated
    with, 12, 23, 24, 55, 80; state legislation
    on, 114–15

treaties, of America with other nations, 243

Treaty of Paris (1783), 10

Treaty of Westphalia (1648), 15

Trenton, Battle of, 123–24, 128

tribunals, 119, 201

Trumbull, John, 244, 248; *The Capture of the Hessians at Trenton*, 243, 244; *The Death of General Warren at the Battle of Bunker's Hill*, 244, 245

Trumbull, Jonathan, 53–54, 58, 62, 74, 101, 106, 132, 135, 169

Trumbull, Joseph, 152

Tryon, William, 117

Tuckerman, Isaac, 170

Turner, George, 198

Turpin de Crissé, Lancelot, *Essay on the Art of War*, 30

typhus, 105, 134, 168

unconditional surrender, 139, 144, 187, 213

Vattel, Emer de, 20–23, 25, 29, 35, 123, 153, 157, 236, 242, 260n18

Vaupel, Samuel, 184–85

vengeance: Americans' desire for, 4, 5, 9, 10, 37, 55–56, 90, 124–25, 137, 138, 142, 159–60, 162–63, 184, 186, 189–90, 216–18, 220, 224, 230, 232, 234–36, 246, 248; Continental Congress and, 156, 232, 234, 236; cycles of, 10, 11, 14, 23, 204, 210, 212–13, 234, 238, 242, 246; founders' desire to control, 241–42; Hessians as object of, 124–25; as justice, 75, 86–87, 125, 137, 142, 189, 192–93, 232; loyalists' desire for, 117–18, 192–93, 199, 231, 246; militias' desire for, 200–203, 206; Native Americans' practice of, 13–14; rejection of, 1–2, 22, 53, 62, 74, 91, 217, 232; resentment contrasted with, 91; retaliation contrasted with, 74; in Seven Years' War, 33; in the South, 10, 189–239; for treatment of prisoners, 43, 50–53, 73–76, 79, 86–87, 89, 134, 135, 159–60, 162–63, 198, 209, 216–18. See also *lex talionis*; proportional retaliation; retribution

Vergennes, comte de, 233–34

violence: in Anglo-American–Native American conflicts, 13–14; defining, 253n6; erasure of, from narrative of Revolutionary War, 240–41, 244; inability of revolutionary leaders to control, 4, 5–6, 241; against loyalists, 109–10, 119–22; national monopoly on, 4, 6, 11, 186, 241; of Revolutionary War, 3–5, 7–8, 10–11, 189–239, 240–49; in the South, 10, 189–239. See also vengeance

Virginia: housing of prisoners in, 171, 174–81, 219–23, 226–27; loyalists in, 110; Revolutionary War in, 2

vision of war, 3; early modern sources of, 14–26; founders' sketch of, 241–42; influences on, 9, 13, 25–26, 35; laypeople's, 73. See also warfare

volunteer soldiers: as provincial regulars, 30; as rangers, 28

Waddill, John, 206

Walcott, William, 136–37

Walker, Thomas, 76

Ward, Artemas, 149

warfare: Christian framework for, 260n18; "civilized" conduct of, 1, 10, 11, 13, 21, 25, 35, 43–44, 46, 56, 68–69, 87, 89–90, 92, 108, 115, 122, 142, 160, 185–86, 248; in colonial America, 26–35; in early modern Europe, 14–26; European vs. colonial American, 26–27; humane conduct of, 21–22, 57, 244; Native Americans' attitudes about, 13–14, 28, 32, 82–84; restraint as characteristic of, 1, 3, 11, 13, 18–19, 21, 22, 25, 32, 35, 37, 43, 46, 52, 87, 90, 92, 190, 200, 247, 258n5; "revolutionary" attitude toward, 3, 138, 142, 157, 186, 236, 248; "savage" conduct of, 2, 22, 32–33, 35–36, 43–44, 212. See also rules of war; vision of war

Warren, James, 168–69

Warren, Joseph, 11, 40, 244

Warren, Mercy Otis, 147, 148

Washington, George: and Asgill Affair, 232–34; attitude of, toward warfare, 13–14, 26,

Washington, George (*continued*)
33, 35, 92, 101, 122–23, 138, 190, 220, 241,
263n45; and Convention of Saratoga, 143,
145, 160–61; and Hessian prisoners, 125–
27; Lee's relationship with, 132–33; on
loyalists, 110; opposed to recruiting loyalists or the British, 203; portrait of, 34, 35;
and prisoner exchange, 6, 60, 97–102, 132,
134–37, 159, 169–70, 177, 229–31, 275n17;
and prisoner management, 63, 67, 130, 149,
152, 165, 223, 236; on prisoners' treatment,
2, 6, 12–13, 43, 61–63, 74, 104, 136, 161, 216–
17, 244; punishment of loyalists by, 115,
117, 118, 122–23; self-education of, in military matters, 30; in war, 47, 92, 93, 123–24,
148, 161, 213; and Yorktown prisoners,
213–17, 219, 226, 232–33
Washington, William, 208
Waters, Thomas, 208
Watson, Brook, 54
Watson, Robert, 276n25
Waxhaws, Battle of, 193–94
Wayne, Anthony, 178
Webb, Joseph, 104
Webb, Samuel, 145
Weedon, George, 126
Weldon, John, 195–96
West, Benjamin, 18, 19; *General Johnson Saving
a Wounded French Officer from the Toma-
hawk of a North American Indian*, 30, 31
West Indies, 128, 191, 204, 210. *See also* Carib-
bean colonies

Wethersfield Company, 40
Whitby (ship), 105–6
White, Philip, 231
Wilkinson, Eliza, 194–95
Wilkinson, James, 143–45, 160
Williams, Ezekiel, 58
Williams, Richards, 105
Williamson, Hugh, 231
Williamson's Plantation, Battle of, 196
Winthrop, Hannah, 148, 150, 152
Witherspoon, John, 157–58
Witt, John Fabian, 263n45
Wood, Gordon, 6–7
Wood, James, 179, 184, 226
Woodford, William, 111

yellow fever, 182
Yorktown, Battle of, 213
Yorktown prisoners, 213–38; attitudes
toward, 220–24, 227, 236; behavior of, 225;
deaths of, 222, 227, 236–38; depiction of
surrender ceremony, 215; diseases experienced by, 220, 222, 240; escapes of, 218,
219; food provided for, 219, 221–22, 225;
freedom of, 236–37; money and resources
for sustaining, 219, 221–24; numbers of,
214, 225, 237; officers of, 214, 222; prospects of exchange for, 228–31; relocations/
marches of, 219–20, 226; treatment of,
213–18, 220–29, 235–36
Young, Alfred, 7
Young, Samuel, 95

Acknowledgments

I always read the acknowledgments. They are an unrivaled window onto the scholarly process. By giving thanks, an author explicitly diagrams the intellectual network and support system that shaped the preceding pages. Much can be gleaned from a close reading of this seemingly perfunctory piece of prose. Perhaps more important, they are very often a delight to read. With the trials of writing in the past, an author's acknowledgments abound with joy and gratitude. It is my hope that my words of appreciation not only inform the reader of how this project came to be but also convey in some small measure the honor and pleasure it has been to call the following individuals and institutions my friends, collaborators, and supporters. Words cannot repay debts, but I have crafted these in the wish that they could.

This book began at Johns Hopkins University, and it is to Philip D. Morgan that I owe my first and foremost thanks. Phil is an unattainable model of scholar and mentor. He was always there when I needed him, but equally important, he gave me the freedom to research and to write for long stretches of time unhindered by meddlesome inquiries. A consummate empiricist, Phil never shied away from demanding copious evidence to support my claims, but he has always allowed me to be the historian I aspire to be. I will never be able to thank him enough.

Before Johns Hopkins, I had the good fortune to work with Alex Roland at Duke University. Alex introduced me to the world of historiography, the dynamics of change and continuity over time, the importance of contingency, and the perils of hagiography. He has continued to serve as an indefatigable mentor ever since. Alex read multiple drafts, offering critique and encouragement in roughly equal measure. Notwithstanding the importance of his scholarly influence, my greatest debts are personal. He and his wife, Liz, welcomed me into their home and embraced me as family. They even introduced me to the love of my life, my wife, Kathryn Maxson Jones. For this and everything else he has done for me, I am eternally grateful.

I am indebted the dynamic group of historians at Hopkins. David Bell, Angus Burgin, Toby Ditz, François Furstenberg, Michael Johnson, John Marshall, Randall Packard, and Gabriel Spiegel all influenced my scholarship in profound ways. I am particularly thankful to David, whose work on the French Revolution has informed my approach to the study of its American predecessor. An immensely generous scholar and brilliant stylist, David poured over my chapters, always urging me toward clarity tinged with audacity. I am thankful for the critique, encouragement, and friendship of every member of the Hopkins Early American Seminar, but especially Joseph Adelman, Zara Anishanslin, Lisa Bob, Sara Damiano, Andrew Devereux, Stephanie Gamble, Claire Gherini, Jonathan Gienapp, Scott Heerman, Craig Hollander, Nicholas Radburn, James Roberts, Justin Roberts, Jessica Roney, Katherine Smoak, and Molly Warsh. Jonathan, Craig, and Claire merit additional appreciation for their unflagging friendship and scholarly companionship. In addition to the early Americanists, I benefited from the good humor and convivial company of Meredith Raucher, Christopher Tozzi, and John Matsui. Writing is often a lonely process, but the above-mentioned individuals helped pull me away from my work and put the entire process in perspective. I am fortunate to call them friends first and colleagues second.

Throughout the more than a decade it has taken me to complete this project, I have been blessed by the support of countless fellow scholars. I am grateful to Sari Altschuler, Fred Anderson, Michael Blaakman, Joel Bohy, Douglas Bradburn, Todd Braisted, Lydia Brandt, John Brooke, Richard D. Brown, Stephen Brumwell, Steven Bullock, Richard and Claudia Bushman, Benjamin Carp, John Coombs, Cornelia Dayton, Paul Erickson, Betsy Erkkila, Andrew Fagal, William Fowler, Joanne Freeman, Paul Gilje, Robert Gross, Ira Gruber, Don Hagist, Hendrirk Hartog, Eric Hinderaker, Don Johnson, Mathew Karp, Matthew Keagle, Catherine Kelly, Carl Keyes, Daniel Krebs, Edward Larson, Wayne Lee, Mark Lender, Andrew Lipman, John Maass, James Kirby Martin, Elspeth Martini, Whitney Martinko, Gina Martino, Holly Mayer, Michael McDonnell, Margaret Newell, Brendan O'Malley, Greg O'Malley, Andrew O'Shaughnessy, David Preston, Jacqueline Reynoso, Margaret Sankey, Eric Schnitzer, Andrew Shankman, Will Slauter, Paul Springer, Anne Twitty, Gregory Urwin, Christine Walker, Joanne Jahnke Wegner, Glenn Williams, and Nicholas Wood. Each of these generous individuals has offered timely advice, source material, criticism, and camaraderie over the years.

I have had the pleasure (and at times the pain) of presenting much of my research to inquisitive audiences at numerous conferences and colloquia. These include the annual conferences of the American Historical Association, Organization of American Historians, North American Conference on British Studies, Consortium on the Revolutionary Era, Omohundro Institute for Early American History and Culture, and Society for Military History. I also profited from discussions of my work at the Massachusetts Historical Society, New-York Historical Society, Virginia Historical Society, Filson Historical Society, Library Company of Philadelphia, American Antiquarian Society, Yale University Early American History Seminar, Hampden Sydney College Society of the Cincinnati Visiting Scholar Program, University of Connecticut Department of History, Fordham University Department of History, Ohio Seminar in Early American History, University of Akron Department of History, McNeil Center for Early American Studies, Fort Ticonderoga Seminar on the American Revolution, and the Fred W. Smith National Library for the Study of George Washington at Mount Vernon.

This book would never have seen print without a staggering amount of financial assistance. In addition to generous funding from the Department of History at Johns Hopkins, I was fortunate to receive research fellowships from the Society of the Cincinnati, the David Library of the American Revolution, the Virginia Historical Society, the Clements Library, the Historical Society of Pennsylvania, and the Massachusetts Historical Society. Numerous archivists and librarians assisted me during my sojourns at these prestigious institutions, but I would particularly like to single out Ellen McCallister Clark, Barbara DeWolfe, Kathy Ludwig, Daniel Rolph, William P. Tatum, Katheryn Viens, and Conrad Wright. Long-term fellowships from the Harry Frank Guggenheim Foundation and the U.S. Army Center of Military History allowed me to complete an initial draft of the manuscript. The process of transforming that draft into a book proved more arduous than I had imagined. Thankfully, I was able to complete much of that process while on fellowship at three outstanding scholarly institutions: the Fred W. Smith National Library for the Study of George Washington, the American Antiquarian Society, and the New-York Historical Society. I was privileged to hold the inaugural Amanda and Greg Gregory Family Fellowship at the Smith Library, the Hench Post-Dissertation Fellowship at the AAS, and an NEH fellowship at the New-York Historical Society. I am immensely grateful to Douglas Bradburn, Paul Erickson, and

Valerie Paley for ensuring my tenure at their institutions was not only produc-
tive but also enjoyable.

I entered this project's home stretch while teaching in the Department of
History at Purdue University. I am blessed to work with brilliant and committed
colleagues. Each has enriched this study in different ways. I am particularly
grateful to David Atkinson, Kathryn Brownell, Frederick Davis, Jennifer Foray,
William Gray, Stacy Holden, Caroline Janney, Rebekah Klein-Pejšová, Wendy
Kline, John Larson, Dawn Marsh, Silvia Mitchell, Mary Mitchell, Yvonne Pitts,
Randy Roberts, Margaret Tillman, and Whitney Walton. The history department under the admirable leadership of R. Douglas Hurt provided ample
funding for research and much-needed time away from the classroom, for
which I am eternally thankful. I would also like to acknowledge the department's tireless staff, especially Fay Chan, Nancy Hughes, and Julie Knoeller.

At the University of Pennsylvania Press, I have been privileged to work
with Robert Lockhart, who has believed in this project from its early stages.
Rather than rush the book out, he allowed me the time needed to substantively
revise it. The anonymous reviewers, who thoroughly commented on the manuscript, have my sincere thanks for improving it greatly. My series editor, David
Waldstreicher, went above and beyond the call of duty. His detailed report
proved invaluable during the revision process. Kevin Brock has my thanks for
preparing the manuscript for submission and for catching several errors. Sections of Chapters 3 and 5 appeared previously as "'The rage of tory-hunting':
Loyalist Prisoners, Civil War, and the Violence of American Independence,"
Journal of Military History 81, no. 3 (July 2017): 719–46 and "'Elated with victory,
and reeking with revenge': The Yorktown Prisoners and the Laws of War in
Revolutionary America," in *Justifying Revolution: Law, Virtue, and Violence in
the American War of Independence,* ed. Glenn Moots and Philip Hamilton
(Norman: University of Oklahoma Press, 2018). I am thankful to the anony-
mous reviewers for their feedback and to the editors for permission to republish.
Catherine Kelly and the anonymous reviewers at the *Journal of the Early
Republic* allowed me to rehearse some of the book's themes in "'The dreadful
effects of British cruilty': The Treatment of British Maritime Prisoners and the
Radicalization of the Revolutionary War at Sea," *Journal of the Early Republic*
36, no. 3 (Fall 2016): 435–65. I encourage those readers who will be disappointed
by this book's terrestrial focus to seek out this article.

My greatest debts are owed to my family, without whom I could never have
endured this process. Kathryn Maxson Jones has lived with this project for as

long as she has known me. Rather than merely tolerate my forays into the "dark side" of America's past, she has accompanied me throughout with good cheer. I am one of the lucky ones to have a fellow scholar for a partner. Kathryn's editorial eye and capacious mind have honed my prose and sharpened my argument. While these pages bear her intellectual mark, it is her perennial enthusiasm and affection that have made this book possible. I cannot help but fall more in love with her each day. Speaking of love, I would not be writing these words had it not been for the unquestioning love and support of my parents, Randy and Connie Jones. They recognized early on that my passion for the past was not a passing fad but was instead my "perfect pitch." Though they might not think of themselves this way, my parents are extraordinary teachers. They raised me and my truly exceptional brothers, Chance and Charles, to value hard work, education, and personal integrity but reminded us not to take ourselves too seriously. All they ever wanted was for us to be the best versions of ourselves and to remember that kindness costs nothing. I could not have asked for better or more loving parents. It is as a proud son that I dedicate this book to them with love and admiration.